# BENTHAM'S PRISON

Jeremy Bentham at the age of 41, from a portrait by an unknown artist (1789). University College London.

# BENTHAM'S PRISON

## A Study of the
## Panopticon Penitentiary

JANET SEMPLE

CLARENDON PRESS · OXFORD
1993

Oxford University Press, Walton Street, Oxford OX2 6DP

Oxford New York
Athens Auckland Bangkok Bombay
Calcutta Cape Town Dar es Salaam Delhi
Florence Hong Kong Istanbul Karachi
Kuala Lumpur Madras Madrid Melbourne
Mexico City Nairobi Paris Singapore
Taipei Tokyo Toronto
and associated companies in
Berlin Ibadan

Oxford is a trade mark of Oxford University Press

Published in the United States by
Oxford University Press Inc., New York

First published 1993

British Library Cataloguing in Publication Data
Data available

Library of Congress Cataloging in Publication Data
Semple, Janet.
Bentham's prison: a study of the panopticon penitentiary / Janet
Semple.
p. cm.
Includes bibliographical references and index.
1. Prisons—Great Britain—Design and construction—History—18th
century. 2. Bentham, Jeremy, 1748-1832. I. Title.
HV8811.S46 1993 365'.941—dc20 92-41295
ISBN 0-19-827387-8

Printed in Great Britain
on acid-free paper by
Ipswich Book Co. Ltd,
Suffolk

For
Andrew, Robert, and Susie

# ACKNOWLEDGEMENTS

I would like to thank Fred Rosen, the Director of the Bentham Project, and Alan Beattie, my supervisor at the London School of Economics, for their guidance, encouragement, and friendship over many years. Without them this book would not have been written. I am also immensely grateful to all my colleagues at the Bentham Project, in particular Cyprian Blamires, Stephen Conway, Jane Haville, and Philip Schofield. They have been unfailingly generous in sharing their knowledge and allowing me to benefit from their scholarship.

I am much indebted to the help of the librarians at the London School of Economics, University College London, and the British Library. I would also like to thank the Dean and Chapter of Westminster Abbey for allowing me access to the Chapter Minutes and to the librarians at the City of Westminster Victoria library for their help with the Grosvenor archive. I am grateful for permission from these libraries, from the Dean and Chapter, and from the Grosvenor Estate to quote from their records. I would like particularly to thank Gill Furlong who has the custody of the Bentham manuscripts at University College for her unfailing patience and courtesy.

I did all my own typing and so I am especially grateful to our friend and neighbour Roy Lawrence who introduced me to an invaluable word processor.

Finally, I must thank my husband, Andrew, who read the typescript and gave me some excellent advice, and my children, Robert and Susie, who prevented me from taking Bentham and his prison too seriously and ensured that life was never dull.

# CONTENTS

# LIST OF FIGURES

*(reprinted by permission of the Librarian, University College London)*

# ABBREVIATIONS AND SYMBOLS

| | |
|---|---|
| BL Add. MSS | Bentham manuscripts in the British Library, Additional MSS 33122 and 33550 |
| Bowring | *The Works of Jeremy Bentham*, published under the superintendence of his executor, John Bowring (11 vols., Edinburgh, 1838–43) |
| *CW* | *The Collected Works of Jeremy Bentham*, general editors, J. H. Burns, J. R. Dinwiddy, and F. Rosen (London and Oxford, 1968–  ) |
| UC | Bentham manuscripts in the Library at University College London. Roman numerals refer to the boxes, arabic to the folios |
| [?] | reading doubtful |
| [. . . ?] | word illegible |

Frequent use, not always attributed, has been made of standard works of reference *The Dictionary of National Biography* and *The History of Parliament*

Niblungs below,
bow to Alberich!
I shall be watching
to see that you're working
day and night
You must be toiling,
sweating to serve
your invisible Lord
who can watch you unseen
and spy on his subjects
You are my slaves now and for ever.

Wagner, *Das Rheingold*

# I

# INTRODUCTION

Bentham's panopticon penitentiary is a project full of contradiction and ambiguity; a prison that is at the centre of philosophical disquisition, managed by a gaoler who has been depicted both as a ruthless capitalist entrepreneur and as a personification of the utilitarian state. It is an individualist enterprise that seems to presage totalitarianism. Scholars have accorded it little interest or respect, yet for twenty years it obsessed the superlative mind of one of our greatest philosophers; it was a tragedy in the life of a man who seemed to his friends happy and successful. Despite its intrinsic fascination there has been no study, adequate or inadequate, of the panopticon prison. This book will deal with the panopticon as an event in penal and political history. Drawing on hitherto unexplored manuscripts it tells the story of Bentham's prolonged negotiations with government and investigates the reasons why the prison was never built. Bentham emerges as a personality very different from the reclusive philosopher of popular mythology. Until the age of 64, he was ambitious to become an administrator and to put his own ideas of penal policy and office management into practice himself. He wanted to apply his 'genius for legislation' to the day to day running of institutions and to play a major role in penal reform not as a philosopher but as a practitioner. The theoretical speculations that now seem his unique contribution to the history of his country were, during many years of his life, a secondary consideration.

In recent years Jeremy Bentham has become a subject of increasing scholarly scrutiny and a focus of controversy. New interpretations of his philosophy and new facets of his personality are emerging. It is imperative that the panopticon prison that occupied so crucial a place in his life and thought should be adequately explored. Much interest has been focused on Bentham's extension of his idea to include provision for the poor in the pauper panopticons. Yet the prison has primacy, in both the time and the importance it assumed in Bentham's life. His proposals for pauper management never had a chance of being accepted. But the prison was very nearly built. It is becoming increasingly clear that it is a vital element in the revision both of Bentham's thought and of penal history. It raises profound problems in relation to his ideas on government, society, democracy, and education. It casts further light on his character and his motives; it is perhaps fundamental to a judgement on the nature of penal reform and so of an important aspect of the European Enlightenment. Yet the published material is still buried in the Bowring edition and the greater mass of unpublished material has hardly yet begun to be considered by scholars.

The panopticon penitentiary has been dealt with only incidentally in the literature. E. Halévy linked the prison with the utilitarian state: 'The prison realises the ideal of a school in which the educator is to be absolute master to determine the external conditions in which the pupil is situated, or of a society in which the legislator is absolute master to create at will all the social relations of the citizens among themselves.' He uses the scheme to support his argument that in Bentham's thought: 'Liberty is not . . . an end of human activity; the doctrine of utility is not, in origin and in essence, a philosophy of liberty.' He argues that contract management based on the interest and duty junction principle would ensure the artificial identification of the interests of the gaoler and the prisoners; this novel instrument of government would enable 'the principles of the doctrine of Helvetius which were despotic, philanthropic, and Utilitarian, but not in the least liberal' to triumph on a point of detail.[1]

Halévy was not the first to question the implications of utilitarianism for liberty. Herbert Spencer had attacked the utilitarians for sacrificing the freedom of the individual on the altar of the supposed interests of the majority, which they equated with the state. In a more profound analysis, A. V. Dicey depicted Bentham as an immensely powerful influence, but his judgement on the merits of this influence is distinctly ambivalent. Bentham was, he wrote, 'the best representative of the humanitarianism and enlightenment' of the eighteenth century and his ideal happiness was 'no far-fetched conception of well-being, but that com-

---

[1] E. Halévy, *The Growth of Philosophic Radicalism*, trans. M. Morris (London, 1928; repr. 1972), 83–5.

bination of an honest and industrious life with the enjoyment of modest wealth and material comfort, which is felt to be an object of desire by any ordinary Englishman'. Yet, when Dicey briefly considered the panopticon, he saw another Bentham, the inventor of 'a mechanical contrivance from which, if rightly used, he, after the manner of ingenious projectors, expected untold benefits for mankind'. In his conclusion, he accused Benthamites of fostering the emergence of a despotic democratic state; they had forged the weapons of collectivism, 'a legislative doctrine, a legislative instrument, and a legislative tendency pre-eminently suited for the carrying out of socialistic experiments'.[2]

This theme has been elaborated by later writers. S. R. Letwin traces the Fabian ideas on social planning and centralized administration to early utilitarian thinkers and she regards the panopticon with a certain fascinated horror; for her, it was Bentham's pet gadget and in his obsession with it, he had forgotten the dangers of unrestrained power; devices of such monstrous efficiency left no room for humanity. 'In his ardour for reform, Bentham prepared the way for what he feared.'[3] Other recent libertarian thinkers use the panopticon to belabour Bentham's whole philosophy as paving the way to the totalitarian state. Gertrude Himmelfarb echoes and emphasizes Halévy's equation of the panopticon with society; for her, the panopticon is the 'existential realization of Philosophic Radicalism' and Benthamite ideas are as destructive to freedom as they are to rights.[4] Manning's more impressive, if as inimical, analysis of Bentham's mind argues that his fundamental concern was for social cohesion and in his fear of instability and disruption he became the advocate of ruthless social engineering in which the will of the majority would prevail and the interests of the minority would be trampled underfoot; there could be no privacy and no tolerance for the deviant. Manning indeed goes so far as to suggest that Bentham would have condoned the elimination of the unfit:

[2] A. V. Dicey, *Lectures on the Relation between Law and Public Opinion in England during the Nineteenth Century* (London, 1905; 2nd edn. 1914), 128–9, 131, 310.
[3] S. R. Letwin, *The Pursuit of Certainty* (Cambridge, 1965), 188.
[4] G. Himmelfarb, 'The Haunted House of Jeremy Bentham', *Victorian Minds* (London, 1968), 75, 77.

In the Benthamite state we may expect that the eccentric will be ostracised and reeducated; the lazy will be punished and the antisocial will be treated in a way calculated to deter their fellows. The question may even arise as to how to dispose of minorities considered to possess little or no social utility . . . The tyranny of minorities Bentham detested, but the tyranny of majorities he considered just.[5]

Himmelfarb and Manning are on the extreme wing of opinion that sees Benthamism as the precursor of totalitarianism. But two recent books by Bentham scholars give some support to their conclusions. The theme of both D. G. Long's *Bentham on Liberty* and C. F. Bahmueller's *The National Charity Company* is the threat to freedom, privacy, and tolerance posed by Bentham's ideas. Long emphasizes the symbiosis between security for the individual and government power that is apparent in Bentham's theories and he contrasts this with David Hume's perception of the eternal tension between liberty and authority. He accuses Bentham of having 'no conception of the possibility of the suffocation of individuality under a blanket of social conformity'.[6] Liberty was merely a means of obtaining security, not an end in itself. As one would expect, the panopticon plays a central part in Long's argument. He describes it as 'this most authoritarian and repressive of his enterprises' and argues that it was consistent with his utilitarianism for it was inspired by the overriding need to sacrifice liberty to security; it was the most severe application of the principle that pervades Bentham's Theory of Reward— that it was necessary to put restraint on man's inclinations so that he may be at liberty to follow them: 'The most profoundly oppressive aspect of Panopticon was not the character of the punishments associated with it but the inexorable and inescapable quality of the remoulding process by which evil-doers were to be, too literally, re-formed into industrious and obedient utilitarian citizens.'[7] Bahmueller's study of Bentham's poor-law proposals is a sustained condemnation of a scheme that would have imprisoned thousands without trial, stripped them of human dignity, and subjected them to ruthless exploitation; 'one wonders', he writes, 'how anyone with even the slightest sympathy for the poor could

[5] D. J. Manning, *The Mind of Jeremy Bentham* (London, 1968), 88.
[6] D. G. Long, *Bentham on Liberty: Jeremy Bentham's Idea of Liberty in Relation to his Utilitarianism* (Toronto, 1977), 218.
[7] Ibid. 187–8.

be other than horrified by Bentham's plan'. Bahmueller is not willing, however, to commit himself to the proposition that the panopticon is a paradigm of Benthamite society; this, he argues, is a complex subject which cannot be resolved until Bentham's writings are published accurately and unknown manuscripts are brought to light.[8] The analysis of the panopticon prison proposals in this book may suggest an answer to this question.

This picture of Bentham as a champion of a stifling social conformity has not gone entirely unchallenged. Margaret Fry's amusing account is more balanced in its assessment. She fears that the panopticon would have doomed many to life-long servitude and would, 'from its complete lack of understanding of human nature, have inevitably worked out as an engine of terrible cruelty'. But she does give Bentham credit for a frigid humanitarianism and 'a fundamental wisdom in his theory of the relation of society to its recalcitrant members'.[9] Roberts has taken issue directly with Bahmueller, arguing that the panopticon poorhouses, by freeing paupers from want and oppression, would have enabled them to develop their potential as human beings.[10] And Poynter in his masterly study of eighteenth-century poor relief, treats Bentham's proposals with respect and even approbation. Although he is repelled by the harsh authoritarian dogmatism of Bentham's schemes, he argues that the plan reveals three Benthams: the exponent of economic liberalism, the planner devising his monstrous nostrums, horrible to modern minds, but also the believer in mutual co-operation between free individuals.[11]

Campos Boralevi deals with the paradox of the seemingly coercive panopticon poor plan with Bentham's insistence on tolerance and justice for women, racial minorities, and sexual deviants. In an interesting and illuminating discussion of his proposals for the indigent, she argues that, given the overriding need for subsistence and security, the panopticon industry houses were 'the best possible *practical* solution for certain individuals'.

---

[8] C. F. Bahmueller, *The National Charity Company: Jeremy Bentham's Silent Revolution* (Berkeley, Calif., Los Angeles, London, 1981), 211, 242–3.

[9] M. Fry, 'Bentham and English Penal Reform', in G. W. Keeton and G. Schwarzenberger (eds.), *Jeremy Bentham and the Law* (London, 1948), 52–4.

[10] W. Roberts, 'Bentham's Poor Law Proposals', *The Bentham Newsletter* 3 (1979), 28–45.

[11] J. R. Poynter, *Society and Pauperism* (London and Toronto, 1969), 109.

The panopticon, she asserts, was not an absolutely good society but a remedy for a specific evil; if there were oppression in Bentham's ideal republic, it would be a symptom of the mal-functioning of the system, for properly organized, the majority could never be a tyrant.[12] A similar theme pervades F. Rosen's analysis of the *Constitutional Code*; he emphasizes the checks on government power and the equation of security with the basic liberties of the subject, freedom from oppression—from any source—and the rule of law. This interpretation of the *Code* raises, by implication, serious doubts as to whether the panopticon can be a paradigm of Benthamite democracy.[13] The work of L. J. Hume places the panopticon at the centre of the development of Bentham's ideas on administration, the role of government in society, and the construction of the legal, rational, democratic state. He argues that the panopticon originated in ideas of indirect legislation, reward, and production economics and helped him to form his theory of organization which so strikingly anticipates twentieth-century ideas of scientific management; that is in the collection and dissemination of information, inspection, efficient communications, and the junction of interest and duty. The rejection of the panopticon, Hume maintains, was the starting-point of his more bitter, radical criticism of British government and his denunciation of misrule, influence, despotism, and the dispensing power of the executive. Hume reconciles Bentham's insistence on contract management in the panopticon scheme with his later view that government might become an efficient administrative instrument, by arguing that Bentham saw contract as suitable for a particular stage in social progress.[14]

Recent work is also forcing a reappraisal of Bentham's charac-ter and of his aspirations. The traditional picture first perpetrated by John Bowring was reinforced by John Stuart Mill. They some-what contemptuously dismiss Bentham as a happy, mawkishly benevolent old man living retired from the world, one who had always been a stranger to the extremes either of pleasure or pain, uninterested in worldly success, playing like a little child with his

[12] L. Campos Boralevi, *Bentham and the Oppressed* (Berlin and New York, 1984), 104. Boralevi's emphasis.

[13] F. Rosen, *Jeremy Bentham and Representative Democracy: A Study of the Constitutional Code* (Oxford, 1983).

[14] L. J. Hume, *Bentham and Bureaucracy* (Cambridge, 1981).

pussies and his mouses. As recently as 1965 Letwin retold this myth. But during the last twenty years, with the publication of Bentham's *Correspondence* in the *Collected Works*, a far more complex and formidable figure is emerging. In his letters, the full importance of his involvement with the panopticon prison scheme can be estimated and he personally is shown in a very different light, as a man very much of the world, capable of sustained negotiation with officials, ministers, and politicians; a man disingenuous, willing to use corrupt methods, devious, tenacious, and, above all, acquisitive. Himmelfarb indeed insists that Bentham's primary motive in pressing the panopticon scheme on a doubtful and reluctant government was greed and that the overriding aim of the prison was sordid gain, not enlightened humanitarianism. Hume argues that Bentham was inspired by the vision of a great fortune. But, although there can be little doubt that money was a compelling motive, it does not follow that it was the sole motive; a thorough study of the panopticon proposals may throw light on Bentham's character and make possible some estimate of the relative importance of altruism and avarice in his personality.

From Bowring to Harrison, writers on Bentham have agreed that the panopticon played a central role in his life, but almost without exception they deprecate it. Leslie Stephen even welcomed the failure of the scheme, which freed Bentham for the pursuit of philosophy: 'He was well out of the plan . . . his failure was a blessing in disguise.'[15] Everett deplored the common sense that turned Bentham aside from the promptings of his genius;[16] and Ross Harrison, though emphasizing the importance of the duty–interest junction principle in Bentham's thought, argues that the panopticon was a digression from the main thread of his life.[17] The prison is often ignored or barely mentioned in studies of his ideas. Baumgardt dismisses it as 'not of basic ethical interest';[18] and even Hume asserts that 'the Panopticon came to dominate his life for several years to an extent that was disproportionate to its place in the structure of his thought'.[19]

---

[15] L. Stephen, *The English Utilitarians* (London, 1900), i. 205–6.
[16] C. W. Everett, *Jeremy Bentham* (London, 1966), 45.
[17] R. Harrison, *Bentham* (London, 1983), 20.
[18] D. Baumgardt, *Bentham and the Ethics of Today* (Princeton, NJ, 1952), 364.
[19] Hume, *Bentham and Bureaucracy*, 241.

This general depreciation is reflected in the accounts of the panopticon; few bother to describe it in more than a few lines and these descriptions are confined to the material published in the Bowring edition. The eventual failure of the project has coloured later accounts and they almost universally assume that Bentham was wasting his time. His concern with the panopticon is treated with a mixture of condescension, incredulity, and disdain or with an unreflecting approval that is almost as insulting. Bentham is not given credit as a rational adult for the ability to understand his own interest and to follow it. Nor is he given credit for knowing where his own talents and ambitions lay. He is assumed to have been mistaken, to have embarked on a doomed enterprise that wasted his time, dissipated his true genius, and depleted his fortune. Yet, however bizarre one may find the idea of the recluse of Hendon transmogrified into Lord Bentham the successful entrepreneurial gaoler living in the midst of his thousand convicts, it should at least be considered that he had serious prospects of achieving his ambitions and serious reasons for pursuing them.

There has been surprisingly little attempt by Bentham scholars to relate the panopticon to penal history. Himmelfarb indeed seems studiously to ignore the contemporary context except where it suits her polemical purpose. Hume's admirably lucid account of the complex negotiations with the government concentrates on the constitutional implications and on Bentham's indignation at what he believed to be the misuse of the dispensing power of the executive to override the will of the legislature.[20] This lacuna in recent Bentham scholarship has been partially filled by the work of penal historians. In revisionist essays, the panopticon is emerging as a project worth consideration. In traditional history, failure was accounted of little importance and, although the panopticon was famous, it was not taken seriously. From the heights of their infallible Political Science, the Webbs condemned the contract system of the eighteenth century, that 'amazing administrative device', as the source of all muddle, waste, inefficiency, and inhumanity. They dismiss the panopticon with a disdain mingled with sadness that 'even at the beginning of the nineteenth century, so wise a man as Jeremy Bentham was

[20] Hume, 'Bentham's Panopticon: An Administrative History', *Historical Studies*, 15 (1971–3), 703–21, and 16 (1974–5), 36–54.

seriously proposing, as the basis of his "panopticon", letting the management by contract to the highest bidder. A hundred years later there were still economists who wished to farm out road maintenance.'[21]

Modern historians, influenced by Marxist analysis, see the panopticon in a very different light and accord it more respect, if not approval. They are concerned more with ideas than with events. The penitentiary is studied as one of the institutions that were emerging during the eighteenth century to discipline the poor. Schools, factories, poorhouses, hospitals, asylums, barracks, even the family, are seen as instruments of social control, a control increasingly necessary as society became fragmented and unstable under the impact of industrial change. This approach has provided fascinating, if at times controversial, insights into the nature of the panopticon. Melossi and Pavarini set out 'to establish the connection between the rise of the capitalist mode of production and the origins of the modern prison'. Jeremy Bentham is scathingly described as, 'a major representative of the ascendant English bourgeoisie'; and his prison as, 'a naive attempt to combine a system of intensified punishment and control with productive efficiency which was never put into practice . . . The *Panopticon* is at one and the same time an architechtonic concept and the embodiment of its own ideology.'[22] Michel Foucault places the panopticon at the centre of his interpretation of penal history. He postulates a discontinuity during the eighteenth century, a sudden change from punishment of the body to discipline directed at the mind or the soul. He contrasts two concepts of the spatial dimensions of power; the old spectacle of monarchy where the subjects gaze at the space filled with the panoply of mystic royal authority, and the new order where power has become invisible and the subjects themselves inhabit a space where they are a spectacle for their rulers. In this new Foucaultian world, subjects have become objects of ruthless curiosity, examination, and manipulation to such a degree that they themselves have been persuaded to become the agents of their own subjection. In his thesis Bentham's panopticon is the

---

[21] S. and B. Webb, *English Prisons under Local Government* (London, 1922), 18.
[22] D. Melossi and M. Pavarini, *The Prison and the Factory: Origins of the Penitentiary System* (Bologna, 1977), trans. G. Cousin (London, 1981), 1, 40.

prototype of a sinister instrument in this new physics of power making possible a furtive exercise of authority to control and subjugate.[23]

Ignatieff also questions the humane and progressive nature of eighteenth-century penal reform. He depicts Bentham's scheme as a link in the chain of rational reform, originating in the ideas of Beccaria and John Howard, but culminating in the horrors of the Pentonville penitentiary opened in 1842. The panopticon was 'the most haunting symbol of the disciplinary enthusiasms of the age'.[24] For Ignatieff, liberalism was Janus-faced; on the one hand extending the franchise to the people in order to widen the bonds of social consent; on the other, repressing the customary liberties of the poor and tightening the grip of the law over the disobedient and the deviant. He argues that the old paternalism was based on a weak state and a tolerance of public disorder, dependent on ritual displays of maximum deterrence to preserve stability. The new order was based on a strong state, an obsession with order, and a reliance on carceral punishment directed at the mind rather than the body in the belief that the criminal could be moulded to bring him back into the social consensus. And the greatest exponent of this new thinking was Jeremy Bentham. Ignatieff has no doubt that there was a symbiotic relationship between Benthamite democracy and social control: 'Bentham's two personae—the advocate of parliamentary reform, and the publicist for the Panopticon—were not contradictory, but complementary.'[25] But he is also in no doubt that the final rejection of the panopticon was a major event in penal history and not the foregone conclusion assumed by Stephen and the Webbs; it established that penal institutions would not be run as capitalist enterprises. Evans, in his study of prison architecture, describes the panopticon as 'more a contraption than a building'[26] and he too emphasizes that it was a mechanical contrivance to obtain and exercise power, a physical extension of Jeremy Bentham,

---

[23] M. Foucault, *Discipline and Punish: The Birth of the Prison* (Paris, 1975), trans. A. Sheridan (Harmondsworth, 1985). See *Utilitas*, 4 (May 1992), 105–20, for my discussion of Foucault and Bentham.

[24] M. Ignatieff, *A Just Measure of Pain: The Penitentiary in the Industrial Revolution, 1750–1850* (New York, 1978), 109.

[25] Ibid. 212.

[26] R. Evans, *The Fabrication of Virtue: English Prison Architecture, 1750–1840* (Cambridge, 1982), 198.

built to magnify his potency. Evans is, however, impressed by Bentham's architectural innovations in the use of glass and iron and in his schemes for integrated heating and lighting. Generally, penal historians have agreed with the great majority of writers on Bentham that the panopticon prison was impracticable and theoretical. It is refreshing to find one writer who dissents. McConville in his study of the administration of English prisons admits that, though the gadgetry and the design may appear far-fetched, the financial and administrative aspects of the scheme were in accord with contemporary practices. He writes of Bentham: 'Essentially he was seeking to bring the entrepreneur gaoler to the service of reformatory imprisonment and his suggestions were ingenious and well worthy of serious attention.'[27]

The central contention of Foucault and his disciples that the reformers of the Enlightenment were actuated by a thirst for regimentation and incarceration is not in its nature capable of disproof. Any expression of gentleness, humanity, or a desire to free the human spirit can be dismissed either as deliberate deception or as a product of a false consciousness that distorted their perception of their own motives and the 'reality' of the world outside. But painstaking unearthing of facts that do not accord with this overall theory can cast doubt on its simplicities. And two recent studies have gone some way to undermine the credibility of Foucault's hypotheses. Roy Porter, in his history of madness, found little evidence for Foucault's 'great confinement' of the insane, at least in England. He concluded that, in the eighteenth century, 'great oddity was in fact still widely tolerated, and there is scant evidence, during the years of Revolutionary wars, of the use of the madhouse as a weapon against plebeians or radicals . . . it was family rather than the state which took action over the disturbed'. Porter admitted however that Foucaultian theory might well apply in the nineteenth century. He saw Bentham as the precursor of the vast lunatic asylums of the next century; he was the patron saint of the 'distinctively institutional asylum architecture, with its elaborate therapeutic, sanitary, and panoptic rationalities'.[28]

---

[27] S. McConville, *A History of English Prison Administration* (London, 1981), i. 134.
[28] Roy Porter, *Mind-Forg'd Manacles: A History of Madness in England from the Restoration to the Regency* (London, 1987), 141, 168.

Margaret DeLacy's detailed study of prison reform in Lancashire raises more fundamental questions as to the ideology of what she calls the group of 'radical historians' who have followed in Himmelfarb's and Foucault's footsteps. She points out that the phrase 'social control' is tautological, for any society must by definition exercise some form of control. And she insists that it is necessary to prove the conscious intent of one group to dominate another rather than take refuge in obscure generalities. The picture that emerges from her research is of far more complex issues than the attempt of one class to repress another; or indeed of the exercise of domination by prison authorities over their inmates. The prisoners were often divided over the merits of reform—many, fearful of the brutality of other inmates, welcomed greater security and seclusion. Political prisoners objected to association with common criminals. She asserts,'The story of prison reform, therefore, is not simply the story of the repression of one group, consisting of prisoners, by another group, consisting of administrators.'[29] She also argues that the radical historians who have attacked the whole concept of imprisonment have failed to suggest a viable alternative. Moreover, they have not studied what actually happened in the prisons. Foucault paid little attention to this problem and even Ignatieff concentrated on the great national penitentiaries of Millbank and Pentonville. The quality of a prison, she believes, was determined not so much by ideology as by the nature of its inmates, the quality of its staff, and the extent of outside supervision. She fundamentally parts company with the revisionist position by suggesting that the proliferation of institutions was not in itself necessarily to be deplored. Cruelty and exploitation were not a monopoly of institutions. DeLacy even has a word in defence of Bentham and the other reformers. She argues that Himmelfarb and her followers, 'have succeeded in depicting Bentham as a greedy, power-hungry, and totalitarian "manipulator"'; and John Howard as a bourgeois dissenter, 'who wanted above all to control the lower classes'. They have dismissed 'the reformers good intentions as a mere screen for class oppression'. DeLacy gives Bentham credit for humanity and she perceptively suggests that the innovative

---

[29] Margaret DeLacy, *Prison Reform in Lancashire, 1700–1850: A Study in Local Administration* (Manchester, 1986), 9.

qualities of his panopticon were designed to temper the hardships of the reformed prisons themselves:

> In many ways, the Panopticon represented a revolt against what Bentham considered a cruel system, and particularly against the sensual deprivations and discomforts imposed in the reformed prison. He objected to the meagerness of the diet, the dark cold cells and the tiny, high gratings, the monotony and unhealthiness of prison labour, the multiplication of petty rules, the solitude, and the enforcement of unprofitable activities merely to harass the prisoners.[30]

Both Porter and DeLacy insist that the picture of the development of both madhouses and local prisons was far richer, more complex, and more interesting than one would expect if Foucaultian ideology possessed exclusive truth.

The essential core of the panopticon writings are the published books, the original *Letters* written in Russia in 1786, and the two *Postscripts* written five years later in 1790 and 1791.[31] There are very considerable divergences between the *Letters* and the

---

[30] Ibid. 16, 172–4.

[31] *Panopticon; or, The Inspection-House: Containing the idea of a new principle of construction applicable to any sort of establishment, in which persons of any description are to be kept under inspection; and in particular to Penitentiary-Houses, Prisons, Poor-Houses, Lazarettos, Houses of Industry, Manufactories, Hospitals, Work-Houses, Mad-Houses, and Schools: With a Plan of Management adapted to the principle: in a series of Letters, written in the year 1787, from Crecheff in White Russia, to a friend in England.* By Jeremy Bentham of Lincoln's Inn, Esquire. Cited as *Letters. Panopticon Postscript; Part I. Containing further particulars and alterations relative to the plan of construction originally proposed; principally adapted to the purpose of a Panopticon Penitentiary-House* (London, 1791). Cited as *Postscript I. Panopticon: Postscript; Part II. Containing a plan of management for a Panopticon Penitentiary-House* (London, 1791). Cited as *Postscript II.* These three works have subsequently been reprinted in *The Works of Jeremy Bentham,* ed. J. Bowring, 11 vols. (Edinburgh, 1838–43), iv. 37–172. *Correspondence (CW),* iii, makes it clear that the original *Letters* were written in 1786 not 1787. At BL Add. MS 33550, 145–230, there are two drafts in Bentham's hand of the original version of the *Letters.* The incorrect date on the title-page has been inserted later. Although these panopticon writings were printed in 1791, they do not appear to have been published in the usual sense of the term, i.e. freely available to the public. When Bentham sent a copy to Lord Auckland (formerly William Eden) in Feb. 1792, he stated in his accompanying letter, 'it has never gone to any Booksellers', *Correspondence (CW),* iv. 361. And in 1803, in *Panopticon versus New South Wales,* he repeats that, although it may have been sold in Ireland, it never found its way into any English shops (Bowring, iv. 240). However, in 1802 a version by Bentham's friend and disciple Étienne Dumont was published in *Traités de législation civile et pénale,* 3 vols. (Paris, 1802), iii. 209–72.

*Postscripts*; and the relationship between them has not been thoroughly explored and is sometimes oversimplified. Himmelfarb argues that the *Postscripts* show the triumph of Bentham's rapacious entrepreneurial spirit.[32] Both Hume and Steintrager suggest that the *Postscripts* merely added practical details.[33] All too often the *Letters* are read as a convenient short version of the whole scheme and the *Postscripts* ignored. A recent version of the texts for French readers brought out under the aegis of Perrot and Foucault dismisses the *Postscripts* as merely elaborations of technical detail which were not worth reproducing.[34] But the relationship is both more complex and more interesting; the *Letters* are a succinct, lucid sketch of a scheme to use an inspection house for a variety of purposes, though particularly as a prison. This original panopticon was very much a contraption, and Bentham described his devices with frivolous and at times facetious glee. But he himself considered that the *Letters* were 'the first rough imperfect sketch: imperfectly contrived and still more imperfectly expressed'.[35] The *Letters* take up a mere 27 pages in the Bowring edition. In comparison, the two *Postscripts* with 105 pages are very much more substantial; they were written in haste; they are repetitious, slovenly, and verbose; at times they descend into turgid circumlocutions that defy meaning. At first glance, *Postscript* I does seem mainly concerned with elaborating the details of the building, with the construction of stairways, and methods of heating and ventilation. Bentham discourages further investigation with sentences such as:

On this account, the upright bars, instead of finding separate horizontal bars at bottom to meet them and afford them support in a line exactly under them, are inflected towards the bottom; and the perpendicular part and the horizontal being both in one piece, the former receives

[32] Himmelfarb, *Victorian Minds*, 45–50.

[33] J. Steintrager, *Bentham* (London, 1977), 80, and Hume, *Bentham and Bureaucracy*, 111.

[34] *Le Panoptique* (Paris, 1977), précédé de L'Œil du Pouvoir entretien avec Michel Foucault, postface de Michelle Perrot. This text consists of a reprint of *Panoptique mémoire par Jérémie Bentham*, Imprimé par ordre de l'Assemblée nationale, Paris, 1791, and a translation by Maud Sissung of the *Letters*. The editors dismiss the *Postscripts* with the words: 'L'édition Londienne comporte en outre un Panopticon Postscript en deux volumes contenant un grand nombre de précisions et de details techniques circonstanciés rédigé en Angleterre après discussion avec les architectes. Nous ne le reproduisons pas ici.'

[35] UC cxix. 72.

sufficient support from the latter, and the first transverse piece that presents itself capable of affording a man a treading place to spring from, runs two or three inches within a perpendicular let fall from the rail.[36]

Yet concealed in the verbiage of *Postscript* I is vital evidence for the evolution of Bentham's ideas on solitary confinement, the powers of prison governors, and the nature of the criminal mind. In any sensible arrangement, the order of the panopticon writings would be reversed and start with *Postscript* II which contains a masterly analysis of the ends and means of punishment based on utilitarian rationality. In a classic statement of the dilemma of any prison administration, Bentham wrote: 'There are few subjects on which opinion is more under the sway of powers that are out of the reach of reason. Different tempers prescribe different measures of severity and indulgence. Some forget that a convict in prison is a sensitive being; others, that he is put there for punishment.'[37] To found the administration of his prison on a rock of reason, Bentham postulated three rules; the rule of lenity which safeguards the well-being of the inmate; the rule of severity which ensures that he suffers; and the rule of economy that prescribes that the whole shall be managed with as much regard to frugality as is consistent with the preservation of life and health and the infliction of punishment. Bentham could not, however, resist the temptation to refine and redefine his ideas, and *Postscript* II also contains long discussions on contract management, the junction of interest and duty, the principles on which convicts should be permitted to associate, the nature of employment in prisons, and the provision to be made for discharged prisoners. He also lavished attention on domestic details of diet, clothes, health, exercise, and, rather as an afterthought, education. One of the aims of this book is to provide a synthesis of the *Letters* and the *Postscripts* that will illuminate the real nature of Bentham's proposals and the development of his ideas.

The publication of Bentham's voluminous correspondence in the *Collected Works* over the past twenty years has provided an invaluable source for Bentham studies; and has made possible for the first time a comprehensive account of the political and legal events that comprise the saga of the panopticon. These letters

[36] Bowring, iv. 90.   [37] Ibid. 121.

provide an essential framework for the new interpretation that is another object of this book. But the richest source for any original contribution to scholarship has come from the wealth of material in the archive at University College London. Fortunately, Bentham kept the jumbled mass of documents, notes, and drafts that are the detritus of his great plan. In one of his saddest comments, he confessed in old age that he could not bear so much as to glance at them: 'I do not like . . . to look among Panopticon papers. It is like opening a drawer where devils are locked up—it is breaking into a haunted house.'[38] Bentham's anguish has met with little sympathy, yet it was real enough. In the nadir of the panopticon's fortunes, he felt he would die 'like a rat in a hole' and he clung to memories of childhood in his lonely misery; a friend, 'gave me once a loaf, which reminded me of my boyhood, and I kept it till it grew green, during Panopticon distress'.[39] J. S. Mill's picture of a Peter Pan figure who 'knew no dejection, no heaviness of heart. He never felt life a sore and a weary burthen. He was a boy to the last,' is essentially false.[40] Bentham was infinitely fortunate that he lived long enough to see his philosophy spread by admiring disciples and to become a thinker celebrated throughout the world. But the success he enjoyed as an old man could only go so far to compensate for the failures and humiliations he endured in his prime. A study of these hitherto unregarded manuscripts can go some way to explaining the depth of Bentham's distress, for they illuminate the full extent of his ambitions. These haunted boxes contain untold riches for Bentham scholarship; they range from scribbled marginal notes to considerable documents, from high fantasy to sober analysis.

The subject of contract prisons has a direct relevance to contemporary debate. A generation ago, they would have seemed a bizarre anachronism. Privatization is now seriously considered. The evils of our gaols, overcrowding, drugs, disease, corruption, and degradation parallel those of the eighteenth century. Then it was gin and gaol fever, now crack and Aids. The problems are the same and the public discussion turns uneasily on the horns of the same dilemmas. Bentham's analysis and remedies could make

---

[38] Ibid. x. 250.
[39] Ibid. 573.
[40] J. S. Mill, *Essay on Bentham*, ed. M. Warnock (Glasgow, 1990), 97.

a valuable contribution to the contemporary debate. It is vital that his ideas should be made widely available. They will provoke controversy but might provide a framework of utilitarian theory within which contemporary solutions can be worked out.

## SUMMARY

This book approaches the panopticon as a historical event rather than as a philosophical concept. It begins with an account of Bentham's early life and an examination of the origins of the panopticon in his writings on penal reform. A separate chapter is devoted to an analysis of the Penitentiary Act of 1779 and *A View of the Hard Labour Bill*.

Chapter 4 explores other ideas on prisons and penal reform that were current in the eighteenth century and upon which Bentham drew in the panopticon writings. It will argue that the panopticon grew from the ideals of the Enlightenment but also drew on evangelical Christianity and *laissez-faire* economics.

Chapter 5 turns to the political situation in which Bentham launched his panopticon and puts the writings into the context of Bentham's own life. It describes the reactions of his family, friends, and members of Pitt's administration.[41]

Chapters 6 and 7 are devoted to a detailed analysis of the panopticon scheme in its entirety, integrating the disparate elements to achieve a coherence that Bentham's own account lacks. Chapter 6 starts with an exposition of the principles that underlay the project and goes on to describe the architecture of the building and to give details of the regime under which the inmates would have lived. The complex problem of solitary confinement is discussed. Chapter 7 deals with the question of contract management and the checks, especially inspection, that Bentham proposed to incorporate into his scheme. It goes on to explore his attitude to criminals and his solution to the problem of crime together with essential safeguards for the well-being of his prisoners and for their subsistence after discharge and in old age.

---

[41] William Pitt (1759–1806), Chancellor of the Exchequer, 1782–3; Chancellor of the Exchequer and Prime Minister, 1783–1801 and 1804–d.

Chapters 8, 9, and 10 draw heavily on Bentham's manuscripts and correspondence to give a detailed account of his dealings with Pitt's and Addington's administrations up to June 1803.[42] The theme of this story is the difficulties of finding a site for a prison given opposition from powerful landowners and the intricacies of the legal and legislative system. This book will suggest that, despite its bizarre quality, the panopticon was not theoretical but a viable project which commanded widespread support. In this aspect, the part played by Samuel Bentham will be given full weight. The project was destroyed by ill-chance and coincidental events rather than by its inherent weakness. Bentham's political naïvety will be apparent, but so will his political dexterity; he was certainly justified in blaming the sinister interests of the aristocracy for ruining his plans, but this he should have expected. Chapter 8 describes first the background of the Penitentiary Act of 1794, and then the details of a Parliamentary bill drafted by Bentham himself which discloses the way he expected the panopticon to work and provides invaluable material on the development of his ideas. Chapter 9 is concerned with the events from 1794 to 1799, in particular the efforts to acquire a site on Tothill Fields and the subsequent reference to the Finance Committee. Chapter 10, while retailing the events that culminated in the rejection of the panopticon in 1803, also uncovers Bentham's own interpretation of the government's actions which he castigated as a perfidious conspiracy against the public interest.

Chapter 11 draws on contemporary newspaper evidence to examine the reasons for the failure of the panopticon. It deals briefly with Bentham's encounter with the Audit Board, and goes on to describe his final defeat at the hands of the Holford Committee, again using manuscript material. It will be argued that even as late as 1812 the demise of the panopticon was far from inevitable.

Chapter 12 returns to Bentham's perception of the panopticon, this time to his private vision of a world organized by and for

---

[42] Henry Addington (1757–1844), cr. Viscount Sidmouth, 1805; Speaker of the House of Commons, 1789–1801; Chancellor of the Exchequer and Prime Minister, 1801–4; Lord President of the Council, 1805; Lord Privy Seal, 1806; Lord President of the Council, 1806–7; Home Secretary, 1812–22; Cabinet Minister without office, 1822–4.

Jeremy Bentham. This account is pieced together from random jottings and gives a fascinating glimpse of his character, the wide scope of his ambitions and his taste in architecture, gardens, and interior decoration. It then goes on to discuss the question of the panopticon as utopia and its relation to the tradition of the pastoral idyll.

In conclusion the significance of the panopticon in relation to penal history and Bentham's utilitarianism is discussed.

# 2

# JEREMY BENTHAM AND THE ORIGINS OF THE PANOPTICON

Jeremy, the eldest son of Alicia and Jeremiah Bentham, was born in Houndsditch in the City of London in 1748. His father, a prosperous attorney and clerk to the Scriveners' Company, amassed a considerable fortune through dealing in property. Jeremy was a small, slight child of remarkable intelligence but prone to nightmares and fearful of the dark, of ghosts, and of hobgoblins. The reality of his life must often have been as fearful as the dreams. His five little brothers and sisters, Thomas, William, Alicia, Rebecca, and Anne, all died in early childhood. Only his brother Samuel, born in 1757, survived. When Jeremy was 11, their mother too died. The death of children was to haunt Bentham for the rest of his life. Seven years after the death of his wife, Jeremiah married a widow with two sons of her own. One of these stepbrothers, John Farr Abbot, died in 1794; the second, Charles Abbot, became a successful and distinguished lawyer and politician.[1] He was to play a significant part in the story of the panopticon. Bentham's relationship with his stepmother was cool and distrustful but for Charles Abbot he developed a wary respect; they were allies though hardly friends.

However, his childhood was not all tragedy. His parents were happily married and he was a much-loved child, his father regarding him with a warm if rather overwhelming pride and affection. There were visits to relations in the country where Bentham learnt that respectful admiration for cats that is so attractive a feature of his character. At the age of 7 he was sent to board at Westminster School. Such was his precocity that at 12 he went to Queen's College, Oxford, and graduated in 1764. His father was

---

[1] Charles Abbot (1757–1829): cr. Baron Colchester, 1817; Chairman, Select Committee on Finance, 1797–8; Speaker of the House of Commons, 1802–17.

fiercely ambitious for his brilliant son: at school and at university he was urged to cultivate useful friendships among the aristocracy. His father dreamed dreams of fame and fortune, perhaps even the Lord Chancellorship, for he had early marked his son down for a career in the law. At the time Bentham seems to have been a dutiful, even deferential son, but the unremitting pressure towards worldly success took its toll. Combined with outward affection was extraordinary bitterness bordering on contempt for his father. Bentham later mercilessly derided his Jacobite leanings: 'My Father was bred up in the principles of it. My Father was pious: but power by whomsoever possessed was the object of his piety. Without much cost in conveyancing, from the Stuarts to the Gwelfs, the transfer of it was made.'[2] And once he left university, Bentham steadfastly refused to gratify his father's wishes. Jeremiah set him up in Chambers, but he could not make him practise. Many years later in another age, Bentham became a Bencher of Lincoln's Inn, but his pathway to that honour was far removed from the one laid down by his father.

Bentham contemplated the legal profession in the 1770s with revulsion. In his view, the system was rotten to the very core; the interests of lawyers were in direct opposition to those of their clients and the general public. The greater the delay, obscurantism, and injustice perpetrated by the courts, the greater would be their remuneration; it was a conspiracy against the public weal; the structure of the law sanctioned delays and denial of justice and covered its faults in a smug patina of mutual admiration. Given these feelings, it is hardly surprising that he could not bring himself to prostitute his talents in law practice. He gave advice on one brief, a suit in equity, to the effect 'that the suit had better be put an end to, and the money that would be wasted in the contest saved'.[3] He preferred to pursue a life of study and writing, living on spasmodic earnings from journalism and an allowance from his father. Jeremiah must have been bitterly disappointed, but he was generous enough not to withdraw his financial support. Bentham never had the spur of necessity to drive him to remunerative labour. His younger brother, Samuel,

---

[2] BL Add. MS 33550, 386. Bowring's version of Bentham's attitude to his father is more sentimental.
[3] Bowring, x. 51.

was in a different case with his fortune to make; he was a man with very different talents, inventive and practical. At the age of 14, he was apprenticed to a shipwright and embarked on a career of varying success as an engineer, inventor, soldier, and entrepreneur. Jeremy loved his brother dearly and was his teacher, mentor, and friend, advising him on any subject under the sun, from chemical experiments to making advances to young women.

As he turned his back on a legal career Bentham had a revelation about his mission in life; he would describe the law as it ought to be; he had, he was convinced 'a genius for legislation'. As a child, he had drawn 'the first draught of that love of justice or hatred of injustice' which was to inspire his life's work.[4] In his twenties he laid the foundations of his philosophy on the principles of utility. 'The greatest happiness of the greatness number' was 'a plain as well as a true standard for whatever is right or wrong, useful, useless, or mischievous in human conduct, whether in the field of morals or politics.' Man was essentially a selfish creature avoiding pain and seeking pleasure and who 'from the very constitution of his nature, prefers his own happiness to that of all other sensitive beings put together'.[5] Bentham spent the rest of his life thinking and writing on the application of these principles to law, government, and institutions. They were all judged on the criterion of whether they conduced to the general well-being. These were revolutionary ideas for they swept aside the widely held and comfortable assurances that law and morality were founded on natural or divine law, prescription, or custom. Everything was to be judged in the harsh light of utility. He derived from the greatest happiness principle the theory that the ends of government should consist of four objectives; subsistence, security, abundance, and equality. Subsistence means sufficient food and shelter without which no life is possible. Security protects person and property against violence and injustice from any source; without security no decent life is possible. Bentham preferred the word security to liberty but within it are included basic civil and political liberties and the freedom to live without fear. He added to this security of expectation which would protect established rights not only to property but also to poor relief.

---

[4] BL Add. MS 33550, 390.      [5] Bowring, x. 79–80.

Abundance meant anything produced beyond essential needs. And the objective of equality meant that this abundance should be spread among the people. Bentham was one of the first to formulate the concept of marginal utility and he believed that the more evenly the good things of life were distributed the greater would be the happiness. But given the natural inequality of talents and the overriding need for security, absolute equality could not be a proper end of government. Nevertheless policies, such as death duties, should be devised that would lead gradually to greater distributive justice.

In 1774 the even tenor of Bentham's life of study and writing was threatened with disruption; he met and fell in love with a Miss Dunkley. She was a girl of only 17 from a respectable middle-class background, but she was an orphan and penniless. His father was horrified; it was one thing to keep his son in idleness but to be called on to support a wife and family was unthinkable. For several months, Bentham hoped through the mediation of his stepmother to change his father's mind. At one time he was planning to give up his chambers and find a house, 'in readiness to receive my Polly'.[6] He even contemplated earning a living by writing; but cooler counsels prevailed. He would not sacrifice his mission to reform the law for his love. He failed to reconcile his father; Jeremiah was indulgent but there was a limit to his indulgence: 'Fortune', he wrote sombrely, 'is absolutely necessary to the Comfort of Life in any Station, more especially in that of marriage which as to wants, is a kind of Multiplication Table.'[7] Bentham slowly disentangled himself from Miss Dunkley; there is no record that he regretted or even remembered her.

This sad little tragedy was followed by high farce. Jeremiah in his ponderous fashion decided to provide his son with a suitable wife. After careful enquiry as to the extent of her fortune, he directed his son towards a Miss Stratton. Bentham was willing to oblige his father; he followed the young lady down to Surrey, purchased a horse, and assiduously rode over wearing his best coat. The lady played the harpsichord while he accompanied her on his violin. Bentham brought little enthusiasm to this courtship; he wrote in bitter cynicism to his brother, 'I did not like her much

***

[6] *Correspondence (CW)*, i. 235.      [7] Ibid. 303.

the first time—I like her much better now: so well that I know not whether I may not give into the Q.S.P. projects: provided always that the fortune be a large one. less than £30,000 in possession or expectancy it must not be.'[8] But although Bentham was hunting a fortune, he played his part with little conviction and refused to compromise his honesty. He would not deceive Miss Stratton as to the true state of his feelings. He wrote to his father: 'If the whole success of the affair depended upon it, I could not bring myself to tell her that concerning my own dispositions, what I did not feel was true.'[9] So he would not assure her that fortune was no object to him. This display of chilly ardour, hardly surprisingly, left the lady unmoved. Bentham's suit was rejected.

Love and courtship had not distracted Bentham from his philosophical labours. In 1776 *A Fragment on Government* was published and enjoyed a transient fame, for the world suspected that it was the work of some eminent lawyer or statesman—perhaps Lord Mansfield. But Jeremiah Bentham was unable to refrain from boasting of his son's achievement and once it was generally realized that the author was an obscure young man, the work ceased to interest the public. This lesson in the harsh consequences of his own unimportance was not lost on Bentham.

He was engaged on more ambitious and wide-ranging speculations on the foundations of government and punishment. The convoluted history of the publication of his works has obscured the origins of the panopticon penitentiary. Its roots were in these theories that Bentham was formulating in the 1770s. Chance and inertia delayed their appearance for almost forty years. The French version of *The Rationale of Punishment*, *La Théorie des peines*, was published under the aegis of Étienne Dumont in 1811; it was mainly based on manuscripts written over thirty years before.[10] When Bentham's ideas are examined chrono-

---

[8] *Correspondence* (*CW*), i. 295. 'Q.S.P.' refers to Queen's Square Place where Jeremiah Bentham lived.

[9] Ibid. 354.

[10] Bowring, i. 388. Account given by É. Dumont of the publication of the *Rationale of Punishment* in 1811, 'Théorie des Peines et des Récompenses, Par M. Jérémie Bentham Jurisconsulte Anglois Rédigée en françois d'après les Manuscrits, par Ét. Dumont'. *The Edinburgh Review*, 22 (Oct. 1813–Jan. 1814), 1–31, published a summary of this work with comments. This was the only version available to English readers until 1830 when the *Rationale of Punishment*,

logically, it becomes clear that his concern with punishment was central to his early ideas on government and that his interest in penal questions was not the product of his brother's invention of a central inspection house: rather, the invention enabled Bentham to give substance to ideas that had been long maturing in his mind. These writings were, according to Dumont, conceived as part of 'a general system of legislation . . . The idea of the Panopticon was as yet unformed'.[11] They are an essential starting-point. They form the philosophical foundation of a justification of punishment and show that his interest in prisons, even down to the details of their administration, preceded any formulation of his own scheme to put them into effect. They also shed light on the development of his ideas on the vital question of solitary confinement and they even hint at the tentative beginnings of the concept of the reconciliation of the interest of prisoners and gaolers that was to be the very foundation of the contract management of the panopticon.

The English version of *The Rationale of Punishment* was finally published in 1830. Its argument was firmly based on the principles of utility and of pain and pleasure. Bentham started from the basic premiss that: 'Punishment, whatever shape it may assume, is an evil.'[12] Both its end and the justification for this end was prevention, and the magnitude of the pain suffered thus needed to be greater than the magnitude of the pleasure expected from the act. Punishment was the basis of government; as he later succinctly stated: 'Punishment is everywhere an evil; but everywhere a necessary one: . . . No punishment, no government; no government, no political society.'[13] Thus, although the thrust of his logic is against cruel punishment as being unnecessary, he sternly rejected arguments based on emotional revulsion, natural rights, or sentimental humanitarianism:

But abolish any one penal law, merely because it is repugnant to the feelings of a humane heart, and, if consistent, you abolish the whole penal code: there is not one of its provisions that does not, in a more

---

Richard Smith's translation of Dumont's work with some use of MS sources was published. This was reproduced as Part II of the *Principles of Penal Law* in Bowring, i. 388–525.

[11] Bowring, i. 388–9.
[12] Ibid. 390.
[13] Ibid. 528.

or less painful degree, wound the sensibility. All punishment is in itself necessarily odious: if it were not dreaded, it would not effect its purpose; it can never be contemplated with approbation, but when considered in connexion with the prevention of the crime against which it is denounced.[14]

Punishment was an 'indispensable sacrifice to the common safety'. But, although the interests of the community justify punishment, the criminal was not outside the pale of society; and his interests could not be disregarded:

It ought not to be forgotten, although it has been too frequently forgotten, that the delinquent is a member of the community, as well as any other individual—as well as the party injured himself; and that there is just as much reason for consulting his interest as that of any other. . . . It may be right that the interest of the delinquent should in part be sacrificed to that of the rest of the community; but it never can be right that it should be totally disregarded.[15]

Safeguarding the interests of the criminal was to be one of Bentham's main preoccupations in his panopticon scheme.

The *Rationale of Punishment* is an analysis, in the classic Benthamite style, of differing forms of punishment, sometimes in revoltingly horrific detail; as Dumont admitted, they 'do not present any pictures upon which the imagination can repose with pleasure'.[16] It is, however, an impressive march through penal policy and practice and provided a solid basis for his conclusion that of all punishment the most acceptable was 'active or laborious' imprisonment. This conclusion was deduced from an analysis based on no fewer than twelve principles. They are worth rehearsing, for they lay bare the solid utilitarian foundation upon which Bentham's later ideas on penitentiaries rest. Punishment should be variable both in intensity and duration; it should be equable, imposing a roughly equal degree of pain independent of circumstance; it should be commensurable (a greater offence should attract a greater penalty); it should possess 'characteristicalness' (have some obvious connection with the crime, perhaps by analogy); it should be exemplary to deter others; it should be frugal (keeping a man inactive in prison is an expensive waste of productive power; shooting him is cheap, but

---

[14] Bowring, i. 412.     [15] Ibid. 396, 398.     [16] Ibid. 390.

'everything he might be made to produce is lost'); a punishment should tend to reform the criminal, not encourage him in his vices; it should prevent him repeating his crime; it should be convertible to profit to compensate for the wrong; it should be popular to avoid public resistance to the law; it should be simply described and easily understood; and it should be remissible for those unjustly convicted—here Bentham takes the opportunity to denounce the death penalty. 'The most perfectly irremissible of any is capital punishment. In all other cases, means of compensation may be found for the sufferings of the unfortunate victim, but not in this.'[17]

On this scale of values, Bentham measured a series of afflictive and restrictive punishments and concluded that: 'Upon examining laborious punishment, we shall find it to possess the properties to be wished for in a mode of punishment, in greater perfection, upon the whole, than any other single punishment.'[18] Labour could be converted to profit, even if combined with the expense of imprisonment, since good management could make the profit equal to the expense; it was equable in that it could be accommodated to different individuals and circumstances; it could be varied; it could lead to reformation, first as it tended to prevent intercourse between malefactors and secondly as it encouraged the habit of industry; it had a element of analogy as many crimes were the product of idleness; and the prisons themselves could be exemplary. In the 1770s, however, Bentham was not yet the passionate enthusiast he became twenty years later and he admitted some drawbacks. Forced labour, he accepted, was not popular, being too easily confounded in the public mind with slavery. He also voiced the objection on which many schemes for profit-making prisons have foundered:

The labour obtained by the force of fear is never equal to that which is obtained by the hope of reward. Constrained labour is always inferior to voluntary labour; not only because the slave is interested in concealing his powers, but also because he wants that energy of soul upon which muscular strength so much depends.[19]

In his panopticon, Bentham would make valiant efforts to devise schemes that would ensure that the prisoners would be inspired

---

[17] Ibid. 402–6.    [18] Ibid. 439.    [19] Ibid. 441.

by the promise of reward, and perhaps he hoped that they could thus be enthused with 'energy of soul'.

The examination of the realities of imprisonment at the time, in accordance with his twelve principles, forms an important section of the *Rationale of Punishment*. Written at the time when John Howard was beginning to expose the scandals of the gaols, it echoes many of his criticisms; one can understand why Bentham at first accorded Howard's work such unstinted admiration.[20] He deplored the incidental evils of prison life—hunger, cold, damp, smells, disease, vermin, indecent practices, noise, and the absence of the consolations of religion. He was particularly incensed by promiscuous association which was no punishment to the hardened offender but rather a tumult which diverted him from the miseries of his situation. Others of more refinement and sensibility would be subjected to untold suffering; it was therefore inequable. It also utterly failed to reform—indeed it corrupted by evil conversation; vicious propensities were aroused and invigorated: 'Prisons, therefore, have commonly and very properly been styled *schools of vice.*'[21] And imprisonment could, quite incidentally, inflict the most grievous of all penalties: 'imprisonment may include every possible evil; from those which necessarily follow in its train, rising from one degree of rigour to another, from one degree of atrocity to another, till it terminates in a most cruel death; and this without being intended by the legislator, but altogether arising from absolute negligence.'[22]

Bentham went on to suggest his own reforms and to sketch very briefly his first 'General Scheme of Imprisonment'.[23] He started from the premiss that promiscuous association could only be obviated by a change in the construction of prisons and he suggested that as there were three types of prisoner so there should be three types of prison. A House of Safe Custody, painted white, for debtors and those held before trial; for second-rate delinquents, whose imprisonment was temporary, a Penitentiary House, painted grey; and for those whose imprisonment was perpetual, who had for ever forfeited their liberty, the

---

[20] *The State of the Prisons*, was published in 1777. The question of Bentham's relations with Howard will be dealt with in Chaper 4.
[21] Bowring, i. 429, Bentham's emphasis.
[22] Ibid. 421.
[23] Ibid. 429–31.

Black Prison. To make prisons exemplary, their appearance should 'strike the imagination and awaken a salutary terror'. His ideas on how this could be achieved reveals his delight in somewhat crude architectural and pictorial symbolism and in devices and details that can too easily be the target of mockery. His prisons were to be decorated with emblematic figures of a monkey to represent mischief, a fox for cunning, and a tiger for rapacity— ideas he elaborated in the *View of the Hard Labour Bill* but abandoned, at least publicly, in his design for the panopticon. Within the Black Prison, to strike terror into the hearts of its inmates, two skeletons were to lie slumped one either side of an iron door, thus reminding them that they were indeed in an abode of death from which there was no escape. This bizarre idea, so reminiscent of the Gothic novel, fits ill with Bentham's sternly rationalistic approach and he admitted himself that it would be ridiculous to a 'man of wit'.[24] It is central to Bentham's penal theory that criminals were of another order of men.

The theory of maximum general deterrence, held so generally in the eighteenth century, had led in practice to an increase in the severity of punishment—it is estimated that by 1770, over 150 offences were punishable by death. But Bentham, temperamentally humane, argued for milder punishment within the framework of his twelve principles. In a masterly manner he marshalled the arguments against the death penalty. It could not be converted to profit and to destroy a man is to destroy his value to the community; it had not the same terrors for all and so was inequable; inflicting death for offences other than murder was not commensurable and so was unpopular, leading to a public disposition to hinder justice; witnesses were unwilling to testify, juries to convict; perjury had become meritorious and the law had fallen into disrepute. These points have become common currency in the debate on capital punishment; but Bentham also deployed two unusual arguments rooted in his distrust of the sinister interests of established power, arguments that have not lost their relevance. First, that the death penalty is dangerous in the hands of evil judges who could by judicial assassination silence for ever witnesses to their crimes. Secondly, that in a society with the legal death penalty, a tyrannical government

[24] Ibid. 431. Horace Walpole's *The Castle of Otranto* was published in 1764.

could the more easily eliminate its opponents as they would be using a method sanctioned by law and custom. Bentham had to admit that for murder the death penalty was both popular and recommended by analogy, but this was overridden by his most powerful objection that it was irremissible; this 'applies to all cases and can be removed only by its complete abolition'. Perpetual imprisonment should take the place of death; first, because it was more economical in that the labour of the criminal could benefit society; secondly, that for many criminals perpetual imprisonment would hold more terror than extinction.[25]

Bentham's insistence on the exemplary quality of punishment lies at the root of the most vulnerable point of his theory. 'The question is not whether a penal code is more or less severe, this is a bad way of looking at the subject. The whole question can be reduced to judging whether or no the severity of the code is necessary.'[26] The judgement on whether death is 'necessary' must also be based on empirical considerations. With rigorous logic, Bentham rejected Beccaria's sentimental arguments for mildness based on natural rights and humanitarianism. But his logic surely leaves the door open to torture, prolonged executions, or any of the other 'complex afflictive punishments' described with such thoroughness in the *Rationale of Punishment*, if they are judged necessary to the security of society.

Bentham himself realized this implication. In an unpublished study, his love of contrivances and his insistence on the exemplary and analogous qualities of punishment betrayed him into suggesting, as alternatives to death, inhuman and degrading penalties that amount to penal torture. The malefactor who had taken advantage of a fire to steal was to be encased in an iron frame shaped like a suit of armour and then turned on a spit to be half-roasted in front of a fire. The highwayman who rode out on a horse to rob was to ride an iron horse, its back as thin as possible with his hands tied and his feet encased in iron boots. Bentham commented that these penal devices had been used in the army for military offences, but:

On account of their severity they have not been much in use of late. On this account as well as that of analogy they seem better adapted to the

---

[25] Bowring, i. 444–50.
[26] *Traités de législation civile et pénale* (Paris, 1802), ii. 418.

purposes to which they are here proposed to be applied. Punishments which are at once of so exemplary and so characteristic a nature, should not be lavished upon slight occasions.[27]

Yet Bentham also stressed symbolism and analogy so as to substitute emblematic terror for the realities of suffering. He suggested that if hanging in effigy could inspire the same fear, 'it would be folly or cruelty ever to hang a man *in person*'.[28] He argued that the greater the apparent evil of the penalty, the less its real evil need be; the greater the striking solemnity of the executions that do take place, the fewer need actually happen; the more analogous to the crime the punishment was, the more exemplary will be its effect.[29]

The problem of the real deterrence of symbols remained. Bentham's treatment of analogy has caused difficulties even for his admirers. He himself expressed doubts:

The species of punishment that command the largest share of public approbation are such as are analogous to the offence . . . The delinquent suffers the same evil he has caused: ought the law to imitate the example it condemns? ought the judge to imitate the malefactor in his wickedness? ought a solemn act of justice to be the same in kind as an act of criminality?[30]

Yet he was fascinated by the idea; some of his suggestions are ludicrous; others are, as we have seen, horrific. The writer of the otherwise laudatory article in the *Edinburgh Review* in 1813 felt that Bentham had been misled by his fancy and took him severely to task for his suggestion that a forger might be publicly displayed with his hand apparently transfixed by a pen, but in reality pierced only by a pin—the ridicule, according to the reviewer, that Bentham sought to attach to the offender would 'here be turned, not against the delinquent, but against the punishment and the law'. Bentham's harsher suggestion that the appropriate punishment for rape was castration, being a penalty that might well come to mind at the very time the offence was in contemplation, was

[27] UC cxliii. 18, 19.
[28] Bowring, i. 398, Bentham's emphasis.
[29] Bentham here came close to the argument of the anonymous author of *Death Not Punishment Enough* (1701), who suggested prolonged executions as a humanitarian measure for they would the more effectively deter from crime and so fewer people would suffer any penalties.
[30] Bowring, i. 412.

dismissed with the words, 'we entirely dissent'.[31] This suggested mutilation, that so much offended against the decencies of the nineteenth-century reviewer, was acceptable in the eighteenth. Lord Kames's influential *Historical Law Tracts* commended the Egyptian code that punished rape by castration as it effectively and humanely answered the end of punishment by preventing the delinquent from repeating the offence.[32]

Fortunately for Bentham's reputation in the more solemn as well as the more prudish nineteenth century, his suggestion of an analogous punishment for a man who had deserted his children remained hidden in his private writings; he was to be set on a pedestal, garlanded with life-size images of his offspring and labelled with an inscription:

'The deserter of his children abjuring the dictates of reason and natural affection takes pattern by the ostrich.' At his right hand shall be the figure of an ostrich standing on a pedestal with its beak close to the culprit's ear. On the pedestal shall be the inscription, 'The ostrich droppeth her egg in the sand and careth not what becometh of her young.'[33]

Dumont stated that he based the *Rationale of Punishment* on Bentham's writings of 1775; he interpolated chapters on the panopticon and transportation from later works. A study of these original manuscripts illuminates the development of Bentham's ideas on imprisonment and reveals some differences and discrepancies. Dumont's version was not taken straight from these pages. The two versions agree substantially on many points. For instance, the injustice of the hardships of imprisonment which, resulting in death, imposed a penalty against the intention of the law, was obviously a question that deeply concerned Bentham;

---

[31] *The Edinburgh Review or Critical Journal*, 22 (Oct. 1813–Jan. 1814), 11, 13.
[32] Henry Home (Lord Kames), *Historical Law Tracts* (Edinburgh, 1761), 49. The copy of this work among Bentham's papers at UCL contains his marginal notes. These notes are of a certain interest. Kames's assertion that the natural restraint of the dread of punishment was greater than any that can be invented by man is criticized as a 'rhetorical declamation'; Damiens had shrieked after, not before, the torture, and Bentham had heard of the horror of these cries from an eyewitness (p. 2). He underlines the point that punishment is a debt due to the public (p. 54) and later notes: 'Pecuniary where it can obtain is the best mode of punishment by the happiness of the injurer being transferred to the injured there is only one portion clearly lost in other cases there are two' (p. 57).
[33] UC cxliii. 28.

there are several reworkings of this theme in the manuscripts. In places the tone of the original belongs more to the eighteenth than to the nineteenth century; it is more robust and franker in dealing with such questions as sex and human excrement. The manuscript speaks openly of the evils arising 'from the obligation of exposing to promiscuous companies of both sexes the parts and operations which modesty requires to be kept concealed—and from seeing practices and hearing discourses of others inconsistent either with modesty or with delicacy'.[34]

Another point glossed over by his editors was Bentham's scepticism. While the manuscript agrees with the later versions that solitary imprisonment 'is peculiarly favourable to the influence of the Religious Sanction', yet the tone is gently mocking:

Sequestered from all the comforts of the world, he will take a stronger interest in the prospect held out to him of the inefffable raptures in another: and he will be the more appalled at that of the torments prepared for the guilty in the regions of eternal night, and that his present situation seems already to be a prelude and a foretaste of those sufferings to come.

And Bentham carefully dissociated himself, and by implication his readers, not only from the criminal but also from the religious terrors that might beset his mind:

The bulk of mankind are not Philosophers; nor is it the Philosopher who exposes himself to be brought into this disgraceful situation. Mysteries which may shock the belief of a Philosopher whose acquaintance with the operations of nature, and the principles of human action enable him to distinguish between the credible, have no such effect upon the minds of the uninstructed multitude.[35]

In a less polished draft, he was much less cautious about his scepticism, he mocked at piety as 'a very cheap drug' and wrote that he would not trouble his readers with what is 'so insignificant

---

[34] UC clix. 188.

[35] Ibid. 196. This is a particularly interesting extract in that it shows a confidence in the law that underlay Bentham's contempt for it; the implication is that philosophers were in no danger of imprisonment, a security that he may not have felt after the French Revolution. Also, it is another example of Dumont's suppression of the irreligious themes in Bentham's thought noted by Halévy (*The Growth of Philosophic Radicalism* (London, 1928), 520).

to the rest of mankind as my own private opinion on matters of religion'.[36]

The treatment of the question of solitary confinement in the *Rationale of Punishment* and the related manuscripts is one of great importance in the history of the panopticon. The original *Letters* paint the most chillingly graphic picture of how solitude could be combined with hard labour, how the prisoners could be alone yet in a crowd. However, Bentham became aware of the dangers of the practice and later changed his mind. The solitude of the *Rationale* was a solitude made dreadful by darkness and the pangs of semi-starvation—another device that Bentham later denounced. Dumont's published version is ambivalent, warning constantly of the dangers and insisting on the temporary nature of the punishment:

The mind of the patient is, by this means, reduced, as it were, to a gloomy void; leaving him destitute of all support but from his own internal resources, and producing the most lively impression of his own weakness, . . . This course of punishment . . . is . . . a sort of discipline too violent to be employed, except for short periods; if greatly prolonged, it would scarcely fail of producing madness, despair òr more commonly a stupid apathy.[37]

Here Bentham is, of course, discussing a solitude different indeed from the well-lit, warm, hard-working cell in the panopticon. But in the manuscripts there are pages that unequivocally approve of absolute solitude, darkness, and a spare diet. In the 1770s Bentham was insisting that the three components were inseparable: 'Solitude, Darkness, and Hard Diet form a compact and consistent body of discipline that ought not to be severed.'[38] Bentham appears at this time to have had no reservations as to this punishment and to have been convinced as to its efficacy in combating the evils of promiscuous association and in tending towards reformation. In a discussion on penitential imprisonment, he described his ideal regime in a bizarre mixture of scientific terminology and biblical rhetoric; he insisted that his convict should see no one *but prison officers*, should lie on straw, and:

[36] UC lxix. 36.
[37] Bowring, i. 425–6.
[38] UC clix. 196. There are three different versions of this idea.

For his diet he shall have nothing but the bread of affliction and the water of affliction. The bread of affliction is bitter bread: the water of affliction is bitter water . . . The particular composition of this bread and water should be determined by some general regulation after consultation with the medical faculty.[39]

The object of these punishments was 'to break the spirit of the patient'. It may be significant that the pages that contain the humane reservation and doubts on solitude in the later versions have been separated from the main body of the original manuscript on which the *Rationale* was based and are to be found interleaved with Richard Smith's copy of 1826.[40] This makes it possible that they are a later revision of his original rigorous ideas.

Among the more significant material in the manuscripts is a discussion of rudimentary schemes to make prison work profitable by reconciling the interests of gaolers and inmates. Halévy has described the panopticon as 'a new application of the principle of the artificial identification of interests the idea of which he had found in Helvetius'.[41] This idea can be found in embryo in the writings of the 1770s. Bentham first dealt with the problems of bringing work to prisons; it would be inconvenient for the master, the gaoler would have no interest in getting the work done and would therefore have to be paid; there was unlikely to be any profit after deducting maintenance. He then went on to suggest that some prisoners might be handed over to masters who could profit from their labour. They would be like apprentices, but the scheme would need, 'nice and minute regulation'. It would need the agreement of the injured party, the magistrate, the offender, and the master. And all would benefit; the injured party would get compensation; the master would profit from the prisoner's work; and the prisoner himself would be working for a master of his choice instead of in prison, and would work well in fear of being incarcerated again; if he were grossly ill-treated, the magistrate might have the power to discharge him. These tentative beginnings of the idea of the apprentice prisoner remained in

---

[39] UC cxliii. 16. Written no earlier than 1778; a reference to the *View of the Hard Labour Bill* makes the Taylor Milne dating of these documents to 1773 clearly incorrect.

[40] UC cxli. 45–92.

[41] Halévy, *Growth of Philosophic Radicalism*, 82.

Bentham's mind; but he concluded that, at present, it would not be possible to use it as an original punishment but rather as an indulgence to be occasionally substituted for hard labour in the penitentiary.[42]

The *Rationale* is a notable work, impressive both in its range and depth, its subtlety and its rigorous logic. But the most extraordinary thing about it was that it lay, like so many of Bentham's other writings, buried, unseen except by a few friends. The story of how Étienne Dumont, met through Bentham's connection with Romilly and Lansdowne,[43] abstracted these manuscripts and later published them in a French version in Paris, has been told many times—notably by Halévy.[44] According to Dumont, Bentham was still disinclined to publish these writings in 1811, and unless they had been brought out 'in the French dress' they would have remained 'shut up in his cabinet. They have lain there thirty years.'[45] This failure to publish was the despair of Bentham's friends. In a much quoted letter, George Wilson had, in 1787, deplored the abandonment of 'Your Introduction, your Code, your Punishments . . . With one-tenth part of your genius, and a common degree of steadiness, both Sam and you would long since have risen to great eminence. But your history, since I have known you, has been to be always running from a good scheme to a better.'[46] But nine years before this, in 1778, Bentham had certainly intended to publish his 'Punishments'; in the course of a long letter to John Foster in St Petersburg, he wrote of the imminent appearance of a Theory of Punishment which: 'For about a year and a half I have been employ'd principally in writing . . . which I hope . . . to send to the press in the course of two or three months. It will form a middle sized Volume in quarto.'[47]

Bentham hoped that this book would inspire reform of the penal system. A hitherto unpublished draft preface written in the

[42] UC clix. 205–6.

[43] Samuel Romilly (1757–1818), knt., 1806; Solicitor-General, 1806–7. William Petty (1737–1805), 2nd Earl of Shelburne, 1761; cr. Marquess of Lansdowne, 1784; Secretary of State Southern Department, 1766–8; Home Secretary, 1782; Prime Minister, 1782–3.

[44] Halévy, *Growth of Philosophic Radicalism*, 75–6.

[45] Bowring, i. 388.

[46] *Correspondence* (CW), iii. 526.

[47] Ibid. ii. 100.

1770s reveals that he was already desirous to be a practical reformer influencing the detailed content of concrete measures, not just an armchair theoretician. He welcomed the 1776 Hulks Act that substituted hard labour on the Thames for transportation, but deplored the fact that it was necessity alone that had forced Parliament's hand. The anger and frustration of an outsider condemned to unremunerative legal theorizing and shut out from the sacred mysteries of the political process are apparent, and with them, a sharp questioning of the secrecy with which Parliamentary business was then conducted:

Men who have the load of affairs engaged in the business of the day, have no leisure for these extensive and fundamental speculations. True: but are there no other men that have. In poetry, in other arts that are their own reward premiums are given with no scanty hand. In the toilsome and difficult Legislation no premiums are given. Better the nation should groan for ever under the affliction of unwholesome Laws, than that the unhallowed hands of the multitude should profane the sceptre of legislation.[48]

The reasons for Bentham's failure to produce his great work on punishment and his general tentative approach to publication are obscure; inertia, self-doubt, his discouraging experience with *A Fragment on Government*: possibly he feared that his ideas were destined to be ignored or misunderstood. This draft preface was designed for his whole code but was concerned mainly with punishment. It is worth quoting extensively for the light it sheds on Bentham's personality and attitudes at the time he was struggling to find his true vocation. It is written in the vigorous, lucid, balanced prose that came naturally to him before his straining after an impossible precision obfuscated his language. He is revealed as a man tortured by misgivings; he was acutely aware that though punishment was a subject of great public interest, his book could not hope to be popular: 'The truth is the bulk of men who read only for amusement are much better pleased to have their passions flattered than their understandings cleared. To write accurately is to impose a task on the reader which few men . . . are willing to go through.' To be popular a book would

---

[48] UC xxvii. 105. Another version reads: 'that the sceptre of legislation should be profaned by the touch how slight so ever of unhallowed hands.' I am indebted to Professor D. G. Long for bringing this passage to my notice.

have to be full of sentimental denuciation of afflictive punishments and lean heavily in favour of the criminal:

But what I meant to write was neither a panegyric, nor a commonplace collection of anecdotes, nor a sentimental comedy, nor a [college] declamation: but a dry treatise of legal policy . . . Well or ill I have thought much, I have copied little: I have some hope of giving satisfaction: I have none of giving amusement. I write not for idlers but for Legislators.[49]

Bentham was fearful that the lack of sentiment and the harsh amoral logic that underlies his analyses would expose him to condemnation and calumny: 'I commit myself to the mercy of the public, with a halter about my neck.' And later in a page headed 'Excommunication', he wrote:

It will be rather hard upon me if after the unpaid labour of many years, and the trouble of writing a great book . . . I should be reprobated as a profligate abandoned man, a man of mischief, a man of whom no good can be expected, because from principles which I imagine we all subscribe to, I have drawn truly or falsely some consequences that are not pleasant to consider.[50]

He was apprehensive that the time was not ripe for a thorough reform of the law, a fear that was justified by the event. 'I have sown the seed; but the harvest I fear, is for another age.'[51] He found sentiment obnoxious: 'There are those who by pronouncing the word *heart* with a certain emphasis think themselves entitled to shut out reason, and to set up their . . . caprices for a law.'[52] He revealed that he himself did at first experience an emotional revulsion against the cruelties of punishment: 'I began in the strain of declamation. When I came to investigate the matter soberly and regularly upon the principle of utility I threw my declamations into the fire.'[53] Given the fears and hesitations expressed in this draft, it is hardly surprising that Bentham did not publish his book on punishment. But there can be little doubt that these delays were damaging to his reputation, limiting the impact of his ideas and vitiating their influence. The delay itself may have had unforeseen consequences of great significance in the fortunes of the panopticon scheme. The *Rationale of*

---

[49] UC xxvii. 105, 106.        [50] Ibid. 106, 108.        [51] Ibid. 101.
[52] Ibid. 107, Bentham's emphasis.        [53] Ibid. 105.

*Punishment* is worthy to be placed beside Howard's *State of the Prisons* or Beccaria's *Crimes and Punishments*, while not even the most devoted of Bentham's admirers would argue that *A View of the Hard Labour Bill* and the panopticon writings are other than inferior. Yet Bentham expended great effort and energy in publishing them in haste and, in the case of the *Letters*, in so incomplete and ill-considered a form that they had to be massively revised. The greatness of the *Rationale* can be measured by his friend Samuel Romilly's changing reaction to Bentham's labours. In 1791 he dismissed them contemptuously as of little account. 'Bentham leads the same kind of life as usual at Hendon,' he wrote, 'seeing nobody, reading nothing, and writing books which nobody reads.'[54] In 1808 the manuscripts written thirty years before came as a revelation. Dumont brought them to show him:

One of them, a treatise on punishments, appears to me to have very extraordinary merit, and be likely to be more popular than most of Bentham's writings and to produce very good effects. I strongly exhorted Dumont to finish it without delay . . . Since the work of Beccaria nothing has appeared on the subject of Criminal Law which has made any impression on the public. This work will, I think, probably make a very deep impression.[55]

Romilly was correct in his judgement. The French version ran to three editions and was translated into Portuguese and Spanish. It was welcomed by the *Edinburgh Review* as a major contribution to penal theory, worthy of comparison with Montesquieu. According to the Webbs, it 'gave to the merely empirical proposals of the prison reformers an intellectual framework connecting them with the wider movement for the reform of the criminal law, and, indeed, also with that for the general reorganization of society on utilitarian principles'.[56]

The panopticon scheme might have had a very different reception if the *Rationale* had been published in due order. It was only after 1811 that Bentham became a prophet honoured in his own

---

[54] S. Romilly, *Memoirs of the Life of Sir Samuel Romilly Written by Himself* (London, 1840), i. 417.

[55] Ibid. ii. 252–3.

[56] S. and B. Webb, *English Prisons under Local Government* (London, 1922), 67–8.

country. And this honour, which he had nearly so carelessly thrown away, he owed largely to Dumont. In 1815 Miss Morgan of Bristol, an intelligent admirer, castigated Bentham for his neglect of his work on penal law. She wrote in tones of incredulity:

The history of these works is perhaps unique in the annals of Literature. Mr Bentham either too fastidious to be satisfied with his own performances, or too impatient to submit to the labour of giving his works that degree of order and arrangement requisite for publication, confided his Manuscript to his friend M. Dumont. . . . Thus have these profound reflections on the Philosophy of Jurisprudence been rescued from that oblivion to which the carelessness of the Author had probably doomed them.[57]

In the 1790s Bentham was not generally considered a great thinker. He must have appeared to many merely one of Lord Lansdowne's more ineffectual and eccentric clients. Bentham also believed that his *Fragment on Government* had mortally offended and frightened the established powers. As he wrote in 1828: 'On the part of the men of politics, and in particular the men of law on all sides, whether endeavour was wanting to suppression, may be imagined.' And he also blamed: 'Advertisements, none. Bookseller did not, Author could not, afford any. Ireland pirated.' As a consequence, the author, after enjoying a brief fame 'was now a nobody'.[58] In his negotiations with the administration this nobody was treated with rudeness and contempt. His friend William Wilberforce related how he had 'seen the tears run down the cheeks of that strongminded man' at the insolence of official underlings: 'How indignant did I often feel, when I saw him thus treated by men infinitely his inferiors! I could have extinguished them. He was quite soured by it, and I have no doubt that many of his harsh opinions afterwards were the fruit of this ill-treatment.'[59] Whether the author of the

---

[57] *The Gaol of the City of Bristol compared with what a Gaol ought to be By a Citizen. With an appendix containing a brief account of the Panopticon, a prison upon a new plan proposed by Jeremy Bentham* (Bristol and London, 1815), 77. See *Correspondence* (CW), viii. 525.

[58] Bowring, i. 256.

[59] R. I. and S. Wilberforce, *The Life of William Wilberforce* (London, 1835), ii. 171. William Wilberforce (1759–1833), MP, 1780–1825; an anti-slavery campaigner, his greatest achievement was the abolition of the slave trade in 1807.

*Rationale of Punishment* would have been so treated is within the realms only of conjecture; but it is possible that Bentham's failure to publish his quarto book on punishment in 1778 helped to nullify what he regarded as his life's work.

# 3

# A VIEW OF THE HARD LABOUR BILL AND THE PENITENTIARY ACT OF 1779

Bentham's preoccupation with prisons has not met with approval. Leslie Stephen is typical in his dismissal of the 'immediately practical work' of the panopticon and his relief at Bentham's return 'to his more legitimate employment of speculative labour'.[1] The panopticon can defy disapproval. But *A View of the Hard Labour Bill* is in a different category.[2] This short pamphlet, seemingly out of the mainstream of Bentham's work, is usually treated of in a few brief sentences and relegated to the lumber room of the archaic and antiquarian. It suffers greatly from the format of the deplorable Bowring edition; the clause-by-clause summary of the bill merges imperceptibly into Bentham's own observations. As it is difficult to distinguish between the legislative proposals and the comment, it lacks coherence and logical progression. Perhaps for these reasons there has been no full study or analysis of the work. However, recent writers have traced in it the origins of fundamental themes of Bentham's thought. For L. J. Hume it is a contribution to the ongoing debate on the nature of the modern state, its instruments and its conditions, and an application of Benthamite principles to a particular situation. He links it with Bentham's other abortive schemes for a Board of Shipping to stimulate inventions and experiments and an Office of Intelligence to collect information

---

[1] L. Stephen, *The English Utilitarians* (London, 1900), i. 209.

[2] *A View of the Hard Labour Bill*; being an abstract of a pamphlet intituled, 'Draught of a bill to punish by Imprisonment and Hard Labour certain Offenders; and to establish proper Places for their Reception' Interspersed with observations relative to the subject of the above draught in particular and to penal jurisprudence in general (cited as *View*), was published in London in 1778. Bentham's intention to republish this pamphlet, together with the other panopticon writings, in 1811 at the time of the Holford Committee, came to nothing (UC cxlix. 187–91). *View* was reprinted, unaltered, in Bowring, iv. 1–35.

on the merits and defects of law. And he argues that the junction of interest and duty is the principle underlying all three schemes.[3] Ross Harrison also contends that the duty and interest junction principle, later developed as a guide to the management of all institutions, originated in Bentham's comments on the provision in the bill making the level of the governor's salary dependent on the level of profits made by the prison.[4] The bill itself, and this was repeated in the subsequent act, gave as the reason that, 'it may become the *interest* as well as the *duty* of each governor to see that all persons under his custody be regularly and profitably employed'. Bentham greeted this 'excellent lesson to legislators' as demonstrating 'genius and penetration'. And he then elevated it into a general principle: 'The means that are employed to connect the obvious interest of him whose conduct is in question, with his duty, are what every law has to depend on for its execution.'[5]

In the dark crannies of the *View* lie hidden some other gems of Benthamite thought. His concern with the plight of Jewish and Catholic prisoners deprived not only of the consolations of their religion but forced day by day to offend against it, was an example not only of an unusual tolerance but of an imaginative sympathy. As Boralevi writes, for Bentham Jews were an existing community with concrete problems, not some abstract hypothesis.[6] Again, his ideas on the collection of statistics meet with the approval of Radzinowicz, who maintains that Bentham's argument that the statistics concerning criminals should be collected with London's Bills of Mortality, and would make useful data for legislators, is 'most striking'.[7] At other points however, scholars have misunderstood the *View*. It is closely linked with the panopticon proposals but the nature of these links is some-

[3] L. J. Hume, *Bentham and Bureaucracy* (Cambridge, 1981), 56, 87, 96.

[4] R. Harrison, *Bentham* (London, 1983), 117. C. F. Bahmueller, *The National Charity Company* (Berkeley, Calif, Los Angeles, London, 1981), 108 suggests that the interest–duty junction principle of management possibly originated in Edmund Burke's *A Plan of the Oeconomical Reformation of the Civil and Other Establishments*, 1780; he would seem to be mistaken as the *View* and the Hard Labour Bill itself have primacy both in time and probability.

[5] Bowring, iv. 12, Eden *et al.*'s emphasis.

[6] L. Campos Boralevi, *Bentham and the Oppressed* (Berlin and New York, 1984), 86.

[7] L. Radzinowicz, *A History of English Criminal Law and its Administration from 1750* (London, 1948), i. 395.

times misrepresented. Boralevi sees the earlier work as an exposition of ideas on penal communities, 'which later on were to become the plans of his famous Panopticon'.[8] Everett asserts that the panopticon was 'calculated to the last detail to answer the purposes of the Act'.[9] Both these statements are misleading simplifications of what is a much more complex connection. Coleman Phillipson makes a more serious mistake in accepting Bentham's later accounts at their face value when he repeats the myth that he subjected the bill 'to a severe criticism'.[10]

The *View* is Bentham's only substantial publication between *A Fragment on Government* in 1776 and the *Defence of Usury* in 1787, the only product of thirteen years when he was in his prime, physically, intellectually, and creatively. For this reason alone it should not be disregarded and, when studied in conjunction with the wealth of manuscript material, it adds considerably to the understanding of his ideas. This short pamphlet raises several questions of interest and importance. Did Bentham's observations influence the contents of the Penitentiary Act of 1779 as he was convinced that they did? What is the connection between the *View* and the panopticon? What were Bentham's motives in publishing this sole work at that time? Why were his accounts of the substance of the tract in later life so wide of the truth? And finally, what light can it throw on his character and his ambitions? In this chapter it will be argued, first, that although Bentham would appear to have been instrumental in persuading the authors of the Act to make some changes, there were other influences at work and the bill was subject to revisions between 1778 and 1779 which Bentham neither foresaw nor advocated. Secondly, that there were considerable differences between his penal theory as expressed in the *View* and that in the panopticon writings; and that, in his old age, his memory of the two works became confused and he confounded the one with the other. Thirdly, that Bentham's knowledge of penal practices was not entirely theoretical but based on at least one visit to the hulks of which he has left a full description. Fourthly, that in publishing this work Bentham may have been motivated by worldly ambition. Also, the manuscripts contain an expanded version of

[8] Boralevi, *Bentham and the Oppressed*, 85.
[9] C. W. Everett, *The Education of Jeremy Bentham* (New York, 1931), 177.
[10] C. Phillipson, *Three Criminal Law Reformers* (London, 1923), 120.

the preface to the *View* which makes it a vehicle for his ideas on Parliament, representative government, and reform, and so a more considerable work dealing with more fundamental issues than prisons.

The extent of Bentham's influence on the Penitentiary Act of 1779 can be gauged by a detailed threefold comparison of the original bill, Bentham's observations on it, and the final statute. The act is of considerable importance in penal history. It was introduced by a group of reformers, among them Charles Bunbury, Gilbert Elliot, and William Eden; they had been helped in the work of drafting by William Blackstone and John Howard. It embodied many of the ideas on prison reform that Howard had advocated in *The State of the Prisons* and was the first-fruit of his exposure of the crying scandal of the country's gaols. It provided for the building of two national penitentiaries in the London area and laid down a series of minute regulations as to site and building, diet, and accommodation, work, management, and inspection. The convicts were to have separate cells at night and, as far as possible, work without associating during the day; the tasks were specified and their labour was to be of the 'hardest and most servile kind'. It was intended that the institution should make a profit from this work. The inmates were to be fed on bread and coarse meat 'or other inferior food', to drink water or small beer and to wear badges on a coarse uniform which would humiliate the wearer and hinder escape. These new penitentiaries were to be managed by a committee of three gentlemen appointed by the Crown; they, in their turn, had to appoint a governor and other officials. Although these three supervisors were duly appointed,[11] the Act became otherwise a dead letter in the sense that the prisons were never built. But it was nevertheless a seminal piece of legislation. The regulations became a model for the Gaols Acts of 1784 and 1791 and for the numerous private Acts for building reformed county prisons.[12] The regime of the

---

[11] These were John Howard, John Fothergill, and George Whatley. By 1781 they had been replaced by Thomas Bowdler, Gilbert Elliot, and Charles Bunbury. Sir Thomas Charles Bunbury (1740–1821), MP, 1761–84 and 1790–1812, was to play an important part in the history of the panopticon. Thomas Bowdler (1754–1825), philanthropist, also had a role to play. He later gained a dubious distinction for his expurgated edition (1818) of Shakespeare's texts.

[12] M. Ignatieff, *A Just Measure of Pain: The Penitentiary in the Industrial Revolution 1750–1850* (New York, 1978), 96.

great national prison at Millbank, started in 1812, was based on the 1779 Act. And as late as 1834, this legislation was cited as proving the British origins of the penitentiary system. It also marked a new departure in the attitude to criminals. In 1776 a Hard Labour Act had been passed to meet the immediate crisis of the end of transportation to America. It enabled convicts to be set to work on the Thames, housed in disused naval hulks. This temporary expedient continued, despite its appalling evils, until 1858. The preamble to this Act justified putting convicts to work on the mercantilist grounds of the inconvenience of 'depriving this kingdom of many subjects whose labour might be useful to the community'[13]—the same argument Bentham deployed against the death penalty. But, in 1779, the preamble of the new act had different justifications, emphasizing that punishment 'might be the means under Providence not only of deterring others . . . but also of reforming the Individuals and inuring them to habits of industry',[14] thus showing a new concern for the individual soul and a new faith in the reformatory worth of work and discipline.

The 1778 bill was a draft circulated privately more than a year before the final and substantially different version was presented to Parliament on 19 April 1779. Bentham's comments, written in three weeks, were published in March 1778. There was, therefore, ample time for his suggestions to be incorporated. At this time, Bentham approved of the bill; he praised its 'foresight and humanity'. Even in a private letter, he was quite uncritical: 'It gave me real pleasure to have to do with a work which I could applaud with so good a conscience.'[15] In marked contrast to *A Fragment on Government*, the general tone of the pamphlet is adulatory, even deferential. It is not surprising that Blackstone was 'extraordinarily civil' and assured him that, although some of the points had already occurred to the authors, his comments had been noted.[16] Bentham certainly believed that he had influenced the contents of the Act;[17] and a detailed comparison does show that several of the alterations correspond to his suggestions. On points of domestic detail (always beloved by Bentham), a garden

[13] Statutes 16 Geo. III, c. 43, p. 484.
[14] Statutes 19 Geo. III, c. 74, p. 58.
[15] *Correspondence (CW)*, ii. 104.
[16] Ibid. 103.    [17] Ibid. iv. 139.

was to be provided, dungeons were to be airy, the prison was to be heated from kitchen flues (no provision for heating had been made in the original bill), and the inmates were to have sheets and a bedstead and could take exercise on the roof. Bentham also pointed to several careless ambiguities; the maximum size of each cell was laid down, but not the minimum; and the bill would, unintentionally, have deprived Duncan Campbell, the superintendent of the hulks, of his post. Both these errors were corrected in the Act. On points of greater substance, Bentham argued that to use daylight as the measure of the working day was undesirable, being too long in summer, too short in winter. The Act laid down a set number of hours according to the season of the year, but still only the eight in winter months that Bentham stigmatized as too few. The clause in the bill that gave Bentham most delight was the provision that the salary of the governor was to be proportionate to the profits made by the prison. Bentham wanted this junction of duty and interest to be extended to the convicts who should be 'allowed some profit, in proportion to the produce of their own labour'.[18] This could be supplemented by extra work. The Act gave powers for any two of the three members of the committee of management to authorize payment of profits to diligent and meritorious offenders for the use and benefit of themselves or their families or to permit them to work during intervals of stated labour. Finally, Bentham may have influenced the provision for discharged prisoners, though not in the way he intended. The 1779 Act contained the first attempt to help convicts over the difficult transition from prison to the outside world. The bill had provided that, on discharge, the prisoners should be given decent clothes and a sum of money (not less than forty shillings or more than £5) and a certificate of good behaviour, if they merited it. Bentham applauded these measures but pointed out that an ex-prisoner without such a certificate would be unemployable, his only resource being the poorhouse, starvation, or crime. In the Act, the certificate was dropped and replaced with the provision that the ex-prisoner would be given more money after a year in honest employment. This, however, had not been Bentham's solution. His was more Draconian; the prisoner who did not earn a certificate would

---

[18] Bowring, iv. 12–13.

either be kept in prison until he succeeded in obtaining one or forcibly enlisted in the land or sea service; this foreshadows his later scheme for subsidiary panopticons for the perpetual detention of discharged prisoners.[19] In 1778 he hoped that very few convicts would fail to earn a certificate after 'so strict and well-regulated a course of discipline'.[20]

Bentham was therefore right in thinking that he had probably improved the bill in several ways. However, many of his suggestions fell on stony ground. The Act, as had the bill, laid down that the convicts were to wear a humiliating uniform; but there was no mention of face dye, Bentham's favourite device to hinder escape; nor of artificial stone bas-reliefs of wolves, foxes, and monkeys to strike terror into the hearts of the ignorant. Bentham himself was dubious about this idea, fearing lest it 'should give a . . . cast of ridicule to the whole contrivance'.[21] Even less surprisingly, Bentham's discussions on the inequality of the pains of continence and on the religious problems of Catholic and Jewish prisoners were passed over in silence, as were his ingenious suggestions for filling the time on Sundays with music, walking in the garden, and Bible reading. Other criticisms of a more political nature were also ignored. Bentham argued against the death penalty for those who attempted to escape on the grounds that perpetual imprisonment would hold more terror. He also expressed concern about the powers of the governor. First, on the grounds that he would have too much power over the awarding of contracts to supply the prison and this might open the door to corruption. And secondly, that an ambiguity in the wording of the bill meant that he would be able to punish convicts with solitary confinement for up to thirteen days without reference to the committee. This part of the bill remained unchanged. Bentham was more worried, however, about the lack of regulation over the hulks. The less stringent measures reflected an extraordinary confidence in the present superintendent and he suggested that the regulations for the hard-labour houses should be extended to the establishments on the river. Not, he assured his readers, that the confidence reposed in Mr Campbell was misplaced: 'yet I should be sorry to see the merit of this individual officer made an argument for entailing powers so unlimited

---

[19] Bowring, iv. 167.    [20] Ibid. 22.    [21] Ibid. 32.

upon what person soever may chance at any time hereafter to bear his office . . . *Jealousy, not confidence, is the characteristic of wise laws.*'[22] By a sad irony it was this very argument that the Holford Committee deployed with such effect against Bentham himself in 1811. The authors of the 1779 Act, fearful of Campbell's considerable political influence, left the distinctions between the hulks and the penitentiaries untouched.[23]

William Eden had circulated his draft bill in the spring of 1778 because he believed that 'The Matter is too complex to be brought to any degree of Perfection except by continued Attention and repeated Alterations.'[24] Other minds and pressures than Betham's were at work and the bill was changed considerably in ways other than those suggested by him before, in the following year, it passed through both Houses of Parliament.[25] These changes are in themselves of importance and form an interesting comparison with Bentham's observations. The preamble to the draft bill had argued against transportation, and Bentham had enthusiastically endorsed this stand; it was unequal, unexemplary, and unfrugal. The 1779 Act omitted this, merely repeating the words of the 1776 Act in stating that transportation to America was attended by many difficulties; but, ominously for the future, the power to transport was extended to 'any parts beyond the seas'. The name of the new prisons was also changed. Bentham had suggested that 'Hard Labour Houses or Labour Houses' would be better than the bill's 'Houses of Hard Labour': 'The technical name', he wrote, 'would by this means be the same as the popular. This would, *pro tanto*, save circumlocution, and guard against error in law proceedings.'[26] However, the authors of the Act had different ideas and the new prisons were to be called 'penitentiaries'. This was a change of some significance; 'penitentiary' has connotations of religious and spiritual repentance quite alien from Bentham's thought. He used the word freely later but was never at ease with the evangelical emphasis on the salvation of the soul

---

[22] Ibid. 29, Bentham's emphasis.
[23] W. Branch-Johnson, *The English Prison Hulks* (London, 1957), 9–10, for Campbell's influence.
[24] *Correspondence* (*CW*), ii. 91. William Eden (1744–1814), cr. Baron Auckland, 1789.
[25] *Journals of the House of Commons*, 37 (1778–80), 372, 412, 415.
[26] Bowring, iv. 7.

of the prisoner which was such a central tenet in the creed of Howard, Wilberforce, Paul, and Holford.

There was also a change of far greater substance than in the name; the original bill provided for a network of prisons throughout the country administered by the magistrates, whereas the Act, less ambitiously, provided for only two penitentiaries in the London area, one for men and one for women, administered by a committee of three appointed by the Crown. The original scheme is of some interest; the country was to be divided into nineteen districts based on the circuit and the counties, each circuit having at least one of the new prisons and each district comprising at least two counties. As Bentham pointed out, the county was too small a unit, the circuit too large. This scheme foreshadowed the nationalization of the prisons and is an interesting early indication of the growing inadequacy of the historic divisions and the need to impose a new pattern if reform of the administration was to be effective. Prisons, however, continued to be administered by the counties until nationalization in 1877. It is paradoxical in the light of the centralizing trend of later reform, that the 1778 bill would have left the control of the new hard-labour houses in the hands of the local magistrates, a committee of whom were to be appointed proportionately at the General Sessions of each county. Bentham approved of the proposed new divisions, but he was aware of the inconvenience that would be suffered by some magistrates because of the length of their journeys to meetings. However, his solution was to pay them salaries; whereas the authors of the bill totally abandoned this attempt to usurp the authority of the county over the prisons and to impose onerous new burdens on the country gentlemen.[27]

Other changes between the first bill and the Act concerned the questions, central in penal history, of visitors and inspection. It was easy to visit eighteenth-century prisons, both for the philanthropist and for the criminal fraternity. Howard was seldom denied access and there was reasonably free commerce with the streets. But casual entry was forbidden to the hulks and both the bill and the Act forbade it to the new prisons. All visitors

---

[27] Ignatieff, *A Just Measure of Pain*, 95, suggests that the subsequent failure to build the penitentiaries was due in part to the opposition of the gentry to interference by central government in prison administration.

would need permission from the prison management. Bentham approved the exclusion of these promiscuous visitants as 'highly eligible'. The inspection of county prisons was on a casual basis, the sheriffs having this duty. But revulsion and fear of disease kept many of them at a distance, with the honourable exception of John Howard. The new labour houses, however, were to be subject to a thorough system of inspection—this was another radical departure. In the bill, the committees were to appoint two official visitors, justices or other substantial householders in the district. Every year one of them was to be changed and none were to serve for more than two years, though after an interval, again of two years, they could be reappointed. They could, if they asked, be paid a gratuity. Bentham approved these measures on the grounds that they would guard against torpor and indifference and too great an intimacy with the governor, but would make the best use of experience. The duties of these visitors were laid down in detail; every fortnight they had to examine the state of the house, see every convict, hear complaints, and inspect accounts. They had powers to examine under oath and impose punishments; they were to report to the judges or the committees. Under the Act, these powers and duties were transferred to any two of the management committee; and any justice in the district had a general right to inspect the prisons. The scheme under the Act is obviously less effective in providing an independent inspection; but, significantly for the future, the Act also provided for an inspector appointed by the Crown who would report to Parliament. The appointment was never made and a system of government inspection had to wait for almost fifty years.[28] As a consequence of the failure to implement the 1779 Penitentiary Act, inspection of the prisons and the hulks remained casual, spasmodic, and alarmingly inadequate.

An analysis of the differences between the bill and the Act therefore shows that Bentham failed to anticipate, let alone influence, the final shape of the Act in several important particulars. It also demonstrates that he failed to take into account the forces that moulded political action, in particular the conservatism, inertia, and immense influence of the country gentlemen. This failure to understand the political nation was to

---

[28] The first government inspectors of prisons were appointed in 1835.

become glaringly apparent in the panopticon negotiations; as Leslie Stephen wrote, 'there were dozens of party politicians . . . who could have explained to him beforehand those mysteries in the working of the political machinery, which it took him half a life time to discover'.[29]

One of the central questions raised by the *View* is how far its ideas on penal theory anticipated the panopticon. It is too often assumed that Bentham was entirely consistent throughout his life, although this assumption is given credence by the evidence of his own words. He regarded the *View* as part of his panopticon writings; his manuscript drafts are filed in folders marked, 'Panopt. Miscell.';[30] and in 1811, he planned to republish the *View* together with the *Panopticon Letters and Postscripts*, the *Letters to Lord Pelham*, and *A Plea for the Constitution*.[31] Speaking in his old age, he implied that there were no contradictions or differences between his early and later theories. But Bentham's memory cannot be relied on and his reminiscences are seriously misleading. In 1823 he asserted reasonably accurately that the pamphlet, 'though free and holding up to view numerous imperfections, was upon the whole laudatory'. His delight at seeing any disposition to improvement 'was sincere, and warmly expressed'.[32] But when recalling the past with Bowring, he boasted of having 'worked' Blackstone and Eden 'to a jelly'; and by 1830 his achievement was on a grander and more heroic scale and his memory accordingly yet more faulty. He had, he believed, lambasted the bill for its reliance on trust management:

the managing hands, whether one or more, not having any interest in the success: gaining nothing in case of profit, losing nothing in case of loss: in a word, their interest was not to be coincident with their duty . . . Actuated by these conceptions . . . I took in hand the plan of the two illustrious statesmen, applied to it the above principle, examined it in all its details, and the result was what appeared to me to be a complete demonstration of its inaptitude.[33]

It is probable that by 1830 Bentham was confusing the *View* with the panopticon writings in which the deficiencies of the Act are fully exposed. As we have seen, much to Bentham's delight at

---

[29] Stephen, *The English Utilitarians*, i. 234.
[30] UC cxix. 1–13.       [31] UC cx/ix. 187–91.
[32] Bowring, i. 255.       [33] Ibid. x. 86, xi. 98.

the time, the 1779 Act did give the governor an interest in maximizing the profits of the prison. Also, his comments in 1778 do not in fact anticipate his reliance on contract management. Indeed, he expressed doubts as to the advisability of giving the governor such wide powers and he commended the provisions that allowed the committees to oversee and negate contracts. He had even graver doubts as to the wisdom of giving Campbell 'powers so unlimited'. This is a far cry from his later insistence that the governor of the panopticon should be given absolute discretion. And, indeed, in 1778 he expressly contradicted the central tenet of contract management; servitude, he argued, could answer the purpose of reformation but not so well, 'under the uncertain and variable direction of a private master, whose object was his own profit, as it may be expected to answer under regulations concerted by the united wisdom of the nation'.[34]

One pillar of the panopticon was contract management, the other, transparent management. The constant surveillance of public opinion, the constant access to the central tower for casual visitors, was Bentham's answer to the problems of inspection. There is no foreshadowing of this in the *View*. Bentham approved the bill's system of inspection by officially appointed visitors and the exclusion of the public from the gaols; and, indeed, went further by condemning English dislike of secrecy in the exercise of coercive powers as being 'unwarranted by the dictates of utility'.[35] The aseptic quarantine imposed on the prisoners in the panopticon is very different from the casual promiscuous commerce with the streets that the bill forbade. The visitors to Bentham's public gallery would be invisible to the inmates and would be unable to smuggle in tools and weapons or help plot escapes. In his transparent panopticon, Bentham hoped to get the best of both worlds, prisons isolated from the outside world but safeguarded by public knowledge of all that went on inside. Another safeguard against the tyranny of authority that became central to his plan of management was life insurance. This also is absent from the *View*. He believed then that the system of inspection proposed in the bill would be 'amply sufficient for obviating any real danger of abusive severity'.[36]

Despite these profound differences, neither the origins of the

---

[34] Ibid. iv. 7.    [35] Ibid. 23.    [36] Ibid.

panopticon idea nor the progress of the negotiations can be understood without reference to the 1779 Penitentiary Act. Bentham certainly believed at first that he had devised a scheme that would indeed answer 'to the last detail the purposes of the Act'. But he had little experience of the application of statute law and one of the most surprising aspects of the events of the 1790s is Bentham's failure, as a lawyer who had made a special study of the subject, to appreciate that the Act would not give him the powers to set up the panopticon. There are nevertheless many points of resemblance between the panopticon and the penitentiaries envisaged by Howard and Eden; and many of the ideas in the *View* anticipated the later scheme. In the *Letters* Bentham commended his panopticon as a perfect device for combining solitude and labour. His vision of the hard-labour houses holds out an implied promise of a utopia of music and gardens created by a junction between interest and duty; within them would be discipline, hard work, profit, and reformation. Although, at this time, Bentham approved of the minute regulations that weigh down the Act, he does suggest that it would be more profitable for convicts in sedentary occupations to follow their old trades. In the panopticon writings, this slight suggestion blossoms into excoriating ridicule of all such attempts to regulate labour by law. It is ironic that Radzinowicz ascribes value to the *View* because it shows Bentham's realization, 'unaided by any practical experience—that the value of a prison system depends equally on broad regulations and on countless provisions touching upon every detail of prison life'.[37] It is a measure of Bentham's failure to communicate his central idea of contract management to posterity that the great expert on criminal history should not realize that he spent twenty years condemning all minute statutory regulation. Bentham's idea of work as the fundamental agent of reformation and his fear of the abyss of idleness was apparent in 1778. Paying lip-service to religious sensibilities, he agreed that in organizing the Sabbath: 'Devotion, it is true, is better on such a day than industry; but industry is better on every day than total idleness, that is, than despondency or mischief.'[38]

---

[37] L. Radzinowicz, *A History of English Criminal Law and its Administration from 1750* (London, 1948–68), i. 380.
[38] Bowring, iv. 19.

Bentham's obsession with the morality of work and the maximization of labour was to reach its highest pitch in his plans for the pauper panopticons.

The treatment of Duncan Campbell and his hulks in the *View* is another point of great interest. In later years Bentham was to dismiss Campbell contemptuously as a projector in the white–negro trade; but in the *View* he is treated more respectfully. Although Bentham was doubtful as to the wisdom of leaving the hulks so unregulated, he went out of his way to insist that the superintendent had not misused his position: 'I have never heard of any fact so much as surmised, that afforded the least reason for deeming that confidence misplaced, and I have much reason for entertaining a contrary opinion.' This seems almost disingenuous at a time when, after adverse reports from Howard, the working of the 1776 Act was subject to a Parliamentary investigation. Bentham may not have wished to appear openly critical of the hulks; he waxed eloquent on the benevolence of Mr Campbell who had voluntarily provided a doctor and on the piety of the Countess of Huntingdon who had sent a clergyman so assiduous in his attention to his sacred duty to the convicts that he 'has distributed Bibles among them; and has endeavoured to direct their attention to the sacred writings, by giving them rewards for performing little exercises proposed to them as tests of their proficiency'.[39]

It is odd to find the sceptic Bentham so enthusiastic for religious instruction and the reformer so blind to the abuses in an institution. It is part, perhaps, of the subservience to established authority that is so marked a feature of the pamphlet. But that is not the whole story. Bentham had gained his 'much reason for entertaining a contrary opinion' and his detailed inside information from a personal visit to the hulks in January 1778. Bentham is often described as a theoretical reformer; in this case he decided to emulate Howard and go to see for himself. His manuscript account is a straightforward description very much in the Howard mode; it does not entirely support the uncritical tone of the published work. The convicts were chained—even the sick;

---

[39] Ibid. 29. Selina Hasting, Dowager Countess of Huntingdon (1707–91) was the founder of a sect of Calvinistic Methodists. She established 64 meeting-houses and left the bulk of her fortune for their endowment.

many were boys, some of them under 12; they were punished by whipping and running the gauntlet. There was 'a very considerable sickness and mortality which Campbell says is concealed as much as possible—the diseases chiefly putrid fever and low spirits . . . mortality greatest among the country convicts'. And, although Bentham asserts that the sleeping quarters were abundantly warm on the freezing day of his visit, yet some of the men's legs were swollen with cold. However, in comparison with other prisons, the hulks that Bentham saw were probably reasonably orderly and clean; Campbell was after all preparing for the Parliamentary inquiry. The *Censor* was a fine large ship, the convicts were all well clothed; their beds 2 or 3 feet apart were of straw covered with canvas and furnished with blankets and rugs—pretty clean, 'from the smallness of the beds it is probable that every man has one to himself . . . hardly any disagreeable smell between decks'. The prisoners were given three meals a day—rice, meat, bread, cheese, and plenty of vegetables; 'the water all filtered we saw the filtering stones, the stone cleaned every day'. And discipline was good; the punishments were rarely inflicted; no strong liquors, no extra provisions from outside, no money were allowed. At work, he wrote:

The men remarkably silent . . . don't talk even to one another—no swearing—Campbell indeed was present all the time we were there. He says they do more work by one half than common workmen and that for the last 6 months they have not cost the public £500 more than the value of their labour, in which he did not include the benefit to the river—allows that he has a good bargain.[40]

The memory of these convicts, their good behaviour under the eye of authority, and the value of their labour may have persuaded Bentham that his panopticon would be both practicable and profitable.

In some ways the most surprising thing about the *View* is that it was published at all. In later life, Bentham suggested that his father was mainly responsible for 'pushing' it.[41] Yet it is clear from his letters that Bentham himself circulated the pamphlet to several influential people including Blackstone and Eden, the authors of the bill.[42] The traditional picture of Bentham, deriving

[40] UC cxvii. 1–2.    [41] Bowring, x. 86.
[42] *Correspondence (CW)*, ii. 103.

from Bowring, J. S. Mill, and Leslie Stephen is of a benevolent recluse, uninterested in money or worldly success. Everett developed this into a mawkish description of a gentle genius, misunderstood but sadly accepting the world's rejection. However, recently a more astringent personality is emerging in the literature. Hume contends that the desire for profit was central in Bentham's fight for the panopticon, and Ross Harrison points out that Bentham was his father's son and had been brought up with the idea of achieving worldly success.[43] It would seem unlikely that the ferociously acquisitive entrepreneur of the 1790s sprang suddenly into life with his father's death; it may be that the death removed an inhibition on an open and ruthless search for success and recognition. In 1778 he may have been willing to pursue ambition with the lackadaisical half-reluctance with which he had pursued a rich wife. Perhaps the *View* written, printed, and published in such uncharacteristic haste was part of a campaign to achieve ambitions that he shared with his father.

There is some support for this interpretation in the manuscripts and *Correspondence*. Hume links the *View* with Bentham's plans for a Board of Shipping and an Office of Intelligence; all were applications of his principles to particular situations.[44] But there would seem to be even closer links between the pamphlet and another earlier abortive scheme for a government newspaper. This is of peculiar interest. Bentham recognized (and this was in 1776) the central importance of the Press; he wrote, 'For an English Minister to neglect the Newspapers is for a Roman Consul to neglect the Forum.'[45] He suggested, therefore, that ministers should secretly subsidize a paper that would, with assumed impartiality, consistently forward their views. Its major object at that time would be to reconcile public opinion to 'constitutional changes and other coercive and unpopular measures as it may be found necessary to adopt with respect to America'.[46] To achieve this end he planned to use several of the less reputable devices of journalism, the inspired leak, the planted story, and the ferocious attack to make it appear that ministers were bowing to popular

---

[43] Hume, 'Bentham's Panopticon: An Administrative History', in *Historical Studies*, 15 (1971–2), 707, Harrison, *Bentham*, 20.
[44] Hume, *Bentham and Bureaucracy*, 87.
[45] UC cxlix. 7.
[46] Ibid. 5.

clamour. He suggested too that the government would derive benefit from stories of the domestic felicity of the King and Queen and their management of their children (given subsequent history not perhaps an entirely happy suggestion). Bentham is here dimly foreshadowing Bagehot's theme of a family on the throne as a force for political stablility. With perhaps conscious irony, he planned to call his newspaper *The Candid Intelligencer*. This scheme is relevant to a discussion of the *View*, first, as it is strongly implied that Bentham was thinking of managing the paper himself, and secondly that one of its tasks would be to comment on 'statutes as they come out; their advantages explained: their deficiencies and their mistakes pointed out: and hints given towards the supplying of the former, and the correction of the latter'.[47] This is exactly what the *View* set out to do. Did Bentham hope that it would persuade someone to give him a job? His letters show that he may well have done. In the spring of 1778, Lord Carlisle, George Johnstone, and William Eden were to be sent to negotiate a settlement with the rebellious American colonies; in March, Bentham sent a copy of the preface of his pamphlet to William Eden and in April he was eagerly trying to persuade Johnstone to take him as an assistant. This may be a coincidence; but it is at least possible that Bentham was hoping that Eden's good opinion would help him to the post. If he was, he was disappointed but philosophical; in telling his friend Foster of his failure, he wrote: 'To love mankind, says Helvetius, one should expect but little of them. I do expect little of them, and am therefore seldom disappointed, and never vehemently.'[48] However, his expressed desire for the sea voyage, for the agreeable company, and for practice in public business may well have spurred Bentham to his three weeks' work on the pamphlet and to the unaccustomed pains of publication.

Bentham felt personally at a disadvantage when dealing with Eden. Earlier, in a manuscript draft, he had written a comparison between himself and the celebrated author of the *Principles of*

---

[47] UC cxlix. 3.

[48] *Correspondence* (*CW*), ii. 105. Frederick Howard, 5th Earl of Carlisle (1748–1825), nominated by Lord North as Chief Commissioner sent to treat with the rebellious American colonies, 1778; President of the Board of Trade, 1779–80; Lord Lieutenant of Ireland, 1780–2. George Johnstone (1730–87), naval officer and MP; Governor of West Florida, 1763–7.

*Penal Law*; a passage that reveals that, although Bentham was aware of the superiority of his own intellect, he was deeply uncertain as to the reception his theories would have from the public; he was out of sympathy with the tone of Eden's ideas and irritated by his effortless success; he praised his work as 'an elegant performance', but went on:

Whenever I agree with him I feel myself at ease; whenever I differ with him it is with pain. I feel how unequal the contest is between us. I feel his hand hang heavy over me. I write from system: and it is the fashion to hate systems. I labour to learn and to instruct: he writes secure of pleasing. He swims with the current: my struggle is to turn it . . . He is one of the ornaments of a court. I have long sequestered myself from the face of men, in the fond hope that I might one day do them service.[49]

The extent of Bentham's desire to conciliate Eden in 1778 is shown by the readiness with which he complied with his objections and fundamentally changed the weight of his preface to the *View*. He did this by the simple expedient of excising large sections of his text. But the bitter regret this caused him is revealed by the frequent annotation of the original in the manuscripts, 'Preface to the View of the Hard Labour Bill uncastrated'.[50] It is yet another indictment of Bowring's failure as an editor that he printed the emasculated version as it was published in 1778, ignoring the version in the manuscripts that Bentham would surely have wished to see the light of day.

This preface falls into three sections. The first is a eulogy of Howard which will be considered in the next chapter. Eden did not object to this, but Bentham thought it was too closely linked with the other sections to be easily detached. The second part of substance is a discussion on the need for wide public debate on new legislation. The third is a demolition of 'the wisdom of our ancestors' argument against change. It was to this last that Eden objected, fearing perhaps that Bentham might prove an embarrassing ally in the fight for what was indeed a radical measure. Eden had broken with tradition by printing and circulating a copy of his bill in order to stimulate discussion. And just at this time Bentham was immersed in penal problems, hammering out in private the ideas that were to form the *Rationale of Punishment*. This was an irresistible invitation to place his views

---

[49] UC xxvii. 107.     [50] UC cxix. 5.

before the public and to bring them to the attention of the eminent and powerful men who were sponsoring the bill. He enthusiastically welcomed this greater openness:

It would be singular enough and rather to be regretted if the capacity of forming a judgment on a measure of this sort depended altogether upon those accidents upon which a seat in Parliament is known sometimes to depend: as if the whole stock of understanding (to say nothing of probity) as well as the whole mass of power in the nation were doomed for ever to be confined within that narrow circle. Such a notion, I must confess were it ever seriously entertained is but too well warranted (as well as usage can warrant notions so ill-suited to the spirit of the constitution) by the privacy with which all parliamentary proceedings have always been endeavoured at least to be enveloped. For my own part however I must confess that without any disparagement to its representatives I can not bring myself to think quite so unfavourably of the great body of the nation.

And in an argument which, if not democratic, is at least a prerequisite of democracy, Bentham went on to assert:

If the *few* indeed are to *decide* ... in the interests of the *many*, it can scarcely one should think be improper that the many should at least be permitted to debate ... I will still suffer myself therefore to hope to see the time when the representatives of the public will no longer disdain to take their constituents into council; and when Bills will be printed for the perusal not of the members of the House only, but of the members of the community.[51]

Bentham was clearly, even as early as 1778, disenchanted with the workings of the 'matchless' constitution and looking forward to a time when the government would be more openly accountable to the people.

Bentham's defence of 'novelties' is more polemical. Eden had disclaimed 'any disposition either to propose or promote novelties in the executive justice of the nation'. Bentham seized on these words. 'The meaning of the passage is not very explicit; but the tendency of it ... seems to be to throw a stumbling block in the way of political improvements.' Eden had also stated that he wished 'to facilitate a business of much national expediency', but how, Bentham demanded, could this not but lead a man to promote novelties? All novelties are either expedient or

[51] UC cxix. 1–2.

inexpedient: 'To reprobate any measure then,' he wrote, 'not because it is inexpedient, but because it is novel, is to combat it with an argument which applies not with any greater force against the worst measure than against the best.' In apologizing for not undertaking a thorough reformation of the criminal law as advocated in his *Principles of Penal Law*, Eden had pleaded, 'it is easier to censure than to correct'. Bentham swept this platitude aside. That fact, he declared: 'we all know well enough without needing a writer, whose rare talents are capable of being so much better employed, to be at the trouble to inform us.' Those endeavouring to improve the laws do not need to be told of the dangers and difficulties: 'The number of those adventurous and eccentric spirits who unbidden and unpaid devote themselves to the service of their country in the most arduous line of duty, is not so great, this patriot band is not so numerous, as to need any discouragements to make it less so.'[52] Thus were Eden's carefully chosen politic words pilloried as devoid of meaning; it is hardly surprising that he took exception to this devastating analysis, protesting that he had merely meant 'to disavow that busy interference with establish'd Systems which except on occasions of necessity like the present is oftener productive of Confusion than Benefit'.[53] If Bentham had indeed intended to ingratiate himself he should have restrained the vehemence of his logic. As it was, he hastily cut out the offending passsages and sent Eden the printed copy with considerable omissions.

The *View* is not an impressive work; it is scrappy and inconclusive. It contains only odd flashes of Benthamite prescience and of practical political wisdom. But it is not sterile or trivial; its very shortcomings make it a work of significance. Bentham's writings on prisons have fallen between two stools; they have seemed of little relevance to philosophers; and because his schemes were abortive, they have held little interest for social historians either. Yet they are central to his life and should have a central place in the revised picture of him that is emerging. The *View* and the related manuscripts are seminal works and an essential source for the public debate on the 1779 Penitentiary Act; they are flawed perhaps, but worthy of more serious consideration than they have yet received.

[52] Ibid. 2.          [53] *Correspondence (CW)*, ii. 92.

# 4

# JOHN HOWARD AND THE ORIGINS OF THE PANOPTICON

The great Penitentiary Act of 1779 originated in two interwoven strands of thought; first, in the rational utilitarianism of the Enlightenment and, secondly, in the ideas of the prison reformers inspired by Christianity and a concern for the individual soul. The panopticon was nurtured in the same soil. Bentham's prison and Howard's penitentiary were a product of the same climate of ideas and assumptions, many of them alien to the twentieth century; in their world, men, as individuals, were responsible for their actions, potentially at least rational, not subject to sub-conscious imperatives, nor the playthings of irresistible economic forces. These premises might now be rejected as naïve, over-simple, and aberrant, lacking a true insight into the human psyche or a true compassion for the casualties of society. But in the eighteenth century they were the widely held, common heritage of intelligent and humane men.

The thinkers of the Enlightenment believed that punishment must deter but also be proportionate to the crime. They took their stand on these principles in reaction to the sanguinary laws that imposed death as a penalty for a myriad of trivial offences, that, on the Continent, inflicted torture as part of the ordinary judicial process, and that sanctioned the cruel horrors of the gaols. The punishment they most favoured was imprisonment with hard labour which they believed would remould criminals into honest men. In their analysis, crime was caused by luxury, drink, and idleness. The associationist psychology of Helvetius and Hartley underlay these assumptions; in their concept of human nature, the psyche was as material as the body, disease could have moral causes, and the indiscipline of the poor could lead to illness as well as to crime. Hospitals and prisons were, therefore, seen as imposing a salutary discipline that would cure the patient of his affliction; abstinence and enforced work would, by altering a man's habits, alter his character. Voltaire had no doubt that not only would this happen but that it was happening. He approved Catherine the Great's policy of sending thieves to Siberia where they became honest men:

We are astonished at the change and yet nothing can be more natural. The condemned are forced to continual labour for a livelihood. The opportunities of vice are wanting . . . Oblige men to work, and you certainly make them honest. It is well known that atrocious crimes are not committed in the country unless when there is too much holiday, and consequently too much idleness, and consequently too much debauchery.[1]

Voltaire also advanced the argument that killing a man deprived the community of the value of his labour:

It hath long since been observed, that a man after he is hanged is good for nothing, and that punishments invented for the good of society ought to be useful to society. It is evident, that a score of stout robbers condemned for life to some public work would serve the state in their punishment and that hanging them is a benefit to nobody but the executioner.[2]

These remarks had been inspired by the work of the great utilitarian theorist, Beccaria, who had a profound influence on Bentham. His basic tenet was: 'It is better to prevent crimes than to punish them. This is the chief aim of every good system of legislation, which is the art of leading men to the greatest possible happiness or to the least possible misery.'[3] To achieve these ends, punishment must be proportionate and exemplary. Beccaria's seminal work, *Crimes and Punishments*, published in 1764, is a sustained plea for more humane practices and a denunciation of torture, 'this infamous crucible of truth', on the grounds of injustice being contrary to the law of nature and utility being an inefficient instrument of judicial enquiry.[4] Men differed in their ability to resist pain, and so 'Torture is a certain method for the acquittal of robust villains and for the

---

[1] J. Heath, *Eighteenth-Century Penal Theory* (Oxford, 1963), 146.
[2] Ibid.
[3] C. Beccaria, *Dei delitti e delle pene* (1764), trans. J. A. Farrer (London, 1880), 242.
[4] Ibid. 150.

condemnation of innocent but feeble men.'[5] He advocated the replacement of the death penalty by perpetual slavery thereby exemplifying the ambivalent nature of the humanitarianism of the Enlightenment. He insisted that the agonies of slavery were more dreadful than those of a quick death and in so doing painted a vivid picture of sufferings as cruel as those inflicted by execution:

> It is not the terrible yet brief sight of a criminal's death, but the long and painful example of a man deprived of his liberty, who, having become as it were a beast of burthen, repays with his toil the society he has offended, which is the strongest restraint from crimes . . . neither fanaticism nor vanity have any place among fetters and chains, under the stick, under the yoke, in a cage of iron; the wretch thus punished is so far from terminating his miseries that with his punishment he only begins them.[6]

Transportation, where these sufferings would not be visible, would fail to deter. By arguing that everlasting slavery was more terrible than death, Beccaria seems to be lacking true compassion, but he had to persuade his contemporaries of the efficacy of the alternative punishment; it had to appear dreadful, so he had to assume a ruthlessness at odds with his character. It was a contradiction that Bentham was to display even more plainly.

In England, more humble writers were concerned with the practical problems of prisons and law enforcement. Written forty years before Beccaria, Bernard Mandeville's short treatise laid the foundation for much subsequent discussion. The tone of his *Enquiry into the Causes of the Frequent Executions at Tyburn* was callously unsentimental, yet there was an underlying pity for the victims of circumstance who lost their lives in such great numbers; the multitude of unhappy wretches put to death, he declared, could not but afflict men of pity and humanity.[7] The criminals were drawn from the great numbers of the 'loose, lazy and dishonest Poor' in which London abounded and he suggested two causes for the increase in crime. First, the reluctance of victims to prosecute, for many preferred to buy back their

---

[5] Beccaria, 151.
[6] Ibid. 171–3.
[7] B. Mandeville, *An Enquiry into the Causes of the Frequent Executions at Tyburn* (London, 1725), 1.

goods rather than be the death of some poor wretch. Secondly, the prison of Newgate was a breeding ground for crime: 'the Licentiousness of the Place is abominable, and there are no low Jests so filthy, no Maxims so destructive to good Manners or Expressions so vile and prophane but what are utter'd there with Applause and repeated with Impunity.'[8] The inmates ate and drank whatever they could purchase—and pawnbrokers and receivers were liberal to thieves in prisons. Anyone could have admittance to them. They were 'debarred from nothing but going out'. Their time was spent in mock trials and cross-examinations that taught the guilty to escape conviction, or on lectures in the art of stealing. This licentiousness spilt over into the streets on days of execution; they were days of jubilee for the whores and rogues of the city. The condemned, fortified by a vast breakfast and unlimited drink, behaved with ribald defiance, jeering at any show of penitence. On the way to Tyburn, the execution carts were stopped so they could be plied with yet more strong liquor. Such executions failed to inspire terror, and so failed to deter— hanging seemed nothing 'but an awry Neck and a wet pair of Breeches'.[9] Mandeville anticipated Bentham's plea for solemn sad executions and dismal processions which would strike terror into the hearts of spectators. To achieve this, he suggested that the condemned should be incarcerated in a dark solitary cell, twelve foot square, with its own privy so that on the day of execution he would emerge pale and emaciated, and be dragged shaking and lamenting to the gallows. In these dark cells, a diet of bread and water would induce repentance, the condemned wretch would be obliged to think of his eternal welfare, and would make a good Christian end. This solitude was not primarily to reform the particular individual—his soul might be saved but his body was forfeit; its real purpose was to deter, he would be an example to convince others of the dreadful nature of his death, of 'the Pangs, the amazing Horror and unspeakable Agonies of his excruciated Soul!'[10]

Mandeville's ostensible argument was that unseasonable mercy was the greatest cruelty, for it encouraged the poor into a life of crime; in that sense it was humanitarian. But his writings are more an example of the callousness of the ordinary eighteenth-

[8] Ibid. 16–17.    [9] Ibid. 37.    [10] Ibid. 42.

century attitude to criminals. He ignored the sensibilities of the poor by advocating handing over the bodies of all those hanged to the anatomists for dissection, though this was a practice widely regarded as a cruel and unnatural extension of punishment fit only for murderers. He also argued that transportation was no longer a sufficient deterrent as rescue was too frequent and the life in America too easy for it to be of any dread to criminals. As an alternative, he suggested that felons should be used to redeem Christian slaves from North Africa or the Barbary coast. The rovers of Barbary 'manage their Slaves as we do our Cattle . . . They laugh at Stubborness and refractory Spirits and their steady Severity is a sovereign remedy against Sloth'. He admitted that this might seem a harsh penalty but it would be exemplary and so 'Thousands that are yet unborn would, deterr'd by the Rigour of those Laws, turn their hands to honest Labour and die in their Beds in their own Country.'[11]

In 1754 an anonymous 'Student of Politics' produced a short tract that anticipated some of Beccaria's theories. He argued that all laws should be based on 'public utility'[12] and that the frequent use of the death penalty was undermining law enforcement. Punishment must deter by exemplary correction; but the debauch and ridicule surrounding executions had made a mockery of the terror they should inspire. He pleaded against the use of capital punishment for so many offences—a life once taken away could never be restored; punishment should be suitable to the offence and take into account the age and education of the offender; and he suggested that malefactors should be 'made slaves according to their different defaults for a longer or shorter space of time'.[13] They would then be of use to the country and a dreadful example to others. For the first five years they should be chained and earn no wages, but after that they could be paid so as to make restitution for the thefts they had committed; and, once the debt was discharged, they could be released. Slavery at home was also preferable to transportation, for the country lost 'young healthy malefactors likely to give to future ages a stronger and better civilized progeny'.[14] He also saw the criminals as drawn from the

---

[11] Mandeville, 49, 52.
[12] A Student of Politics, *Proposals to the Legislature for Preventing the Frequent Executions and Exportations of Convicts* (London, 1754), 29.
[13] Ibid. 26.    [14] Ibid. 39.

class of idle itinerant poor and suggested Draconian methods to deal with the problem; methods that put Bentham's National Charity Company in perspective. All vagabonds, beggars, fiddlers, ballad singers, and others should be rounded up and returned to their parishes. If they wandered off they would be made public slaves; and to facilitate the enforcement of the law, *all* the poor should wear badges and, if found without, they should be whipped and, on the second offence, made public slaves.

The most cogent statement of the links between poverty and crime was made by Henry Fielding, a magistrate for Middlesex and Westminster. His analysis was coloured by country-party ideology, in that he blamed the degeneracy of the age on trade and luxury; the most numerous of the poor, he argued, were those able but not willing to work, those who tried to emulate the wickedness and profligacy of their superiors:

the very dregs of the people, who aspiring still to a degree beyond that which belongs to them, and not being able by the fruits of honest labour to support the state which they affect, they disdain the wages to which their industry would entitle them; and abandoning themselves to idleness, the more simple and poor spirited betake themselves to a state of starving and beggary, while those of more art and courage become thieves, sharpers, and robbers.[15]

Love of pleasure, gaming, and drunkenness created poverty and crime; and the most effective measure for stopping the progress of vice was to remove the poor from the temptations that beckoned in every street in London. To achieve this end, Fielding suggested that the magistrates of Middlesex should devote the poor-rate to building a vast combined workhouse and prison which would have contained 5,000 paupers and 1,000 convicts. The industrious poor were expected to commit themselves voluntarily, and vagrancy, poverty, idleness, or crime would have been reasons for incarcerating other inmates. Their labour would have been hired to contractors who would have set them to work inside the house.[16]

The theories of the Continental Enlightenment and the

---

[15] Heath, *Eighteenth Century Penal Theory*, 92.

[16] H. Fielding, *A Proposal for Making an Effectual Provision for the Poor* (London, 1753).

concerns of English commentators were drawn together by William Eden, many of whose ideas were shared by William Blackstone. Eden's seminal work, *Principles of Penal Law*, provided the framework of debate for a generation; perhaps indeed until Jeremy Bentham's work on punishment saw the light in the next century. This bland reasonable statement of the reformer's position argued that utility, 'the good of all is the great object of all', should be the basis of government and prevention of crimes should be the object of the lawgiver; it was an essential of political freedom that laws should be known and clear to common understandings. 'The political liberty of a state consists in the security of the people and that security bears a proportion to the justice, and wisdom of the penal code, which protects innocence by the chastisement of guilt.'[17] Punishment should therefore be proportionate to the offence. Eden had grave doubts as to the efficacy of transportation which, he contended, was often beneficial to the criminal but always injurious to the community for it deprived the state of a subject. It failed to deter for America was too civilized, fertile, and healthy to hold any terrors and he suggested several alternatives. The malefactors could be employed in public works or, in an echo of Mandeville, sent to Tunis or Algiers in return for Christian slaves, or transported to found colonies in West Africa. On imprisonment, and this was before he fell under Howard's influence, he advocated several obvious reforms, such as the separation of debtors from criminals and those awaiting trial from those convicted. But he was against using imprisonment as a regular punishment on the grounds that the offender would become a burden to the community, his morals would be corrupted and, being hidden from the eyes of the people, his sufferings would not be exemplary. Eden's main theme was the injustice of the death penalty for trivial offences, for it brought the law into disrepute, leading to a hardening of the sentiments of the public. Eden made his point with an example that was to become famous: 'But when in the eighteenth century it is made a capital crime to cut down a cherry tree in an orchard; the thinking part of mankind must listen to such a law with irreverence and horror.'[18] He concluded with

---

[17] William Eden, *Principles of Penal Law*, 2nd edn. (London, 1771), 82–3.
[18] Ibid. 310.

a plea for reform of the penal code, for all men are interested 'in the assignment to every particular offence, of the smallest punishment compatible with the safety of society'.[19]

There is a certain emollient quality in Eden. Though he was a master of the pretty phrase, he was no crusader. His book lacks rigour and avoids contention in a way very alien to Bentham despite the concurrence of many of their views. Eden is inclined to rely on sentiment in the place of logic when arguing his case; cruel and prolonged executions are 'contrary both to sentiment and morality'; mutilation 'inconsistent with decency and humanity'; and castration as a penalty for rape an example of barbarity and again 'inconsistent . . . with decency'.[20] Despite his welcome for the content of Eden's ideas, Bentham found their tone uncongenial; in a private note he described him as 'smooth as oil'.[21] But Eden nevertheless had laid the theoretical foundation for the reform of the penal code by contending that every wanton, unnecessary suffering inflicted by the legislature was tyrannical and unjustified. 'The accumulation of sanguinary laws', he wrote, 'is the worst distemper of a State. Let it not be supposed that the extirpation of mankind is the chief object of legislation.'[22]

Eden's *Principles of Penal Law*, followed by the more practical works of Howard and Hanway, produced, by the time of the panopticon, a certain consensus of ideas on prisons. William Paley independently came to conclusions similar to Bentham's. He argued that the ends of punishment were amendment and example and these might be achieved by solitary confinement and hard labour, for as he wrote: 'An aversion to labour is the cause from which half of the vices of low life deduce their origin and continuance. Punishments ought to be contrived with a view to the conquering of this disposition.'[23] The criminals, he believed, should be allowed a share of their earnings and, after discharge, the state should secure their maintenance for it was impossible for those released from gaol to earn an honest livelihood. But Paley did not share Bentham's optimism and was dubious about the possibility of reformation: 'little has ever been effected, and

[19] Ibid. 330.
[20] Ibid. 25, 62, 262.    [21] UC xxvii. 107.
[22] Eden, *Principles of Penal Law*, 306.
[23] Heath, *Eighteenth-Century Penal Theory*, 258.

little, I fear, is practicable.'[24] He also wished to retain capital punishment for minor crimes, fearing that any change would disrupt society; he was dismayed that the frequency of executions was lessening the abhorrence of crime. But, in direct contrast to Bentham who consistently argued for more public display and less real suffering, Paley's solution was to increase the horrors of execution in private by, for instance, casting murderers into a den of wild beasts, 'where they would perish in a manner dreadful to the imagination, yet concealed from the view'. This, he contended, with a tortuous logic, would deter, 'without offending or impairing the public sensibility by cruel or unseemly exhibitions of death'.[25]

Samuel Romilly voiced more gentle and humane sentiments suggesting that crime was a product of a flawed society and that all members of it were comprehended in the guilt: 'if we negligently suffer a thousand forces of profligacy, and encouragements to vice, to surround these helpless creatures on every side, what a refinement of cruelty is it to hang the thieves and profligates whom we have made.' His remedy was to provide employment and to discourage drunkenness and idleness, 'which are the forerunners of every other vice'.[26] And he envisaged Howard's penitentiary as a refuge for these unfortunates; solitary confinement and labour would subdue the obdurate, and 'it would be a kind of asylum to that very large description of offenders, who are rendered such by the defects of education, by pernicious connexions, by indigence, or by despair'.[27]

Finally, Patrick Colquhoun, a metropolitan police magistrate who was to play an important role in the later history of the panopticon, quite independently came to conclusions remarkably similar to Bentham's. Crimes, he believed, had their origin in the vicious and immoral habits of the people; the legislature should be in the place of a parent and should lead errant children into the paths of virtue. Convicts should be employed in public works and the provision of a place after discharge, where the ex-felon could find honest employment, would be a work of great public benefit:

[24] Heath, *Eighteenth-Century Penal Theory*, 258.       [25] Ibid. 261.
[26] Ibid. 264.       [27] Ibid. 270.

The conditions of a convict would even in some respects be superior, inasmuch as he would have medical assistance and other advantages tending to the preservation of health, which do not attach to the lower classes of the people, whose irregularities, from not being restrained, and whose pursuits and labours, by not being directed by good judgment and intelligence, often produce bad health, and extreme poverty and distress.[28]

The man who most of all directed Bentham to a penitentiary as a field for practical endeavour, and who also exerted the most profound influence on other prison reformers and penal theorists, was John Howard. Born in 1726, the son of a wealthy upholsterer in London, he was left sufficiently well provided to buy estates in Bedfordshire and to live as a country gentleman. In 1773 he was appointed High Sheriff; one of his tasks was to oversee the county gaol. During the course of his duties he was horrified to find that innocent prisoners, acquitted of all charges in open court, were nevertheless dragged back to prison because they were unable to pay the gaolers' fees—fees necessarily incurred while awaiting trial. Howard suggested to the magistrates that such fees should be defrayed out of the rates but was told that this was impossible without a precedent. So he set out on his first journey to neighbouring counties to discover their practices. It was the first of many journeys across England and the Continent until he died of fever in Russia in 1789. It has been estimated that he travelled almost 60,000 miles and expended over £50,000 of his fortune. The prisons he found in England were all too often dens of terror, filth, and disease. He estimated that more died of gaol fever than were hanged. In some counties, imprisonment for debt was tantamount to a death sentence. In many gaols there was no separation between the classes of prisoner: debtors, those awaiting trial, witnesses, and the convicted, men and women, were promiscuously incarcerated. The ancient distinction between the gaols and bridewells had virtually disappeared and those sentenced to corrective labour were all too often idle. Gaolers made their living through fees and 'the tap'—the right to sell liquor to the prisoners. The inmates extorted 'garnish' in

---

[28] P. Colquhoun, *A Treatise on the Police of the Metropolis . . . By a Magistrate* (London, 1796), 297. Patrick Colquhoun (1745–1820), metropolitan police magistrate, 1792–1818.

money, clothes, or sexual services from each other. In some prisons there was no allowance for food, so the poor would starve without private charity. Gaolers would extort their fees from unhappy prisoners by loading them with chains; the day-to-day running of many gaols was largely in the hands of the inmates. The very evils that the eighteenth century identified as the causes of crime—profanity, drink, gaming, and idleness—were rampant in the gaols themselves; they were clearly dens of vice and seminaries of crime.

One of the first-fruits of Howard's investigations was the Gaols Act of 1774, which empowered magistrates to pay the fees of those acquitted and made some attempt to preserve the health of the prisoners. But if Howard had only denounced the evils of the gaols in general terms, he might soon have been forgotten; what gained him immortality were the methods he used. Each prison was subjected to the same inquisition, the same questions were asked, the same points noted. In 1777 he produced the first instalment of the *State of the Prisons*, a vast compendium in which information was systematically set out and facts and figures were carefully tabulated to enable comparisons to be made between different gaols in different counties. Howard was the harbinger of social science. In the following years, this information was constantly added to and updated. Howard also produced his blueprint for an ideal prison which is in many ways the fore-runner of the panopticon. It should be sited on an eminence near to a good water supply. Cleanliness was of the utmost importance in the prevention of disease; the prison should be regularly whitewashed, swept, and mopped with hot vinegar; on arrival each inmate should be washed and perhaps dressed in prison uniform; clean clothes and bedding must be provided. There should be infirmaries and workrooms; solitary cells at night were essential for the protection of prisoners from the violence of their fellows and to give them opportunities for reflection and repentance. The different classes of prisoners must be separated to prevent sexual immorality and the corruption of the young by the hardened offender. For those sentenced to corrective labour, idleness was unacceptable—they should be kept at work ten hours a day, mealtimes included; such work was unlikely to be profitable, indeed profit must take second place to reformation, but could be a means to inure to habits of industry and might set the steps of the sinner on the road to repentance. A chaplain to cure souls was as essential as a doctor to cure bodies. Sober and diligent workers were to be rewarded by better diet and lodging and be given a character on discharge. Howard argued that gaolers should cease to be dependent on the profits from fees and the selling of drink and should be paid an adequate salary; they should be sober, respectable, and constantly in residence. Inmates should never have positions of authority over each other. Thus, the inmate community would be destroyed and the gaolers distanced from the criminal world. Gaols should be under the supervision of magistrates who would give their services voluntarily and be actuated by the desire to serve the public. And the prisons should be regularly inspected by magistrates expressly appointed for the purpose, who would have a duty to make reports to the bench. The subsequent history of English prisons and the trend of legislation are clearly foreshadowed in Howard's proposals. Its salient features were the banishment of the evils of debauch, the separation of prisoners from one another, the breaking of the links between gaolers and the inmates, the increasing authority of local and central government over the details of management, and a system of inspection by independent philanthropic, but officially appointed, visitors. The corollary to these developments was the ending of free commerce with the streets; the prisons became secret claustral institutions from which the casual benevolent intruder was banished. It is the final irony that John Howard would have been excluded from the very prisons that his influence helped to establish.

There are many similarities between Howard and Bentham. Physically he was a spare, small man with a sallow complexion. He had the same love of detail, down to recipes for whitewash. He approached facts scientifically, carefully reading, recording, and tabulating. He was an ascetic; personally abstemious, he avoided any animal food or alcohol, even oysters or beer; his diet consisted of tea, milk, butter, bread, fruit, and vegetables. He loved gardens and gardening and, like Bentham, collected plants and seeds from foreign countries. Although a fervent dissenter, he was tolerant of other religions and did not reject those of another faith. An early biographer wrote of him: 'whilst in the exercise of that active benevolence which has immortalized his name, he would as freely have risked his life to relieve the miseries of a Papist, a Mussulman, or an Hindoo, as that of a Calvinist, a Baptist, or an Independent.'[29] Temperamentally humane, he disliked capital punishment and believed it should be confined to murder, arson, and housebreaking with violence—all offences against the person rather than against property. In his early writings on punishment Bentham frequently cited Howard as an authority on all questions of prison discipline. Even before their meeting in 1778, he had expressed unstinting admiration; he planned to pay Howard the considerable compliment of dedicating to him his book on punishment. There is a rough draft in his papers which shows how close he believed their affinity to be:

I take without your leave or even knowledge, the liberty of prefixing your name to this performance. When I began putting together these sheets I little thought to see a dedication at the head of them; not knowing any Great man whose livery I would wish to wear. On this address at least it will not be easy to fix a charge of flattery: for, your esteem excepted, I am not in want of anything which . . . it is in your power to give me . . . The obligations I owe to you are great and many: some as a member of the community, . . . From your example I have derived encouragement in many a fit of despondency, and argument in many a debate . . . My sentiments, as far as I have travelled over the same field of speculation I find to be in almost every instance congruent to his.[30]

He also planned to pay tribute to Howard in *A View of the Hard Labour Bill*; in his 'uncastrated' preface, he used the example of Howard to argue for greater openness in discussion of legislation and to castigate Eden's smooth politic apologia for the bill:

*Mr Howard*, the prisoners' friend (and who, in an age of devotion, would have been their Saint) *Mr Howard* by a course of the most hazardous and painful researches that perhaps it ever entered into the heart of a man not spurred by fanaticism to engage in, has set on foot a reformation in our police, for which the latest posterity will be bound to bless him. Would it have subdued his resolution . . . had he been told . . . that prisons were very dangerous and unwholesome places . . . that to establish any general and consistent plan for their regulation was a

[29] J. B. Brown, *Memoirs of the Public and Private Life of John Howard the Philanthropist* (London, 1823), 618.
[30] UC clxix. 75.

novelty; that there might indeed be some abuses in them; but that 'it had been always found much easier to censure than to correct'.[31]

The most revealing account of Bentham's reaction to Howard can be found in his private correspondence where he expressed an esteem that bordered on reverence. In the spring of 1778 he wrote a lengthy letter to John Foster,[32] then living in Russia, in which he insisted that Howard's book must be given to the Empress Catherine, and then went on to describe their meeting. After reading the *View*, Howard had called on him and Bentham was very greatly flattered by this attention from one whom 'I had not the least personal acquaintance with'. This letter is absorbing, partly as a picture of Howard, but also as showing Bentham struggling to come to terms with non-utilitarian altruism. 'He is, I believe, take him all in all, one of the most extraordinary men that this age can shew.' Bentham then described Howard's ascetic regime when on his travels: sleeping only every other night, eating only bread, butter, milk, and vegetables, eschewing strong liquor, fearing no disease; 'He spends £100 a month of his own money when travelling.' Yet this philanthropist was no foolish fanatic:

He is no crack-brained enthusiast: the qualities of his head are scarcely inferior to those of his heart. His book is a model for method and for the sort of stile that is competent to his subject . . . His discourse is fluent . . . his eye piercing. . . . He is accurate to an extreme: takes nothing from report: and asserts nothing but what has come under the cognizance of his senses.

Bentham continued with some observations on his own future and ambitions, trying to measure himself against Howard:

From all this rhapsody you would be apt to infer that I fancied myself a great man. The fact is, I live in the same dirty chambers, and am as poor as when you knew me. Law mending *sine privilegio* is a sad trade for a man to thrive by: such as I am, I have given myself to the Public . . . Mr Howard is sacrificing his time, his security, and his fortune. Fortune I have none: the sacrifice of my security is not at stake: why should I grudge the sacrifice of my time? Mr Howard and the public honour he has met with, are of more use to me than you would imagine to prove to my friends that I am not crazy.

[31] UC cxix. 4.     [32] *Correspondence* (*CW*), ii. 98–115.

But, although Bentham often subsequently laid claim to kinship with Howard, 'as a kind of brother of the trade',[33] their paths were to diverge. On management, contract, and inspection he was to become increasingly dissociated from the mainstream of Howard's ideas. This tension reflects differences in the beliefs and personalities of the two men. Howard's motives were of another world. He almost ostentatiously rejected public acclaim; when a monument to him was proposed, he denounced it as 'a hasty, sad, unkind measure', and sombrely asked: 'Could none of my friends, who know how much I hate show and parade, have stopt it?'[34] Bentham, in contrast, craved public recognition and the outward trappings of success. He arranged for his own body to be erected after death as a monument, as an auto-icon, to inspire the philosophers of the future. He still sits perpetually enthroned in his wooden box in the cloisters of University College London. Howard's spirit was not raised by Fame, but by the love of God and the hope of salvation. A similar evangelism, quite alien to Bentham, was to be a guiding light to the next generation of prison reformers and to be one of the rocks on which the panopticon was eventually to founder. Howard's altruism has been dismissed as a manifestation of an obsession with his own sins; but his religion was irradiated with humility and he was quite free of the unctuous self-righteousness that is so repellent an ingredient of some nineteenth-century religiosity. He had a true sympathy with the criminal: 'I consider that if it had not been for divine grace, I might have been as abandoned as they are.'[35] Each criminal, he believed, was a rational and immortal being, reformation must be the primary end of punishment, and reformation meant that a man should accept the salvation of God. These beliefs underlay the whole of his penal theory.

Bentham does not appear to have felt any of the guilt for his own sins or for the sins of the world that weighs down the heart of the Calvinist Christian. But John Howard was one of the very few people who inspired in him a certain humility. For all his lip-service to the welfare of humanity, Bentham's benevolence lacked passion, dedication, and the courage for the ultimate

---

[33] *Correspondence* (*CW*), iii. 182.      [34] Brown, *Memoirs*, 452.
[35] Ibid. 529.

sacrifice. Howard expended his own fortune with no hope of return; he risked, and forfeited, his life. Bentham recognized that here were qualities to which he could not aspire and which he would not denigrate:

In the scale of moral desert, the labours of the legislator and the writer are as far below his, as earth is below heaven. His was the truly Christian choice; the lot, in which is to be found the least of that which selfish nature covets, and the most of what it shrinks from. His kingdom was of a better world; he died a martyr, after living an apostle.[36]

Despite his saintly qualities, Howard left an ambiguous legacy; there is no adequate modern biography, so the contradictions in his personality and his achievements have yet to be explored. These surfaced immediately on his death. His obituary in the *Gentleman's Magazine* condescendingly deplored the 'not un-expected, yet certainly untimely, death of the eccentric, but truly worthy, John Howard'. It went on to publish the scandal that has dogged Howard's memory, that his severity had caused the madness of his son. The writer was also doubtful as to whether all his labours would achieve any permanent improvement in the prisons; this, 'Time only can shew.'[37] In subsequent issues of the magazine, Howard's friends leapt to his defence, angrily refuting the accusation of cruelty to his child, but the doubts remained, and have cast a shadow on Howard's reputation ever since. His principles of prison reform have been even more sharply questioned; he has been held responsible for the transformation of the casual, open, eighteenth-century prison into the total carceral institution of the nineteenth. Professor D. G. Long, one of the few writers to recognize Bentham's debt to Howard, poses the question of how Howard's humanitarian approach can be reconciled with the oppressive regime of the panopticon;[38] but there is no contradiction. Pentonville, arguably the apogee of Howard's influence, created a silent sanitary penitentiary, in stark contrast to the riot and debauch of Newgate but perhaps as

---

[36] Bowring, iv. 121.

[37] *The Gentleman's Magazine and Historical Chronicle*, 60 (1790), Part I, 276–8. As another coincidental link between the Benthams and Howard, Prince Potemkin sent his own physician to minister to Howard in his last illness and ordered that a death-mask should be taken. See Ch. 5, 99–100.

[38] D. G. Long, *Bentham on Liberty* (Toronto, 1977), 185–6.

cruel. In the twentieth century, with the benefit of hindsight, Arthur Gardner could praise Howard as a scientist rather than a saint, as a great collector of facts. He even denied his claim to be a prison reformer at all, belittling him as 'a pioneer in a field of research almost entirely neglected until the advent of his day'; and the military monastic prisons he created are disparaged as 'perhaps more righteous in intention than happy in results'.[39] The orthodoxy of modern revisionism is as unsympathetic. According to Rod Morgan, prisons are 'one of the more potent facts and symbols of human repression and despair'. And it was Howard's vision that created them and which has been, 'productive of as much cruelty, misery and vice as it prevented'. Ignatieff, with a more sophisticated sense of history, argues that Howard might have rejected Pentonville, but it was his child nevertheless.[40]

At the centre of the assessment of Howard's legacy is the question of solitary confinement. Solitude, or some sort of separation, became the accepted practice in reformed prisons in Britain, America, and on the Continent. Its use has inspired the greatest abhorrence. George Ives expressed this emotional revulsion in exaggerated terms, accusing the 'little band of earnest men and women zealous reformers', of inaugurating 'a machine for the infliction of suffering compared with which the old barbarities were short and relatively merciful'.[41] This controversial practice had its origin in the reformatory of St Michele built in Rome by Pope Clement XI in 1703. St Michele was intended for refractory children rather than criminals, parents were expected to pay for the privilege of their children's sojourn, and the inmates were carefully selected. In some ways, this building was strikingly similar to the panopticon. Like a church with cells built into the outer walls, it was a manufactory as well as a house of correction and the inmates were occupied in the various processes of cloth production. Robin Evans thus describes its design:

[39] Arthur Gardner, *The Place of John Howard in Penal Reform*, Howard League for Penal Reform (n.p., 1926), 1, 14.

[40] R. Morgan, 'Divine Philanthropy: John Howard Reconsidered', in *History*, 62 (1977), 388–410. Ignatieff, *A Just Measure of Pain*, 209. Morgan, rather oddly given the evidence, asserts (p. 398) that Howard gave 'no indication that he would have disapproved' of solitude by day as well as by night.

[41] G. Ives, *A History of Penal Methods* (London, 1914; repr. Montclair, NJ, 1970), 171.

At the east end was an altar, at the west end a whipping post and a sign demanding silence. Between were lines of benches to which certain children were chained and set to work spinning wool. Others were kept in their cells all the time. Each cell had its own privy in the thickness of the outer wall, each had a barred window facing into the central area from which the altar could always be seen, so that Mass could be celebrated without necessarily letting the children out. It was as if a cloister had been crammed into the interior of a church, the aisles filled with ranges of cells, and the whole sandwiched in a factory.[42]

It is possible that we have here the origin of Bentham's central chapel which his inmates could attend without stirring from their cells. He was familiar with it, for Howard visited and approved of this institution, particularly commending the motto, 'Parum est coercere improbus poena nisi probus efficias disciplina'—'It is of little advantage to restrain the bad by punishment unless you render them good by discipline.' The idea of this monastic penal discipline was advocated in protestant England by Bishop Joseph Butler, an influential churchman and philosopher. In a sermon at St Bridget's in Easter Week, 1740, before the Lord Mayor, the Aldermen, Sheriffs, and Governors of the several Hospitals in the city of London, he anticipated Beccaria, arguing that, 'the only purposes of punishment less than capital, are to reform the offenders themselves, and warn the innocent by their example'. And he asked:

whether it be not a thing practicable . . . to exclude utterly all sorts of revel-mirth from places where offenders are confined, to separate the young from the old, and force them both, in solitude, with labour and low diet, to make experiment how far their natural strength of mind can support them under guilt and shame and poverty; this may deserve consideration.[43]

This sermon was subsequently published and had a wide circulation.

Prison reformers advocated solitary confinement for three main reasons: first to protect the inmate from intimidation, violence, and sexual assault, one of the less savoury aspects of eighteenth-century prisons was that rape was a normal 'garnish' levied on

---

[42] R. Evans, *The Fabrication of Virtue* (Cambridge, 1982), 60.
[43] J. Butler, *Sermons by Joseph Butler DCL*, ed. W. E. Gladstone (Oxford, 1897), 264.

men, women, and children; secondly, to prevent corruption by association of the young by the hardened offender; and thirdly, and for many this was the prime reason, to induce repentance by hours of solitary reflection. As the genesis of the penitentiary is studied more closely, it is becoming increasingly apparent that Howard was not the original or sole progenitor of its ideology.[44] The principle had many advocates and became the received orthodoxy of a wide range of eighteenth-century reformers. Oliver Goldsmith's saintly Dr Primrose, when unjustly imprisoned for debt, established a moral ascendancy over the motley gang of other inmates who, before his advent, had been sunk in riot and debauchery. By preaching and example, he was able to establish a regime of morality, sobriety, and work. And at night, in his solitary cell, he was able to indulge in reflection and submission to the will of Heaven and to the laws of his country. John Bender argues that these scenes in *The Vicar of Wakefield* were an important contribution to the development of the idea of the penitentiary and that it was this reformist aspect of the novel that most concerned contemporaries when it was first published in 1766.[45]

Another pioneer advocate of solitary confinement was the Revd Samuel Denne. In 1771 at the time of the rebuilding of Newgate prison, he published a pamphlet that attempted 'to shew the good Effects which may reasonably be expected from the Confinement of Criminals in Separate Apartments'. Its object was to persuade the Aldermen of the City of London to allow the prison to be redesigned on a cellular pattern. This pamphlet is of peculiar interest in that it looks back to the eighteenth-century preoccupation with the corruption of the lower orders by luxury, gaming, and strong drink and forward to the religious and practical concerns of the nineteenth century. To some extent it anticipates both Hanway and Howard. Denne closely followed Fielding's analysis of the causes of the great increase in crime. He maintained that luxury was the parent of theft and that the

---

[44] M. Ignatieff, *A Just Measure of Pain* (New York, 1978), 54. Ignatieff is misleading in his assertion here that Hanway was the first to advocate the idea of using solitary confinement for offenders under sentence.

[45] John Bender, 'Prison Reform and the Sentence of Narration in the *Vicar of Wakefield*', in Felicity Nussbaum and Laura Brown (eds.), *The New Eighteenth Century* (New York and London, 1987), 168–88.

punishments meted out were failing to deter; the roads were infested with footpads and highwaymen, burglary was an every-night occurrence, and atrocious murders were common events. He contended that the evil courses of the upper classes led the poor to crime: 'there is', he wrote, 'a broad and well-beaten passage from places of public diversion...to prison.'[46] He deplored the great increase in playhouses, opera houses, masquerades, and assemblies; these diversions of music, dancing, and gaming had spread outward from London to the remotest parts of the kingdom; Tonbridge, Bristol, Scarborough, Cheltenham, and Bath all had their assembly rooms: 'all these scenes of dissipation and luxury, and extravagance, must be attended with ruinous consequences both to the public and to individuals.'[47] Plays such as *The Beggar's Opera*, which glorified crime and criminals, were particularly obnoxious; and Denne suggested that Parliament should tax places of diversion to check their increase and, with the proceeds, pay for gaols with separate cells. With vivid metaphor, he argued that the prisons corrupted individual inmates and were a source of contagion infecting the whole community. 'For these rank weeds thrive fast in this hot-bed of vice; and, when grown to maturity, they scatter a large quantity of their noxious seed, which can hardly ever be eradicated.'[48]

Denne was anxious to prevent the spread of physical as well as moral contagion; he argued that there was a duty to preserve the health of prisoners and humanity urged that they should be subject to no greater hardships than were necessary. 'The abominable foulness of our gaols has long been a matter of complaint', and prisoners were kept in conditions worse than dog kennels and pigsties. Separate cells, he argued, would be easier to keep clean and the spread of gaol fever would be easier to check. But a disorder worse than the fever was 'the complete corruption of the morals of almost all the persons who are sent into them'.[49] The moral quarantine of single cells would make the work of visiting clergymen more effective for their exhortations to repentance would be heard with greater respect and any

---

[46] Samuel Denne, *A Letter to Sir Robert Ladbroke, Knt. Senior Alderman and One of the Representatives of the City of London* (London, 1771), 1, 45. Robin Evans cites Denne (misnaming him Robert) several times but fails to discuss his ideas on solitary confinement.
[47] Ibid. 44.     [48] Ibid. 21.     [49] Ibid. 10, 15.

inclination towards penitence would be reinforced by solitude, not undermined by the mockery of other offenders. And in solitude the felon awaiting execution could repent of his sins. Denne maintained that gaols were so generally regarded as academies of wickedness that even minor offenders were assumed to be hardened villains after serving a short sentence; but if they could be kept in solitude, uncontaminated by evil association, they would leave gaol untainted and employers would be more willing to offer them honest work.

Denne was quite clear that separate cells were not solely for the benefit of the criminal, for they would be a cruel punishment, particularly for the hardened offender: 'I am much deceived,' he wrote, 'if a more terrible penalty could be inflicted on them.' The pangs of conscience would inflict 'exquisite distress and torment'. And he went on to draw a noteworthy comparison between lunacy and crime; crime was a form of madness where the passions and appetites overcame reason. But criminals had deliberately and voluntarily abrogated reason and so deserved 'to be treated like animals of an inferior rank; like beasts of prey, to which level they have reduced themselves'.[50] But, like lunatics, they could be cured; and just as doctors prescribed close confinement and strict temperance for the insane, so should magistrates for their more refractory patients. Denne was in the mainstream of enlightenment thought. He quoted Blackstone, Thomas More, and Beccaria to support his questioning of the justice of the death penalty for minor offences; solitary confinement, he urged, should be tried instead. He expressed grave doubts as to the other alternatives that had been suggested. The public spectacle of men held in perpetual slavery, he felt, would not be acceptable to freeborn Englishmen. Mandeville's suggestion of sending English felons as slaves to the Barbary coast offended against his feelings of humanity; and torture 'must make a reader tremble who is not dead to all those tender feelings which the God of nature has impressed upon the mind of a Being created in his image'.[51] He concluded with a plea to the City of London to try the experiment of solitary confinement: 'As the edifice is designed to last for many ages, let not posterity have cause to censure, and to lament in vain, the inattention, the

[50] Denne, *A Letter . . . City of London*, 50–9.          [51] Ibid. 78.

neglect, or ill-timed economy of their forefathers.'[52] In the event, ambitious plans for a cellular prison were shelved and the new Newgate was built with a grandiose exterior but with an interior on the old pattern of dark passages and open wards. And posterity did indeed lament the misjudgements of its builders.

Another influential exponent of solitary confinement was Dr John Jebb, a fellow of Peterhouse, Cambridge, and a man of somewhat extreme enthusiasms. (In 1786 he was ostentatiously buried in unconsecrated ground in the presence of the Duke of Richmond and two bishops; William Wilberforce was expected but failed to attend.) Jebb worked tirelessly for the 'establishment of true political Freedom in every part of the globe', advocating short Parliaments, equalized representation, and an unrestricted franchise, not only in Britain, but in Ireland, India, and America. He was an admirer of the humane methods of punishment advocated by Hanway and Howard. And he insisted on the necessity of solitude, silence, and pure air in prisons. To a certain extent, he anticipated panopticon architecture by suggesting buildings 'into whose recesses the eye of vigilance can penetrate with greater ease'. But he followed Howard in maintaining that prisons should be entirely under the control of the magistrates and gentlemen of the districts and should be inspected by committees of gentry and clergy. He was deeply distrustful of the army and any involvement of the military in any aspect of police. 'Better, far better,' he wrote, 'that all the present evils and disorders, however grievous, should continue, than that under specious pretences, liberty, the choicest gift of heaven to man, without which no other blessing can convey real enjoyment to the rational mind, should be impaired . . . by the introduction of a French system of police, even in our gaols.'[53]

The most fervent eighteenth-century advocate of an absolutist system of solitary confinement was Jonas Hanway. This engaging eccentric has until recently rarely been given credit for his substantial contribution to penal theory; the entry in the *Dictionary of National Biography* barely mentions his work in this

---

[52] Ibid. 82.
[53] John Jebb, *Thoughts on the Construction and Polity of Prisons and Hints for their Improvement*, Preface by Capel Lofft (London, 1786), pp. xx, 7, 10.

field. But, if concurrence of ideas is any indication, he was an important influence on Bentham who paid him the compliment of careful study. Hanway was a philanthropist and traveller. In his youth he undertook extensive journeys throughout Russia, Persia, and the Near East, and published accounts of his experiences. He then settled in London where, according to Dr Johnson's cruel comment, he 'acquired some reputation by travelling abroad, but lost it all by travelling at home'.[54] He was a cranky enthusiast; he bitterly opposed the naturalization of the Jews and aroused the great doctor's ire by denouncing the practice of tea drinking as a degenerate oriental habit that was enervating the nation and undermining the strength of the industrious classes. He was one of the first men to walk through London sheltering from the rain under an umbrella, defying the jeers and abuse of chairmen and hackney coach drivers. But he championed other more serious and worthy causes with the same courage and lack of concern for appearances. He was particularly concerned with the plight of children. In 1756 he founded the Marine Society for the purpose of training boys for service in the navy. He published several tracts drawing attention to the sufferings of the children apprenticed to chimney sweeps. He also interested himself in the welfare of prostitutes; in 1758, he founded the Magdalen Hospital where these unfortunate women could find an asylum and the chance to earn a respectable living. In the panopticon writings, Bentham cites the Magdalen as a spectacle that attracted visitors; he relied on the same curiosity to supply the public inspection of his prison. Hanway was also an enthusiast for inoculation against smallpox and, perhaps most admirably of all, an early and passionate opponent of the slave trade.

Hanway was naïve and deeply religious, but nevertheless shared many of Bentham's ideas on penal reform and also some of the assumptions that underlay them.[55] He eloquently expressed fear and outrage at the level of crime. He traced every evil in society to the breakdown of order. And he lamented the

---

[54] J. Boswell, *Life of Johnson* (London, 1791), ed. R. W. Chapman (Oxford, 1980), 440.

[55] Jonas Hanway (1712–86). These ideas were expounded in three works: *The Defects of Police* (London, 1775); *Solitude in Imprisonment* (London, 1776); and *Distributive Justice and Mercy* (London, 1781). See also Bowring, iv. 78.

terror in which people were living, when a man could not travel without fear of a pistol at his head, and must go continually accompanied by armed guards. This, he insisted, destroyed liberty and was a species of slavery.[56] Hanway's analysis of the causes of crime followed the conventional pattern; drinking, gambling, idleness, and self-indulgence were at the root of the problem, but all classes were to blame for the reckless hedonism of the age. 'The present time is distinguished as the age of Pleasure: her altars are erected in every street and corner: the common people are initiated into her mysteries.'[57] The remedy was work; honest employment was the foundation of order in society. Hanway's suggestions for the provision of the poor anticipated some of the themes of Bentham's National Charity Company. As man is born to labour, the poor should be inured early in life to a regime of industry and self-denial; children should be set to reap and sow, knit and spin.

Hanway was moved by pity for the children of London born only to die. 'I think every infant in distress, is my country!'[58] Where possible, he wanted to move people out into the country where fewer would die. He pointed to the horrific mortality in London, in some workhouses all the children died, families might lose all twelve of their offspring. He blamed this on several factors, poverty, drink, dirt, and attendant disease. In a perceptive comment he ascribed the deaths of infants to the sulphur from sea coal. He maintained that the mortality rate of children of the better classes in cities was similar to those of the poor in the country—a finding borne out in later statistical studies. His solution was a colonization of England. If people were removed from London, 'we might see many a desart tract smiling in corn and pasture'.[59] In common with Bentham, he insisted that the country could support many more on the land and advocated intensive cultivation; the pleasure parks and horses of the gentry consumed land and grain that could be better utilized by people. Hanway's, like Bentham's, poorhouses would be places of abstinence. For Hanway, one of the great advantages of the country over London was that the poor would be removed from the temptations of the metropolis, drink, gaming, and profligacy; and their diet must be spare—butter, sugar and, of course, tea

---

[56] Hanway, *Solitude*, 63.    [57] Hanway, *Defects*, 265.
[58] Ibid. 256.    [59] Ibid. 252.

must be firmly excluded. Hanway advocated properly regulated workhouses where labour would be obligatory and he suggested that information should be collected from the parishes in order to ensure uniformity—Bentham's involvement in the poor law started with just such an attempt. Hanway generally emphasized the need for fuller and more accurate information on prisons as well as workhouses and indeed on all matters of police—the need for accurate factual information is, of course, one of Bentham's major themes. Hanway wanted all beggars and vagrants to be placed in workhouses and labour enforced by a regime of solitude, bread, and water; if they still would not work, they would be removed to prison. Hanway showed the same desire as Bentham to maximize labour; the children preserved in the healthy country workhouses would be a valuable commodity and all, including the old, should, if at all possible, work. Even blind beggars if they cannot knit or sew could be made to turn a wheel. Bentham's pauper panopticons have many obvious parallels with these ideas; Bentham may well have taken some of Hanway's inchoate suggestions to use as a foundation for his vast systematized regulation of the poor.

Hanway, like Bentham, calculated the worth of a life in monetary terms. Solitude with hard labour in prison, he argued, was economical for execution and transportation deprived the country of the value of labour. He calculated that in the past thirty years 'we have suffered the loss of 10 or 12,000 of the ablest subjects by death or transportation: these computed at £200 each amount to full £2,000,000!'[60] He condemned the reliance on these punishments as the insanity of the age. He was sickened by the youth of so many of the offenders for most of those ending on the gallows were little more than boys, each of them with a body fit for labour and a soul crying out for salvation. Hanway had no doubts as to the alternative: 'imprisonment and labour are the true substitutes for hanging and transportation.'[61] And to achieve this he pleaded for more prisons. 'Let a great number of prisons be forthwith built, larger, stronger and better calculated for the purpose of a secure confinement and a more rational and humane correction.'[62] And, after discharge, these men could be recruited into the navy.

[60] Hanway, *Defects*, 281.     [61] Ibid. 225.     [62] Ibid. 3.

Hanway had clear ideas as to the nature of the regime in these new prisons; similar to Howard's, they also anticipate many of the characteristics of the panopticon. His prisons would be healthy and sanitary; and the inmates taught that cleanliness was a virtue. They would be built on a hill; in each cell a water supply and a privy would be provided; they would be heated by steam from the boilers, furnished with iron bedsteads and outside would be a garden for the privileged prisoners to work in. A chapel was an essential, stalled so that the prisoners could see and hear the preacher but not each other. The name of each inmate would be known only to the head gaoler. And, above all, they would be kept in utter solitude, sequestered from all visits and all company except that of the warders and the chaplain. In this passionate advocacy of this crushing of the evil in the criminal between the anvil of solitude and the hammer of religion, Hanway, rather than Howard, is the forerunner of the nineteenth-century builders of Pentonville. He was convinced that solitary cells would isolate criminals from infection, from 'the poisoned breath of companions in wickedness';[63] it would teach repentance; and it would deter for it would indeed be dreadful: 'solitary imprisonment is the most terrible . . . the most humane, religious, efficacious, method, that can be adopted.'[64] He insisted on the absolute nature of the solitude necessary. Although, in 1776, he described Howard as his guiding star,[65] he later criticized the 1779 Penitentiary Act for not enforcing a rigorous solitude. It should, he declared, be amended, 'to accomplish the great purpose in view, as real solitary imprisonment and religious instruction, supported by well-regulated labour'. He feared that if there were any association, 'the terror of Solitary Imprisonment, will yield to the convulsions of a common prison'; and that work in association during the day would mean that 'the whole structure, built with one hand, were pulled down with the other'.[66] This criticism of the Act was to be paraphrased by Bentham when he complained that the work of the night in solitude was undone during the day, 'the history of Penelope's web reversed'.[67]

[63] Hanway, *Solitude*, 70.    [64] Hanway, *Defects*, 213.
[65] Hanway, *Solitude*, 61.
[66] Hanway, *Distributive Justice*, 206, 207, 222.
[67] Bowring, iv. 138.

For Hanway, the overwhelming object of solitude in imprisonment was the salvation of souls; it would open the gates of God's
mercy to the offender. But he does not ignore the practical
argument that it would protect the inmate from physical violence;
prisoners, he asserted, had been known to suffer appalling
injuries to their bodies, including the gouging out of their eyes,
as well as corruption to their souls and morals from evil communication. The solitary cell would give life, health, and God's
grace. And, to the man awaiting execution: 'The walls of his
prison will preach peace to his soul; and he will confess the
goodness of his Maker, and the wisdom of the laws of his
country.'[68] The chaplain would be the messenger of God's mercy.
In Hanway's prison he was assigned a position of authority that
again presages the nineteenth century. Work was essential for it
would fill up the dreadful void of solitude and also enable the
inmate to earn a living on return to the world; but it was the
visiting clergyman who would discover the temper of each
inmate, judge when it was fit that he should be released, and
estimate his progress towards a true repentance. Those rejecting
the proffered consolation of religion would be subject to whipping, a harder diet, and prolonged confinement.[69]

Hanway ascribed the evils of his day, luxury, profligacy, and
crime, to the moral befuddlement consequent on the decay of
religion. Bentham, in his early writings on punishment, admitted
the power of the religious sanction and agreed with Hanway to
the extent that solitude and a spare diet would create circumstances most conducive to its efficacy: 'there cannot be a more
favourable opportunity for the instructions and exhortations of
Religion . . . Threats before unheeded, promises formerly un-
attended to will now acquire an undisputed empire over his
will.'[70] He did, however, subject Hanway's writings to criticism,
but by Bentham's standards it is mild and of form rather than
substance. He gave Hanway full credit for humanity and expressed a respect for his ideas, even if he found fault with their
prolixity and lack of order and was dismissive of their religious
overtones. He wrote in one of his unpublished manuscripts:

Unhappily that active and intelligent friend of humankind does not
possess the qualities of a good writer in altogether so great perfection as

---

[68] Hanway, *Solitude*, 109, 88.        [69] Ibid. 41–4.        [70] UC clix. 196.

those of a good man. There is often a great deal of truth in his reflections, and of force in his expressions. But the . . . want of conciseness and method in his writings seems to be an obstacle to their meeting with that success among political men which the matter of them often merits. The strong tincture of Religious Zeal that mixes itself everywhere with his political speculations is such as will be no great recommendation of them to a certain class of readers.[71]

In the original panopticon plan of 1786, Bentham was as fervent an advocate of absolute solitude on rational grounds as Hanway was on religious. In contrast, Howard had begun to have grave misgivings, for humanitarian and pragmatic reasons. As he continued his researches, he came across instances where his own theories had been put into practice in a way that dismayed him. At Reading gaol, he found that prisoners had been left in solitary cells for over a year; at Sherborne, in the new bridewell, prisoners were allowed out of their cells for only an hour a day. Howard carefully distinguished between the provision of separate rooms and the punishment of solitary confinement and he firmly dissociated himself from the practice unless carefully limited and regulated. He asserted that it was dangerous and inhumane to incarcerate inmates alone for more than two or three days; this must be contrasted with nineteenth-century regimes that condemned men to as much as eighteen months in solitary as a matter of course. Howard advanced his argument with sense and compassion:

I wish all prisoners to have separate rooms; for hours of thoughtfulness and reflection are necessary . . . I am glad to take this occasion of making some remarks on *solitary confinement*. The intention of this, I mean by day as well as by night, is either to reclaim the most atrocious and daring criminals; to punish the refractory for crimes committed in prison; or to make a strong impression, in a short time, upon thoughtless and irregular young persons . . . It should therefore be considered by those who are ready to commit, for a *long* term petty offenders to *absolute* solitude, that such a state is more than human nature can bear, without the hazard of distraction or despair . . . The beneficial effects on the mind, of such a punishment, are speedy, proceeding from the horror of a vicious person left entirely to his own reflections. This may wear off by long continuance, and a sullen insensibility may succeed.[72]

[71] Ibid. 197.
[72] J. Howard, *An Account of the Principal Lazarettos in Europe* (London, 1789), 169, Howard's emphasis.

As we will see, this passage made an immediate impression on Bentham and caused a fundamental change in his proposals. Several of Howard's other disciples followed him on this point. Charles Bunbury, who commended the panopticon in the House of Commons in 1793, insisted that he was no friend to solitary confinement and feared that it was too often imposed for slight offences. And Lord Loughborough, the Lord Chancellor himself, in a tract on prisons that did little more than repeat Howard's principles, argued that, although there should be entire separation at night, association during the day should be allowed.[73] Other reformers, however, inclined more to Hanway's position. George Onesiphoros Paul, whose great prison at Gloucester was one of the most influential structures ever built, advocated a more severe regime. He argued that separation by day as well as by night was the prerequisite for all improvement for it inclined to reform, prevented the evils of association, induced repentance, and facilitated the imposition of prison discipline. During the 1790s as the practice of solitary confinement became increasingly unpopular, Howard's reputation inevitably suffered. In 1800 James Martin, a liberal humanitarian Member of Parliament, stigmatized Howard as the man who had devised the solitary cells; he 'was certainly one of the worthiest men who ever existed; but if he had been one of the worst, he could not have suggested a punishment of a more cruel and mischievous description'.[74] Howard had drawn a distinction between separate cells at night and solitary confinement; unfortunately in the prisons, this distinction became meaningless. The gaolers of the eighteenth century were not trained and educated men and, by the nature of their distasteful and dangerous task, they were unlikely to be caring and compassionate; and the prisons were becoming increasingly overcrowded. In the circumstances, the existence of solitary cells almost ensured their abuse. For this Howard was certainly responsible, but unintentionally; he had foreseen the problem and had warned against it.

The eighteenth-century movement for penal reform was quite

[73] *The Parliamentary History of England*, 30 (31 May 1793), 958. A. Wedderburn (Lord Loughborough), *Observations on the State of the English Prisons and the Means of Improving Them* (London, 1793).

[74] *Parliamentary History*, 35 (22 July 1800), 470. Sir George Onesiphoros Paul (1746–1820), philanthropist and prison reformer.

remarkably unsuccessful. Blackstone, Eden, and Romilly appear
in the twentieth century to have won the argument, but in their
own day they failed to inspire political action to relax the sanguinary laws. Indeed, despite the force of their arguments on the
cruelty and absurdity of hanging a man for felling a cherry tree,
the number of capital offences in fact rose from 160 in 1765 to
225 in 1815. Romilly's persistent and courageous advocacy of
a more rational and humane code of laws achieved virtually
nothing in his lifetime though his example was to be an inspiration in the future. The reformers had to contend with inertia,
fear, and a callous lack of concern for the fate of petty criminals.
Also, powerful arguments were deployed to defend the existing
practices. In 1785 Martin Madan was arguing against the use of
the royal pardon on the grounds that the certain prospect of
retribution was the best deterrent. And in the next century, the
Chief Justice, Lord Ellenborough, was to resist any attempts to
moderate the criminal code on the grounds that only by the
infliction of cruel terror could order be preserved. On the provision of a humane and rational substitute for the death penalty,
there was again retrogression rather than progress. The temporary expedient of the hulks became established and added a
new dimension to the evils of incarceration. Parliament was
unmoved by the arguments of the reformers that transportation
was wasteful, unexemplary, and disproportionate. In 1779 a
committee of the House of Commons investigated the possibilities of other localities for penal colonies. They argued that
it was justified to send atrocious criminals, particularly those
reprieved from the gallows, to areas where disease flourished;
one of the areas considered was the west coast of Africa, which
would have been tantamount to a death sentence. The committee
also concluded that establishing a colony in healthy places was
agreeable to the dictates of humanity as well as being advantageous to navigation and commerce. In the end, Botany Bay was
fixed upon as healthy, fertile, and distant; and the first fleet sailed
in 1787 in defiance of the reformers. The efforts to improve
conditions in the' gaols were only marginally less ineffective.
Increasingly, imprisonment was being imposed as a penalty and
so the pressure to build and extend the gaols was becoming
greater. Howard's ideas inspired some local improvement and
some magistrates were shamed by his visits into ameliorating

conditions. But too often these improvements proved temporary. At the end of the century, the code of laws remained sanguinary and disproportionate; punishment remained random, chaotic, and capricious; and the structure of the system of county, borough, and private goals from which the evils arose, remained substantially unchanged.

Bentham's panopticon originated in the theories and principles of the eighteenth-century prison reformers. He wrote within the conventions he held in common with Howard, Hanway, and Paul. The panopticon was in some ways conservative, at times only elaborating on well-worn themes; at others it was startlingly innovative. Bentham was deeply versed in the literature and influenced, perhaps more than he would have admitted, by the assumptions and theories of other writers. As the years after his meeting with Howard in 1778 passed, the tension between their ideas became more apparent. There does not seem to have been much further personal contact but there are some references to their friendship of which Bentham never ceased to boast. In 1780 he considered dedicating the *Introduction to the Principles of Morals and Legislation* to Howard, promising him the honour that, 'your name and mine will be handed down to posterity on the same page'.[75] But Bentham was to become more doubtful as to Howard's principles and more impatient of his influence. As his ideas matured, the straitjacket of the 1779 Penitentiary Act became increasingly galling. And Howard's shortcomings became more apparent the closer his theories were studied and Bentham became aware of the superiority of his own intellect. Howard himself realized his limitations, confessing: 'I am the plodder who goes about to collect materials for men of genius to make use of.'[76] Bentham saw himself without any difficulty as the man of genius who with rigorous logic would impose order on the inchoate mass of Howard's facts and point the way to a system that would achieve his ends.

The panopticon writings were a sustained criticism of Howard's penitentiary; it was a town rather than a building, vastly extravagant; and the methods of management were profoundly misconceived; of Howard's publications he wrote: 'They afford a rich fund of materials; but a quarry is not a house. No leading

[75] UC xxvii. 126.     [76] Brown, *Memoirs*, 607.

principles—no order—no connexion.'[77] Howard himself glanced at the original panopticon *Letters* in manuscript and seems to have made only minor objections on the grounds of light and ventilation. Bentham had this information only on hearsay, and admitted: 'Neither at that time nor have I since had any opportunity of explanation on that subject with my venerable and much-lamented friend.'[78] Whether Howard would have defended his principles of management cannot be known; but certainly their baleful influence was to blight the fortunes of the panopticon. Although Bunbury and Bowdler, both disciples of Howard, were converted by the eloquence of Bentham's logic, others were not. Paul and Loughborough remained unconvinced. And it was Howard's ideas on management by appointed commissioners and a salaried governor and inspection by duly appointed visitors that prevailed. But perhaps the most fundamental rift was over religion; this goes to the root of the whole nature of the rival penal systems. For Howard, as for Hanway, salvation was the primary end of punishment as it was of human existence. For all his stern insistence on the grindingly hard labour to be extracted from convicts, Howard never lost sight of their immortal souls; so the reform of the prisoner must always take priority over profit. In contrast, Bentham saw no way of judging a man's moral improvement except by measuring the improvement in his work. In an unpublished comment, he confided that 'Reformation is at bottom nothing but prevention.' And sceptical, as she perhaps was, he echoed Queen Elizabeth's disclaimer of wanting a window into men's souls: 'A man's disposition is no further of any consequence than as his acts are the result of it . . . In truth it is only from a man's acts that his disposition can be judged of: or indeed to speak out: it is a man's actions only that exist: his disposition is but a fictitious entity.'[79] More ruthlessly and crudely practical in the panopticon *Letters*, he asserted: 'I must confess I know of no test of reformation so plain or so sure as the improved quantity and value of their work.'[80]

For Bentham, the object of a man's life was to avoid pain and maximize pleasure; the idea of redemption through suffering was repugnant to him; Christianity was a sanction to be used for

---

[77] Bowring, iv. 121.  [78] UC cxix. 72, 74.
[79] UC clix. 267, probable date 1775–6.  [80] Bowring, iv. 50.

keeping order, not a consolation for the oppressed. He would have made use of this sanction but dissociated himself from the faith on which it is based. Bentham's felon was in his cell to work, not to pray; Howard's prisoner would have solitude to reflect alone and to repent of his sins alone; Bentham's would be constantly under inspection, constantly subject to the external pressure and manipulation of his gaoler, never free to face his guilt or his Maker and to suffer the agonies of repentance in private. It was a chasm that proved unbridgeable.

# 5

# THE FIRST PHASE
## 1786–1793

The political arena in which Bentham fought for his panopticon was dominated by the Prime Minister, William Pitt. He was the sun around which lesser ministers and officials revolved; he was the fountain of power and success. Bentham always recognized this cardinal fact; he addressed himself to Pitt in the first flush of his new discovery; it was Pitt who, in the summer of 1793, visited Queen's Square Place with Dundas to look at the model of the panopticon, casually signified his approval, and agreed that Bentham should go ahead and make his arrangements; and that scene became indelibly fixed in Bentham's memory. Bentham, trusting to his word, unwisely committed himself to considerable expenditure of his own money on the project, believing he would most certainly be promptly reimbursed. As the weary years rolled on, it was Pitt's word of support that he craved, that he knew would open the doors of success, but that was denied him. And, finally, it was Pitt, that most faithless of ministers, whom he ferociously denounced as the originator of his troubles. The 'Picture of the Treasury' was a picture of Pitt's treasury.

As an administrator Pitt displayed contradictory qualities; his biographer writes: 'Pitt could be vigorous and thorough; he could also be volatile or evasive. It depended on the state of his interest, itself very largely at the mercy of events.'[1] There can be little doubt that had he enthusiastically supported the panopticon project it would have gone ahead. During his time of office, new legislation put a heavy burden on ministers and officials, pressure on Parliamentary time was great, and contentious and complicated matters were too often shelved. The morass of legal and political difficulty in which the panopticon became engulfed was

[1] J. Ehrman, *The Younger Pitt: The Years of Acclaim* (London, 1969), 322–3. Henry Dundas (1742–1811), cr. Viscount Melville, 1802; Home Secretary, 1791–4; Secretary of State for War, 1794–1801; First Lord of Admiralty, 1804–5. He was impeached for malversation in 1806.

certainly complicated. It is not surprising that Pitt lost interest and failed to summon up the political will that might have overcome the difficulties.

Henry Dundas was the other major political figure to appear in the panopticon saga. His responsibility for the conduct of the war with France has left him with an unenviable reputation for conceit, inefficiency, and negligence. Perhaps unjustly, for his administration of the Home Office before he became Secretary of State for War in 1794 was marked by a high level of competence.[2] He was an old ally of Pitt and had been crucially concerned in the manœuvres that led to his emergence as prime minister in 1783. At his side he fought the great Parliamentary battles that had consolidated the government's grip on power. As Pitt's second-in-command he was a most powerful and influential minister. The basis of that influence was his management of elections in Scotland which provided Pitt with his majority in the House of Commons. As a political manager, Dundas performed a vital role; he was also a personal friend, encouraging the Prime Minister in the drinking bouts for which they were both notorious; a scurrilous couplet has Pitt asking.

> I cannot see the Speaker, Hal, can you?
> What! Cannot see the Speaker, I see two.[3]

Several other of the protagonists in the panopticon drama were members of the group of men formed around Pitt in 1782–3 as he came to power; a group used to working closely together, held by ties of interest and loyalty. The dividing line between politicians and civil servants was not yet clear, officials owed their appointment to influence, and were often attached to the person of the minister rather than to the service of the Crown. Evan Nepean, the under-secretary at the Home Office who, with Dundas, was concerned with the early travails of the panopticon, started life as a ship's purser. He was brought into the government service by Lord Shelburne in 1782, but attached himself to Pitt and became one of his close associates. In 1794 he accompanied Dundas to the War Office and in the following year was appointed Secretary to the Admiralty. The Treasury was also administered by Pitt's

[2] R. R. Nelson, *The Home Office 1782–1801* (Durham, NC, 1969), 19.
[3] Ehrman, *The Younger Pitt*, 585.

friends. Both George Rose, the Senior Secretary and Charles Long the Junior, had close personal ties with the Prime Minister going back for many years—indeed, Long had been a friend of Pitt when they were both at Cambridge. Rose's alliance with Pitt was cemented during the crisis year of 1782. Rose had conceived a profound dislike of Shelburne and had temporarily lost the secretaryship in the Treasury. He later wrote:

I had experienced very uncomfortable feelings from the temper and disposition of Lord Shelburne; sometimes passionate or unreasonable, occasionally betraying suspicions of others entirely groundless, and at other times offensively flattering. I have frequently been puzzled to decide which part of his conduct was least to be tolerated.[4]

This antagonism culminated in a quarrel so bitter that Rose vowed 'never to be in a room with him again while in existence'. In July of that year, 1782, Pitt asked for his friendship and support; 'From that moment I considered myself as unalienable from Mr Pitt.'[5] And in December, Rose was back at the Treasury, where he continued administering the country's finances and managing elections until the government's resignation in 1801. There is no evidence that Rose allowed himself to be influenced by the memories of that old quarrel when he was dealing with Shelburne's protégé, Jeremy Bentham; but he cannot have forgotten it. Charles Long was also inspired by an intense loyalty to Pitt. 'I have really no wish', he wrote in 1801, 'beyond that of following your fortunes whatever they may be.' And after the Prime Minister's untimely death, he lost all taste for politics.[6] William Wilberforce was in a different category. He had made the acquaintance of both Pitt and Rose in the early 1780s and continued to be a close friend of both men. But his conversion to evangelical Christianity in 1785 precluded a normal

---

[4] G. Rose, *The Diaries and Correspondence of the Right Hon. George Rose*, ed. L. V. Harcourt (London, 1860), i. 25. Evan Nepean (1752–1822), Under-Secretary of State for Home Affairs, 1782–94; Under-Secretary of State for War, 1794–5; Secretary to the Admiralty, 1795–1804; Governor of Bombay, 1812–19. George Rose (1744–1818), Senior Secretary to the Treasury, 1783–1801. Charles Long (1760–1838), Secretary to the Treasury, 1791–1801; Member of the Board of Trade, 1802; Lord of the Treasury, 1804–6; Joint Paymaster General, 1807–17; Paymaster General, 1817–26.

[5] Rose, *Diaries*, 30.

[6] R. G. Thorne, *The History of Parliament: The House of Commons 1790–1820* (London, 1986), iv. 449.

career of political advancement. Henceforth, he devoted his energies to humanitarian causes, notably the abolition of the slave trade. Even before he met Bentham he was a fervent advocate of the penitentiary system. In 1786 and again in 1788 he urged Pitt to action on the building of the national penitentiary, but was put off by promises and fair words.[7] He later became a close friend of Bentham and a supporter of the panopticon. On several occasions he tried to build bridges between the two men. In considering the political fortunes of the panopticon, it has to be remembered that many of the men Bentham was dealing with came from this group of politicians knit together by ties of interest, loyalty, and friendship dating back many years. They were above all, Pitt's men; Bentham was an outsider.

The eleven years between the passing of the 1779 Penitentiary Act and the launching of Bentham's panopticon was a time of hesitation and experiment in the development of prisons. The national penitentiary was not built. The death of William Blackstone in 1780 removed a powerful promoter of the cause. The committee of the first three commissioners, John Howard, George Whatley, and John Fothergill was racked by disagreements as to the site, and by 1781 had been replaced by Sir Charles Bunbury, Sir Gilbert Elliot, and Thomas Bowdler. A site in Battersea on the Spencer estate was chosen and approved by the Lord Chancellor, the Lord Mayor, and twelve judges in accordance with the terms of the act. But in 1784, the project was finally abandoned. Its alarming cost, estimated at around £200,000, was too great for the government to contemplate. However, the same three commissioners continued to be vested with the legal powers to build and manage a prison on the Battersea site and Bowdler and Bunbury were to play a significant part in the fortunes of the panopticon. Although the government shied away from the expense of a national penitentiary, local magistrates were more active. In 1784 and 1791 Gaols Acts were passed encouraging the counties to build prisons in accord with Howardian principles. Altogether forty-two new gaols and houses of correction were built in the years between 1779 and 1787, notable among them those at Petworth in Sussex and at Gloucester. The latter was the work of the magistrate and

[7] W. Wilberforce, *Private Papers of William Wilberforce*, ed. A. M. Wilberforce (London, 1897), 16, 21.

influential prison reformer Sir George Onesiphorus Paul who was destined to play a role in the later history of the panopticon. But improvement of the local gaols was not an adequate solution in the face of a rising conviction rate and a rapid increase in the prison population. The numbers in the hulks rose to over 2,000 and, in an attempt to alleviate the situation, the government resorted again to transportation. In 1787 the first fleet sailed to Botany Bay, followed in 1791 by the ill-fated second fleet. Bentham was unfortunate in his timing; had he himself launched the panopticon in London in the 1780s he might have more easily persuaded the government to let him take over from the three commissioners; but ten years later the consolidation of Howardian prisons in the counties and revival of transportation augured ill for his schemes.

Bentham's panopticon *Letters* written in Russia in 1786 were one of the products of expansion of the county gaols. The differences between the *Letters* and the *Postscripts* can, in part, be explained by the different circumstances of their writing. The frivolous and somewhat superficial *Letters* written in Krichëv were far removed both geographically and practically from the harsh realities of English politics and prisons; whereas the *Postscripts* were written in London and were the product of the need to persuade government of the viability of the project and the desirability of entrusting Jeremy Bentham with its execution. Bentham had joined his brother Samuel at the beginning of 1786 ostensibly in the hope of interesting Catherine the Great in his code of laws. But, characteristically, he made no push to obtain an audience with her. Russia was the land of opportunity for many Englishmen at this time. Samuel had found favour with Prince Potemkin, the Empress's favourite and chief minister, and was in charge of several of his projects, not only fighting in the war against the Turks but also as a general factotum, attempting to put into practice Potemkin's grandiose visions of model farms and manufactories.[8] It was in an attempt to employ ignorant Russian peasants effectively in manufacturing that Samuel devised a circular inspection house that would enable each

---

[8] I. R. Christie, 'Jeremy Bentham and Prince Potemkin', *The Bentham Newsletter*, 10 (1986), 17–21, gives an amusing account of Samuel's embarrassment when Jeremy became involved with Potemkin's schemes.

workman to be supervised from a central observation post. Bentham always emphasized that the panopticon was his brother's invention;[9] and in all his subsequent schemes Samuel was to be closely involved and to share in the credit and the profits. The news from England that transportation was to start again and an advertisement in the *St James' Chronicle* asking for designs for a house of correction in Middlesex were the two immediate occasions for the writing of the *Letters*. They were dashed off in high spirits without reference to books and detailed how the device of inspection could be applied to penitentiaries, work-houses, madhouses, lazarettos, hospitals, and schools. Already there was a promise of a utopia: 'you should see a new scene of things spread itself over the face of civilized society?—morals reformed, health preserved, industry invigorated, instruction diffused, public burthens lightened, economy seated as it were upon a rock, the gordion knot of the poor laws not cut but untied—all by a simple idea in architecture.'[10]

But from its very inception, the panopticon was to be a source of mortification. In December 1786 Bentham sent his brain-child to London, little doubting that it would be greeted with an enthusiasm equal to his own. The *Letters* were addressed to his father who was on the Middlesex Bench; and they were sent with permission to publish. It was Bentham's intention that his father should communicate the plan to his fellow magistrates. For once Jeremiah Bentham seems to have been disinclined to push his son into public notice. Bentham wrote also to George Wilson commending his 'sort of Flying Castle, or, to speak more to the times, an air balloon, it sweeps over all sorts of ground'.[11] Wilson, wearied of the difficulties of publishing for someone else at such a distance, resolved 'to have no concern in the publication of any other work which you may think proper to send over'.[12] Despite his irritation he soon forgot this resolution; his coolness towards the panopticon can be contrasted with the alacrity with which *A Defence of Usury*, sent to him in May 1787, was seen

[9] M. S. Bentham, *Life of Brigadier-General Sir Samuel Bentham KSG* (London, 1862), 83–4, paid tribute to the scrupulous way in which he gave his brother credit for the invention, in marked contrast to James Mill's account in the *Encyclopaedia Britannica* which ignored his role.
[10] Bowring, iv. 66. At BL Add. MS 33550, 145–230 are drafts of the *Letters*.
[11] *Correspondence (CW)*, iii. 514.
[12] Ibid. 532.

through the press and published in the same year. Bentham's father seems to have been no more enthusiastic than his friend. His son was hurt by his lack of encouragement and by his failure to bring it to the notice of the Middlesex magistrates. His attitude was in marked contrast to the fond pride with which he had boasted of *A Fragment on Government* in 1776. Bentham waited in vain for a word of praise. He wrote plaintively: 'My letters on the inspection house . . . I was in hopes could have been favoured with some notice. If they have failed of giving you pleasure they have failed of one of their main objects.'[13] Later he complained 'that what inclination you appear to have to publish my letters on the Inspection-house is grounded not on any personal satisfaction such a publication would afford you . . . but on the anxiety you conceive to subsist on my part to see it take place for some purpose or other respecting us or one of us'.[14] Bentham did have such a purpose and, given the low public standing of gaolers, his father may well not have wished either of his sons to be involved in it. Earlier in 1787 Bentham had drafted a letter in Samuel's name to Pitt suggesting that, if his idea were to be made use of in England, 'I could almost wish to lend a hand to the accomplishment of such a business.'[15] This letter was never sent, but it shows that from the outset Bentham envisaged the panopticon as a field for the exercise of his brother's talents.

Bentham returned to London in February 1788, a man in search of a role, 40 years of age, contemplating an uncertain future and a past that seemed one of ill-directed effort and almost unrelieved failure. For two years he seems to have forgotten about the panopticon. At first, feeling like 'a fish out of water',[16] he occupied his time working on his code of laws, buying an expensive harpsichord, and finding lodging in a farmhouse at Hendon, his 'hole in the ground' to which he could retire to write when the demands of life in London became too intrusive. The following year he, his head and heart altogether in France, was, with many of his contemporaries, distracted by the cataclysmic events there, and he spent many hours commenting upon them.[17] He also published his *Principles of Morals and Legislation*, and the Anti-Machiavel letters attacking Pitt's policy towards Russia.

---

[13] Ibid. 542, see also 550.  [14] Ibid. 547.
[15] Ibid. 535.  [16] Ibid. 618.  [17] Ibid. iv. 33.

Probably the most important influence in his life at this time was the friendship of Lord Lansdowne and of the ladies of his family. Lansdowne on his first arrival in London had been 'vastly civil'[18] reproaching himself for not giving Bentham a place while he was in power. And in June 1789 he tentatively suggested that Bentham might find a use for his talents as a Member of Parliament. Bentham demurred at both suggestions, feeling that he was not fit for a place and that his weak voice would prevent his being an effective MP. But he appears to have believed that Lansdowne would one way or another provide him with opportunity. The illness of Lady Lansdowne and her death in August necessarily postponed any possibility of these half-promises being honoured that summer; but it was to Bentham that Lansdowne turned in his grief and who provided him with company and consolation.

The first attempt to build the panopticon was taken on Lansdowne's iniative. He felt himself to be under an obligation to Bentham and went some way to discharging it by sending the panopticon *Letters* to Sir John Parnell, Chancellor of the Irish Exchequer in August 1790. Parnell's response was favourable, he wrote to Lansdowne, 'I have never read a more ingenious Essay . . . I am so convinced of the Utility of the Plan, that I believe it would be adopted in Ireland, but I do not know whether I am at liberty to have the treatise copied.'[19] While Bentham willingly, and copiously, gave Parnell his advice on the printing and implementation of his project, he does not seem to have been particularly gratified by Lansdowne's initiative and indeed may well have been disappointed that his help was not more substantial, for within two weeks he wrote a remarkable sixty-page letter accusing Lansdowne of having broken faith with him. He had expected to be brought into Parliament but when the Marquis had the opportunity, after recently gaining control over the second seat in Chipping Wycombe, he had chosen instead to give the seat to Sir John Jervis, a man in Bentham's eyes, manifestly incapable: 'a very good man on board of ship,

---

[18] *Correspondence* (*CW*), iii. 617.
[19] Ibid. iv. 137. Sir John Parnell (1744–1801), Chancellor of the Irish Exchequer, 1785–99.

but what is he to do, or what did he ever do in Parliament?'[20] Most of the letter is taken up with abuse of Lansdowne's other members. They were incompetent, inferior knaves, yet not even obsequious, and openly contradicted their patron; Lansdowne himself was taunted by his failures in politics; he will never be Prime Minister again. In this letter, Bentham's mask of calm philosophy had slipped and revealed naked resentment and ambition. He has felt the humiliation of being pointed out in public before ladies and servants as a fit object of charity and yet he has gained nothing; he has disappointed his father and is bitterly envious of his stepbrother, Charles Abbot, who has a already been offered a seat in Parliament. He was not ambitious for money: 'The only thing I have coveted for these many years has been the opportunity of trying whether I could make myself of any use to the country and to mankind in the track of *legislation*.'[21] And it was clear that he wanted a field in which he could put his ideas into practice. 'Do you really then think me', he wrote, 'incapable of every thing but proposing impracticable projects, and throwing out odd ideas that would not have occurred to any body else? Is *good*...absolutely synonymous to *impracticable*?'[22] Lansdowne, in his reply, gently protested that he had no idea that Bentham had parliamentary ambitions, believing 'your Happiness to depend on your perfect Independence'.[23] But he promised, now he knew, that he would bring him in at the first opportunity. Bentham wisely discounted this promise as 'Birmingham halfpence' and, although he remained on friendly terms with Lansdowne, he does not appear to have asked again for any favour.

It was only gradually that Bentham came to see the panopticon project as a vehicle for his ambitions. He did not contemplate becoming the contractor-governor in Ireland; his lengthy letters to Parnell were mainly concerned with how peculation could be checked, and indeed he disclaimed any wish to become involved with the day-to-day business, for 'I am not fond of accounts nor

---

[20] Ibid. 158. Sir John Jervis (1735–1823), cr. Earl of St Vincent, 1797; Admiral of the Fleet; MP for Lansdowne's seat Chipping Wycombe, 1790–4; he commanded the fleet against the Spanish at the great victory off Cape St Vincent, 1797.
[21] *Correspondence* (*CW*), iv. 152, Bentham's emphasis.
[22] Ibid. 167, Bentham's emphasis.
[23] Ibid. 181.

of pecuniary responsibility.'[24] If he had gone to Ireland at all, he would have gone as a member of the Irish Parliament; but this suggestion of Lansdowne was not seriously contemplated. The panopticon prison was far from being his only concern at the time. In September 1790 he wrote to Parnell: 'Do you happen to want a plan of Education just now, or a plan of anything else? These are my amusements. One thing is pretty much the same to me as another.'[25] He was, however, becoming increasingly interested in the management of a prison and, early in 1791, for the first time suggested that he himself should be the contractor-governor of a national penitentiary in London. He wrote to Pitt proposing to carry into execution his improved system, confessing that for many years the subject had occupied 'a warm place in my thoughts . . . before any personal views had mixed with it . . . where is the stranger who will enter as deeply as the contriver into the spirit of the contrivance?'[26]

This letter marks the beginning of Bentham's campaign for the panopticon, a campaign that would end only with the Holford Committee's rejection twenty years later. The first stage of this campaign takes us to the summer of 1793 when Pitt indicated his approval and asked Bentham to go ahead with his arrangements. During these eighteen months the idea of the panopticon gained a hold on Bentham's mind so strong that not all the years of disappointment could shake it. Nearing his death, he still yearned for his prison. The growth of his personal ambition had complex roots. George Wilson's reproaches on the waste of his and Samuel's opportunities and talents must have been a factor. The feelings of social inferiority which he struggled to overcome in his relations with the Bowood ladies may have inspired a desire for great wealth—and a title. The death of his father in March 1792 not only gave him capital to finance his project but may have removed an inhibition about the pursuit of worldly success. The writing of the *Postscripts* in 1790 and 1791 was also of significance. They had their origin in the printing of the *Letters* in Dublin forced on him by Parnell's desire to publicize the project. When Bentham came to reconsider his plan five years later he found it inadequate. It was but 'the original rude sketch'.[27] The building needed fundamental changes, and they were dealt with

---

[24] *Correspondence (CW)*, iv. 174.     [25] Ibid. 195.     [26] Ibid. 229.
[27] Ibid. 290.

in the first postscript; but the second postscript entailed a re-working of the principles of management. It is possible that only then did Bentham realize how completely the panopticon could achieve the ends of punishment and create a perfect instrument for the exercise of power.

The other factor that led to Bentham's commitment to managing the panopticon was his brother's career. Samuel Bentham, the original inventor, was also a vital influence during 1791 and 1792. He was a very different person from Jeremy, a soldier with a turn for mechanical invention, a practical, not over-scrupulous man of business, confident and successful with women, openly ambitious and worldly. Despite these differences the two men were held together by the ties of great affection. For Jeremy, love of Samuel was probably the strongest emotion in his life. He wished to protect, guide, and provide for his young brother. In 1787 he had left him in Russia pursuing a successful career. But in October 1788 Samuel, in the course of a long letter giving an account of his part in the campaigns, confessed to the heart-sickness of an exile: 'I am certainly well off and in all probability shall always be well off in this country, yet I have a terrible longing to come home.'[28] In May 1791 he achieved his desire, arriving back in London, but with his future uncertain. He immediately involved himself with his brother's project, writing in June that he hoped panopticon would be finished, 'till which no new objects must take our attention'.[29]

Bentham was anxious to find scope for his brother's genius; he had unbounded faith in his manifold inventions which ranged from veriminicular boats (long barges slotted together) to double axletrees, from invalid chairs to improved treadwheels. The panopticon was only one of many schemes. In May 1791, just at the time when Samuel was expected in London, he drafted a letter to George III bringing to his notice his brother's amphibious vehicle for which he made extravagant claims: 'Bridges rendered needless; rivers, the broadest and most rapid, no obstacles to the largest army,—all by a modification given to the structure of a baggage-waggon! Expense saved too, instead of increased. The contrivance as simple as it has been proved to be effectual.'[30] He goes on to commend the panopticon to the

---

[28] Ibid. 12.  [29] Ibid. 317.
[30] Ibid. 289. This letter was probably not sent.

King, though less effusively, as another of his brother's useful devices. Three years later, when deeply committed to the panopticon project, he dismissed the profits expected from the prison as 'trifling' in comparison to those that could be made by a system of luggage ports served by 'your divided axle-tree carts'.[31] Unfortunately for the brothers' material prosperity these carts dismally failed tests on the road. 'Poor unhappy divided-Axle-tree!' Bentham wrote, 'Mr Smith's report of it is terribly unfavourable.'[32]

Samuel Bentham was closely involved in the first phase of the panopticon project; the shadier side of the business such as bribery was left to him, as 'anything of that sort will come better from an intriguing Russian like you, than from a reformer like your betters'.[33] But his most important contribution was in planning the use that was to be made of the labour of the prisoners. He had invented a machine for wood- and stone-working, which the physical exertions of the men was to set in motion; neither dexterity nor goodwill would be necessary. This became an integral part of the enterprise. The 'raree show', which the brothers set up in a room in Queen's Square Place to demonstrate the panopticon to influential people, consisted of models of the inspection house and of Samuel's machine. And it was from the produce of this machine that the great profits were to be made. The panopticon was to be a joint venture; Jeremy would put up the money and devise management methods while Samuel would provide the business acumen and inventive genius to oversee the workshops. They would be partners, joint contractors, and would have lived together in the panopticon governor's mansion, each with their separate study but sharing the responsibilities of the prison.

Bentham's letter to Pitt in January 1791 outlining his proposals was followed by silence. At this point Bentham was philosophical about the delay. He wrote to his brother in April: 'I gave in a proposal to our Potemkin two months ago; but the Potemkins never give answers.'[34] He was beginning to establish contacts in the political world. His friend Reginald Pole Carew became a

[31] *Correspondence (CW)*, v. 69.
[32] Ibid. 72. Another of the Benthams' projected enterprises was 'The Indicator', a summary of advertisements from newspapers, UC cviii. 2–99.
[33] Ibid. iv. 327.      [34] Ibid. 262.

close ally; he circulated his proposal to several other MPs and peers including William Wilberforce. The most important convert he made at this stage was Sir Charles Bunbury. Bunbury was already a veteran in the field of penal reform. He had been chairman of the 1778 Parliamentary committee of inquiry into the hulks and he was, as one of the commissioners appointed under the 1779 Act, entrusted with the vital powers to acquire land to build the penitentiary. Bentham sent him the *Postscripts* as they were printed and Bunbury was persuaded to become an enthusiastic and stalwart supporter. Although Bentham concentrated on building a prison in London, he was still considering other possibilities. In May 1791 it became clear that Parnell's initial enthusiasm had waned and the panopticon was unlikely to be built in Dublin; this does not seem to have grieved Bentham, he had little opinion of the Irish government, describing them as 'a sad crew'.[35] He also suggested to his friend James Anderson that he might himself become a contractor for a panopticon prison in Edinburgh. Anderson declined and warned him to beware of becoming involved in the political machinations of William Pitt, a warning that the future was to prove only too well founded: 'As to Pitt, he is a very Jew,—he will say . . . the very reverse of what he intends to do, if he thinks it can effect any little object.'[36]

Bentham was also considering joining with his brother in building and managing a panopticon in Paris to replace the Bicêtre, and in November he sent a French version of the panopticon proposal to the National Assembly. It was to his French correspondent, Jacques Pierre Brissot de Warville, that he described the panopticon in the notorious phrase, 'a mill for grinding rogues honest, and idle men industrious'.[37] This venture also came to nothing. The Assembly thanked Bentham for his works, 'plein de vues utiles sur les prisons'[38] but assumed that he was offering to manage the institution without reward—a prospect that would hardly have tempted him, or Samuel, away

---

[35] Ibid. Reginald Pole Cárew (1753–1835), Commissioner for Auditing Public Accounts, 1799–1802; Under-Secretary of State at the Home Office, 1803–4.

[36] Ibid. 297.

[37] Ibid. 342. The proposal that Bentham sent to the Assembly was drafted by Dumont and published in 1802 in *Traités de législation civile et pénale*, iii. 209–72.

[38] *Correspondence* (*CW*), iv. 340.

from London. The year 1791 ended with a letter to Pitt politely requesting an answer to his January letter; the London penitentiary remained the only viable prospect for building the panopticon.

The year 1792 brought a great change in Bentham's financial circumstances; his father died leaving him a comfortable fortune enabling him to live as a gentleman in Queen's Square Place. Bentham had spent most of his life resisting his father's efforts to push him into fame and fortune, and he appeared at times almost wilfully determined to remain poor and obscure. With his father's death, perhaps his need to eschew wealth and public recognition faded and his proper ambitions were allowed to emerge. Certainly his determination to build the panopticon grew stronger. His improved financial position enabled him to offer to meet the cost of the building himself. He became more sophisticated in his dealings with the administration; he tried indirectly to put pressure on Pitt by approaching him through the officials at the Treasury, writing to George Rose warning him that Bunbury was determined to bring up the matter of the penitentiary in the House of Commons unless the government acted. This was the first of a long series of communications with Rose who was to play a central role in the subsequent fortunes of the panopticon. Bentham was understandably reluctant to become involved in a public campaign to win government approval for his enterprise. The reputation of gaolers was low, besmirched by their association with the criminal world, that of contractors little better. Bentham was painfully aware that he would lose caste unless the panopticon project was presented as a measure of reform. He wanted to be in the company of John Howard rather than Duncan Campbell. From the very first he had hinted to Pitt that the King should award him some mark of distinction, presumably a peerage, to ensure that he suffered no loss in honour or reputation. He was very anxious to be distinguished from 'the tag rag and bobtail of White–Negro drivers'.[39] As the years of soliciting the government went by Bentham was to lose some of this delicacy of feeling.

In May 1792 the Home Secretary, Henry Dundas, first began to take an interest in the panopticon. Bentham had sent him the

[39] *Correspondence (CW)*, iv. 367.

panopticon writings and was intensely irritated to hear that he had accepted a loan of another copy, clearly having completely forgotten the books lying unopened at home. Again there were long silences and delays; Bentham, anxious as much for his brother's interests as his own, wrote begging for a clear decision; an unequivocal refusal would be preferable to continued uncertainty. 'While this business hangs in suspense, my Brother, whose assistance I should stand much in need of is kept from going to Russia where he is loudly called for.' And he himself was prevented from going to build panopticons in Paris.[40] In other letters, Bentham expressed fears that the nexus of interest between the Home Secretary, the Treasury, and the contractor for the hulks, Duncan Campbell, would prevent his plan getting a fair hearing. Eventually, in September 1792, Dundas visited Queen's Square Place, saw the panopticon models and the machinery and approved. According to Bentham, he agreed that the prison could be built on the site already chosen in Battersea under the powers of the 1779 Act. At this point it seemed to Bentham that he now only had to secure money from the government and the agreement of two of the original commissioners. Gilbert Elliot was absent in Scotland, but Thomas Bowdler might be available. 'By only signing a paper, any two of the three intended Supervisors of whom he is one, could put us in possession of the ground, supposing the money to be forthcoming, at a minutes warning.'[41]

But despite Bentham's optimism and Dundas's approval, the scheme again got caught in the doldrums; for almost ten months there seems to have been little progress. Bowdler was tracked down and signified his willingness to help in acquiring the land, but the money was not forthcoming. The government again seems to have dragged its feet; and expenditure had to be approved by Pitt and the Treasury. In May 1793 Bunbury finally broke his silence; in a major speech in the House of Commons he attacked the scandals of transportation to Botany Bay which entailed great suffering and left many felons waiting for several years in the hulks and the overcrowded gaols. He urged the government to adopt the ingenious plan proposed by Mr Bentham, by which 'well regulated prisons calculated to reform offenders,

[40] Ibid. 369.    [41] Ibid. 395.

and to convert the dissolute and idle into good and industrious subjects, would be provided ˙at a cheaper rate than vessels in the Thames'.[42] At the same time Bentham was reporting that 'Various of Pitt's friends . . . have been at him with mallets, beating Panopticon into his head.'[43] Their efforts finally achieved success when in July, Dundas and Pitt visited Queen's Square Place and in the presence of Samuel and Jeremy Bentham asked them to make their arrangements and go ahead with their plans.

Bentham had waged a successful campaign, manipulating the political processes, approaching ministers through the 'proper channels', persuading officials like Rose at the Treasury and Evan Nepean at the Home Office to further his plans. He was encouraged by general approbation. 'The "Panopticon" plan' he wrote, 'is approved by everybody.'[44] The proponents of the original national penitentiary were won over. Howard himself had offered only minor criticisms on light and ventilation before departing on his last journey; the fundamental points of central inspection and contract management were left undisputed. Bunbury was a convert and Bowdler, the second commissioner, shaken in his views by the force of Bentham's logic, confessed: 'The defects in the Penitentiary Act are certainly numerous . . . I assure you I think the Legislature is indebted to You for shewing so very clearly, how ill suited the Act is to the purpose for which it was intended.'[45] The architecture of the inspection house was also generally approved. Robert Adam commended it as infinitely superior to Blackburn's ideas and Lord St Helens, who had seen many of the most celebrated provincial prisons including Paul's county prison at Gloucester, believed that none of them was 'in any degree comparable to yours', and was persuaded that 'its adoption would be a most important public benefit'.[46] In the summer of 1793 the panopticon seemed to have a fair wind behind it and to face only a few slight obstacles. And Bentham seemed near to realizing his ambition to create a field of practical endeavour in which he and his brother could labour for the public good.

[42] *Parliamentary History*, 30 (31 May 1793), 958.
[43] *Correspondence* (*CW*), iv. 432.
[44] Ibid. 320.
[45] Ibid. 437.
[46] Ibid. 409. Alleyne Fitzherbert (1753–1839), cr. Baron St Helens, 1791; a professional diplomat and an old friend of Bentham.

# 6

# PROPOSAL AND CONTRACT I

The proposition that Pitt and Dundas approved so casually in the summer of 1793 is far from straightforward or easily comprehended. It is tempting to confine oneself to a quick reading of the *Letters*, but this can lead to serious misunderstandings. To appreciate the nature of the panopticon and its place in penal theory and to understand Bentham's protracted negotiations with Pitt's administration, it is necessary to study his proposal in its totality. The rough sketch contained in the *Letters* was subsequently altered in several material ways in the *Postscripts*; it was then massively condensed in a printed *Proposal*, which is in the nature of a prospectus; and finally cast into legal form in the draft contract which Bentham hoped to make with the government. The following two chapters will attempt a synthesis from these disparate sources and will also draw on Bentham's private notes where they shed light on his ideas. This has not been done before and will provide scholars with a coherent and accessible description of the panopticon. The project will be analysed by themes; this chapter deals with the principles on which the structure rested, going on to a description of the building itself and the regime of the prison and then to a discussion of the controversial question of solitary confinement. Chapter 7 deals with the plan of management, the powers of the governor, and the checks to be imposed on him, in particular the inspection principle and the insurance schemes. Bentham's theories on the criminal mind, the nature of work, and the provision for discharged prisoners will be explained. It must be realized, however, that one aspect of the panopticon cannot be separated from another. Each proposal is not an isolated entity but a cog in a mechanism. Each part is symbiotically linked. The principle of lenity, the position of the governor's urinal, the junction of interest and duty, and trays of steamed potatoes are bound inextricably together. The panopticon must stand, or fall, as a whole.

## PRINCIPLES

Bentham's principles of management are simple. The foremost ends of imprisonment, deterrence, and reformation must be served; but the security of the inmates from violence, ill-treatment, and negligence must be ensured; escapes must be prevented, but moral and intellectual welfare should be safeguarded; and there must be provision for future subsistence and good conduct. He devised three fundamentals to achieve these ends, lenity, severity, and economy. By the primary rule of lenity the prisoner must be deprived only of liberty not of health or life; he should not be starved, overworked, chained, or beaten, or kept in such conditions of cold, damp, and filth that he would sicken or die. This cardinal principle of any humane prison system is the foundation of the panopticon. Though it may be questioned whether Bentham's establishment would have achieved these benevolent ends, he believed it could and there can be no doubt that he abhorred the squalor and cruelty that unjustly inflicted a terrible death for minor offences. He wrote eloquently with real feeling on this evil: 'Styled less than capital, they are in fact capital, and much more; the result of them being not simple and speedy death . . . but death accompanied and preceded by lingering torture.'[1] So the prisoner must be kept healthy, warm, and adequately fed, yet he must also suffer. By the second rule, that of severity, his condition 'ought not to be made more eligible than that of the poorest class of subjects in a state of innocence and liberty'.[2] This is not the principle of less eligibility that became notorious with the New Poor Law after 1834, but of equal eligibility. Bentham did not envisage grinding his convicts down to below the level of the poorest of the poor. Economy should be the prevalent consideration unless it conflicted with the rules of lenity and severity. On this third principle Bentham expended much eloquence and ingenuity. This is hardly sur-

---

[1] Bowring, iv. 123.   [2] Ibid.

prising since expense was the main reason why the penitentiary, sanctioned by the 1779 Act, had not been built; so unless Bentham could persuade the politicians of the frugality of his scheme, it too would fail. Economy was also a necessary prerequisite for the profits that would make the prison viable. 'As to the rule of economy, its absolute importance is great—its relative importance still greater. The very existence of the system ... depends upon it.'[3]

Parsimony is not an attractive quality and when exercised at the expense of others less fortunate, it becomes repugnant. It is easy, as Gertrude Himmelfarb does so emotively, to picture Bentham as a penny-pinching skinflint, ruthlessly exploiting prisoner and pauper alike. But, although it is natural to recoil from his more repulsive devices to ensure frugality, it must be remembered, first, that for Bentham economy was a cardinal virtue of all administration; and that, secondly, in the panopticon it was subservient to the well-being of his prisoners. Bentham himself was more concerned with the objection that his prison would not be harsh enough. The tension between a benevolent concern for the welfare of inmates and the need to inflict misery upon them has underlain the public debate on penal reform since the time of Howard. There is no final answer to this dilemma and prisons remain profoundly contradictory institutions. Stories of overcrowding, neglect, and oppression often fail to arouse interest, let alone indignation. Indeed, indignation seems more easily roused by the amenities of 'soft' prisons; and many have agreed with Sydney Smith that the discomfort and discontent of the inmates should be the first object of any convict prison.[4] Bentham's attitude was more humane. He believed that it was easier to inflict suffering than to alleviate it and that his prisoners would suffer enough. He admits that they might seem better off than the poor outside: 'All men in a state of innocence and liberty do not in fact enjoy a full supply of necessaries.'[5] But they could if they dispensed with luxuries; and the poor have a privilege the prisoner is denied, freedom. In a private, unpublished fragment, Bentham for once extolled liberty as an

---

[3] Ibid. 125.

[4] 'State of Prisons', in *The Edinburgh Review or Critical Journal*, 35 (Mar. 1821–July 1822), 286–302.

[5] Bowring, iv. 124.

absolute good. 'One blessing yet is wanting without which all comforts lose their relish—liberty.' In his delight in the matchless splendour of his panopticon penitentiary, Bentham often seems lacking in sympathy and sensitivity to the miseries of its inmates, but in the following note he reveals an understanding of the nature of the sufferings it would inflict:

Should I like to be in their case? What man at liberty could answer otherwise than in the negative. They are in health. They suffer neither hunger thirst nor cold; true; but not a moment of their time is at their own disposal. . . . what they do is for their ultimate good; true: but in the mean time they do nothing as they please. They are not worn down by excessive labour: true: but except what is absolutely necessary for meals and sleep there is not a moment of their time during which they are not either at work or under discipline. They work and what they do is more for others than for themselves.[6]

Bentham preferred to concentrate his attention on the comforts of his charges and on the frugality of his administration. But the three principles form a nexus; lenity, severity, and economy were interdependent: 'The measure of punishment prescribed by the rule of severity, and not forbidden by the rule of lenity, being ascertained, the rule of economy points out, as the best mode of administering it, the imposing some coercion which shall produce profit, or the subtracting some enjoyment which would require expense.'[7]


## THE BUILDING

Foucault described the panopticon as 'a cruel ingenious cage', a pitiless contraption designed for control and subjugation.[8] But Bentham's vision was of a beautiful building, a stately pleasure dome comparable to the Rotundas at Ranelagh and Dublin, or the circus at Bath. There was, he insisted, no reason why the panopticon should not be a cheerful place; a sketch of it in his papers depicts a faerie palace, tinted in muted shades of pink and

---

[6] UC cxix. 82.
[7] Bowring, iv. 125.
[8] M. Foucault, *Discipline and Punish: The Birth of the Prison* (Paris, 1975; Harmondsworth, 1985), 205.

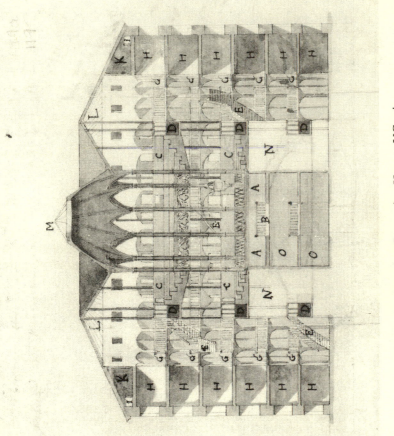

Fig. 1 Section of an Inspection House, UC cxix. 119

grey (see Fig. 1).[9] This would adorn any neighbourhood. 'It will', he wrote, 'add singularity to beauty; it will crown the eminence; it will give life and ornament to the country. It will be a lantern; it will be a bee-hive; it will be a glass bee-hive; and a bee-hive without a drone.'[10]

The basic structure of this building is well known. It was to be circular or polygonal in shape with the cells around the circumference. At the core would be a central inspection area of galleries and lodge, disjoined from the main building, linked to the outer perimeter only by stairways, none of the floors or ceilings coinciding. From this lodge, authority could exercise a constant surveillance while remaining itself invisible. For Bentham, this structure was a living entity, an artificial body, the inspection lodge its heart, its passageways its nerves and arteries. In the *Letters* the structure was very much a contraption, a simple idea of architecture that would itself transform the world. A doubtful recipe for utopia, it also fails to carry conviction as a viable building. But in *Postscript* I, Bentham not only elaborated but also gave substance to his architectural concepts and changed them in several material ways. And yet, although he lavished attention on structural detail, the building itself had been ousted from its position of prime importance by the scheme of management. 'The management was indeed the end: the construction of the building but one amongst a variety of means, though that the principal one.'[11] Iron and glass were to be extensively used in his revised scheme; the pillars, arches, staircases, and galleries were to be made of cast iron, for it was lighter, more flexible, less bulky and might be cheaper than stone or brick. It would not harbour putrid infection and was resistant to fire, as were the plaster floors that he preferred in place of wood. Glass was also to be used extensively in skylights and there would be two large windows for each cell.[12] In the *Proposal*, Bentham summarized his vision: 'The Building circular—a Iron cage glazed—a Glass Lantern, about the size of Ranelagh!'[13] In this use of glass and iron, Bentham was in the vanguard of the technology of his time. Iron was a newfangled material for large-scale building, the

---

[9] UC cxix. 119.     [10] UC cxviii. 52.     [11] Bowring, iv. 122.
[12] Ibid. 97–8.     [13] UC cxv. 32.

first iron bridge had been built only twelve years before.[14] And developments in the techniques of glass manufacture were making possible more extensive use of the material. Architecturally, the panopticon foreshadows Paxton's Crystal Palace rather than Pentonville.

The panopticon's sanitary arrangements were less visionary. As in Hanway's proposed prison, each cell was to contain an earthenware pipe covered with an iron lid, for 'necessary evacuations'. It would lead down to a common sewer. Water would be pumped up to an annular tank situated under the roof of the building; it could then easily be supplied to each cell. Hoses, connected to the tank, could drench the building in case of fire. Large windows would ensure that light would penetrate even to the innermost recesses of the inspection area and at night lamps backed by reflectors outside the central lodge would cast light into the cells; thus extending 'to the night the security of the day'.[15] Outside, a kitchen garden, where favoured prisoners would work, would provide the establishment with vegetables.

In his methods of heating the building, Bentham again relied on a novel device, warm air. After devoting many pages of *Postscript* I to discussion and argument, he suggested that a new iron stove patented by Moser and Jackson, of Frith Street, Soho, should be tried. In this fire was applied to the outside of a vessel to heat air passing through the inside; the warmed air would then be distributed throughout the building.[16] In this method of heating Bentham was again a harbinger of modern progress. When, in 1840, Charles Barry incorporated hot-air heating in his palatial monument to triumphant Radicalism, the Reform Club in Pall Mall, it was a well-established system; but in 1790, it was an innovation in the experimental stage.

Conversation tubes were another modern device that Bentham planned to install as a communication system within the prison. According to the *Letters*, they were to run between the inspection lodge and each cell, enabling the governor to instruct and admonish each inmate. But by *Postscript* I, they were, less ambitiously, to connect the lodge and the inspection galleries.

---

[14] At Coalbrookdale, Shropshire in 1779.
[15] Bowring, iv. 41.
[16] Ibid. 67, 110–18.

They would be a tool for constantly enforcing a clockwork regularity on the administration of the prison. 'Certainty, promptitude, and uniformity', Bentham declared, 'are qualities that may here be displayed in the extreme. Action scarcely follows thought, quicker than execution might here be made to follow upon command.'[17] He delighted in the novel technique of these tubes; they were installed in his own home and played a role in the *Constitutional Code*. He had a blind faith in their efficacy and the practicality of using them over long distances. It is a measure of the immensity of his grand panopticon design that, at the start of the war with France in 1793, he suggested to the Home Office that his prison could be the nerve-centre of a network of such tubes stretching for hundreds of miles underground, forming a national system of intelligence and defence.[18]

One of the main changes between the *Letters* and *Postscript* I was in the location of the governor's house. In the *Letters*, Bentham envisaged him living in the central lodge, which would be, 'a complete and constant habitation for the principal inspector . . . and his family'.[19] This impractical suggestion was abandoned in the *Postscript*, and living quarters, fit for a gentleman, abutting on to one side of the circle of cells and projecting from it, were substituted. This change was suggested by the architect, Willey Reveley, whom Bentham consulted over the proposal to build a panopticon in Dublin. This change would have enabled the central area to be opened out to light and air, and would have created a 'dead part' within the building which Bentham proposed to use for staircases and passages, a vestry, an organ, a clock tower, and a belfry.

The central inspection lodge remained the focal point of the building both architecturally and administratively; and on it Bentham lavished his inventiveness to ensure that the inspector could survey the cells while remaining invisible himself. In the end, he devised a structure more claustral than the cells themselves in which he would have immured himself and his staff. The

---

[17] Bowring, iv. 85.

[18] *Correspondence* (*CW*), iv. 485–90. To Evan Nepean. Nepean, at the Home Office, was in charge of naval intelligence and also of public order and the control of riots in London. See R. R. Nelson, *The Home Office, 1782–1801* (Durham, NC, 1969), 117.

[19] Bowring, iv. 45.

lodge was to be shaped like two short-necked funnels joined together at their necks, the top sloping walls screening the interior from the view of the upper cells, the bottom forming the room screened from the lower cells; the narrow circle at the funnel's neck was at eye level, pierced by holes covered, perhaps, by smoked glass, through which the inspectors could peer at their charges, but impenetrable from the outside. In this lower room, 54 feet in diameter, the inspector could read, write reports, keep accounts, and receive visitors. It would contain offices for the sub-governor, the chaplain, the surgeon, and possibly the head schoolmaster, divided only by movable screens which would not reach the ceiling. At all times the central aperture must remain clear. Here the officers of the prison could meet, talk, and eat together. 'Why not,' asked Bentham, 'as well as fellows in a college?'[20] Access to this nerve-centre was through folding doors, up a staircase, then through an opening in the floor. As the levels of the inspection tower did not correspond to those of the cell area, to get out into the yards entailed a journey of frightening complexity, across 'the inspector's inner bridge', down 'the inspector's drop' to 'the inspector's landing place', and through 'the inspector's straits'; a journey only possible for the active and slim as the drop was only 2 feet wide; 'two feet is no great thickness: but a man of greater corpulency is certainly not fit to bear an executive part in the government of a prison'.[21] How he would have accommodated any eminent person of greater girth who came to inspect his prison, Bentham did not say. The aim of this labyrinth of galleries, stairs, and passageways was not only to keep prisoners under constant observation; it was also to protect the warders by keeping them separate from the inmates. This was a prison, 'where a keeper never need see a prisoner without either a wall, or a grating, or a space of seven feet between them'.[22]

In his central lodge from which the interior of the prison was visible, Bentham would have effected what Robin Evans describes as 'a dramatic change of purpose'.[23] William Blackburn, the great architect who designed many of the county

---

[20] Ibid. 85.
[21] Ibid. 85, 92–3.
[22] Ibid. 87.
[23] Evans, *The Fabrication of Virtue* (Cambridge, 1982), 146–7.

prisons that put Howard's principles into practice, always incorporated a central governor's lodge that was the focal point of the prison, usually at the hub from which his radial wings extended. But his lodges overlooked the spaces between the buildings, the courtyards, and passages, not into the interior itself. In the next century, his design was copied at Millbank and Pentonville, making these penitentiaries radically different from the panopticon. But total surveillance, on Bentham's principles, is with the help of closed-circuit television and remote control devices, the practice in some of the most modern prisons.

In his provision for a chapel, Bentham can be seen to have succumbed to the religious attitudes of his day. In the *Letters*, he refused to contemplate a separate permanent chapel and suggested a movable pulpit and sounding board; the inmates were to remain in their cells for divine worship. 'No thronging nor jostling in the way between the scene of work and the scene destined to devotion; no quarrellings, nor confederatings, nor plottings to escape; nor yet any whips or fetters to prevent it.'[24] In *Postscript* I, however, he asserted: 'The necessity of a chapel to a penitentiary-house, is a point rather to be assumed than argued.'[25] And despite the expense, a regular chapel in the centre visible from the second, third, and fifth rows of cells is to be provided; and Bentham has to allow some of the prisoners to be moved to the areas in front of these cells for divine service.

The panopticon of the *Letters* seemed a fragile and vulnerable structure; Lord Westmorland, the Lord Lieutenant of Ireland, laconically dismissed it with the objection: 'They will all get out.'[26] Stung by this casual criticism of his pet scheme, Bentham in his *Postscripts* added bars to the windows and an elaborate system of outer defences to keep the prisoners in and the mobs out. The security of prisons from external attack was a matter of great moment—the Gordon riot mobs had stormed Newgate and freed the prisoners only eleven years before. In his plans for fortification, Bentham revealed a characteristic concern for efficiency above all else, combined with a startling disregard for ancient safeguards for public safety and freedom of assembly. Taking on the mantle of a military strategist, he addressed

---

[24] Bowring, iv. 43, 47.
[25] Ibid. 78.
[26] Bowring, xi. 104. See also *Correspondence* (*CW*), iv. 234.

himself to the problem with ruthless thoroughness. A system of outer walls, palisades, and ditches constantly patrolled by sentinels would ensure that the prison could be approached only along a walled avenue. At the first sign of a hostile intrusion, the porter's bell would summon the whole armed force of the prison to man the front; anyone approaching along this defile would be exposed to the fire of the defenders and would be shot down. The safeguards of the Riot Act were jettisoned. 'There needs no riot-act; the *riot-act* has been read by the first man who has forced himself within the gates. . . . The avenue is no public highway . . . those who force themselves within it do so at their peril.'[27]

Bentham hoped that some of the military force guarding the panopticon would be regular soldiers. It was the convention of the time that the magistrates called in the militia to guard the prisons only in emergency. But Bentham wished to have the panopticon protected constantly by the army. In this he showed an insensitivity to political reality in a world where the use of the Army to quell mobs was regarded with the utmost suspicion, and it was widely believed that it was justifiable for soldiers to fire only as a last resort in self-defence. The War Office was reluctant in the extreme to allow the Army to be used without the express authority of the magistrates.[28] No doubt this was one reason why Bentham, as governor of the panopticon, planned to ask for his name to be inserted in the Commission of the Peace for Surrey.[29] He was impatient of the men whose 'zeal for liberty' deluded them into opposing the use of the Army, it was efficient and effective and so, 'against whom should it be made use of with less scruple, than against felons and their allies?'[30] Bentham's attitude to the Army reveals how out of sympathy he was with the traditional Whig distrust of military power and how great the gulf was between him and his contemporaries, like John Jebb, who were zealous for liberty, a gulf which, as a private jotting showed, extended far beyond the immediate question of guarding prisons. Under a pencilled heading, 'Anti-military policy bad', he compared the old English and the modern French policies, the one

---

[27] Bowring, iv. 106.
[28] T. Hayter, *The Army and the Crowd in Mid-Georgian England* (London and Basingstoke, 1978), 11–12, 22, 28.
[29] *Correspondence* (*CW*), iv. 455.
[30] Bowring, iv. 165.

keeping the military odious to the people, the other making them as one with the people. He concluded that the French: 'seems the broader bottomed, the more generous and more enlightened of the two: and more suited to modern situations and to modern times.'[31]

## THE REGIME

Bentham described the regime of his prison with such minuteness that it is possible to reconstruct every detail in the daily life of its inmates. On arrival they would have been stripped, washed, and clothed in accord with health, comfort, and decency. This was the standard practice in contemporary reformed prisons. For Bentham cleanliness was not only a matter of health but of moral purity. In words with a Christian resonance, he emphasized: 'Between physical and moral delicacy a connexion has been observed, which, though formed by the imagination, is far from being imaginary . . . Washing is a holy rite: . . . Alas! were it but as easy to wash away moral as corporeal foulness.' The new arrival would have been subjected to an initiation ceremony rather than a bath:

On reception . . . thorough cleansing in a warm bath—thorough visitation by the surgeon. . . . Clothing new from top to toe . . . Ablution—regeneration—solemnity—ceremony—form of prayer:—the occasion would be impressive. Grave music . . . psalmody at least, with the organ. To minds like these . . . what preaching comparable to that which addresses itself to sense?[32]

During their stay, the inmates would be kept scrupulously clean, their hair close shaven, their clothes frequently washed. They would blow their noses only into handkerchiefs and spit only into spitting boxes. They would have to wash their hands before and after meals. They would wear wooden shoes and their coats would have one sleeve short above the elbow, the other long to the wrist. This would enable an escaped felon to be quickly and easily identified by the different appearance of his

---

[31] UC cxix. 107. This was written 1791–2 and so would be referring to the royal army of the *ancien régime* not to the people-in-arms of the Revolution.
[32] Bowring, iv. 158.

arms—a temporary mark more acceptable than the face washes Bentham had proposed in 1778. The contract stipulated that each prisoner should be properly dressed and supplied with new clothes every year and a clean shirt at least twice a week. The inmate would be placed in a constantly lit cell where he would stay immured, very safe and very quiet; where he would sleep, work, and pray; where he would be nursed when sick and punished when contumacious. There were to be no refectories, workshops, or sanatoria in the panopticon. Bentham admitted that this restriction to one room was severe; he appealed in mitigation to his personal experience. 'All this and more, it has more than once happened to myself to be in the same room for a considerable time together, and I cannot say I ever found any bad consequence from it.'[33]

The cells were to be no larger than necessary, between 9 and 13 feet deep depending on the storey they were on, and 6 feet wide for the single cells in the *Letters*, 14 feet for the double cells in *Postscript* I.[34] Into double cells, Bentham contemplated placing two, three, perhaps four prisoners. The height of the cells presented him with a problem; he wished to make it 8 feet but the 1779 Penitentiary Act had stipulated that the height of the cells must not be less that 9 feet. He poured scorn on this provision in a characteristic piece of special pleading; the panopticon so warmed and aired would be healthy with even lower ceilings. 'I am almost ashamed of the eight feet I ask.'[35] He pointed to the low ceilings in the hulks and the confined spaces between decks in Captain Cook's ships; yet, barring the odd pestilence, men in the hulks were as healthy as the rest of the population and very few of Cook's sailors died. And he excused confinement to one room by the fact that, for most of the Irish, one room housed man, wife, children, dogs, and pigs. These parallels are hardly exact; sailors, Irishmen, and even convicts in the hulks were not confined for months and years to their quarters. But Bentham did realize the necessity of fresh air and exercise to keep his prisoners healthy. However, that too could be made subservient to economy and profit. The prisoners could, to everyone's advantage, take their exercise walking in a wheel, an exercise as healthy as walking uphill, easily supervised and immediately

[33] Ibid. 118.    [34] Ibid. 42, 68, 75.    [35] Ibid. 120.

useful, for the action of the wheel could pump water to the annular tank at the top of the building. They could do this for at least an hour every day, probably in two separate stints; the exercise could be regulated with military precision and: 'To mark the time, and to preserve regularity the better, the assistance of martial music may be called in.'[36] This question of airing caused Bentham much heartsearching; he does not appear to have been concerned with the degrading nature of wheel-walking or of the claustrophobia likely to be induced by a regime where men were only taken from cells down narrow passages to exercise enclosed in a wheel. What did concern him was the apparent need to provide airing yards for the prisoners on Sundays, a day when work would offend against religious sentiment. In *Postscript* I he expounded a complicated scheme for marching yards divided by walls which in *Postscript* II is rejected on grounds of expense.

The convicts were to be allowed seven and a half hours' sleep, and eleven on Sundays, though Bentham thought this too generous; as he pointed out in a letter to Pitt, Coke had allowed his student only six hours and that should suffice for felons.[37] He drew also on anecdote, praising the stamina of a servant at an inn whom he had chanced to meet:

I happened once to fall into conversation upon this subject with a maid-servant at one of the London inns frequented by night-coaches. She went to bed once a-week at most, nor then slept longer than other people. The other nights all the sleep she had was two or three hours dosing in a chair. No ill health—no complaint of hardship. Such is the power of habit; and so moderate, in comparison of the demands of luxury, are the calls of nature.[38]

In his manuscripts, he cited Mirabeau as stating that German peasants slept only five hours.[39] Bentham deplored the indulgence of lying in bed on both moral and physical grounds; 'the animal frame is relaxed,' he complained, 'the spirits sunk, and the Constitution debilitated and impaired; the habit of indolence is at the same time formed and riveted, and the texture of the

---

[36] Bowring, iv. 160.
[37] *Correspondence (CW)*, iv. 227.
[38] Bowring, iv. 163.
[39] UC cxix. 81. The reference is to H. G. Riquetti, Count de Mirabeau, *De la Monarchie prussiene sur Frédéric le Grand* (London and Paris, 1788).

mind vitiated along with that of the body'.[40] The question of the beds themselves caused Bentham much agonizing; again the 1779 Act stood in his way, the bedsteads had to be iron; Bentham queried this, why not wooden? Or even better, hammocks, on the grounds of economy and convenience. In the contract, Bentham undertook to provide separate beds and bedding, 'of sufficient warmth, and kept in a state of constant cleanliness; clean sheeting or blanketing being supplied to each at least once in every month'.[41]

Apart from sleep and exercise, the inmate of the panopticon would work fourteen hours at sedentary labour and spend one and a half hours eating his two meals a day, half an hour for breakfast, and an hour for dinner. The diet was a matter of prime concern both for Bentham and for the government officials he negotiated with. Bentham was clear on the principles of his dietary; by the rule of lenity, no man should go hungry; by the rule of severity, the food must not be palatable; by the rule of economy, the cheapest available. Bentham disliked the idea of a diet scanty enough to impose the pangs of hunger, 'I should speak honestly, and call it *torture* . . . it is applying the rack to the inside of the stomach, instead of the outside of a limb.' Yet he stigmatized Howard's dietaries as absurdly lavish: 'Butcher's meat . . . four times a-week, to felons whose diet is to be their punishment!'[42] Bentham's solution was to feed his prisoners on any cheap food available and to give them as much as they wished to eat. In his *Correspondence* and private jottings several schemes for economical diet are adumbrated. In a letter to James Anderson, he revealed a plan to feed his convicts on potatoes cooked in iron trays which could then be loaded on trolleys, conveyed to the cells, and eaten from.[43] He also suggested privately to himself that putrid fish 'sweetened' with charcoal could be served to the prisoners.[44] The government lawyers were more concerned with this question of food than with matters of greater moment. Methods of inspection and hours of work went through on the nod, but the prisoners diet was subject to rigorous questioning. The first article of the *Proposal* had promised, 'a constant supply of wholesome food not limited in quantity'.

---

[40] Bowring, iv. 163.   [41] UC cxv. 86.   [42] Bowring, iv. 154.
[43] *Correspondence* (CW), iv. 303.   [44] UC cvii. 70.

When the terms of the contract were being negotiated, Richard Ford, a magistrate and MP who managed the business of London police for the Home Office, was asked to look over the terms on behalf of the government. He questioned the powers of the governor on this article. Wholesome food should be explained more specifically, as the clause 'would be reposing too great a discretion in any Governor, who is not only irremovable, according to the contract, but whose successor is so'.[45] In answer to this, Bentham suggested the details of a suitable prison dietary:

Each prisoner shall be supplied every day with wholesome food: viz: bread, interchangeable with rice, pease, potatoes, or other roots commonly used for human food, or with messes made of oatmeal or other meal, or grain commonly used for human food, as much as he shall choose to eat; together with a competent allowance of meat, or fish, or soups or other messes made of any such animals and parts of animals as are usually employed for human food:

But in listing foods, Bentham had not met Ford's objection nor abandoned the principle of his absolute discretion. He saw the control over diet as an instrument which he could not relinquish and he went on, 'without stint to every man . . . who shall exert himself with ordinary diligence . . . but in case of idleness or misbehaviour the quantity as well as the quality' would be reserved to the choice of 'the said Jeremy Bentham and his successors as a means of engaging the said prisoners, without the spur of corporeal severity, to set their hands to labour'.[46]

Bentham did therefore contemplate using the pains of hunger to force compliance, but he hoped to do more by reward. His inmates would be able to purchase more palatable food out of their earnings, this again would encourage them to work for present gratification. Whatever reward could be earned by diligence, Bentham's charges would never be allowed the indulgence of alcohol, not even small beer, or of tea. Water, and water alone, was to quench their thirst. Neither were they to be allowed to smoke. Bentham's prohibition of tobacco was on health grounds, that of drink on moral grounds. He cursed the

---

[45] UC cxv. 108. Richard Ford (1758–1806), barrister, MP, and Police Magistrate at Shadwell and Bow Street.
[46] Ibid. 112.

evil of the demon alcohol in terms that would not disgrace the most rabid of temperance reformers. Public houses were 'fountains of liquid poison'; and drunkenness, 'that murderous infatuation, in comparison of which every thing else that goes by the name of vice is virtue'.[47]

Yet, though he would have deprived his prisoners of the consolation of tobacco and beer, he hinted that the pangs of sexual continence might be too heavy a burden to bear. In a much quoted passage, he suggested that marital sex might be permitted.

Must the iron law of divorce maintain throughout the whole of so long a term an unremitted sway? Can the gentle bands of wedlock be in no instance admitted to assuage the gripe of imprisonment and servitude? Might not the faculty of exchanging the first allotted companion, for another far otherwise qualified for alleviating the rigours of seclusion be conceded, without violation of the terms . . . of the sentence?[48]

This humanity would have an ulterior motive, for the indulgence might be an incentive to good behaviour. It would have posed problems in a panopticon and in a private note, Bentham discussed solutions: 'strict search by an inspector of the same sex for security and a canvas curtain or extinction of light for decency afford sufficient [. . . ?] for the prevention of abuse.'[49]

In the *Proposal*, Bentham emphasized that in his panopticon, the cruelties of whipping and irons would be banished. How then was he planning to control his prisoners? He recognized the need for some punishment but argued that, with constant inspection, the need should be minimal; boredom and the promise of reward would encourage work. Punishment, if it became necessary, should be analogous. 'Outrageous clamour may be subdued and punished by gagging; manual violence, by the strait waistcoat; refusal to work, by a denial of food till the task is done.'[50] In his private papers, Bentham described a gagging machine of two horizontal paws, fastened by a lock.[51] Finally, Bentham did contemplate using absolute solitude as a punishment, but reluctantly, as this was unremunerative and so at variance with the rule of economy. 'If you must torment them, do it in a way in

---

[47] Bowring, iv. 224, 169.
[48] Ibid. 136–7.
[49] UC cxix. 117.    [50] Bowring, iv. 164.    [51] UC cvii. 73.

which somebody may be a gainer by it. Sooner than rob them of all society, I would pinch them at their meals.'[52]

Bentham undertook to educate his charges and, in his *Proposal*, the provision of a school is given prominence. Yet in the panopticon writings this occupies only a short section at the end of *Postscript* II. The facetious final section of the *Letters* is concerned with schools organized on a panopticon model and is not relevant to the prison; for Bentham this was a *jeu d'esprit* and should not be taken as a serious statement of his educational theory. In the penitentiary, children—and as he pointed out many felons were children—and the illiterate, 'at least among the men', were to be taught only subjects that could be put to practical use, reading, writing, and accounts. They were to have these lessons on Sundays. If any showed a particular talent, especially for music, it would be cultivated. This limited learning would have a twofold object and would be in the interest of both the inmate and the governor for it would help the convict to earn a living after discharge and would make his labour a more valuable commodity while he remained in prison. Interest and duty would inspire the governor in his task of education for, 'it would be for his own advantage to give them every instruction, by which the value of their labour may be increased'.[53]

Bentham's vision of the building and the regime of the panopticon is profoundly ambivalent. It was a place of suffering in which every care was taken of the health and comfort of the inmates. They would have a doctor to tend their ills and a chaplain to dispense the solace of religion. They would inhabit a place of warmth, airiness, and light with a garden for growing vegetables; a place created by the marvels of modern technology; a place full of music where men would exercise to martial tunes and sing at their work. The song 'Our Worthy Governor' would extol the virtues of their master and all the good things he had done. But if he had failed in his duty and left undone the things he ought to have done, the song would become a 'merited satire and accusation before all the world'.[54] Yet the panopticon was also a place where men would toil for fourteen hours a day, immured in tiny cells, deprived of the most basic privacy. They

[52] Bowring, iv. 74.　　　[53] Ibid. 161–2, UC cxv. 32.
[54] Bowring, xi. 107.

would tread wheels, eat only potatoes, and drink only water. Contradictions are inescapable in any well-meaning prison; and they are all too clearly defined in the panopticon. Bentham's powerful intellect and his insistence on the most minute and concrete detail cast too bright a light for comfort on the evils of carceral institutions. He raises dilemmas that are too often obscured by sentimental vagueness and pious generalities.

## SOLITARY CONFINEMENT

The penal reformers of the Enlightenment are often held responsible for the creation of the Victorian penitentiary. The crowded filthy squalor of the old gaols was replaced by institutions, clean and sanitary perhaps, but where the inmates were incarcerated in tiers of tomb-like cells, the deep silence broken only by the muted footsteps of ghostly masked figures. Ignatieff begins his study of the relation of the penitentiary to the industrial revolution with an emotive description of its apogee, the regime at Pentonville, the utter silence, the utter isolation from humankind, the machine-like precision of the food trolleys, the ruthless regimentation of every apsect of life. 'Even those', he wrote, 'who thought they had got used to solitude found themselves dreaming about the prison long after. They would hear the bolts crashing shut in their sleep—and the screams.' This was the culmination of punishment directed at the mind rather than the body, the culmination of 'efforts to devise a perfectly rational and reformative mode of imprisonment'.[55]

The panopticon is haunted by the same 'gloomy paradox of crowded solitude' by the chilling vision of men packed together and yet alone. As Bentham jestingly put it: 'In the condition of *our* prisoners . . . you may see the student's paradox, *nunquam minus solus quam cum solus*, realized in a new way: to the keeper, a *multitude*, . . . to themselves, they are *solitary* and *sequestered* individuals.'[56] It is often assumed that Bentham was simply an exponent of solitary confinement. In 1921 Ernest Bertrand, the governor of the central prison at Louvain, an

---

[55] Ignatieff, *A Just Measure of Pain* (New York, 1978), 11.
[56] Bowring, iv. 59, 47, Bentham's emphasis.

enthusiastic advocate of the cellular system, credited Bentham with its revival.[57] And in 1968 Anthony Babington ascribed to Bentham a belief in the efficacy of long periods of solitary confinement in reforming the criminal.[58] Bentham's reputation on this question can be explained partly by his writings in the *View* and in the *Rationale of Punishment* but also by the fact that in the more widely read *Letters* he does unhesitatingly and unreservedly approve the practice. However, between writing the *Letters* and the *Postscripts* he changed his mind. His unequivocal rejection of solitary confinement is one of the most important developments in his ideas on penology between 1786 and 1790. He came to believe that the panopticon was too efficient a system to be used to impose unmitigated solitude, for 'it enables you to screw up the punishment to a degree of barbarous perfection never yet given to it in any English prison'.[59] Yet solitude seemed essential to the eighteenth-century penal reformers for the prisoners' own protection and to avoid the evils of promiscuous association. And Bentham realized that such association could not be tolerated; inmates would terrorize and corrupt one another if allowed to mix freely together. His solution was to place two, three, or perhaps four prisoners in a cell. This would create carefully assorted companies of men who would eat, sleep, work, pray, and exercise together; form innocent attachments to each other and give each other aid and comfort: 'Each cell is an island:—the inhabitants, shipwrecked mariners, . . . partners in affliction, indebted to each other for whatever share they are permitted to enjoy of society, the greatest of all comforts . . . Quitting the school of adversity, they will be to each other as old school-fellows.'

This somewhat mawkish picture of a reformed-criminal old boy network can hardly have been convincing to those who feared that prisons would be schools of vice. But Bentham was driven to this expedient by two imperatives of different force. First, humanity and the fear of the damage prolonged solitude would do to men's minds. Second, the economic consideration that this

---

[57] S. and B. Webb, *English Prisons under Local Government* (London, 1922), 217.
[58] A. Babington, *The Power to Silence; A History of Punishment in Britain* (London, 1968), 95.
[59] Bowring, iv. 71.

flexibility would enable the workforce to be used more efficiently. Bentham seems to have been actuated mainly by the realization that solitude 'is productive of gloomy despondency, or sullen insensibility. What better can be the result, when a vacant mind is left for months, or years, to prey upon itself.'[60] He had become convinced that solitude was 'torture in effect' and should be applied only for short periods, as a punishment not as part of a regular prison regime. Even in the *Letters* certain reservations are apparent when he argued that solitude should not be inflicted in prisons for safe custody only.[61] By August 1790, he was expressing grave doubts as to its use for convicts, in words that make it quite clear that his major preoccupation was the well-being of the inmates. In a letter to Sir John Parnell, to whom he would have been expected to emphasize economy, he suggested movable partitions between cells:

It might be better it should not be absolutely out of every body's power to alleviate the punishment . . . by allowing two or more to live together. This might seem a mighty trivial concern to some persons writing and reading like you and me at our ease: but to the poor devils in question it might make the Difference betwixt rapture and despair.[62]

However, having decided on this change of plan, Bentham was at no loss to think up more hard-headed reasons. He realized that money would be saved on construction and that seclusion in companies would enable a greater diversity of employment and would allow experienced workmen to teach boys. Absolute solitude could then be used as a punishment; and the prisoners could be grouped so as to impose a check on each other.[63] He also seized this further opportunity to attack the 1779 Penitentiary Act which would have imposed absolute solitude at night in separate cells while permitting corrupting association during the day: 'It is the history of Penelope's web reversed: the work of the night is unravelled by the day.'[64]

In the *Letters* Bentham had assumed rather than argued the desirability of solitary confinement. Other influences, apart from his own fertile invention and powerful intellect, were at work to change his mind. Above all, Howard himself had expressed grave

---

[60] Ibid. 74–5.     [61] Ibid. 59.     [62] *Correspondence (CW)*, iv. 190.
[63] Bowring, iv. 74–6.     [64] Ibid. 138.

reservations as to the way separate cells were being used to incarcerate prisoners in absolute solitude. Bentham quoted his words to support rejection. His brother may also have raised doubts in his mind. According to Maria Bentham, Samuel's wife, her husband was averse to solitary confinement except as a humane means of temporary punishment; he believed 'that employment under the least possible *apparent* restraint' would be the most effective way of reclaiming felons.[65] There can be no certainty as to which influence was predominant; Bentham's own account says the final word: 'In the letters, I assumed solitude as a fundamental principle. I then copied, and I copied from recollection. I had no books. I have since read a little: I have thought more.'[66]

Bentham then was no exponent of silent sequestered imprisonment; indeed, he is the author of one of the most moving and perceptive denunciations of the practice:

When the external senses are restrained from action, the imagination is more active, and produces a numerous race of ideal beings. In a state of solitude, infantine superstitions, ghosts, and spectres, recur to the imagination. This, of itself, forms a sufficient reason for not prolonging this species of punishment, which may overthrow the powers of the mind, and produce incurable melancholy. . . . This course of punishment . . . is . . . a sort of discipline too violent to be employed, except for short periods: if greatly prolonged, it would scarcely fail of producing madness, despair, or more commonly a stupid apathy.[67]

More robustly, long after the panopticon was no more than an unhappy memory, he ridiculed the innate absurdity of the practice. 'To think that by vacancy of mind mental improvement can be assured! It is by well filling it, not by leaving it unfilled, that I (in Panopticon) should have operated.'[68]

Solitary confinement brings into sharp focus the problem of the moral position of the revisionist historians. Foucault and Ignatieff both denounce, in ethical terms, the individuals like Bentham and Howard who struggled to reform the gaols, because the outcome was a carceral institution of total control. They are blamed for the consequences of their actions not for their

---

[65] M. S. Bentham, *Life of Brigadier-General Sir Samuel Bentham, KSG* (London, 1862), 100.
[66] Bowring, iv. 71.    [67] Bowring, i. 426.    [68] Bowring, x. 530.

expressed intentions. This interpretation of penal history must be challenged. Men long dead are not responsible for the actions of another generation. Howard was a prison reformer in the sense that he set out to ameliorate conditions in accord with his lights; can he justly be blamed for the sins committed in his name by others living in other circumstances and subject to other imperatives? It was not part of an inevitable process that the ideas of the great reformers of the eighteenth century, Howard, Paul, Bentham, and Hanway, should have produced Pentonville. Their influence could have worked differently, could have weighed differently on men other that Whitworth Russell and William Crawford.[69] It must be reiterated that neither Howard nor Bentham advocated solitary confinement for long-term prisoners. Neither would have tolerated the penitentiary regimes of the next century. The responsibility for Pentonville must lie with the men who approved, built, and administered it. Prisons raise dilemmas from which there is no easy escape; Howard's influence on their evolution may have been deleterious, but his intentions were good. So were Bentham's. At the heart of the matter is the innate evil of carceral institutions; perhaps there can be no such thing as a humane prison and that the only morally acceptable way to reform them is to raze them to the ground. But no generation has found this possible. Destruction must remain an ideal achievable only in the anarchic society of a Kropotkin or a William Morris. Meantime, men of goodwill must try to ameliorate conditions in a piecemeal fashion, identify evils, and suggest remedies, as Howard and Bentham did in their day.

---

[69] William Crawford and Whitworth Russell were the first government inspectors of prisons appointed under the Prisons Act of 1835. Their reports were largely responsible for the regular imposition of solitary confinement and the building of Pentonville.

# 7

# PROPOSAL AND
# CONTRACT II

## MANAGEMENT

'I would do the whole by *contract*,' declared Bentham, 'I would farm out the profits . . . to him who, being in other respects unexceptionable, offered the best terms.'[1] It is in this scheme of management that the panopticon deviates most radically from the future of administration as it evolved during the nineteenth century. In the event, the state took over the running of organizations such as prisons, appointing their own salaried personnel, subject to government inspection and parliamentary scrutiny. This came to be so self-evidently the correct path of progress that Bentham's insistence on the virtues of contract management and his defence of farming appeared to the Webbs aberrant, if not bizarre. They were condescending, almost contemptuous:

The Political Science student has nowadays no difficulty in seeing that the appalling condition of the prisons in the eighteenth century . . . is to be ascribed less to any culpable neglect of the sheriffs and the Justices . . . than to the amazing administrative device . . . of converting the keeping of a prison into a profit-making private business.[2]

But now, with the reaction against state provision of services and the privatization of public utilities, such as electricity, water, and indeed prisons, the arguments deployed by Bentham have a new relevance to twentieth-century controversies. In the panopticon writings at least, Bentham is the forerunner of the application of modern free-market ideology.

In the 1790s contract was the ordinary method of administration over a range of public services, in particular prisons and

---

[1] Bowring, iv. 47, Bentham's emphasis.
[2] S. and B. Webb, *English Prisons under Local Government* (London, 1922), 18.

punishment. The white–negro trade of transportation to America had been managed by contractors; the experts consulted by the parliamentary committees of enquiry into the founding of new penal colonies were captains of slaving vessels. The first fleets to Botany Bay were let out to private contractors. The hulks were managed by a contractor. And, although the county prisons were financed from the rates and supervised by the magistrates, the keepers would usually pay for their positions and derive their reward from fees extracted from prisoners, the selling of drink and other indulgences, and the manipulation of supplies. Bentham's contract management was following well-tried precedent; it was not a novel or peculiar innovation.

The 1779 Penitentiary Act was, however, a radical initiative and did anticipate the future in that it provided for a salaried governor and laid down strict and minute regulations. Bentham realized that this act would be quite incompatible with his scheme and throughout the *Letters* and the *Postscripts*, he launched a bitter and increasingly intemperate attack on the Act both in its general concept and its details. This aspect of the panopticon writings is a paean, lauding the advantages of market forces as against state control. In a passage that deserves to be better known, he derided the whole concept of legal regulation of trades:

There are two points in politics very hard to compass. One is, to persuade legislators that they do not understand shoe making better than shoemakers; the other is, to persuade shoemakers that they do not understand legislating better than legislators. The latter point is particularly difficult in our own dear country; but the other is the hardest of all hard things everywhere.[3]

He condemned, root and branch, the whole structure of regulation in the Act the errors of which were the 'fruits of legislative interference in matters of domestic and mercantile economy'.[4] Profit and economy alone should regulate hours of work and the choice of trades. Howard was treated with a condescension amounting to disdain; his dietaries were over-lavish, his architectural plans were grandiose, producing a 'penitentiary town', unwieldy, complex, and horrifically expensive; felons did not need

---

[3] Bowring, iv. 52.    [4] Ibid. 153.

dining rooms, workrooms, or sanatoria; powder rooms would be suggested next. The 1779 Act would also have created a vast, salaried, administrative structure of governor and deputy governor, taskmasters, underkeepers, store keepers, and committees— a pyramid to add to the fund of corruption and sinister interest:

Along with uninterested management goes a salary. . . . This salary is so much thrown away. 'And will not a contractor equally require payment?' Doubtless: but where will he look for it? To the fruits of his own industry, not of other men's . . . I said *thrown away*; but it is worse than thrown away: it is so much thrown into the treasury of corruption, otherwise called the stock of influence.[5]

Legislative regulation, Bentham argued, produced absurdities. The Act laid down that the diet must include bread but did not safeguard the prisoner against poisoning or starvation; and it made modern methods of heating illegal. Such absurdities once they became law were difficult to change; it would take two or three years and another Parliament to undo the mistakes of minute regulation. Not surprisingly, Bentham came to the conclusion that the Act 'proscribes my mode of building one, and my mode of managing one, in almost every circumstance'.[6]

So Bentham would have jettisoned the committees and the regulations of the Penitentiary Act. In their place, one contractor-governor would concentrate all power in his own hands. He would appoint all subordinates, including the doctor and the chaplain; he would decide on the details of the prisoners' regime; he would regulate their work and impose his own discipline. He would hold his office for life and could bequeath it to his successors; and he would have 'all the *powers* that his interest could prompt him to wish for, in order to enable him to make the most of his bargain'.[7] Bentham rejected board management for it bred disagreement, disunity, and procrastination. 'Monarchy, with publicity and responsibility for its only checks: such is the best, or rather the only tolerable form of government for such an empire.'[8] The zeal of this monarch would be kept alive by the strongest of all appetites, lust for money. Bentham argued cynically, that love of power grows sleepy, benevolence and public spirit cool, love of novelty dies, but, 'pecuniary interest

[5] Bowring, iv. 129, Bentham's emphasis.　　[6] Ibid. 117.
[7] Ibid. 48, Bentham's emphasis.　　[8] Ibid. 85.

grows but the warmer with age'.[9] Contract management was the heart of the panopticon project, for it effected the junction of duty and interest. By its alchemy it would be possible: 'To join interest with duty, and that by the strongest cement that can be found.'[10] And it was conducive to economy for it banished peculation and negligence.

In insisting on a contract national penitentiary, Bentham was confronting a mountain of prejudice and respected opinion against farming. He was also arguing against the future, for it was his opponents who were to triumph on this issue. And he was crossing swords with one of the most influential thinkers of his time, Adam Smith; and combating one of its most deeply felt prejudices, the humanitarian revulsion from the cruelties incidental in farming the poor, a revulsion so strong that the practice had been outlawed in 1782. Bentham argued for contract or 'interested' management on three grounds; it would be more economical; it would avoid creating a new pyramid of salaried places; but, above all, it would be more critically scrutinized. He elevated this last point into an axiom of government that foreshadowed the fundamental tenets of the *Constitutional Code*. 'Jealousy is the life and soul of government. Transparency of management is certainly an immense security; but even transparency is of no avail without eyes to look at it.'[11] He turned the rhetoric of the opponents of farming against themselves; contractors are of all people the most likely to inspire distrust. 'Every contractor is a child of Mammon: a contracting manager of the poor is a blood sucker, a vampire; a contracting jailer, a contracting manager of the imprisoned and friendless poor . . . must be the cruellest of vampires.'[12] Such people therefore would be subjected to the most stringent inquiry and the most profound suspicions and so would be the most closely scrutinized. Bentham confronted the prejudice against farming the poor by arguments that have a particular interest in the light of his subsequent extension of the panopticon to pauper management. He insisted that his prison differed in fundamentals both in principle and in scale; first, its end was punishment, not comfort; secondly, it was open to unexampled inspection by thousands of people—few parishioners bother to look into a poorhouse; and thirdly, the

---

[9] Ibid. 128.  [10] Ibid. 125.  [11] Ibid. 130.  [12] Ibid.

manager of a poorhouse in a parish would be a rustic petty tradesman, inferior in class, education, and humanity to a man chosen to be the manager of a national penitentiary. Bentham saw himself as peculiarly eligible for this position; in an odd jotting, he listed his qualifications for the job, and, with unconscious irony, extolled his contribution to the 1779 Act and cited Howard and Blackstone as referees:

JB    A man of responsible circumstances, of unexceptionable character, of a liberal education, of an honourable profession—not altogether unknown in the literary world who quitted that profession to no other purpose, than to devote himself exclusively to the service of mankind, a man who was the friend of Howard and in the confidence of all his plans and whose services in the original framing of the Penitentiary Act stand recognized under the hand of Blackstone.[13]

In his manuscripts at this date (1791) there is also a passage where he joined issue directly with Adam Smith on the question of farming taxes using arguments against salaried officials that have a direct relevance to the contract management of the panopticon. Adam Smith had insisted that farming can never be the best and most frugal way of collecting a tax. 'No? Never? What should hinder it?' Bentham asked. It must be compared with salaried board management:

By employing as few officers as the business can be done by: by giving to each officer as little as he can be made to serve for . . . Compare this with the sinecures, with the fixed salaries, with the enormous salaries, with the pensions on superannuation, with the manufactured superannuations, with the hundred pound bills for whipcord, and the thousand pound bills for stationery of board management. Compare this with the difference betwixt fine gentlemen's industry and working men's industry—betwixt the exertion of a man who has another as sharp as himself to look after him, and one who has nobody to look after him but the picture of a man with a ball in one hand and a stick called a sceptre in the other. Make these and a few more comparisons and judge whether in contract management there can be any want of pure sources to draw profit from.[14]

And Bentham goes on to expose the basic inconsistency of Smith's position. 'Adam Smith condemns Contract management for the revenue. The same Dr Smith treats with just derision

<hr/>

[13]  UC cxix. 20.      [14]  Ibid. 26.

those legislators who are for meddling with private economy with the economical concerns of individuals.'[15]

Bentham's final answer to the problem of salaries was to devise a system in the *Constitutional Code* whereby positions would be bestowed on the applicant (given he was qualified) who was willing to do the job for the lowest pay. This idea derives from an experiment he was planning for the panopticon. In his manuscripts is a draft advertisement for a surgeon offering: 'Board, Washing and Lodging and a Salary of £ / / a year.' The applicant was invited to fill in the blank space and told that where qualifications and character were equal, preference would be decided by the terms. A similar advertisement for a clergyman is prefaced by a stern warning: 'The situation being a public and distinguished one it will be in vain for any one to apply whose moral character will not bear the strictest scrutiny.'[16] A strict hierarchy would have prevailed in the management of the panopticon. The officers would dine in the inspection lodge; there would be two sittings, the upper officers dining first and withdrawing to the other semicircle while their underlings ate. The menus were to be carefully graded, the upper being allowed wine, the lower beer; the upper, pies and puddings every day, the lower only on Sundays.[17]

These discussions of farming, salaries, and contract management mark an important stage in the evolution of Bentham's ideas on government. L. J. Hume has authoritatively and convincingly argued that it was distrust of the whole structure of interest, place, and sinecures in eighteenth-century government that led Bentham to reject state administration at this stage in his life. Yet he was later able to envisage a government organized in such a way that could make it an efficient, economical machine. This new light on the management principles of the panopticon would lend support to Hume's conclusions. But Bentham never lost his distrust of salaries and pensions. Competitive tendering for government appointments is a fundamental tenet in the *Constitutional Code*; an idea that seems as remote from contemporary

---

[15] Ibid. 29. See also Bowring, ii. 249–51, where the same point is made more temperately.

[16] UC cxviii. 137, 139.

[17] UC clvii. 32, 54.

reality now as contract management of public utilities seemed to Sidney and Beatrice Webb seventy years ago.


## INSPECTION

To prevent the absolute power of his 'monarch' degenerating into tyranny, Bentham devised an elaborate system of checks, the major one being transparent management. The ever-open eye of inspection would sustain the powers of the governor, and create the tension between interest and duty without which the whole edifice would collapse. Bentham's system of inspection had five different aspects; first, the prisoners were watched by authority to ensure discipline and good behaviour; secondly, the governor would watch the actions of his subordinates; thirdly, these subordinates would watch the governor; fourthly, the inmates would spy on each other; and fifthly, the whole structure would be thrown open to the public. The only darkness in this dome of light was that the eyes of the prisoners were veiled, they could not see their inspectors, their visitors or the inmates of other cells. And they could never know when the eye of inspection was upon them. In this, the panopticon differs from the Benthamite state. Sheldon Wolin has argued that with only a slight change the warder of the prison could be equated with society; a society that would enforce social conformity, coercing self-regarding men to consider the interests of others.[18] But in the Benthamite state it would be those who exercised power who would be scrutinized, not those subject to power as in the prison. This is not a slight change.

The inspection of the prisoners was to be absolute, 'every motion of the limbs, and every muscle of the face exposed to view'.[19] And Bentham's faith in it was as absolute. It would obviate the need for irons; it would stop conversation through any barrier or in chapel; it would prevent the possibility of escape or attack on the warders. The building was at every point a device to ensure the reality of inspection. Even the water closets in the governor's home were positioned so that, 'he is *necessarily*

---

[18] S. Wolin, *Politics and Vision* (Boston, 1960), 342–8.
[19] Bowring, iv. 47.

obliged, as well as without trouble enabled, to give a look into the prison once a-day at least, at uncertain and unexpected times'.[20] Bentham planned to enforce discipline by playing a game of cat and mouse with his prisoners; in a revealing footnote he wrote:

I will keep an unintermitted watch upon him. I will watch until I observe a transgression. I will minute it down. I will wait for another: I will note that down too. I will lie by for a whole day . . . The next day I produce the list to him. You thought yourself undiscovered: you abused my indulgence: see how you were mistaken. Another time, you may have rope for two days, ten days: the longer it is, the heavier it will fall upon you. Learn from this, all of you, that in this house transgression never can be safe.[21]

By such methods Bentham believed he could subjugate hardened criminals.

Inspection was also a device to ensure the good behaviour of subordinate officials and to prevent their tyrannizing over the prisoners; they too would be under the eye of the governor. As Bentham explained:

In no instance could his subordinates either perform or depart from their duty, but he must know the time and degree and manner of their doing so. It presents an answer, and that a satisfactory one, to one of the most puzzling of political questions—*quis custodiet, ipsos custodes?*[22]

The governor might himself be a tyrant; but every subordinate encouraged to eat and work in the central lodge would know of his every misdemeanour: 'The legitimate authority of the governor and sub-governor will here receive assistance, their arbitrary power restraint, from the presence of their associates in office. A governor . . . will blush, if not fear, to issue any tyrannical order in presence of so many disapproving witnesses.'[23] The prisoners themselves would find it in their interest to ensure the good behaviour of their fellows. One of the advantages of having two or three prisoners together in a cell was that they could act as a restraint on each other: 'so many comrades, so many inspectors; the very persons to be guarded against are added to the number of the guards.'[24]

---

[20] Ibid. 88, Bentham's emphasis.   [21] Ibid. 81-2.
[22] Ibid. 45.   [23] Ibid. 85.   [24] Ibid. 164.

The final application of the inspection principle was of the whole of the prison by the whole of the outside world. The central tower would enable judges and magistrates to inspect the prison quickly and safely. They would no longer be deterred by disgust at the squalor or by fear of disease. In private marginal notes, Bentham detailed how he would have made these visitors perform their duties with efficiency and diligence: 'Turn into questions the several regulations the observance of which is to be subject of the enquiry of the Visitors—obliging them to write a separate answer to each viz: at least Yes or No. The rules being printed a blank column may be left to receive their answers and their signatures.'[25] The design of the building would also enable any member of the public safely to enter the prison and to view every prisoner in it: 'I take for granted as a matter of course, that . . . the doors of these establishments will be, as, without very special reasons to the contrary, the doors of all public establishments ought to be, thrown wide open to the body of the curious at large—the great *open committee* of the tribunal of the world.'[26] Thus Bentham anticipated almost to the very words, the public opinion tribunal that was to scrutinize and judge government in the *Constitutional Code*.

In the unreformed gaols of the eighteenth century, free commerce with the streets was some safeguard against the ill-treatment of prisoners. But it had its dangers; promiscuous visitors could smuggle in tools and help to plot escapes. It was for this reason that, in 1778, Bentham had approved the exclusion of the public from the national penitentiary. But in 1786, he hoped to get the best of both worlds, the safeguards of free visiting combined with the isolation of the inmates from the outside world. In the *Postscripts*, he elaborated on his original ideas; as well as casual visitors to the inspection lodge, the public would be encouraged to attend divine service on Sunday in the same way that they visited other London institutions such as the Magdalen and the Asylum. The spectacle would be as affecting and interesting; and, if these worshippers could be persuaded by the order and cleanliness of the penitentiary to contribute to its upkeep, so much the better. To encourage donations, everything, 'must be kept as nice as a Dutch house'. And the visitors 'would

[25] UC clvii. 26.     [26] Bowring, iv. 46, Bentham's emphasis.

keep up a system of gratuitous inspection, capable of itself of awing the keeper into good conduct, even if he were not paid for it'.[27]

Bentham's *Proposal* emphasized the importance of public access to his prison not only on Sundays but on other days at mealtimes and times of work, 'providing thereby a *system of superintendence, universal, unchargeable and uninterrupted*, the most effectual and *indestructible* of all securities against abuse'.[28] And in a letter to Dundas, in August 1794, Bentham argued that the panopticon must be built near London, 'the great seat of inspection'.[29] It is the more surprising that the contract makes no mention of inspection, not even by magistrates, let alone members of the public. It is a measure of the the government's lack of concern for the well-being of felons that the Act of 1794 and the contract would have left Bentham's panopticon quite uninspected by law; any public access would have been entirely dependent on his sense of duty. And it might have caused him problems, the nature of which can be seen in a letter designed to allay Lord Spencer's fears that the neighbourhood of the panopticon would become a resort for criminals. 'No man who does not come decently clad, will be admitted: every man will be liable to be searched . . . every man will be liable to be questioned.'[30]

Bentham's emblem for his inspection house was an ever-open eye encircled by the words, 'Mercy, Justice, Vigilance'.[31] This image reverberates chillingly down the centuries. In the subsequent evolution of the penitentiary, inspection took the place of the massive walls, iron bars, and chains of the old prisons. Arthur Griffiths, the historian of Millbank prison, extolled the stringent discipline, 'the sleepless eye' of constant surveillance.[32] Ignatieff maintains that the ruling image both of the penitentiary

---

[27] Ibid. 78–9.

[28] UC cxv. 32, Bentham's emphasis.

[29] *Correspondence* (*CW*), v. 60.

[30] Ibid. iv. 456. George John Spencer, 2nd Earl Spencer (1758–1834), Lord Privy Seal 1794; First Lord of the Admiralty, 1794–1801; Home Secretary, 1806–7.

[31] Ibid. 219. See UC cxix. 124 for Bentham's own sketch. This same emblem of the eye in a triangle is painted in the centre of the great dome in the Cathedral of St James in Santiago de Compostela.

[32] A. Griffiths, *Memorials of Millbank and Chapters in Prison History* (London, 1875), i. 34, 237.

and of the panopticon was, 'the eye of the state—impartial, humane, and vigilant—holding the "deviant" in the thrall of its omniscient gaze'.[33] It was this complete control achieved by maximum transparency that made Foucault describe the panopticon as an ideal instrument in the physics of modern power; it enables the subject to be examined and manipulated and, because he can never know when the eye of inspection is upon him, discipline is internalized, he collaborates in his own subjection. In the twentieth century it is easy to inspire fear and revulsion with images of ceaseless vigilance; it has too often been the instrument of totalitarian tyranny. And it is the stuff of fictional terror, of the ever-wakeful, ever-watchful eye of Tolkien's Dark Lord and of Orwell's Big Brother. But surveillance is a tool of administration like any other and can be put to a bad or a good use. Condemnation, implied or explicit, of Bentham must rest on his ideas, not on the spectres raised by the sinister resonances in minds sensitized by the horrors of twentieth-century events. In the panopticon, men were stripped of all privacy, but Bentham was aware that this was a punishment and that it caused revulsion.. He discussed this question in his manuscripts. First he rehearsed the reactions of a sentimental gentleman who:

To a temper formed to humanity . . . happens to have added the elevated birth, the refinements of education and an enthusiastic love of liberty, inflamed by the circumstances of the time: a never-closing inquisitorial eye figured itself to him as a new invented instrument, the only one that was yet wanting to be added to the horrors of the Bastille.

This gentleman had pictured the suffering of the inmates:

Not to have a moment exempt from the scrutiny of an inquisitorial eye! Not to have a moment of liberty even of that scanty and melancholy remnant of liberty which till now has been respected even in a prison! This punishment is a punishment worse than death: a punishment too horrible, too intolerable even for the worst of criminals.

In answer to this Bentham argued that this was a judgement based on personal feelings and that he, Bentham, would not object to surveillance. 'Supposing myself to have no forbidden enterprise in view, nor while I forbore such enterprises any abuse

---

[33] Ignatieff, *A Just Measure of Pain* (New York, 1978), 113.

of power to apprehend, the idea of an inspector's presence would in the one case be a matter of indifference in the other case even of comfort.'[34] To this argument from his own character, he added another point that habit can accustom men to inconveniences; prisoners would not suffer from such 'morbid delicacy'; they would become inured to the irksomeness of inspection. But the main justification, which Bentham frequently reiterated in his advocacy of the principle, was that inspection would replace the cruelties of iron fetters and fetid dungeons.

In his plan for inspection by the open tribunal of the world to safeguard the welfare of the inmates, Bentham was at odds with the future; even more at odds than over contract management, for his idea of free public access to a spectacle has no place in modern penal theory or practice. In 1811 the Holford Committee rejected Bentham's plans for universal inspection as giving inadequate protection to the prisoners. Their opinion became the accepted wisdom of the nineteenth century and faith was put in the sense of professional and religious duty of doctors and chaplains, and in the public spirit of magistrates, government inspectors, and official visitors. Investigation of prisons was more and more strictly controlled and confined to an official élite; and after they were taken over by the state, in 1877, they became, in the Webbs' words, '"a silent world," shrouded, so far as the public is concerned, in almost complete darkness'.[35] In the twentieth century, the Official Secrets Act still threatens any official who reveals, without proper authorization, what goes on within the gaols. Since centralization, 'prisons have usually been as effective in shutting out the enquirer as they have in keeping in the prisoner'.[36] It is the ultimate irony that the Home Office would certainly exclude Howard from the very prisons which his influence has helped to establish. The inmate culture of the eighteenth century and the free commerce with the street had been some safeguard against official tyranny. It was pitifully inadequate. Unfortunately, the new system was also pitifully inadequate. Doctors, chaplains, visitors, and inspectors colluded with officials to conceal abuses and cover up scandals. In 1872 a

---

[34] UC cxix. 78. The identity of this gentleman of sensibility has yet to be determined.

[35] S. and B. Webb, *English Prisons*, 235.

[36] M. Fitzgerald and J. Sim, *British Prisons*, 2nd edn. (Oxford, 1982), 6.

Howard Association pamphlet denounced abuses in the secret wards of the convict prisons; it was 'a uniform practice, on the part of the convict authorities, to ignore complaints, deny abuses, and represent themselves as exemplarily efficient'.[37]

Other carceral institutions were shutting their doors to the world. The mockery of the insane by the casual visitors to Bedlam is repellent to modern minds, but it had been some safeguard. In the 1770s unrestricted visiting was ended and admission was granted only to ticket holders. But in Roy Porter's judgement: 'the gain produced by ending the tormenting of patients may have been outweighed by the loss caused by reduced contact between inmates and the public and by diminished public accessibility.' The worse cruelties, he believes, may well have been perpetrated after this time. The York Asylum, opened in 1777 as a shining example of enlightened humanitarianism, soon became a place of great secrecy where death, atrocious ill-treatment, profiteering, and embezzlement were all too easily concealed.[38] Despite official inspection, lunatics, and those whose relatives and doctors deemed lunatics, were immured in shrouded asylums, invisible and unheard. In the panopticon writings, Bentham anticipated the perils of secrecy and foresaw the cosy relationship and close sympathy that would arise between officials and official inspectors. He argued that public spirit would not be sufficient to ensure that duties were properly performed and abuses prevented: 'To contract-management was to be sub-stituted trust-management,—in other words, the trustees being constituted authorities, nominees of other superior constituted authorities, management by patronage; or, in still ulterior words, to management by functionaries in whose instance interest coincided with duty—trustees whose interest was at daggers-drawn with duty.'[39]

Despite its shortcomings, Bentham's idea of an inspection gallery freely accessible to the public is worthy of more con-sideration and respect than it has received. It drew on an old tradition. In London, the asylums, the hospitals, and the Magdalen were public spectacles. Bentham's contemporaries

---

[37] Howard Association, *Defects in the Criminal Administration and Penal Legislation of Great Britain and Ireland* (London, 1872), 81.

[38] R. Porter, *Mind-Forg'd Manacles* (London, 1987), 129, 135.

[39] Bowring, xi. 103.

would have found nothing odd in his proposal for open chapel services, for it had respectable precedent. Lock's Hospital for venereal disease had been founded in 1746 with the double object of curing the patients and converting them to a godly way of life. The services in its chapel were therefore an essential part of the regimen. The public were admitted, though the patients in this case remained invisible. But at the Magdalen, established by Jonas Hanway as an asylum for reformed prostitutes, the public could enjoy the additional titillation of worshipping in the company of penitent whores. And the fashionable world flocked to the entertainment.[40] Bentham hoped to make prisons another such public spectacle. As it was, the Howardian reform movement shut the prisons to the outside world, silenced the inmate élite, and ended the commerce with the street that had exercised some check on custodial power. Had it been adopted, Bentham's transparent management might have altered the emphasis of reform of all carceral institutions; and might have gone some way to prevent the drear catalogue of straitjackets, dousing, hallucinations, self-mutilation, and suicides that disfigure the history of penal institutions in the nineteenth and twentieth centuries.

## OTHER CHECKS ON THE POWER OF THE GOVERNOR

Bentham relied on public inspection to keep his prison clean and his prisoners safe from the worst excesses of brutality; but he wrote into his scheme other checks on the considerable powers of his governor. It would be in his interest to keep the prison free of disease for he would be obliged himself to live in its midst and so would be at risk from any contagion. 'Encompassed on all sides by a multitude of persons, whose good or bad condition depends upon himself, he stands as a hostage in his own hands for the salubrity of the whole.'[41] This was a weighty consideration only forty years after the Black Assize when over fifty people, judge, jurors, lawyers, and spectators at the Old Bailey had died from

---

[40] Betsy Rodgers, *Cloak of Charity: Studies in Eighteenth Century Philanthropy* (London, 1949), 49–52.
[41] Bowring, iv. 62.

an infection carried by prisoners from Newgate. Another check on the governor was that he would have been answerable to the court of the King's Bench. This basic provision runs unchanged through the panopticon writings, the *Proposal* and the contract. He would be required to present a report on the moral, medical, and economical condition of the establishment, and to answer any question posed by anyone on any aspect of his management. In expatiating on this point, Bentham took the opportunity to criticize the rules of evidence on self-incrimination. In the *Proposal*, he insisted that all questions could be asked even those, 'the answer to which might tend to subject him to conviction, though it were for a capital crime, not excepted: treading under foot a maxim, invented by the guilty for the benefit of the guilty, and from which none but the guilty, ever derived any advantage'.[42] This controversial polemic was omitted in the contract. In setting up the King's Bench as an umpire, Bentham was following established practice. The 1779 Penitentiary Act laid down that the justices of the peace were to report any waste or mismanagement to this court. Duncan Campbell was under its jurisdiction and, in the next century, the rules of Millbank prison had to be submitted to the court. It was a device notorious for its ineffectiveness. All Campbell's reports and records were systematically ignored. In 1799 the Lord Chief Justice himself complained that representations from convicts in the hulks were never acted upon:

The Act of Parliament requiring this return to be made, I suppose meant something. I have heard this return read a number of years, four times every year, containing the same story, and precisely in the same words. This Act of Parliament which requires this return to be made, supposed that cases might occur which would require the interposition of this Court, and that this should not be considered as a mere job.[43]

This farce had then been played for over twenty years and Campbell's reign was coming to an end: the contract system of the hulks was finally abandoned in 1802. Even the lackadaisical officials of the government thought to question the effectiveness of this device in their negotiations with Bentham. In 1795 Ford,

---

[42] UC cxv. 32.
[43] *The Times*, 11 Apr. 1799, in UC cxviii. 451, endorsed 'Duncan Campbell censured'.

in his observations on the contract, pointed out that there was no provision to enforce the court's orders and suggested that the governor should enter into a bond to abide by its decisions. This Bentham willingly agreed to and, indeed, insisted that he would surrender his office in case of an order given by the court for misbehaviour.[44]

Reports to the King's Bench were a concession to the usual practice of the time; but of far greater moment and originality were Bentham's schemes for insurance. These are at the heart of the junction of interest and duty. The governor had a basic legal obligation not to starve or mistreat his prisoners but, by the insurance scheme, he would have had a positive inducement to keep them alive. Bentham worked out his plans in detail. An estimate would be made, based on the Bills of Mortality, of the number of convicts likely to die in the course of a year. The contractor would be given £10 for every likely death and, at the end of the year, he would forfeit £10 for every actual death. Therefore, if mortality in the panopticon were more than average, he would lose money, if less, he would gain. In a comment more than usually crassly insensitive, Bentham explained: 'make but my contractor's allowance large enough, and you need not doubt of his fondness of these his adopted children; of whom whosoever may chance while under his wing to depart this vale of tears, will be sure to leave one sincere mourner at least.'[45] By the time the contract was drafted, the reward, or the penalty, had increased tenfold to £100.

Monetary gain, or loss, was the basis of other devices to ensure that the governor performed his duties efficiently and zealously. If he allowed a prisoner to escape (irresistible violence from without excepted), he would forfeit £50. If the panopticon discipline failed to reform an inmate and, after release, he were reconvicted, the governor would suffer a penalty on a sliding scale; £1 if the offender had been imprisoned for one year, up to £25 for five years or more. This money would be applied to indemnify those injured by the subsequent offence; Bentham saw these payments as having a twofold function, they would:

operate as a motive to the Governor to attend to the moral and religious part of the plan of management . . . and as . . . an inducement to parties

[44] UC cxv. 108, 112.    [45] Bowring, iv. 53.

injured especially among the poorer classes to come forward in the character of prosecutors: that is, that it would serve to sit in the scale against the many and powerful considerations that tend to withhold a man from taking upon him that expensive, laborious and unpleasant function.[46]

Thus Bentham was hoping to overcome one of the major barriers to the certain and uniform enforcement of the law in the eighteenth century, the reluctance of the injured party to prosecute.

The details of these insurance schemes caused Bentham trouble. It was difficult to find the right basis to assess the likely number of deaths among his convicts. In the *Proposal*, he stated that the proportion would be grounded on the number 'among persons of the same ages in a state of liberty within the Bills of Mortality'. But when it came to drawing up the contract no mention was made of this limitation; perhaps Bentham hoped to drive a hard bargain with the government. But Ford took up this point, arguing that it would be disadvantageous to the public as most deaths in the Bills of Mortality were of children under the age of 10. Bentham agreed to alter the terms to exclude those under 10 but asked for this provision to be suspended for the first year as the intake from other gaols would bring disease and the building would be unseasoned. This life insurance scheme raised other problems and doubts in the negotiations with the government. In a letter to the Duc de Liancourt, Bentham mentioned it as 'a clause which, with great difficulty, I got allowed'.[47] The reasons for the pressure against the scheme are complex. Lord Spencer had indicated that he might allow the panopticon to be built on a piece of his land between Battersea Bridge and Lambeth. Bentham objected to this site as notoriously unhealthy. It would seem that the administration were suggesting that the insurance scheme should be abandoned so as to overcome Bentham's objection. But Bentham felt that he must practice what he preached; in a letter to Wilberforce, he explained:

Lord Spencer has since offered to me . . . to give up his opposition if I would accept of a *marsh*, admirably convenient for me in a pecuniary view, but as certainly pregnant with the destruction by hundreds in a year of those whom I would wish to reform, and not to poison . . . I

---

[46] UC cxv. 135.      [47] *Correspondence* (*CW*), v. 160.

wished to rid myself, once for all, of the temptation to commit safe
murder for great gain; and, accordingly, after a hard struggle, prevailed
to have retained in the contract the clause binding me . . . to pay £100 for
every death.[48]

In his private papers is a draft of his reasons for retaining the
insurance clauses, which explain the vital importance he attached
to the junction of interest and duty in the creation of a humane
prison. He argued convincingly and with remarkable perception:

The nature of things does not afford another expedient of equal efficacy
for effecting that intimacy of union between interest and duty the want
of which has been the sole and universally acknowledged cause of the
miseries and abuses which have been so notoriously prevalent in prisons.
It applies to this purpose the united powers of *reward* and *punishment*,
without the expense of the one or the *hardship* of the other: . . . Legal
penalties can attach only upon specific *acts*: upon the wounding, starving
or poisoning men outright—They afford very little security against
destructive *habits*; against the being killed by inches or by neglect: worn
out by want of rest or nourishment: poisoned by bad provisions or
unwholesome trades and occupations.[49]

The best and the worst of Bentham's attitudes were thus contained in the life insurance scheme. In it he revealed a kindly
determination to ensure the health of the inmates combined with
a willingness to calculate the monetary value of the miseries
of death. The scheme obeys the internal logic of the junction
of duty and interest yet offends against sentiment and human
dignity. But to Bentham, it must have appeared a sensible,
practical, and far from novel solution to a real problem. He knew
well the sufferings inflicted on convicts when duty and interest
were disjoined. In 1791 the second fleet to Botany Bay sailed
with 1,763 convicts; on arrival over 300 were dead or dying. This
was not surprising, for the contractor to whom they had been
entrusted was paid a lump sum for each man, so the less they ate
and the sooner they died, the greater would be his profit. The
terrible mortality on the Atlantic slave ships was also causing
public outrage at this time. Bentham's insurance device was in
accord with current practice for dealing with such problems. In

---

[48] Ibid. 210–11, Bentham's emphasis.
[49] UC cxv. 107, Bentham's emphasis.

subsequent sailings, the contractors were paid extra for each healthy convict to land in Australia. And in 1794 the Slave Trade Act attempted to improve conditions by paying a premium for each slave landed alive. These methods were short-lived, becoming anachronistic as salaried officials took over from contractors in the administration of prisons and transportation. But, as with inspection, it is at least arguable that Bentham's insurance scheme might have been more effective in safeguarding the welfare of prisoners than the unholy alliance of warders, chaplains, and doctors that ruled the secret wards of the nineteenth-century convict prisons.

## THE CRIMINAL MIND

Bentham called the panopticon, 'a mill for grinding rogues honest'.[50] This repellent image colours many people's reaction to the scheme. It seems to deprive the criminal of humanity, degrading him to level of a machine, a machine moreover that was to be subjected to a process of ruthless manipulation. For Foucault, this mill was a technological device, a laboratory of power for the subjugation of men. He, and other revisionist historians, link the penitentiary with the evolution of the whole apparatus of social control developed in response to the needs of the emerging industrial capitalist society. Hospitals, barracks, schools, poorhouses, factories, and model villages are seen as instruments in the hands of authority to control, manipulate, and discipline the deviant and the poor. Bentham's theories on the nature of man, the criminal mind, and the causes of crime are therefore crucial in understanding the panopticon and its place in the ideology of the penitentiary. They also touch on one of the most intractable problems of the panopticon. On the one hand, Bentham postulates rational utilitarian man who, knowing his own interest, is capable of following it; on this he bases his theory of democracy. On the other hand, the inmate of the panopticon is deprived of choice, indeed in the pauper panopticons brought up in ignorance of the outside world, deliberately deprived of the knowledge that would enable him to make a rational

---

[50] *Correspondence (CW)*, iv. 342.

choice in accord with his own interest. Bentham's cry was '*fiat experimentum*'; but how could the pauper experiment in the cloistered world of panopticons? Bentham's psychology and his analysis of the causes of crime go some way to explaining the ambivalence in his thought. It is defensible that prisoners should be deprived of choice—indeed Bentham sees this as part of their punishment; the extension of this punishment to paupers can be more easily understood after consideration of his ideas on the criminal mentality.

For Bentham, the criminal was a member of the community whose interests should be considered; at one point he even argued that the criminal should not be excluded from the franchise.[51] Yet the criminal was also a defective being. Bentham, like other thinkers of the Enlightenment, subscribed to the theory of David Hartley that the pysche was as material as the body; disease could, therefore, have moral causes. In the same way, moral delinquency, crime, and the poverty closely allied to crime, could also be the product of physical causes, idleness, drink, and debauchery. A regime of self-denial, abstinence, and discipline could 'cure' the defective mechanism of the human frame and the human mind. Criminals were like children, their development arrested and distorted, standing in need of control—and inspection. The fullest account of these ideas comes not in the original panopticon writings but later in *Panopticon versus New South Wales*, where Bentham wrote:

They may be considered as persons of unsound mind, but in whom the complaint has not swelled to so high a pitch as to rank them with idiots or lunatics. They may be considered as a sort of grown children, in whose instance the mental weakness attached to non-age continues, in some respects, beyond the ordinary length of time.

He argued from this premiss that death is a totally inappropriate punishment; the criminal should be treated as a refractory patient. He went even further, anticipating the fashionable twentieth-century idea that criminals are not innately evil, but mentally sick: 'Among savages, when to a certain degree a man is sick in body, he is cast forth, and thought no more of. In a nation civilized in other respects, the same barbarity is still shown to this

[51] Bowring, iii. 559.

at least equally curable class of patients, in whose case the seat of disorder is in the mind.'[52]

Yet Bentham realized that poverty and crime were closely linked; the criminal was likely to be poor and many had yielded, 'for once to the momentary impulse of some transient temptation'. They could be 'distinguished from many of their neighbours more by suffering than by guilt'.[53] Gilbert Geis gives Bentham credit for realizing the social causation of crime.[54] But underlying this humanity was a harsher belief that destitution as well as crime could be an act of will. If the poor laboured industriously, eschewed strong drink, gambling, and debauchery, they would avoid the extremes of want. But they were led into temptation and corrupted by idleness and alcohol. In this, Bentham was merely echoing the almost universally held views of his time. But he optimistically and perhaps naïvely believed that the wicked and the idle could be reformed by being removed from all such temptations and subjected to the engine of the panopticon. The discipline would enforce apparent submission and in so doing would transform it into real submission. 'Men become at length what they are forced to seem to be: propensities suppressed are weakened and by long-continued suppression killed.'[55] Habit, one of the great forces controlling the lives of men, would inure them to honest labour and even, he argued in a private note, reconcile them to the deprivation of privacy and freedom consequent on inhabiting a panopticon. 'In time they will be accustomed to it, and the galling roughness of their chains will be smoothed away by use.'[56]

At the core of Bentham's concept of the criminal is a moral perception that differs radically from much of the humanitarianism of the twentieth century that sees the criminal as a victim. He did not see the individual as flotsam and jetsam tossed on the tides of history. Haskell, in his criticism of the incoherence of Foucault's theory, argues that the reformers of the Enlightenment believed in a 'blameworthy self' and had no conception that

[52] Bowring, iv. 175, 186.
[53] Ibid. 76.
[54] Gilbert Geis, 'Jeremy Bentham', in Hermann Mannheim (ed.), *Pioneers in Criminology* (London, 1960), 57.
[55] Bowring, iv. 140.
[56] UC cxix. 82.

voluntary actions could be caused by forces outside the human will. 'But the crux of the difference can be evoked by posing a single question. *Can voluntary acts be caused?* The convention that prevailed in educated circles before the closing decades of the 19th century quite consistently implied a negative answer to that question: since that time all consistency has been lost.'[57] For Bentham and other reformers of the Enlightenment, criminals, like other men, were potentially rational beings responsible for their own actions; they had violated the laws and could not go unpunished. This concept of the 'blameworthy self' justified the infliction of suffering; but that suffering should be meted out in careful measure. As Haskell writes, what the reformers 'opposed . . . was unnecessary suffering, suffering to no good end, and against this they often fought like tigers'.[58] Bentham's central belief was that the rational mechanism of human morality could be refashioned, the criminal mind literally re-formed. The overwhelming corrupting influence in the lives of the poor that tempted them into crime was idleness; and the cure for idleness was work.

## WORK IN THE PANOPTICON

Work was therefore to be the great engine of reformation in the panopticon as well as the source of profit to the governor; idleness was the cause of crime and work was a cure for idleness. Quality of work was Bentham's criterion of reformation and habits of work would themselves reform. They would change behaviour. 'Habits of Industry', he wrote, 'are perhaps the only criterion of their again becoming proper members of society.'[59] Although he envisaged forcing his prisoners to work at first by withholding their food, Bentham believed that, as work became a habit, it would become a pleasure. He denounced the central concept of the 1779 Penitentiary Act that work should be a punishment. Work should reform men, inure them to habits of

---

[57] Thomas L. Haskell, 'Foucault, Humanitarianism and the Blameworthy Self', 27–8, unpublished paper given at the Conference on the Welfare State, Murphy Institute, Tulane University, in Feb. 1986, Haskell's emphasis.
[58] Ibid. 27.
[59] UC cxix. 19.

industry, and transform them into honest citizens. He questioned the whole philosophy of hard labour. 'The policy of thus giving a bad name to industry, the parent of wealth and population, and setting it up as a scarecrow to frighten criminals with, is what I must confess I cannot enter into the spirit of. I can see no use in making it either odious or infamous.' Work must therefore be pleasurable: 'To me it would seem but so much the better, if a man could be taught to love labour, instead of being taught to loath it.'[60] His insistence here on the pleasures of work would seem to call into question whether he wholeheartedly subscribed to the classic utilitarian thesis that man could be driven to labour only by the spur of necessity and want. H. L. A. Hart argues that Bentham believed that man would always be forced into painful labour.[61] But Bentham may have changed his attitude, coming to believe that the alchemy of the panopticon could transform painful into pleasurable labour, or at least mitigate the suffering it inflicted.

In his search for profitable and pleasurable labour. Bentham argued that the clauses of the 1779 Act regulating the nature of work to be done in the penitentiary should be jettisoned, profit and profit alone should be the criterion in the choice of trades. The inmates must be inspired to labour by reward: 'Reward, not punishment, is the office you must apply to. Compulsion and slavery must, in a race like this, be ever an unequal match for encouragement and liberty.'[62] So they must share in the profits and must benefit immediately from harder work by being able to buy indulgences and better food. But the inmate was not to be allowed to spend all his earnings on present gratification. Bentham worked out a scheme that was written into his draft contract whereby a prisoner should have, as of right, a quarter of his earnings and half of this should be set aside by the governor to purchase him an annuity for his old age.

The governor was, however, to keep three-quarters of the earnings of the prisoners and from these the profits of the prison would arise; a major section of the contract gave powers to employ prisoners for his benefit. It was therefore in his interest to

---

[60] Bowring, iv. 144.
[61] H. L. A. Hart, *Essays on Bentham* (Oxford, 1982), 24–5.
[62] Bowring, iv. 144.

work his prisoners as hard as possible, for as long as possible, and at the most lucrative trades possible. He must be free not only from restrictions on choice of trades but on hours of work also. Bentham was determined to exploit the labour of his felons and to take full advantage of his position as a monopolist. In a statement worthy of the most ruthless capitalist entrepreneur, he wrote: 'What other master is there that can reduce his workmen, if idle, to a situation next to starving, without suffering them to go elsewhere? . . . and who, so far from being able to raise their wages by combination, are obliged to take whatever pittance he thinks it most for his interest to allow?'[63] In *Postscript* II he set out the details of what this would entail. His prisoners were to work fourteen hours a day at a sedentary trade and another hour walking in a wheel. 'Fifteen hours out of the twenty-four, without the smallest hardship.' He himself had seen the honest poor work such hours 'in health and cheerfulness'.[64]

Although Bentham insisted on the governor's complete liberty to choose among a variety of sedentary trades, in practice much of the work in the panopticon would have been as uniform and monotonous as the rest of the regime; for Bentham planned to use the energy of his prisoners as he would a steam engine. He explained later:

I had . . . in conjunction with my brother, Brigadier-general Bentham, expended some thousand pounds in bringing to maturity a system of inventions of his for executing by machinery . . . the most considerable branches of wood-work, besides many branches of stone-work and metal-work. . . . The system was in such forwardness that we were upon the look-out for a steam-engine. Human labour, to be extracted from a class of persons, on whose part neither dexterity nor good-will were to be reckoned upon, was now substituted to the steam-engine.[65]

From his private notes it would appear that Bentham envisaged an intensive use of wheel-powered machinery. Samuel Bentham's wood-sawing machine (Fig. 2) would have been of vast dimensions; and, given the technology of the time, would have needed a large walking-wheel to activate the vertical motion of the piston. And Bentham planned several such machines. In his private marginal notes, he listed corn-grinding, threshing, and

---

[63] Ibid. 56.     [64] Ibid. 163.     [65] Bowring, xi. 167.

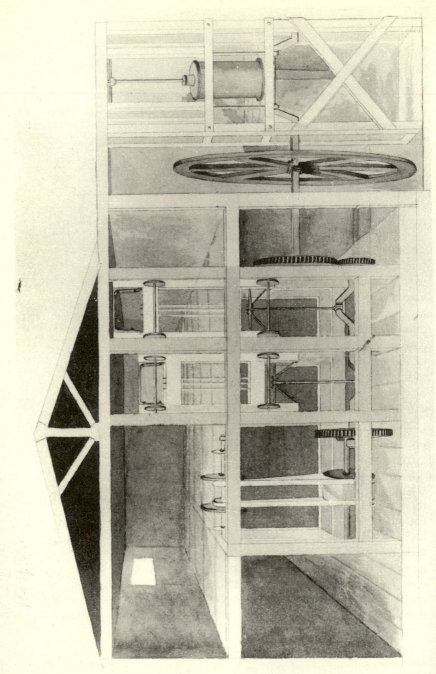

Machine Sewing Machine, one of S.B.'s', UC cxvii. 24

chaff-cutting in addition to woodwork, stonework, and water-raising. A note in Samuel Bentham's writing shows how he planned to apply the force of men's strength to turn his machines:

At the same time as men walk on the outside of a lantern wheel to apply their weight in an uninterrupted motion another such lantern wheel might present itself above the former at a convenient height for men . . . to steady themselves by. Then, if the motion of these two wheels be made to communicate and keep pace together, the men might hang any part of their weight on their arms to ease their legs without diminishing . . . the effect. If the wheel was of large diameter, they might hang by their hands to the upper bars while their feet were on the lower.[66]

These wheels were to be kept in motion continuously and so meal times would vary as men did their shifts. Whether this drudgery would have achieved the purposes of reformation by inculcating a love of labour seems questionable. The nature of much of the toil in the panopticon would have been little different from the cranks and treadmills that became notorious in nineteenth-century gaols. This would seem to contradict Bentham's central tenet that labour could and should be pleasurable and that a prisoner's moral reformation could be measured by the improved quality of his work; for, if neither dexterity nor goodwill are needed, how can quality be improved?

## DISCHARGE OF THE PRISONERS

Bentham's care for his prisoners extended beyond the end of their prison terms. With his network of pecuniary safeguards, he had made himself responsible for their subsequent behaviour, losing money if they were ever reconvicted of an offence. It was therefore to his advantage that the ex-convicts were neither tempted nor forced to return to a life of crime. He devised a complex scheme to retain substantial control over the lives of the former inmates. The security of society and the perennial difficulty for the ex-felon of finding honest work were other

---

[66] UC clvii. 32, 46. I am indebted to Dr Stephen Conway for his opinion on the handwriting. The paper is headed with the word 'Panoptic' and the letters 'SB' in pencil.

motives that inspired him in his search for methods to ensure
continuing honest behaviour. The provision in the Hard Labour
Bill that would have given prisoners clothes and money on discharge was the first attempt to help convicts over the difficult
return to ordinary life. In 1778 Bentham had approved these
ideas, but subsequently he changed his mind and poured scorn on
such aid; it was 'like giving board money to the school boy';[67] a
point that he elaborated on in *Postscript* II. 'The penitentiary
act sets a whole regiment of such beggars on horseback . . .
Can prudence, can economy, be expected generally to prevail
during the ecstasy that will so naturally mark the period of
emancipation?'[68]

The genesis and evolution of Bentham's answer to this problem
can be traced in his writings from the time his mind first turned to
penal questions. The idea of a relationship between master and
convict to their mutual advantage was present in embryo in the
writings of the 1770s. In the *Letters*, he suggested that the contractor and the prisoners might continue 'their manufacturing
connexion, after the dissolution of every other'.[69] The stigma of
prison would make it difficult for the workman to get employment elsewhere and he would have to accept lower wages. 'He
would therefore probably come cheaper to his former master
than another man would.' In a manuscript draft he elaborated on
this: 'When the term of his confinement was at an end he might
be provided with a small house in the neighbourhood with work
at the same rate that he had it allotted to him in prison.'[70]

In *Postscript* II these vague ideas had flowered into a full-
blown scheme covering every eventuality and providing a series
of alternative routes that could be taken by the 'emancipated'
prisoner, none of which would have left him more than a pitiful
modicum of freedom. He could enlist in military service in the
army, the navy, or the East India Company; this plan was based
on current practice. After 1776 the courts sometimes sentenced
criminals to service in the army or navy as a substitute for
transportation in an attempt to ease the overcrowding in the
gaols. His proposals also follow closely established practice in the
disposal of prisoners whose death sentence was commuted. These

---

[67] UC cxix. 21.        [68] Bowring, iv. 171.
[69] Ibid. 55.        [70] UC cxix. 19.

pardons were nearly always conditional, usually on transportation. But the Home Office papers show a variety of other fates.
Service in the navy was sometimes stipulated, as was, increasingly
frequently after 1790, service in the army. The East India
Company rejected all requests to take convicts up to 1792 but
was accepting them by 1794. Of even more interest, some convicts
were pardoned on condition that they gave security for good
behaviour or would consent to do hard labour for a period,
generally a year. Likewise employers would give security for
men they wished to hire. Sometimes, those who had signed
the petition for pardon would be asked to answer for the good
behaviour of the convict.[71] This last practice may have been the
inspiration of Bentham's scheme for ensuring employment for
the ex-prisoner, who would have had to find some responsible
householder willing to put up £50 as surety for his good behaviour. The Draconian powers of master over apprentice were
to be given to such householders. The full powers of the Vagrancy
Acts were to be available for his recapture in case of escape and
for imposing penalties on anyone found harbouring him. The
recognizance of £50 was renewable year by year and, if not
renewed, the ex-convict was to be returned to the panopticon. In
a long footnote, Bentham revealed how he saw this scheme
working to the advantage of the governor. He would be in a
perfect position to give such sureties and to judge the worth of a
workman and to make the best use of his abilities. And he could
set up subsidiary panopticons for the reception of the discharged
felon.[72] In effect, the man would be exchanging one prison for
another; in his new institution he could neither absent himself
nor become intoxicated, for that would deprive his master of the
benefit of his services. But there would be some alleviations. He
might not have to work quite such long hours, a curtain would
shield him from the eye of inspection during times of recreation
and sleep. 'The comforts of matrimony' could be enjoyed. And
on Sundays he could have perfect liberty. Bentham describes this
life as 'a state of free service, only somewhat better guarded than
ordinary against misbehaviour and abuse'.[73]

---

[71] R. R. Nelson, *The Home Office, 1782–1801* (Durham, NC, 1969), 97–8.
[72] Bowring, iv. 166.
[73] Ibid. 169.

He admitted that this life was one of hardship. In a passage that seems to fly in the face of the principles of equal justice, he suggested that men of greater refinement could be bought out of this servitude in the subsidiary panopticon by their friends: 'Men accustomed to a style of life superior to that of the common run . . . may by the generosity of a disinterested bondsman, find themselves clear of every obligation of service. A father may thus rescue his son, an uncle a nephew, a brother a brother, from the hardships of a degrading servitude.'[74] Bentham was on the defensive about his discharge proposals; he himself admitted that they were not faultless: 'The end in view here is to ensure the good behaviour and subsistence of convicts after the expiration of their punishment, regard being had to economy, humanity, and justice. If perfection be still at a distance here, shall we find anything nearer to it in the colonization scheme, or the penitentiary act?'[75]

This question is worth consideration. Bentham saw the discharged felon as caught in a trap; in the short term of drunkenness and riot; in the long term of crime or the poorhouse. And in his mind, the major justification for his proposals was that they would entail only the proper enforcement of existing statute law. The Vagrancy Acts gave magistrates the power to whip and imprison persons with no visible means of support. In both his published and his private writings, Bentham returned again and again to this theme:

It is evident, that . . . almost every person who happens not to have responsible friends, must of necessity upon his discharge from the Hulks, or from the Penitentiary House find himself whether he will or no, in the predicament of a rogue and vagabond . . . and the same causes which at first brought him into that predicament must by their continuance bring him into that of an incorrigible rogue.[76]

Predictably Gertrude Himmelfarb reserves her severest condemnation for proposals that would have incarcerated the pauper criminal in the subsidiary panopticons for the term of his natural life, making a mockery of release (though no worse a mockery than the injustice that sent Howard on his travels, the system that returned an innocent man, acquitted in open court, to prison for

[74] Bowring, iv. 168.     [75] Ibid. 169.     [76] UC cxix. 20.

non-payment of the gaoler's fees. And this abuse had been ended less than twenty years before). The subsidiary panopticons must be considered in the context of Bentham's thought and of contemporary practices. Bentham was in many ways a realist. The humane aspiration to provide an honest livelihood for prisoners after release was, in his mind, dependent on its being in the interest of someone to provide it. He saw the profit that would accrue to the governor as being essential for the provision of the ex-convict. To ensure that profit some sanction to enforce labour would be necessary—hence the despotic powers he would have allowed the panopticon authorities. Bentham also believed in the ideal of the Enlightenment, that laws should be equitably, uniformly, and certainly enforced. The confusion and capriciousness of English law were anathema to him. The Vagrancy and Settlement Acts made the whole of England a prison for many of the poor; the distinction between crime and poverty was blurred by the existing law. As Bentham wrote:

I will not pester you with further niceties applicable to the difference between *houses of correction*, and *work-houses*, and *poor houses* . . . between the different modes of treatment that may be due to what are looked upon as the inferior degrees of *dishonesty*, to *idleness* as yet untainted with dishonesty, and to blameless *indigence*. The law herself has scarcely eyes for these microscopic differences.[77]

It is sometimes argued that the saving grace of these laws was that they were enforced only randomly and sporadically. But the unequal and uncertain enforcement of laws does not render them nugatory. Whole communities were impoverished by decisions of local magistrates. Many individuals suffered injustice and many were incarcerated in fetid workhouses; many more were hounded from place to place on the authority of the local overseers of the poor. It can have been little consolation to these victims to know that many of their fellows escaped. Respect for abstract justice or for the human dignity of the indigent was not a noticeable quality among Bentham's contemporaries. An uncritical acceptance of the eighteenth-century rhetoric on the customary liberties of Englishmen, combined with a sentimental nostalgia for the illusory freedoms of pre-industrial society have brought the Enlighten-

---

[77] Bowring, iv. 59, Bentham's emphasis.

ment ideals into disrepute. Yet comprehensible law fairly and uniformly enforced is a more rational and worthy objective than a jumbled mass of obscure law enforced occasionally and capriciously.

The other eighteenth-century reality that Bentham's discharge proposals must be seen against is transportation. The men and women sent to New South Wales very rarely returned and, even at the expiry of their terms, many were kept in bondage in the colony. Again, as Bentham pointed out at length in his writings on transportation, the amount of suffering inflicted on the individual was a matter of blind chance, varying from a terrible death during the voyage to an early emancipation and a comfortable life in a new world. The attitude of the public must also be taken into account. The main purpose of transportation was to rid the country of the criminal. And this axiom continued to be a cornerstone of penal policy until the opposition of the Australian colonies brought transportation to an end in the middle of the nineteenth century. Pentonville itself was built to reform by solitude and religious exhortation felons who were destined not to release in England but to a new life in Australia—cleansed of their wickedness. It is an indication of the fertility of Bentham's invention that, despite his vehement disapproval of transportation, he anticipated even this use of the penitentiary. He suggested that the panopticon discipline would be an ideal preparation for the new life—and given the shortage of skilled labour in New South Wales, he may well have been right. 'How useful it might be . . . to the colonization scheme. In this case, the trades the prisoners were employed in, and the instructions of all sorts they were made to receive, might be adapted to that object and made subservient to their final destination.'[78]

Bentham was not unaware of the major objection to his discharge proposals. He admitted in his private writings that, 'such obligation if inflicted by law may seem a hard and unjust extension of the original sentence'. But he reiterated his answer that, in the context of transportation and the Vagrancy Acts, his discharge proposals were realistic, fair, and humane. In a manuscript note, he wrote:

[78] Bowring, iv. 169.

but the utmost of such a hardship and injustice is trifling in comparison of that which they undergo at present by the provision of the law. It is upon this very provision that all advantage in this point of view reaped from the colonisation plan actually depends: if in consequence of being legally sentenced for 7 years, a man is physically detained for life, then the provision takes place: if no such provision takes place, and he returns to the country after the expiration of the sentence, the security is gone. With the three options the condition of a convict . . . would be three times as good as that in which many numerous descriptions of persons to whom no crime is imputed, are placed by a variety of laws now in force: witness the Vagrant Act 17 G.2, 15 under which a man merely for begging or for want of employment may be consigned in the first instance to the House of Correction for above 6 months: for the second offence to the same place with unlimited whipping, for above two years, and for the 3rd to transportation for seven years.[79]

Ignatieff argues that the failure to build a national penitentiary in accordance with the 1779 Act was due in part to the reluctance 'to abandon the banishment of notorious offenders for a system of imprisonment that would result in the eventual return of the convicts to the community. . . . For a society that had long accepted the incorrigibility of offenders, it was difficult to adjust to a punishment that presumed their eventual reintegration into the labor market.'[80] It is to these considerations that Bentham's plan addressed itself; he insisted that, reformed or not, his felons would still be given the means of subsistence and prevented from future mischief:

The *securing* the public against the future ill-behaviour of a discharged convict has hitherto been looked upon as a problem, insoluble except by death, or some other punishment which, under the name of temporary, should be in effect a perpetual one . . . upon this plan, be he ever so incorrigible, the public will have nothing to fear from him, since, till he has given satisfactory proof to the contrary, he will not be let loose.[81]

[79] UC cxix. 89.
[80] Ignatieff, *A Just Measure of Pain*, 95–6.
[81] Bowring, iv. 168, Bentham's emphasis.

# 8

# THE PANOPTICON BILL
# OF 1794

Beggar-Whipper General
William Cobbett

Although the prospects for the panopticon seemed fair in the summer of 1793, there were some ominous signs. Early in the year Pitt's government had been dragged reluctantly into war with revolutionary France, a development that seemed to have made little impression on Bentham at the time, but which was to determine the fate of his prison. Then, in August, the first of the legal difficulties that were to bedevil his scheme surfaced, forcing the administration to introduce a new Penitentiary Act. The events surrounding this legislation have not hitherto been adequately described, but they form one of the turning-points of the panopticon saga. The wealth of manuscript material at University College read in conjunction with Bentham's voluminous correspondence enables a new interpretation to be suggested; and one that shows Bentham's continuing concern with the discharged prisoner and the security of society. These exciting documents contain the apotheosis of the panopticon in Bentham's own parliamentary bill. It is not generally realized that Bentham spent five months, from October 1793 to February 1794, absorbed in drafting his own attempt at legislation. This considerable work has remained buried in the haunted boxes of the panopticon papers and is virtually unknown to scholars. When it is eventually published, it will take its place among the more significant and prescient of Bentham's works. But whether it will substantiate his claim to have a genius for legislation is another matter.[1]

In the spring of 1794 three possible panopticon statutes existed;

---

[1] The MSS are in two boxes; a draft in Bentham's own hand in UC cxxiv and jumbled copies of this in UC cxix (b) in several different hands; there are also several pages of notes and comments.

the draft Act that eventually became law later that year; and Bentham's own two bills, a short bill consisting of only three sections and a considerably longer bill starting with the clauses of his first bill but continuing with further details. The relationship between these three drafts has never been elucidated and indeed has been misunderstood. Taylor Milne in his Introduction to volume iv of the *Correspondence* implies that Bentham's shorter bill was the basis of the subsequent statute. He describes how Bentham 'stayed on at Queen's Square Place until early April, completing the draft of a new Penitentiary Bill', difficulties arose, but 'by the beginning of May these had been ironed out and a shorter version of the bill was brought before the House of Commons'.[2] Gertrude Himmelfarb is even more definite; she criticizes the Penitentiary Act of 1794 which vested care, management, superintendence, and control in a single contractor-governor and blames Bentham for it. 'The Act was tailor-made to Bentham's specifications—as it might well be, since it was he himself who tailored it.'[3] Hume in his sharp questioning of this account comes near to the true picture when he asserts that there were substantial differences between Bentham's proposals and the Act.[4] In fact, they were two quite separate exercises. A study of the manuscripts together with the published correspondence makes it possible to piece together the story behind the Act. Bentham at first hoped that his original long bill would be enacted; he then truncated it, taking the first three sections to form a short bill which he saw as a preliminary measure; one of the copies is endorsed in his hand: 'Panopticon Bill (so much as is sufficient for the present session).'[5] But this too was jettisoned and replaced by the government measure; again Bentham's endorsement makes this clear:'Original Pan. Bill No. 1 containing Sec. I, II, & III being the sections superseded by the present Penitentiary Bill before the House.'[6] Bentham's own recollections support this version of the course of events. 'I drew a bill,

---

[2] *Correspondence* (*CW*), iv. xxx.
[3] G. Himmelfarb, 'The Haunted House of Jeremy Bentham', in *Victorian Minds* (London, 1968), 66.
[4] L. J. Hume, 'Revisionism in Bentham Studies', *The Bentham Newsletter*, 2 (1978), 12.
[5] UC cxix. 137.
[6] UC cxxiv. 2.

short, compact, and as I thought, complete. But the bill so drawn was rejected with ignominy.'[7]

This original panopticon bill and Bentham's commentaries on it are of immense interest. They are a goldmine of information about Bentham's ideas on bureaucracy. They are an extraordinarily prescient discussion on the problems of the administration of welfare. They touch incidentally on disparate questions such as evidence and the role of Parliament. And they even contain hints of Bentham's radicalism at this stage in his life. But above all, they are the final flowering of his prison scheme and show more clearly than his published writings, first why the panopticon engrossed so much of his life and thought, and secondly that his poor-law proposals and the National Charity Company were not just another application of his brother's device of an inspection house but arose directly from the panopticon penitentiary. This chapter will first describe the background to the 1794 Penitentiary Act; the second major part will be concerned with the contents of the bill; and thirdly, the subsequent fortunes of the government measure will be related.

Bentham nursed an ambition to help draft legislation. He had passionately desired to become a Member of Parliament; and he also envisaged himself as a legislative consultant to the government. *A View of the Hard Labour Bill* had been a critical commentary on proposed legislation and Bentham was inordinately proud of the influence he believed he had exerted on the subsequent statute. In May 1793 he wrote a letter offering his services to the Home Secretary, Henry Dundas, in the drafting of bills. He wished for no emolument but would subject himself to a trial of abilities: 'Let a business of any kind, with such instructions as were thought necessary, be put into my hands: let the same business with the same instructions be put into the hands of any other person. Each having drawn his Bill, let the other be called upon to give his observations on it.'[8] Dundas's immediate reaction is not recorded, but Bentham's offer was perhaps not forgotten, for later that year, when it became apparent that a new Penitentiary Act would be necessary, Bentham was at long last given his opportunity. He welcomed it with open arms, boasting: 'I am at present occupied in drawing a bill, at the

---

[7] Bowring, x. 251.     [8] *Correspondence (CW)*, iv. 430.

recommendation of authority, for Mr Pitt to bring in upon the opening of the session.'[9] Sadly, despite his confidence and high hopes, his bill was a dismal failure.

The legislation of 1794 and the slough of trouble that engulfed Bentham's project had their roots in the problems of land acquisition and the terms of the 1779 Act. Bentham's attempts to deal with these problems suggest that his abilities as a practising lawyer were limited and that he was politically naïve, seeming almost wilfully determined to misunderstand the parliamentary process and the weight of interest to which the administration was inevitably subjected. The 1779 Act had given the government powers to build a national penitentiary: the Crown was to appoint three supervisors who were empowered to chose a site and to build and manage the prison. The site had to be approved by the Lord Chancellor, the Speaker, the Lord Mayor, and twelve judges; and compensation was to be settled by jury. In 1782 a site on Battersea Rise was finally approved but the penitentiary was never built, largely owing to the immense expense. But when Bentham launched his panopticon scheme, the three supervisors were still in legal existence. As we have seen, Bentham was convinced that, with the consent of Bunbury and Bowdler, the site in Battersea could be acquired for the building of the panopticon under his management.[10] In this Bentham was wrong in law, for the government lacked powers. This difficulty was pointed out in a letter from John Reeves, a legal adviser to the government, on 5 August 1793:

I have looked into the Penitentiary Act 19 Geo. 3 c. 74 . . . And it appears to me that Mr Bentham's Proposal does not at all square with the design of the legislature. It was certainly intended by the Parliament to provide for a public Institution to be regulated by Public Officers— such is the nature of the supervisors . . . Mr Bentham's on the other hand, is a private concern, and the very principle, upon which the activity and vigour of the design are to depend for motion, is that the prisoners and everything in the prison are his private concern. I do not think Mr B's plan can be carried into execution under the Authority of that Act.[11]

[9] Ibid. 483.
[10] Ibid. 395.
[11] Ibid. 438. John Reeves (1752?–1829), Chief Justice of Newfoundland, 1791–2; King's Printer, 1800. His *History of English Law* in 5 vols. (1783–1829) was a standard work in its time.

This was a fearful blow to Bentham's hopes. He wrote of 'the sudden appearance of the difficulty'.[12] Yet he should not have been thus taken by surprise, for he himself had insisted on the shortcomings of the 1779 Act and had complained that it would have proscribed contract management.[13] This sudden realization that the Battersea Rise land could not be compulsorily acquired without new legislation induced Bentham to try his eloquence on the owners to persuade them to give up their land voluntarily for his purposes; the See of York was the freeholder and Earl Spencer held long leases. Bentham wrote two letters similarly sycophantic in tone, first to his old headmaster, Archbishop Markham, and secondly to Lord Spencer. These letters are long, even by Bentham's standards; they extol the excellencies of his prison and appeal to a disinterested zeal for the public good which, despite his utilitarian creed, Bentham felt should animate the souls of men and determine their actions. Markham responded courteously but took up a position of inactive neutrality from which he refused at any time to be moved. But from Spencer, Bentham met with a wily tenacious opposition that was, in the end, to shatter his hopes and bring his schemes to nought.

Spencer's determination to hold his land is eminently understandable. Battersea Rise, not now perhaps the most desirable of residential areas, was, at the end of the eighteenth century, still pretty country, the lavender hill rising steeply from the river within easy reach of London. It was a pleasant and salubrious neighbourhood, and for these reasons Bentham wanted to build his pleasant and salubrious prison there, especially as it was near the metropolis, the great Seat of Inspection. For just these reasons the value of the land was rising rapidly and it was increasingly being let out on building leases. Spencer's pecuniary interest was involved in holding on to his land and in protecting the whole area from the pollution of a prison and the damage this would do to the value of property. Bentham expended much eloquence in combating these fears, but failed to convince. Regrettably, the negotiations with Spencer started badly. Bentham gave the impression of being, if not untruthful, at least tendentious on a material point. He wrote: 'now I am urged to have the buildings in readiness in *six months*, under a penalty of

---

[12] *Correspondence* (*CW*) iv. 440.    [13] Bowring, iv. 117.

five thousand pounds.'[14] Spencer replied promptly absolutely declining to relinquish his land in haste and expressing doubts as to Bentham's veracity. 'I can hardly conceive it possible that you can really be subjected to a penalty for not doing what seems to be absolutely impracticable without the authority of Parliament.'[15] Despite Bentham's frantic disclaimers that he had meant that the penalty was conditional on the scheme's going ahead, Spencer continued to believe that an attempt had been made to mislead him. It was an unfortunate start to what was to be a most unhappy association. Bentham continued to press argument, eloquence, and offers of compensation, but Spencer remained adamant. His refusal made new legislation unavoidable.

It was in these circumstances that Bentham was asked to draft the legislation; and his bill formed part of his strategy to defeat the Spencer interest. He saw it as an appeal to Parliament as a disinterested arbiter; in a manuscript comment, he wrote: 'Apprized that the delay would be the loss of the season to the measure, he chose to abide the determination of Parliament. He refused favour, and threw himself upon strict justice. Strict justice therefore and no more is what he ought to have.'[16] This was a serious political misjudgement, Parliament was not an independent tribunal dispensing abstract justice but an arena where conflicts of interest were resolved—and the Spencer interest was very powerful. Apart from his position as a great landowning aristocrat, the Earl was a man of ability and intellect who was to become a formidable First Lord of the Admiralty. A friend of Pitt at Cambridge and a fellow member of the Goosetree Club, he had been one of the original circle that had formed around Pitt on his first entering the House of Commons. He was now an influential member of the group of Whigs attached to the Duke of Portland—a group that supported the war with France and was soon to split from the Foxites and enter the government.

Bentham threw himself heart and soul into his appeal to Parliament. In January 1794, in the midst of his labour, he wrote to his

[14] *Correspondence* (*CW*), iv. 448, Bentham's emphasis. William Markham (1719–1807), Headmaster of Westminster School, 1753–65; Archbishop of York, 1777–1807. Bentham was at Westminster, 1755–60.
[15] Ibid. 450.
[16] UC cxix. 188.

brother: 'Panopticon Bill is now to me what Specification was to you: though, thank Heaven, not quite so bad.'[17] It was indeed a mammoth task; and Bentham produced an elephantine bill, argumentative, polemical, and packed with labyrinthine detail. It was grossly long; the list of contents alone filled four pages. It contained fifteen sections, 257 clauses, the whole comprising as many as 50,000 words. It included no fewer than thirty-one forms numbered from A.1 to I.2.[18] The bill also incorporated features to make it more accessible to the public; it was broken down into numbered sections, each given a short title. According to Bentham, the language was designed to be unambiguous, redundant words were weeded out and their place taken by long preambles; Bentham could not resist arguing his case and these preambles were polemics designed to disarm criticism in Parliament. 'What I have saved on *pleonasms*, I have spent on *reasons* . . . reasons are stubborn things, and must be taken as they come.'[19] Bentham argued that if they made the bill unwieldy, they could always be cut out: 'Cancelling taking less time than the investigation of deficiencies, over amplitude and minuteness has been preferred to shortness.'[20] In this Bentham again shows a misunderstanding of the role of Parliament. Parliament is not a drafting or revising committee; a bill is not a discussion document but rather an expression of the intention of the executive worded substantially in the form in which it will eventually become law.

However, Bentham was immensely proud of his creation and seemed to have no doubt that it would be accepted by the administration. Copies were widely distributed to his friends and to members of the government in March; but at the end of the month, he was complaining that the condition of the project was worse than stationary, and reproaching ministers for not bringing

---

[17] *Correspondence* (*CW*), v. 2. William Henry Cavendish-Bentinck (1738-1809), 3rd Duke of Portland: Prime Minister, 1783; Home Secretary, 1794–1801 Lord President of the Council, 1801–5; Prime Minister, 1807–9.

[18] This compares with the 110 clauses, about 21,500 words, of the Poor Law Amendment Act 1834 or the 13,500 words of the 1779 Penitentiary Act. It was not unknown to incorporate forms in statute in the 18th c.; the Vagrancy Act of 1744 contains two; Gilbert's Act 1782, fourteen. The practice seems sensibly to have been discontinued in the 19th c.

[19] UC cxix. 314, Bentham's emphasis.

[20] UC cxxiv. 6.

in the bill at the beginning of the session. It was probably at this point that he produced his short bill; his hopes revived when Nepean called to collect a copy to show Pitt. But two days later, on 15 April, he was writing to his stepbrother Charles Abbot that his bill had been rejected and a new one was to be drafted: 'I hope to God you may have been able to do something with the S.G.: if not, we perish—Just what you expected has happened: Mr L. is exercising a negative upon the Bill, a negative which I fear will be effectual.' Charles Long, Junior Secretary at the Treasury, 'is working and working to put it into a Parliamentary Shape . . . whatever he makes of it I shall not object to, unless the S.G. steps in to deliver me out of his hands.'[21] On 22 April William Bentham (a distant cousin) and William Cruise, conveyancers of Lincoln's Inn, were instructed to draw up a bill in conventional terms.

From this time onwards, Charles Long took over as the main contact between Bentham and the government. It was another unfortunate start to what was to be another disastrous association. It is clear that whatever the merits of the bill as a piece of ideal legislation, it never stood any chance of being acceptable to government lawyers. Bentham's friends realized this. Abbot had cautioned him; and Samuel Romilly, with masterly tact, combined praise with a clear note of warning: 'There is', he wrote, 'a great deal too much merit in the bill for it to have the smallest chance of passing.'[22]

Bentham's complaints of the inefficiency and procrastination of the government have generally been accepted by scholars. On this particular point, Hume wrote: 'The work of drafting gave Bentham his first real taste of the hard-pressed Administration's capacity for delay.'[23] But Hume does not seem to have realized that a completely new bill had to be drafted between the middle of April and 9 May when Dundas introduced it in the House of Commons. In this instance at least, the administration cannot

[21] *Correspondence* (*CW*), v. 27–8. Mr L. William Lowndes, Parliamentary Counsel to the Treasury, 1789–98; S.G.: the Solicitor-General, Sir John Mitford (1748–1830), cr. Baron Redesdale, 1803; Solicitor-General, 1793–9; Attorney-General, 1799–1801; in the House of Lords he became a pillar of reaction and opposed every proposal for legal reform suggested by Romilly.

[22] Ibid. 18.

[23] Hume, 'Bentham's Panopticon: An Administrative History', in *Historical Studies*, 15 (1971–2), 709.

fairly be blamed for delay; they might indeed be commended for the speed with which they moved. They had wanted a simple tidying-up measure to give them powers to proceed; Bentham had drafted a major, seminal Act that had no hope for getting through Parliament.

The 1794 Penitentiary Act produced by the government lawyers was short and in essence simple. It gave the Treasury powers to acquire land, in legal terms similar to the 1779 Act, and to make a contract for a profit-making prison. It was a slipshod and irresponsible Act; there were no statutory provisions for fundamental safeguards for the health and welfare of the prisoners, and no provision whatever for inspection or control. Bentham's proposals were very different; his bill would have empowered Jeremy Bentham to acquire land, but it would also have written into statute basic restrictions on the powers of the governor. As he warned: 'powers so ample . . . ought to be kept in check by an adequate and never-failing controul.'[24] In his bill the government was directed to make a contract that would have ensured the welfare of the inmates and circumscribed the authority of the governor. He had to provide a proper diet, clothing, separate bedding, medical assistance, and a resident chaplain and surgeon. The prisoners were to be allowed to earn; and a proportion of such earnings were to be set aside for their old age. On their release, the governor had to provide employment for the able-bodied and subsistence for the infirm. He had to pay 'head money' for each death to ensure attention to their health and a penal sum in the event of any subsequent crime to ensure attention to their reformation. These are the fundamentals of the panopticon which Bentham believed would join duty with interest; and he proposed to write them into the law of the land. In the long bill there was also a lengthy section that would have made the supervision of the court of the King's Bench a reality, in particular Bentham undertook personally to attend the court; and any magistrate in the county was free to enter the prison at any time to inspect and enquire into the welfare of the inmates.[25]

The chief part of Bentham's bill, however, was not concerned with the management of the prison but with the fate of the prisoners after discharge and with the creation of the bureaucratic

---

[24] UC cxix. 208.  [25] Ibid. 209, 210.

machine that his schemes would have entailed. The implications were fully worked out in sections on Superannuation Annuities, Post Liberation Options, the metasylum, Friendly Guardianship, Identification Marks, Escape, Felony Indemnification Money, Prisoner's Settlements, Correspondence Facilitated, and, finally, a section on Personal Clauses. There are two very different, though not necessarily contradictory, aspects of Bentham's proposals for discharged prisoners. First, there is an intelligent, wide-ranging, and prescient concern for their welfare, presaging many of the methods and attributes of the modern welfare state. Secondly, there is the creation of a web of regulation to ensnare the ex-convict and his family in a world of servitude; where, although their subsistence would have been guaranteed, almost all liberty of choice would have been lost. By the terms of his contract with the government, Bentham would have been obliged to provide pensions for old age or incapacity; these he called superannuation annuities. His exhaustive elaboration of this scheme in his bill exemplifies his benevolent bureaucracy and concern for the welfare of his charges. The pensions were to be financed from the earnings of the prisoners who would be allowed a quarter of their wages, half of this quarter could be spent on present gratification but the other half would be set aside under the control of Jeremy Bentham and his successors. This fund could be supplemented by charging the general public to enter the prison and by charitable gifts. Bentham hoped and believed that these annuities would provide a complete provision, something in the region of £8 to £10 a year.[26] According to the contract, the commencement and amount of such payments were to be determined by two referees, one appointed by the Treasury, the other by Bentham himself.[27] In a comment Bentham revealed that he envisaged some measure of redistribution in the scheme, a man would not have the automatic right to take out what he had put in but the money available would be spread in accordance with need to provide a minimum provision for all:

Some will be young, others already old . . . The constitutions and habits of some will enable them to keep on earning a subsistence to a later period of life: others will require this period to be accelerated. All these inequalities must in some measure be removed: for while any are

[26] Ibid. 151, 210.     [27] UC cxv. 86.

indulged with an *abundant* provision, none ought to be left without a *sufficient* one. The first thing then to be done is to establish a *minimum*; below which no man's allowance shall be reduced.

To achieve this some would lose:

The young must be pinched in favour of the old . . . those who have a long sentence to undergo in favour of those who have but a short one: perhaps too those who have a better constitution in favour of those who have a worse. But as in all these instances the burthen will fall heaviest on those best able to bear it . . . none it is hoped will think themselves aggrieved.[28]

Thus, Bentham presaged the idea of a minimum provision and also the fixed old age pension that is not directly tied to contributions.

In his methods of administering these superannuation annuities, Bentham also anticipated several of the attitudes and devices that became commonplace in the nineteenth and twentieth centuries. A somewhat overbearing paternalism is evident in his exhortation to the annuitant:

This annuity, being intended for the support and comfort of your Old Age, and as a sure and perpetual supply, and not to be hazarded in the pursuit of superfluous wealth, much less to be dissipated for the purposes of extravagance, can not nor any part thereof be alienated: that is either given, sold, exchanged or mortgaged.[29]

The pension would normally have been paid at the Penitentiary House, but at the request of the annuitant, the governor could pay it at any post town. This provision would enable the man to choose where he lived, so as not to banish him from his connections.[30] To achieve this admirable end, Bentham devised a system that anticipated the bureaucratic methods of the twentieth century. Payments were to be made through the post office by means of no fewer than seven forms, C.1 to C.7.[31] The first form, the grant of the annuity, was preceded by two pages of instruction for the recipient. The second was a form for the annuitant requesting payment at a certain post town. The third was for the postmaster to certify as to the identity of the annuitant; the

---

[28] UC cxxiv. 14, Bentham's emphasis.     [29] UC cxix. 214.
[30] UC cxxiv. 8.     [31] UC cxix. 213–16.

fourth, a receipt from the post office in London of the governor's payment; the fifth instructed the postmaster to pay the money; the sixth was an order from the post office backing the order; and the final one was a receipt from the annuitant to the post office of the money paid. For this work, the postmaster was to be paid a fee, out of the annuity. Receipts were to be in triplicate, one for the postmaster, one for the governor, and the third for the General Post Office in London to be preserved in the muniment office.[32] In this sophisticated use of the post office, Bentham anticipated modern practice at a time when the machinery was at its most rudimentary; it was only in 1792 that a private scheme run by postmasters had devised the first money orders to facilitate the sending of small sums from one part of the country to another.[33]

The paternalist aspect of Bentham's schemes is most clearly apparent in his plans for prisoners after discharge. In the printed *Proposal*, the widely distributed leaflet designed to publicize the panopticon, Bentham promises 'to ensure to them a *livelihood* . . . by setting up a *Subsidiary Establishment*, into which all such as thought proper, should be admitted'.[34] This phrase hides a reality very different from its obvious meaning. In *Postscript* II Bentham had adumbrated several possible roads for his prisoners to take. In the bill these alternatives are spelt out in detail. The released man could join the army, the navy, or the service of the East India Company; he could be bound to an employer, a Friendly Guardian, who would have to put up a surety of £50; or he could transfer to a subsidiary panopticon, the metasylum, administered by the governor. What he could not have was freedom to tramp the highways, scratch a living by casual work or begging, emigrate, go to sea, or return to thieving. The liberty of choice of such a man was thus severely circumscribed. In one of his more lengthy preambles, Bentham justified this compulsion with a variety of arguments of varying force. Such a man, he argued, used from infancy to habits of dishonesty and dissipation, might well refuse the honest work available in favour of begging or crime; the employment must be truly secure for it would be

---

[32] Ibid. 152.
[33] Herbert Joyce, *The History of the Post Office* (London, 1893), 420–1.
[34] UC cxv. 32, Bentham's emphasis.

easy for a false appearance of work to be obtained by collusion with companions in idleness and iniquity; the provisions of the Vagrants Act in any case, gave powers to punish and imprison all those without the means of subsistence; and those criminals transported were in practice confined for life in the colony; the number of options on offer demonstrated that they were not an extension of punishment; the care taken to enable prisoners to find a Friendly Guardian gave them as much liberty as was compatible with the public safety; and, finally, the provision for superannuation annuities for their old age would be a compensation for even severer obligations.[35] Subsequent clauses of the bill spelt out the administrative machinery that would have prevented the ex-convict from escaping the clutches of the system. While still a prisoner, he would be informed of the options by access to a list; if he were rejected by the three services and could not find a Friendly Guardian, he would be bound to the metasylum.

The vetting of the Friendly Guardians best exemplifies Bentham's elaborate methods of bureaucratic control. The Friendly Guardian had major responsibilities and obligations; he had to maintain his ward, he was answerable for his good behaviour and liable to pay indemnification money if he committed a crime. The bond of £50 was renewable year by year and he was under an obligation to inform the governor of any change in the circumstances of himself or of his ward. In return, he had the power of a master over his servant, and, if his ward absconded, he could obtain a warrant from a magistrate to enforce his return. He could, if he wished, surrender him to the metasylum.[36] Bentham devised elaborate precautions to ensure that any Friendly Guardian was a person of responsibility, honesty, and good standing. He had to be a householder of known character and good fame, to pay taxes, and be worth £200. It is interesting that Bentham explicitly provided that both Jews and unmarried women were eligible to be Friendly Guardians. The process of accredition was ponderous, entailing the use of fourteen forms; this onerous responsibility Bentham decided to place on the local magistrates. Applicants were to be examined under oath as to their name and age, if they could not

---

[35] UC cxix. 153–4.     [36] Ibid. 229.

produce a registration of baptism, they had to account for its absence (compulsory registration of births was still forty years in the future); information on religion, marital status, names and ages of children, present and past occupations, and abodes was required; tax vouchers were to be produced. Both in these methods and the concepts behind them, Bentham was attempting to bring regularity and order to society, to categorize people and to gather and keep information that could be used to enforce the authority of the governor of the panopticon. If for any reason the relationship between the ward and his Friendly Guardian was broken, the ward returned to the metasylum. Bentham continued to emphasize the importance of the collection of accurate statistics on personal matters; he later attacked the Church's monopoly as it limited the registration to those whom the clergy deemed fit to be born, marry, or die. When national registration was finally established in 1836, the collection of information was made the responsibility of the new Poor Law Guardians.[37]

It was for good reasons that Bentham called his post-liberation establishment the 'asylum for all'. It was a refuge where subsistence was provided in return for honest work; it was the last resort for any prisoner not choosing to fight, who failed to find a Friendly Guardian, or indeed who refused to make any choice at all. From being 'Penitentiary Man' he became 'Metasylum Man'. Bentham emphasized that all had a right to employment in the metasylum. They also had the obligation to work, to behave soberly, honestly, dutifully, obediently, and diligently. If a metasylum man refused to work, the governor could chastise him as a master would a servant or a magistrate could inflict a whipping or imprisonment. He could also be so punished for absconding from the metasylum and anyone aiding or harbouring him could be fined—as Jeremy Bentham planned to become a Surrey magistrate he may have seen himself in the position of meting out such penalties. The governor was to pay 'Metasylum man' wages, keeping a proportion towards his superannuation annuity. He was to provide him with clothes, lodging, washing, sustenance, and medicine.[38] Every year the governor could award a certificate of good behaviour which would act as a recom-

[37] Bowring, vi. 64. Registration Act 1836, 6 & 7 William IV, c. 86.
[38] UC cxix. 222–7, 273.

mendation and, after three such certificates, absolute emancipation could be granted—but this was entirely at the discretion of
the governor—the inmate had no rights. Bentham envisaged his
metasylum as a reservoir of skilled labour to which employers
would resort to find workers, undertaking the burdens of Friendly
Guardianship in return for the secure control they would have
over their operatives. The metasylum would, Bentham wrote in a
note,

be a sort of *Register Office*, where Masters will be coming in abundance
to bid against me for good hands . . . The *leavings* of the public will
therefore be all I can depend upon. This disadvantage I have taken upon
me with my eyes open, to save the plan from the reproach of keeping
men in a state of perpetual servitude.[39]

Perhaps he felt that he had not entirely rebutted this charge for,
in another note, he justified his post-liberation options on the
grounds that, by the Friendly Guardian system, a man could gain
any degree of independence which in the judgement of his friends
he could be trusted with, and in any case, his situation should be
compared to men pressed into the navy or balloted for into the
Militia.[40]

Bentham's preoccupation with his discharged prisoners can be
explained by the fact that he had a considerable pecuniary interest
in their good behaviour. He stood to lose a great deal of money if
the panopticon inmate returned to a life of crime. He was obliged,
under the terms of the contract, to pay compensation to injured
parties on a sliding scale, the longer the prisoner had spent in the
penitentiary, the greater the amount of money Bentham would
owe. This plan was part of his effort to ensure the junction of
interest and duty, for the governor would have a pecuniary
interest in the reformation of his charges. He could not, however, rely solely on the reformatory influence of the panopticon,
profound though his faith in its efficacy was. Elaborate precautions were taken to ensure the subsistence and good behaviour of
the ex-convict and to limit the amount of compensation that
Bentham would have been liable to pay. His obligation ceased on
the inmate entering the army or navy or the service of the East
India Company, but would revive if he were returned to the

---

[39] UC cxix. 187, Bentham's emphasis.    [40] UC cxxiv. 9, 10.

metasylum. To facilitate the administration of the system, lists of the panopticon prisoners were to be displayed in every court. And to enable the inmates to be identified with certainty, they were to be permanently marked. Bentham expended a considerable amount of ingenuity in working out the methods, the justification, and the uses of this device which seemed inescapable within the logic of his penitentiary and metasylum. The whole structure of indemnity and superannuation depended on a certain means of identifying individuals. In *A View of the Hard Labour Bill*, Bentham had suggested temporary face-dyes to hinder escape, but had rejected any permanent mark as oppressive and unjust. But, by 1794, he had come to the realization that a permanent mark was essential for the smooth administration of his welfare system. He enacted in his bill that every prisoner on admission to his prison would be tattooed with his name and date and place of birth on the upper part of his left arm where it would be generally hidden from view. In a lengthy preamble, he excused this provision on several grounds; it was the practice among seafaring men; it would obviate the need for irons; it would help prevent escapes and future crimes; it would be a reassurance to Friendly Guardians; and it would help in the payment of indemnity money and superannuation. The tattooing would be done with 'as little pain or uneasiness as may be'.[41] In his notes, Bentham described this marking as: 'one of the mildest as well as most efficacious instruments of public security that the nature of things affords. I can not but be proportionally solicitous of its adoption . . . if prejudice should take umbrage and raise the cry of cruelty, I would with all my heart be the first on whom the operation should be performed.'[42] He went on to argue that this tattooing could not be compared with branding for it was not a punishment; neither would it be a lasting mark of infamy that would prevent the prisoner ever becoming a useful member of society, for his future was secured in any case. Bentham remained enamoured with this device and, if the panopticon had ever been built, its inmates and its officers alike would have been marked. In 1804 he was writing:

In Panopticon, it was a sheet anchor: my plan was, by all imaginable and lawful means . . . to get the prisoners to submit to it, as part of the

[41] UC cxix. 264–5.     [42] UC cxxiv. 11.

uniform of the establishment: and to prevent its being considered as a punishment, or a hardship, I intended to have set the example in my own person, and, if possible, in those of my subordinates.

But to Bentham's bewilderment, the idea seems to have met with ridicule: 'Real public spirit is so rare—horror of singularity, to any useful purpose, so general, that there is not, perhaps, one man in a thousand to whom any degree of public utility would afford sufficient compensation for depriving himself of so good a pretence for setting up, or joining in, a horse laugh.'[43]

In the twentieth century an identification mark on a human arm is more likely to raise a shudder of abhorrence than a horse laugh. A device so hideously evocative of Auschwitz must be seen as a fearful stigma of an evil tyranny. But, for Bentham, it was a benign instrument for the general good that would increase personal liberty. In his discussion of 'Indirect Methods of Preventing Crimes', he argued that as sailors were tattooed for the utilitarian reason that their corpses could be identified after shipwreck, why should not everyone be so marked? 'If it were possible that the practice should become universal, it would be a new spring for morality, a new source of power for the laws . . . This means . . . would become favourable to personal liberty, by permitting relaxation in the rigour of proceedings.' And, again with remarkable prescience, Bentham suggested that such marks could be used to devise alternatives to imprisonment; thus foreshadowing the development of probation, the uses of fingerprinting, and the present debate on electronic devices to restrict the liberty of offenders outside prison walls. 'Imprisonment', he wrote, 'having for its only object the detention of individuals, might become rare, when they were held as it were by an invisible chain.' He was aware that there could be misuse. He admitted that during the French Revolution many had owed their lives to disguise; and public opinion 'opposes an unsurmountable obstacle to such an institution'. But public opinion could be patiently guided and the great could set an example: 'If it were the custom to imprint the titles of the nobility upon their foreheads, these marks would become associated with the ideas of honour and power.'[44]

[43] *Correspondence* (CW), vii. 266.     [44] Bowring, i. 557.

The necessarily tortuous relationship between the welfare network of the panopticon and the existing poor law caused Bentham much tribulation; no fewer than fifty-six clauses of his bill dealt with this subject. In his discussion of the difficulties and complexities can be found the genesis of the National Charity Company. It also becomes apparent that the extension of the panopticon organization from prisoners to paupers arose as much from the dynamics of the scheme itself as from the public debate on the poor laws. The clauses in the section on Prisoner's Settlements charted exactly how the obligation and responsibilities of the governor and the parishes would interlink.[45] On admission to the penitentiary, the prisoner was to be questioned by a magistrate as to his own and his family's place of settlement. When this had been discovered, the judgement, in quadruplicate, was to be sent to the overseers of the poor in the parish, to the sessions of that county, to the sessions in which the penitentiary was situated, and to the governor. The overseers had three months in which to question the decision and appeal against it to the penitentiary house sessions. The family was then chargeable on the parish. On discharge, if the prisoner entered the metasylum, he would not gain a settlement in that parish, and his maintenance would be the responsibility of the governor for ever. If his wife and children came on to their parish, a proportion of his wages could be stopped for their maintenance. However, if the metasylum man so desired, he could petition, with the consent of the governor, for his family to lose their settlement and be conveyed to the metasylum. If any member of his family was found to be a vagrant, they would be returned not to their place of settlement, but to the metasylum. Thus the tentacles of Bentham's bureaucracy would have reached into every corner of the land clutching in its grasp the wives and children of convicted criminals.

One of the more disturbing aspects of the panopticon bill was that Bentham contemplated using brutal methods to ensure the smooth administration and viability of his plans. A warder who became intoxicated or who fell asleep at his post would have been subject to a disproportionately heavy penalty. He could be imprisoned for up to a year on conviction before a single

[45] UC cxix. 288–301.

magistrate, but on conviction by indictment the penalty was life imprisonment. The decision of the governor on how to proceed against his negligent servant would therefore determine the extent of his punishment.[46] In an observation, Bentham defended this clause against the charge that it was 'most outrageously severe', on the grounds that the true measure of punishment is prevention and that the mischief caused by such negligence might be the escape of many prisoners. The penalty should also take into account the possibility that the negligence might have been feigned to hide collusion between the warder and the prisoners.[47] Bentham also seemed willing to resort to the extremes of corporal punishment. In a series of proposals most damaging to his reputation as a humanitarian, he enacted a range of penalties for attempting to escape, starting with lengthening of the prison sentence and culminating in the infliction of 1,000 lashes for a man who had used force to effect escape. The logic of this was that any prisoner confined for life would not be deterred from attempting escape except by a 'strict terror'; and such penalties were, in any case, an ordinary part of military discipline. Bentham's argument here was realistic in the terms of the eighteenth century, and he may have been attempting to make his proposals acceptable and to avoid the infliction of the death penalty. He stressed that hanging might be counter-productive, and 'in the case of a desperate and abandoned Prisoner might operate as an incitement to the offence'. Bentham was also prepared to use whipping to extract information; if the inmate lied during the investigation as to his place of settlement, he could be whipped; and, if he refused to answer questions, he could be flogged, 'till he comply'.[48] Professor Twining has demonstrated that Betham could justify torture in principle;[49] he could also contemplate inflicting it in practice.

The panopticon writings contain incidental material on the development of Bentham's theories on evidence. In the *Proposal*, he had attacked the rule of self-incrimination. In his bill other points are touched on. The testimony of criminals, that is a

---

[46] UC cxix. 268.
[47] Ibid. 183.
[48] Ibid. 269, 268, 289.
[49] W. L. and P. E. Twining, 'Bentham on Torture', in *Bentham and Legal Theory*, ed. M. H. James (Belfast, 1973), 39–90.

panopticon man and his accomplices, should be admissible, 'any law or rule or notion of law to the contrary notwithstanding'.[50] In his detailed provision for the legal proceedings arising from disputes as to settlements Bentham subtly defended hearsay evidence. Such evidence, he maintained, should be admissible and so subject to the penalties for perjury, for 'whatever is called knowledge is . . . nothing more than a higher degree of *belief*'; it could never be ascertained where knowledge began and belief ended, so it followed that an expression of an inferior degree of belief could be false and perjurious.[51]

The bureaucratic machinery of the panopticon bill raises interesting questions. Bentham planned to extend the use of existing structures of local authority not, at this stage, to create new ones. His struggles with these difficulties and his dissatisfaction with the fallible instruments at his disposal may well be one of the reasons behind the extension of the panopticon to poorhouses. The National Charity Company would itself have administered its systems of coercion and welfare; and its network of poorhouses spread over the country would have obviated the need to employ the post office, local overseers, magistrates, and vicars. Accrediting Friendly Guardians would have put onerous new duties on magistrates and the post office was to be the channel for superannuation payments; even the Church had a function to perform. In the section on 'Correspondence Facilitated' Bentham confronted the further legal and practical problems that would have been posed by his complex arrangements. The panopticon correspondence would have been carried free of charge and to ensure, as far as possible, the safe delivery of mail to the local overseers, the postmasters were instructed to deliver the panopticon letters to the minister at divine service on Sunday. Thus religion and the clergy were to be recruited to play their part in Bentham's bureaucratic structure. It was also to be enacted that every letter put in the post should be presumed to have arrived. Printed forms were to contain abstracts of the law so that no person should, through ignorance, 'lose lawful advantage, much less to suffer any punishment by reason of such ignorance'.[52] To provide evidence of posting, Bentham proposed

---

[50] UC cxix. 158.     [51] Ibid. 296–7, Bentham's emphasis.
[52] Ibid. 303, 306.

that the penitentiary house should keep two books, a Receipt Letter Book and an Issuing Letter Book. The entries in these were to be numbered and authenticated by the stamp and initials of the postman and the penitentiary clerk. Copies of all letters sent and received were to be kept. The problems of establishing identity and keeping a check on the ex-convict were also dealt with. Every prisoner would be given a discharge certificate; so, if a man with the panopticon mark upon his arm were found without such a certificate, he would be treated as a deserter, liable to be apprehended and conveyed to the penitentiary. However, to avoid subjecting the innocent to such inconvenience, the governor would provide spare copies of such certificates.[53] Marked men were not permitted to change their names under the penalty of desertion. In one of the more bizarrely convoluted provisions of the bill, Bentham gave *anyone* the right to compel the baring of the left arm to display the mark and made any who refused liable to a fine. However, the person exercising such compulsion for 'wantonness or malice' was also liable to a fine.[54] Members of the great tribunal of the public, the inspectors of the panopticon prison, also risked being ensnared in the web of bureaucracy and extended penalty. A visitor to the inspection gallery would have to write his name, address, and occupation in a book, the purpose of which was: 'for the discouraging of persons of evil fame resorting to the said House to the molestation thereof and of the neighbourhood of the same.'[55] If they refused, they could be detained until they agreed. If they gave false information, they could be fined or imprisoned. The governor was empowered to cross-examine any visitor and any visitor was liable to be searched. Despite these hazards, Bentham proposed to charge for admission.

In his bill, Bentham's style at times descends into a fog of obfuscation characteristic of the worst excesses of bureaucracy. Methods for the delivery of the governor's wardship assignment of a Friendly Guardian are described thus:

and moreover if he should have received from the said Governor a proper blank certificate declarative of such Act of delivery which Certificate may be according to the Form marked (F.14) shall according to the

---

[53] UC cxix. 274, 276.     [54] Ibid. 280–1.     [55] Ibid. 269.

truth of the case fill up such Certificate and shall retransmitt the same signed by him to the said Governor at the said Penitentiary House.[56]

Bentham does not mention the need for education in the bill but he was obviously assuming that there would be widespread sophisticated literacy among the people affected by his schemes.

Of possible biographical interest are the Personal Clauses of the bill; they contain a superb example of Benthamite logic with a hint that he may not altogether have forgotten his ambition to become a Member of Parliament. He argued that the law forbidding contractors from sitting in Parliament should not apply to the governor of the panopticon; for the true object of the law was to secure the freedom and independence of Parliament and so a contractor dependent on the goodwill of the government should be excluded. But the governor of the panopticon held office during good behaviour and so was dependent not on the favour of the government but on 'the dispensations of strict and public justice'. He would also have deserved well of his country and have contributed greatly to the improvement of police; for such extraordinary service, a disability was no fit reward.[57]

Bentham's panopticon bill was not only a vast compendium of his ideas on the treatment of criminals and of the texture of a complex bureaucracy, it was also a vehicle for radical theory, a Trojan horse for law reform. The bill, as well as dispensing with rules of evidence, would have excluded the panopticon from the provisions of certain Acts, in particular the Statute of Apprentices. Bentham was hoping to demonstrate their inutility by experiment and example and so pave the way for their repeal.[58] There is also in his notes hint of a more general radicalism. The long preambles were to serve the purpose of explaining and justifying the Act to the public so making the law more accessible to the many who would be affected by this Act: 'The people . . . have not been much used especially in the modern periods of our legislation . . . to see any thing like an indication of regard for either their reason or their affections: but were the spectacle suffered to exhibit itself, I can not think they would be displeased with it.'[59] This sentence can be found in a version in Bentham's own hand and was carefully scraped away in the copy

---

[56] Ibid. 235.     [57] Ibid. 312.     [58] Ibid. 314.     [59] UC cxxiv. 19.

meant for public consumption and an anodyne sentence inserted on top. This excision was perhaps not surprising in the year in which Habeas Corpus was suspended and it certainly supports the theory that Bentham's radical ideas were suppressed rather than abandoned in the years after 1792.

The length, complexity, and wide-ranging nature of Bentham's panopticon bill go some way to explaining the tenacity with which he held to the project, and the bitterness of his disappointment as it finally sank into obscurity. His vision of inspiring by practical example a great wave of law reform was destroyed. His hopes of administering a vast organization, the last details of which he had already worked out, were dashed. His forms, his system of penalties, his books, and his pensions were, for the time being, cast on to the dust-heap of frustrated ambitions. The bill and its many copies and its supporting notes were left to moulder in his files.

Meanwhile, on 9 May 1794, Dundas, not Pitt, introduced the government's Penitentiary Bill to the House of Commons; according to Bunbury its sole purpose was 'securing the Ground'.[60] But it was opposed by a determined group of influential men, Dent, Baldwin, and Thornton. They were themselves resident in Clapham and so had a personal interest in preventing the prison being built in their neighbourhood. Bentham complained sadly that the administration had deserted the measure and that it 'was carried by *me* through the House of Commons'.[61] Worse was to follow in the Lords. There the Spencer interest ensured that a vital amendment was carried; the Treasury was empowered to acquire the Battersea Rise site, but the words, 'or any other as convenient and proper Spot of ground', were inserted, thus making it very difficult to acquire that particular site by compulsion. Bentham realized at once the consequences of this wrecking amendment; the bill, he wrote to his brother on 15

---

[60] *Correspondence (CW)*, v. 32.

[61] Ibid. 33, Bentham's emphasis. William Baldwin (1737?–1813), Duke of Portland's private secretary, 1794; MP, 1795–1806; Counsel assisting the Secretary of State having the Department of the Colonies and Counsel on all questions relating to criminal business at the Home Office, 1796–d. John Dent (1761?–1826), MP, 1790–1826. Henry Thornton (1760–1815), MP, 1782–1815; banker, economist, and philanthropist. He joined Wilberforce in attacks on the slave trade and was an influential member of the Clapham sect.

June, 'has been botched'.[62] It had been botched with the connivance of the administration. Two days later Bunbury explained the parliamentary constraints behind the retreat; 'I understood the opponents had agreed to let the Bill pass *on Condition* the Buildings were not to be erected on that particular spot belonging to Ld Spencer and the See of York.'[63]

Bentham's first reaction to this setback was sensible and realistic. 'No—indeed', he wrote to his brother, 'I do not think we shall have the land.'[64] Unfortunately his attitude changed; with the other Portland Whigs, Spencer joined the government in July, and it was perhaps the realization that he was now dependent on the goodwill of the powerful wealthy aristocrat who had wrecked his plans that betrayed Bentham into a serious blunder. On 16 August he sent a long, intemperate, and offensive letter to Dundas accompanied by a vast memorandum, insisting that he still had a legal right to the Battersea site and threatening to abandon the scheme if it were not delivered up to him. He attacked Spencer's integrity and accused the government of truckling to powerful interests, and Charles Long in particular of being careless of the public good and profligate with public funds.[65] Further delay would reflect, he asserted:

great dishonour on that part of his Majesty's Administration which is in your hands. That in particular it might be alleged, and however falsely— yet with too much *colour* of truth, that the principal if not only cause of such procedure, was the relation which the question was known to bear, to the interests of a noble Earl lately called into High office.

The appearance of injustice, Bentham insinuated, suggested that there was a secret influence at work, that 'there were one Law for a Peer, and another for a Commoner—one Law for a Member of Administration, and another Law for the rest of his Majesty's equally loyal subjects'.[66]

These missives naturally caused deep offence and certainly brought Bentham no nearer to acquiring any site in Battersea. Unfortunately he persisted for another two years in his vain pursuit of this mirage. In December 1794 Spencer's position in the government was consolidated with his appointment to the

---

[62] Ibid. 42.  [63] Ibid. 46, Bunbury's emphasis.
[64] Ibid. 44.  [65] Ibid. 54–69.  [66] UC cxviii. 65.

vital post of First Lord of the Admiralty in the place of Pitt's brother, Lord Chatham, who had to be removed for incompetence. Samuel Bentham's appointment as Inspector-General of Naval Works in 1795 brought him into close contact with Spencer and he became friendly with Lavinia, Lady Spencer. He was thus in position to warn his brother that the Earl's opposition was 'unsurmountable'.[67] But Bentham remained unconvinced, until, on 29 August 1796, Spencer wrote in unequivocal terms that left room for neither misunderstanding nor hope: 'I always had and still continue to have very strong objections against your pursuing your plans at Battersea . . . I am determined to keep my Estate unless compelled by law to give it up.'[68] If Bentham had recognized earlier Spencer's determination to hold fast to his land, he would have pursued alternative sites with vigour after the débâcle of June 1794, and his prospects of success would have been much brighter.

The episode of the ill-fated panopticon bill must both enhance and diminish Bentham's reputation. But perhaps primarily it suggests that he had, at this stage in his life, a genius for bureaucracy rather than for legislation. Much of the bill belongs to the realm of regulation—indeed of office practice—rather than law. As a final point, a brief reference to Bentham's ideals of law is illuminating as a comparison between his theory and his practice. In the earlier panopticon writings he had lambasted minute statutory regulation; and in his general theory of law he extols the virtues of simplicity and clarity and attacks ambiguity, obscurity, and overbulkiness. 'Lengthiness is particularly vicious when it is found in connexion with the expression of the will of the legislator.' Overbulkiness is in the interest only of lawyers and leads to 'the most consummate uncognoscibility'. A worthy code, he wrote,

would not require schools for its explanation, would not require casuists to unravel its subtilties. It would speak a language familiar to everybody: each one might consult it at his need. It would be distinguished from all other books by its greater simplicity and clearness. The father of a family, without assistance, might take it in his hand and teach it to his children.[69]

[67] *Correspondence* (*CW*), v. 153.     [68] Ibid. 247.
[69] Bowring, iii. 208, 246, 209.

Bentham's principles and his practice in the panopticon bill appear irreconcilable; the long hidden draft legislation adds another problem and another paradox to the question of the place of the panopticon in his thought.

# 9

# HANGING WOOD AND
# TOTHILL FIELDS

The Penitentiary Act of 1794 had laid on the Treasury the responsibility of acquiring land and negotiating a contract. But the two years following its passing were bedevilled by the seemingly hopeless search for a suitable site. They were also marked by a significant shift in the focus of Bentham's negotiations with the government. Dundas, Nepean, and the Home Office retired from the centre of the stage, while Rose, Long, and the Treasury emerged into the limelight. Dundas, as Home Secretary, had been responsible from the outset for the conduct of the war with revolutionary France, but in 1794 he was relieved of other responsibilities and appointed Secretary of State for War. So, although for a few months he continued to be Bentham's contact at ministerial level, he substantially withdrew from the negotiations and plunged himself, with a notable lack of success, into the waging of war, presiding over an unprecedented series of military disasters. The war also claimed Nepean; he accompanied Dundas to the new War Department and, in 1795, he became Secretary to the Admiralty. Until the summer of 1796, Bentham continued to address pleas to both to exert their influence in his favour, but the panopticon was no longer their responsibility.[1] Dundas and Nepean had been favourably inclined and Nepean remained helpful and sympathetic. But with the transfer of the negotiations to the Treasury, Bentham was abandoned to the tender mercies of George Rose and Charles Long, neither enthusiastically committed to the penitentiary nor inclined to exert themselves to overcome the problems that beset it. It is also significant that, after Dundas, Bentham had contact with no one of a similar stature. Dundas was a powerful minister, a figure of weight in the Cabinet. Pitt refused to concern himself with Bentham's business and so it was relegated to the notice of Rose

---

[1] *Correspondence (CW)*, v. 234, 245.

and Long, who were primarily officials. They were Pitt's men, indebted to him for their places. They were, however, at this stage, reasonably well disposed to help Bentham's scheme forward and, outwardly at least, believed it would benefit the public. It was a different matter with the lawyers concerned. The law officers, Sir John Scott, the Attorney-General, and Sir John Mitford, the Solicitor-General, were, if not obstructive, unhelpful and contributed largely to the procrastination that drove Bentham to despair.[2] Scott was sceptical, believing that the panopticon was impractical and romantic and he was also concerned with the fundamental legal problem of reconciling the 1794 Penitentiary Act, empowering the government to execute a contract for a prison, with the 1779 Act, which would have instituted a prison managed by commissioners appointed by the government. When asked to approve the draft contract, he delayed from January to May 1795 and then noted without enthusiasm: 'I think this draft is conformable to the late Act—and I approve it as being so—How far the late Act and the Act of 19 Geo 3 c. 74 are meant in any and what respects to stand together or can be both executed I presume is not submitted to my consideration.'[3]

William Lowndes, another close associate of Pitt and legal Counsel at the Treasury entrusted with drafting of parliamentary bills, was also an opponent of the panopticon. But the greatest bane in Bentham's life was Joseph White, the Solicitor at the Treasury—'Lord White' or 'his magnificence' as Bentham ironically described him.[4] White behaved with gross arrogance, boorish ill-manners, and a crass disregard for the amenities of civilized society. In the summer of 1796 he was concerned with the business of engrossing the contract. For private delectation, Bentham wrote a description of his dealings with White, displaying talents for dialogue and a sharp observation of detail that suggest that he could have turned his hand to novel writing had

---

[2] Sir John Scott (1751–1838), cr. Baron Eldon, 1799, Earl Eldon 1821; Solicitor-General, 1788–93; Attorney-General, 1793–9; Lord Chief Justice of the Common Pleas, 1799–1801; Lord Chancellor, 1801–6, 1807–27. In the later years of Eldon's career delays in Chancery became a matter of public scandal. Bentham was one of his severest critics. See 'Indications Respecting Lord Eldon', Bowring, v. 348–82.

[3] UC cxv. 102.

[4] *Correspondence (CW)*, v. 234.

he been so inclined. At one of their meetings White arrived two and a quarter hours late to find Bentham lying in wait for him on the pavement:

I joined him near the foot of the staircase. His countenance and deportment haughtily sullen and silent—Not a syllable nor a gesture in way of apology or regret for the breach of appointment. On our entrance into the Chambers, he throws himself covered into his elbow chair. I stood by the side of it uncertain. Taking up my draught of the clause he . . . began making alterations in it saying it was to accommodate the Attorney General . . . I was obliged to put a sudden stop on observing him with the insertion of words the effect of which would have been to make the annuities—these superannuation annuities—commence immediately upon discharge . . . Without a syllable of reply, but with a countenance full of gloom, he strikes out the obnoxious words.

White then insisted he had to show the revised clause to the Attorney-General. Two days later Bentham called again:

Mr B. Well Sir, have you been able to see the Attorney-General yet about this business of mine.
Mr White No. I have not.
Mr B. Can you guess when you shall be able to see him about it?
Mr White Perhaps in the course of next week.
Mr B. I hope at any rate it will be early in the next week.
Mr White I shall see.[5]

Bentham had not only to bear the cross of pedantic and obnoxious lawyers but he also, at this time, lost the company and support of his brother. In 1795 Samuel Bentham was given a roving commission to inspect naval works and in the following year was appointed Inspector-General. While Bentham was still hoping to cajole or browbeat Spencer into giving up his land, the prospect of another site was dangled before his eyes. For a few brief months in the summer of 1796 his hopes were raised, only to be dashed again by aristocratical influence. The site was Hanging Wood; and the story of his attempt to acquire it illustrates the perennial difficulty of finding land for a prison. It also gives an insight on how the ancient countryside around London was being destroyed at this time.

---

[5] UC cxv. 123–7. This account is endorsed: '1796 Aug. 15 to 20 Panopt. J.B.'s Journal of Transactions and conversation with Joseph White Esq.' Joseph White was Treasury Solicitor, 1794–1806.

In July 1796 Bentham informed Long of a discovery he had made of a tract of land along the river upstream of Woolwich Dock Yard, bounded on the south by the London to Woolwich road.[6] This land, belonging to the Bowater family, was available, but Bentham wanted to erect the actual panopticon building south of the road on a hill covered with ancient woodland, called Hanging Wood. For Bentham, the site had every advantage except that it was rather far from London, the great seat of Inspection, and certainly considerably further than Battersea Rise. This elevated land was owned by Sir Thomas Spencer Wilson who lived a short distance away in the great Jacobean mansion of Charlton House. With his usual optimism, Bentham discounted any possible objection from the inhabitants of the area, for trees would screen the building from view, and only the very topmost turret would be visible from any of the adjoining villas. Considerably overestimating the distance, he insisted that Charlton House itself was at least a mile away. Bentham took comfort also from the prison hulks moored at Woolwich, which would surely have made the sight of convicts a familiar one. The state of the wood also gave him grounds for hope. This was ancient natural woodland, not plantation, and had been let out on a destroying lease. Fences had been pulled down, trees uprooted, and sand extracted; the whole prospect was one of dereliction. Sir Thomas Wilson himself was rich and would have been influential had he not had the misfortune to be deranged, subject to a morbid melancholy. Bentham, unaware of this, wrote appealing to his public spirit, as he had to Spencer's, begging him, 'to take a pride in embracing with alacrity the occasion of making one of those sacrifices of private inclination to public benefit, which every good subject is prepared to make'.[7] It was an appeal that fell on ears even deafer than Lord Spencer's. Sir Thomas was beyond interest or enjoyment, but his wife, Lady Wilson, reacted vigorously against the proposal to build a prison in her wood. Her agent, John Stride, called on Bentham to warn him of her repugnance; the land in question was a favourite walk of hers and its loss would occasion her an uneasiness so great as to undermine her health. The threat of a lady's uneasiness might not have deterred Bentham, but Lady Wilson had stronger

---

[6] *Correspondence* (*CW*), v. 230-2.     [7] Ibid. 236.

weapons. Her three daughters had all married men of power and influence and one of them, Lord Arden, a Member of Parliament and a Lord of the Admiralty, sallied forth to fight his mother-in-law's battle. Bentham referred him to the Treasury but Arden would not be denied: 'Lord Arden (Devil take the fellow) . . . would come, and John was blockhead enough to let him in upon me.'[8]

The interview was profoundly unsatisfactory to Bentham, Arden impressed on him the family's opposition to the penitentiary and dwelt on the powerful friends and influence he could and would exert against it. Bentham, realizing that the Treasury would not proceed in the face of such resistance, turned again to Lord Spencer's land in Lambeth: 'It is with the sincerest regret I find myself thrown back upon your Lordship's Marsh, spite of my utmost efforts to emerge from it.'[9] The final, emphatic refusal of any Spencer land was his only reply. Bentham made a last desperate attempt to persuade the Wilson family to accept the panopticon in Hanging Wood. He wrote an impassioned plea to John Stride begging Lady Wilson to reconsider and offering to create an improved, delightful, and private walk extending perhaps to the river bank: 'the greater part would necessarily remain susceptible to additional beauty in the shape of Walks and Plantations in which, as in every other case of Rural Economy, use and ornament might be made to go hand in hand.'[10] And he begged the honour of a visit from the lady so that she could herself inspect his models and contrivances. To reinforce his pleas, he delicately offered Stride £100 a year if he could overcome the lady's prejudice. Neither courtly attention nor bribery attained their object. Stride replied non-committally; but Lady Wilson did not visit Queen's Square Place, and Hanging Wood joined Battersea Rise and Lambeth Marsh as sites that sinister aristocratical influence had forced Bentham to discard.

After the final banishment from the promised land of Battersea Rise and the fiasco of Hanging Wood, Bentham began to realize

---

[8] *Correspondence* (*CW*), v. 243. Charles George Perceval, 2nd Baron Arden (1756–1840); Lord of the Admiralty, 1783–1801; Registrar of the Court of Admiralty, 1790–1840; Master of the Mint, 1801–2; Commissioner of the Board of Control, 1801–3; Lord of the Bedchamber, 1804–12.
[9] Ibid. 246.
[10] Ibid. 249.

the difficulties by which he was beset. As he plaintively complained: 'A *fit* site obtainable for *such* a purpose *without a dissentient voice* is the site of the *Golden Tree* and the *Singing Water*: and after a three years' consideration, I beg to be excused from searching for it.'[11] He decided to abandon the search in salubrious suburban areas and took himself to Tothill Fields, an area of waste only yards from Westminster with easy access to the river; an area of vile mean streets and marshy unproductive land, notorious as a resort for thieves and vagabonds, squalid with festering rubbish. Surely here the panopticon could be built without antagonizing the neighbourhood: 'It would render the spot instead of an *eyesore*, an *ornament* to the *vicinity*: by substituting to the miserable Poor House, a *magnificent* and *elegant* structure, and, to the present combination of *swamps* and *laystalls*, a cultivated spot, laid out upon a Plan in which *ornament* would be combined with *use*.'[12] In this he was sadly mistaken. His choice of site became immediately enmeshed in legal difficulties and encountered formidable opposition.

The attempt to acquire Tothill Fields and the consequent reference to the House of Commons Select Committee on Finance raise several questions; why was the project referred to the committee in the first place? What did Bentham hope to gain from it and how far, if at all, did he achieve his aims? Light is also cast on the fundamental matter of the contemporary perception of the panopticon.

Bentham first suggested Tothill Fields to Charles Long in September 1796, as all hope of Hanging Wood disappeared: 'From one of the *pleasantest*, I descend at once to one of the *vilest*. I can descend no lower.'[13] Bentham's attention had been drawn to Tothill Fields by the fact that the Earl of Salisbury was selling adjoining land on Millbank, some of which would be needed for the essential access to the river. The site Bentham wanted for the panopticon was waste land, the main interested parties being the Dean and Chapter of Westminster Abbey as Lords of the Manor and the parishes of St Margaret and St John whose inhabitants had the right of pasture and the tipping of rubbish. From the first, it was realized that this, being common

---

[11] Bowring, xi. 115, Bentham's emphasis.
[12] UC cxxiii. 221, Bentham's emphasis.
[13] *Correspondence (CW)*, v. 259, Bentham's emphasis.

land, could not be compulsorily acquired under the terms of the 1794 Penitentiary Act and so new legislation would be needed. Despite this, the great men of the Treasury, Long, Rose, and in the end even Pitt, all signified their approval. Unfortunately for Bentham, the Church authorities were not so acquiescent. The parishes opposed the scheme and the Dean of Westminster, Bishop Horsley, a wily, pugnacious prelate who held the See of Rochester in plurality was far from enthusiastic. In October 1796 Bentham wrote to him asking for his help, in and out of Parliament, to enable this scheme of inestimable public benefit to be realized. In his letter, he insisted frequently that it was Pitt's wishes and Pitt's choice of site. Horsley's first reaction to this was to write to Pitt for confirmation. Bentham wrote to Wilberforce: 'if the Bishop is fully impressed that Mr Pitt really wishes it, it will be done—otherwise not.'[14] Pitt does seem eventually, on Wilberforce's prompting, to have signified his approval to the Bishop, but perhaps not with great enthusiasm for Horsley continued obstructive and determined to protect the financial interests of his benefice. The interests of the Dean and Chapter of Westminster on the one hand and of the parishes on the other were to some degree conflicting. The Dean and Chapter as 'Lord of the Waste' had a doubtful right to grant building leases, though this was disputed by the parishes. This contention had in the 1760s destroyed the possibility of development by the Adams brothers who, according to Bentham, 'came forward with a much *greater* project, according to which the whole of Tothill Fields . . . was to have been divided into streets lined with Capital Houses'. This plan, 'pregnant with magnificent Ideas and emblazoned in brilliant colours' came to nought.[15] The Dean and Chapter in 1796 may well have hoped that such a site would have been developed for something more attractive than a prison. On 16 November the Chapter met and decided that only the minimum amount of land would be allocated for the penitentiary, the rest being, after enclosure, reserved for improvement by the Dean and Chapter and the parishes.[16] As Bentham pointed out to

[14] *Correspondence* (*CW*), v. 298. James Cecil (1744–1823), 7th Earl and 1st Marquis of Salisbury. Samuel Horsley (1733–1806), a considerable scholar and theologian; Bishop of Rochester and Dean of Westminster, 1793–1802; Bishop of St Asaph, 1802–6.
[15] UC cxxiii. 219–20, Bentham's emphasis.
[16] *Correspondence* (*CW*), v. 302.

Rose, this obstructive attitude made a new bill to acquire an adequate amount of land essential.

Another problem that emerged was that the boys of Westminster School, then as now the responsibility of the Dean and Chapter, had been accustomed from time immemorial to play cricket on Tothill Fields. Bentham promised to provide them with a fine new pitch more extensive than of Mr Lord's cricket ground in Marylebone. Bentham's discussion of this problem was informed by personal experience from his own school-days:

To the *Westminster Scholars*, it would afford an advantage as flattering as it would be new and unexpected. At present whatever benefit they reap from the use of that dreary and ill-looking expanse, in the way of sport and exercise, is subject to the perpetual intrusion of *mean dangerous* and *unwelcome* company, of all sorts: a source, an apparent one at least, of corruption, which of itself has been known to operate with effect in the minds of Parents, as an objection to their intrusting their Children to that School.[17]

Within two months of the proposal to build on Tothill Fields being first mooted, clouds were gathering. In November Charles Abbot warned Bentham that 'Ld. Grosvr's opposition is thought to be the most formidable.' Belgrave House, the residence of his son Viscount Belgrave, a Commissioner of the Board of Control, was within half a mile of the site, though Bentham insisted it was well screened from view.[18] Rose was concerned that it would be very difficult to proceed in a hostile manner against the Dean and Chapter.[19] And Wilberforce feared that his friend lacked the political influence to prevail; he willingly gave Bentham the benefit of his political experience. In his warnings he foresaw the troubles that were to engulf the new legislation:

I fear that you would be hardly able to carry a Bill thro' both Houses in the face of the Dn. and Chrs. opposition: I say *you*; I ought not to have

[17] UC cxxiii. 221, Bentham's emphasis.
[18] *Correspondence* (*CW*), v. 300, 260. Richard Grosvenor (1731–1802), 1st Earl Grosvenor, was famous as a horse breeder. He had the misfortune to be forced to repudiate his wife because of her scandalous affair with George III's brother, the Duke of Cumberland. Robert Grosvenor (1767–1845), Viscount Belgrave, succ. father as 2nd Earl Grosvenor, 1802; cr. 1st Marquis of Westminster, 1831. MP, 1790–1802; Commissioner of the Board of Control, 1793–1801. His careful management of his estates, including the development of Belgravia, laid the foundations of the wealth of the Dukes of Westminster.
[19] Ibid. 312.

it to *say*; but I doubt if it will be practicable to prevail on Ministry to bring forward the proposal themselves, as they ought, and to support it with all their force.[20]

Bentham was indebted to him for more than good advice on political realities. Wilberforce was, at this time, active in his service, visiting Bishop Horsley, exhorting George Rose, and, above all, ensuring that Pitt's support for the penitentiary was conveyed to the Dean and Chapter. Wilberforce was not just concerned for his friend's interests in this world. His care extended to his immortal soul, for he was embarking on a doomed effort to convert Bentham to evangelical Christianity. Bentham realized his ulterior motive, wryly confiding in his brother: 'Wilberforce wonderfully cordial and confidential—but is laying plots for converting me—I was hard put to it this morning to parry him.'[21] Bentham was convinced that the obstacles put in his path were the results of selfish personal motives blind to the public good; Wilberforce had another explanation:

I must say, few things have more impress'd my mind with a Sense of various bad Passions and mischievous weaknesses which infest the human Heart, than several Circumstances which have happened in relation to your Undertaking. A little, ever so little, Religion would have prevented it all and long ago have put the public in possession of the practical Benefits of your plan.[22]

Bentham remained unconvinced—and unconverted.

Despite these ominous warnings, Bentham was confident. He persuaded himself that the Dean and Chapter would make only a token opposition now that they were assured of Pitt's commitment. He won over James Wyatt, the architectural adviser to the Dean and Chapter. And, above all, in December, a start was made in drafting a new bill, though at Bentham's expense. At the end of 1796, it had been approved by Lowndes and sent to the Treasury and the Law Officers. All seemed in train for its introduction to Parliament early in the next session. Bentham had been gratified by a letter from Patrick Colquhoun, a metropolitan police magistrate and authority on problems of law enforcement,

[20] *Correspondence* (*CW*), v. 309, Wilberforce's emphasis.
[21] Ibid. 301.
[22] Ibid. 309.

offering his assistance 'to promote the Completion of this very useful Establishment'.[23]

The year 1797 started with Bentham confident that the bill would be introduced within a few weeks; he was to be bitterly disappointed. It was a lost year for the panopticon prison; it was also a dark year in England's history. Mutiny in the navy, rebellion in Ireland, financial crisis, and military disasters threatened the country with invasion and Pitt's government with catastrophe in the loss of the King's confidence on which its existence depended. Even Bentham recognized that 'the cloud which hung over the country' might have priority with public men over the penitentiary project.[24] But the disaster which struck the panopticon project was not just a product of a distracted administration. For the first five months of the year, Bentham tried to get the Attorney-General and the Solicitor-General to consider his bill. In May they rejected it. Scott disliked the whole scheme, it was 'romantic' and the bill, 'the most unlike an Act of Parliament he ever saw'.[25] Mitford, generally more sympathetic to Bentham, also disapproved. In Bentham's papers is a copy of this short simple measure; the powers of the 1794 Act to acquire land anywhere in Middlesex, Kent, Essex, and Surrey were 'Hereby Declared to extend not only to cultivated and other lands . . . But likewise to lands in the state of Waste which might be subject to the rights of Common.' At the end of this document, Scott's and Mitford's comments, dated 2 May 1797, have been carefully copied by Bentham himself and tell clearly why they rejected this sweeping measure:

We have separately considered this act: and it appears to us that no act can be passed applicable to wastelands indefinitely throughout four counties, which will not be liable to so many objections that it appears to us the legislature cannot with due attention to the interests of individuals pass it into law. If a particular spot were pointed out, notices given (as in cases of enclosure bills) . . . a particular act might perhaps be passed . . . which would not be so objectionable, especially as the parties

---

[23] Ibid. 325. This letter was addressed to Samuel Bentham showing how closely he was connected with the panopticon in the eyes of a well-informed observer.
[24] Ibid. 368.
[25] Ibid. 365–6.

interested would then have an opportunity of pointing out particular inconveniences.[26]

So Bentham, again at his own expense, had to draft a second bill, this time a long complex measure detailing the land to be acquired and the obligations undertaken. And by the end of 1797 he was in the same position as he had been a year earlier, sending the second bill to the Treasury and the Law Officers. Again he was wearily soliciting consideration for it. On 5 February 1798 another blow fell. This bill, specifically relating to Tothill Fields, was judged to be an enclosure bill and so subject, by the rules of the House, to different procedures: in particular, it would be necessary to display notices on church doors for three consecutive weeks in August and September before the bill could be introduced in Parliament. It was therefore impossible to bring in the bill without a delay of yet another year. The government had grievously bungled. From the first, it was clear that common land was involved, yet bills had been considered for fourteen months by government lawyers. In the previous year, the law officers had casually mentioned a possible need for notices, but the Treasury had failed to realize the implications. It was crass ineptitude and Bentham, sensing that he had the Treasury at a disadvantage, expressed his anger. He wrote a bitter letter to Rose complaining that the delays were threatening him with financial ruin and suggesting that, as compensation for his losses occasioned by government procrastination, he should be given the contract to manage the hulks, in the place of Duncan Campbell. Bentham did not see the awarding of this contract as a favour but rather as an indemnification the government in justice owed him, and one that would save them money. In no way would it be an alternative to the panopticon, but a strictly temporary arrangement that would 'afford me an opportunity of initiating myself into the business, and the transition from the Hulk plan to the Penitentiary House plan would be smoother'.[27] He suggested that the notice to terminate Campbell's contract and the notices for the new bill should be issued at the same time

---

[26] UC cxxiii. 167–84. The summary of Bentham's life in *Correspondence* (*CW*), vols. iv and vi, fails to make clear that two quite different bills were involved.

[27] *Correspondence* (*CW*), vi. 8.

to demonstrate the government's good faith. Rose replied by return with a conciliatory letter, clearly embarrassed by the 'difficulties' that Bentham had encountered and assuring him of his goodwill. But he did not give a straight answer to Bentham's request for the hulks. Driven to a stratagem that has become the time-honoured refuge of the harried bureaucrat, he suggested an inquiry—a reference of the whole business to the Commons Select Committee on Finance. Somewhat ambiguously Rose promised that 'the Public would be satisfied that it should either proceed or at once be given up as they should report'.[28] It is unlikely that the government would have been willing to entrust the hulks to Bentham. Campbell had been in charge since their inception in 1776 and his management was under question. They were generally reckoned at the Home Office as well as among penal reformers to be sinks of vice and seminaries of crime. In 1799 the Lord Chief Justice himself was to complain that for years the termly reports to the King's Bench were a meaningless fiction.[29] The government was contemplating a far-reaching change in management and in 1802, after Campbell's departure, they appointed Aaron Graham, a magistrate, to oversee the hulks and report directly to the Home Office.[30] Bentham's plea to be given the hulks as a private contractor on the same terms as Campbell was therefore unlikely to be acceptable.

According to Hume, the reference to the Finance Committee was engineered by Bentham as part of his strategy to deploy his influence. But it seems more likely that it was a device used by the administration to buy time until the end of the parliamentary session. Bentham's first reaction hardly bears out the supposition that he had been intriguing for such an inquiry. In a somewhat intemperate letter, he hinted to Rose that any inquiry into why he had not got Battersea Rise—the site recommended by twelve Judges—would bring obloquy on the government and might cause contention between the house of commons and the Cabinet. To Wilberforce, he was more outspoken: 'Meantime I will state to you distinctly where everything centres with me—it is in the sink of perdition—the Hulks . . . what do you think of Mr Rose's

[28] Ibid. 10.
[29] Ibid. 144.
[30] W. Branch-Johnson, *The English Prison Hulks* (London, 1957), 36.

sending me to the Committee? . . . He might as well have sent me to the Pope—Can there be any thing more perfectly in the power of Mr Pitt?' And with a certain foresight, he opined that 'Plying the Committee, would be like bringing an Action upon a Judgment: a man gets another judgment for his pains.'[31]

However, Bentham could not resist the temptation to air his grievances and in a few weeks' time he was busy preparing his answers for the committee. In the meantime, his fertile mind, at work upon the prospect of managing the hulks, had hatched another expedient; a temporary wooden panopticon to be built on a sandbank on the Thames near Greenwich. This would be similar to the hulks, but would allow the convicts to be under inspection; he begged the government for £10,000 deductible from the £24,000 they would have owed him for the permanent building—there should therefore be no extra expense to the public; for as soon as the permanent building were up the public would be reimbursed.

Bentham got no immediate answer to his request for the temporary panopticon, as he had got none for the hulks. But, as the weeks passed, he became immersed in preparations for the committee hearings and considerably more optimistic as to its effects. He believed it would spur on the irresolute Treasury to override opposition to his bill. If it had been Rose's intention to distract Bentham, and his friends, from the failings of the administration, he had succeeded. Bentham became deeply involved in the preparation of evidence and in the possible implementation of its recommendations. The remit of the Finance Committee was to enquire into methods of saving public money; its chairman was Charles Abbot, Bentham's able and successful stepbrother; and two of its members were known to him, Reginald Pole Carew was a personal friend, and Henry Thornton a friend of Wilberforce. The committee was not just concerned with the penitentiary scheme, but more widely with the expense of police. Its other business was to enquire into Colquhoun's proposal for a Board of Police Revenue which would have centralized and rationalized the collection of government dues and brought marginal trades suspected of having links with the criminal world, such as hackney coaches, livery stables, secondhand dealers, and

[31] *Correspondence (CW)*, vi. 15.

pawnshops, under regulation. The committee recommended the setting up of a Board of Police Revenue and further praised schemes dear to Bentham's heart, the registering of lodging houses, a Police Gazette, and an annual report of police from each county.[32]

The primary purpose of the 28th Report of the Finance Committee was to find ways of saving public money, but the commitee went somewhat outside its terms of reference and produced a study of different penal methods and a discussion of their merits. They gave unequivocal support to the panopticon project and urged the immediate execution of the contract so as not to 'deprive the public . . . of the benefits of a plan which they cannot but look to as likely to be productive of the most essential advantage, both in point of Economy and police'.[33] This conclusion was based first on financial considerations, and backed by an armoury of figures; it was more economical than either the hulks or transportation.[34] The committee endorsed without discussion the principle of a contract prison and indeed were particularly attracted by the clause whereby after the death of both Jeremy and Samuel Bentham, the annual charge might cease, for by that time the project would be so profitable that contractors would be competing to manage it. Patrick Colquhoun, when questioned on this point, had no doubts. The penitentiary, he asserted, 'would be the means of training both sexes to productive labour, to such a degree as to render it an object to new Contractors, after the system becomes fully matured, to take upon them the management of convicts merely for the profit of their labour'. The reports to the King's Bench would make commercial information available as to the value of the contract and 'render the labour of Convicts a species of property, finding its true value in a competition of purchasers'.[35] The report dryly

---

[32] UC cl contains many pages devoted to evidence for the committee on this subject, and to a Police bill.

[33] Bowring, xi. 167. *Twenty-Eighth Report from the Select Committee on Finance: Police Including Convict Establishments. Reported by Charles Abbot 26th June 1798.* Cited as *Report.* An extract from the *Report* and Bentham's evidence was printed in Bowring, xi. 165–70.

[34] Bentham had doubts as to the value of any comparison when the cost of imprisonment as a punishment in county gaols was impossible to ascertain. See UC cl. 338.

[35] *Report*, 362.

commends the plan, 'which bids fair to put an end to all expense upon the extinction of the lives of two middle aged persons'.[36]

However, the committee was not only concerned with the public purse, for the panopticon penitentiary had, in its eyes, other virtues than economy. It would tend towards reformation and it had one great advantage in 'the certain employment and industrious livelihood which it ensures those whose terms of confinement are expired'. Thus, the metasylum was commended by a committee of the legislature. The committee's reason for praising Bentham's discharge proposals was the alternative of setting free a flood of criminals; for the hulks would discharge 254 of their unreformed inmates every year to prey upon the public. If, in addition, many of the convicts returned from New South Wales, 'the prospect would indeed be dreadful'. Finally, the committee was impressed by the full publicity and inspection to which the prison would be subject, 'that constant facility of inspection which will in an unusual manner be afforded by the very form and construction of the building'.[37] It recommended that Tothill Fields should be acquired and the building erected as soon as possible. Bentham's evidence, given with some apprehension, was supported unequivocally by Colquhoun. He had, a few years before, suggested to the Home Office a Village of Industry to employ minor criminals and discharged prisoners, but generously admitted that the panopticon was much superior to his own scheme and urged its adoption as an incalculable advantage to the public, both for economy and the improvement of morals. Colquhoun, in his capacity as Police Magistrate, saw much of the evils of the hulks and was forthright in his condemnation of these seminaries of vice and wickedness; they quite failed to reform their inmates: 'I have seldom or never known an instance of their return to honest industry; on the contrary, many of them have been detected immediately afterwards in the commission of new crimes.'[38] The report followed Colquhoun in stigmatizing the hulks as corrupting morals and encouraging crime. The committee also, which more concerned Bentham, gave its blessing to his taking over these sinks of iniquity. In his evidence, he argued at some length that management of these convicts would be an acceptable form of compensation for the

---

[36] *Report*, 351.     [37] Bowring, xi. 166.     [38] *Report*, 360.

delays and losses he had suffered, and that it would be an earnest of the government's good intentions and ease the transition from the hulks to the panopticon. Bentham was very anxious that the committee should include a recommendation on this subject; and, after some urging, Henry Thornton, now an ally, contrived to insert the words: 'A mode of compensation has indeed been proposed by the contractor, which, so far as it goes, has the advantage of not being attended with any expense to the public, and to which it does not appear to your Committee that any substantial objection can be made.'[39] Bentham no doubt wished to get his hands on the lucrative contract for the hulks but only as a step towards the realization of his dream. In a letter to Rose, he revealed his plan: the men in the hulks were to be moved with all speed to the wooden structure of the temporary panopticon preparatory to the erection of the permanent building.[40]

The committee also cast doubt on the wisdom of transportation. It complained that information from the colony had been scanty, and made the point that the only advantage of this method of punishment was that the distance made it difficult if not impossible for the criminals to return—an argument that Bentham, at this juncture concerned with practicalities, passed without comment, but was later to denounce as justifying an extension of punishment from a certain term to life, an extension unsanctioned by Parliament, illegal, and unjust.[41] But, the committee argued, even that advantage would be lost for, as the colony improved, return would become easier. In the meantime, the country not only lost the labour of convicts, but also had to spend considerable sums in New South Wales on defence against internal disorder.

The Finance Committee report was, therefore, thoroughly satisfactory from Bentham's point of view. It endorsed his scheme and condemned its rivals. However, it could not meet all his requirements. Bentham was at Hendon during much of the summer of 1798 and he spent some of those weary months writing his own version of the report. This exists in rough drafts in his papers; there is no fair continuous copy, there are different

---

[39] Bowring, xi. 167. See *Correspondence* (*CW*), vi. 47–9, for exchange of letters with Thornton.
[40] *Correspondence* (*CW*), vi. 52–3.
[41] Bowring, iv. 186–7.

versions and signs of reworking. He does not appear to have circulated it to his friends. It would seem possible that he was writing for his own private amusement.[42] In this shadow report he pays off old scores in the forms of parliamentary language; he casts down his enemies, exalts his friends, stands forth himself as a heroic, magnanimous figure, and reveals his somewhat startling plans for the hated colony of New South Wales.

Bentham started by analysing the four different chronical punishments: simple imprisonment, transportation, confinement in the hulks, and confinement in a penitentiary. He came, inevitably, to the conclusion that imprisonment with forced labour was cheap and productive, 'it is only by bad management, . . . unanimated by those motives and unfurnished with those lights, which no other principle but personal interest has strength and perseverance to supply, that this nature can be changed'.[43] He went on to insist on the necessity of punishment in all aspects of human existence:

The stores of reward being limited and even its efficacy precarious, to bring about everything by reward and discard punishment altogether would be an enterprise altogether inconsistent with the slightest knowledge of human nature. Not only in the Penitentiary House, but even in the Boarding School, and in the very nursery—in the bosom of the fondest parent punishment must be constantly in prospect.[44]

Punishment must be inflicted only so far as it is necessary to bring about the desired end—in this case, the extraction of labour. Bentham then summarized the history of the attempt to build a penitentiary, revealing the ambiguity of his attitude to Howard; at one point he mocked the original scheme as: 'two Towns: containing between them as many Houses as there were to be prisoners . . . Economy the humble virtue of private life, was either negligently passed by unheeded, or disdainfully rejected as a clog upon the exertions of official discipline.'[45]

However, at another point, he boasted that 'Mr Bentham was already a veteran in the field of Penitentiary speculation. He had been in habits with Howard: and his printed observations on the original Penitentiary Act, before it had as yet reached the House in the shape of a Bill, gave birth to several amendments.'[46]

[42] UC cl, cli.　　[43] UC cl. 339.　　[44] Ibid. 341.
[45] Ibid. 350.　　[46] Ibid. 363.

His approval of Colquhoun and Bunbury, both of whom had seen the light, was without qualification. Colquhoun, who had given up his own scheme as soon as he had become aware of Bentham's, was praised for his honourable generosity and Bunbury for his good sense in realizing the shortcomings of Howard's penitentiary:

It is not often that two men applying their minds without concert to the pursuit of the same object . . . arrive at so perfect a coincidence: it is still less frequent among authors of concurrent plans for either to come forward and give preference to the other: but on this occasion another incident of the same kind that presented itself to the recollection of some of the Members of your Committee, was that in the year 1793 or 1794 an honourable gentleman who was to have bourne a distinguished part in the execution of the original Penitentiary plan was the Member who before the Bill for that purpose had been brought in by Mr Secretary Dundas was the first to introduce Mr Bentham's plan to the notice of the House.[47]

If Bentham was lavish in praise of the friends of panopticon, he was harsh, if circumspect, in his condemnation of its enemies. His shadow committee was impelled to ask him how a plan of such manifest benefit had been so long delayed. Mr Bentham nobly tried to shield the Treasury and Earl Spencer from the just wrath of Parliament, his 'appearance was tardy and his answers reluctant'.[48] But he was forced to admit that the failure to secure the site on Battersea Rise had been the main obstacle. His committee, turning to the Treasury, found that they were willing to proceed, there being no question of the propriety of the scheme, but the choice of a site had presented a difficulty. Bentham's report castigated the supineness of the Treasury; no difficulties had existed that they were not authorized, indeed required, to overcome. As for the cause of the administration's procrastination, his report did no more than hint at the crying scandal of Spencer's behaviour; on that, 'it is not the wish of your Committee to withdraw the veil'.[49]

In dealing with New South Wales, the shadow report becomes of far greater significance, revealing plans for the colony that

---

[47] Ibid. 366. Charles Bunbury was the member.
[48] Ibid. 367.
[49] UC cl. 370 and UC cli. 489. There are several versions of this passage.

Bentham never made public. He started by summarizing the history of transportation from the time of Charles II. Irritated by the sentimentality that was willing to swallow the camel of the reality of servitude while straining at the gnat of penitentiary contract labour, he wrote: 'By transportation Slavery . . . was indeed established, but being established out of sight it was not regarded as a grievance.'[50] But Bentham did not condemn New South Wales on the emotive grounds of establishing a new slave colony, but on the solid grounds of expense. He was also irritated by the ambiguities with which this expense was justified, it was never clear for what purpose the colony was founded:

> Ask if the Colony provides any prospect of paying its own expenses— oh, but it is an engine of punishment to be substituted to the Hulks. Ask whether as an engine of punishment it be not an expensive one—Oh, but it is a Colony to boot, and a fifth quarter of the globe added to the British Empire.[51]

Bentham's plans for the future of the colony can be better understood if read in conjunction with another unfinished work of his, a draft pamphlet dated September 1798, entitled, 'Political Prospects or What is to be done? or What is to become of us?' This polemic is a dramatically worded warning of the threat of national bankruptcy; in this age, 'pregnant with dark and disastrous events . . . one great calamity hangs over all our heads . . . with an impact more or less threatening to all—its name is Bankruptcy'. He hinted that colonies were increasing this threat; and might also be an obstacle to a necessary peace. 'In regard to Colonies, the practical inference is, that whether we give up any of our old ones or no, it is not worth while to continue the war for the sake of acquiring or preserving any new ones.'[52] This pamphlet was clearly intended for public consumption, and his meaning as to the future of the colonies is obscure. But in his writings on the Finance Committee, he unequivocally insisted that New South Wales might have to be jettisoned: 'it is impossible for your Committee not to be led to the supposition that there may be a time when the throwing it off may present itself to Parliament as a measure absolutely indispensable.'[53] He put forward three alternative expendients to rid Britain of this

---

[50] UC cl. 342.            [51] Ibid. 359.
[52] UC cvii. 151–74.       [53] UC cl. 360.

intolerable burden, expedients that he feared would seem novel and romantic because without precedent. They were selling or transferring to some foreign power; sending some member of the Royal family, or some other personage of high rank, to rule the colony on condition of residence; or establishing a government, monarchical, republican, or copied from the Constitution of this country, that would be run by the colonists themselves. He advocated independence in these words: 'the members of the governing body being taken from among the inhabitants of certain descriptions or of all descriptions—the evacuating the spot altogether as far as the establishment paid by this country military, naval and civil is concerned leaving the colonists to settle the business of government by themselves.'[54]

One is left to speculate on who might have bought Australia; perhaps the Americans who were to purchase Louisiana from the French in 1803, and, if they had, how the history of the two countries and the world might have been changed. Even more intriguing is which of George III's deplorable sons might have ended his days in Botany Bay as monarch of New South Wales. Bentham did realize that these proposals were unlikely to be practical politics except in a dire national emergency. And it is not possible to claim prescience for his prediction of colonial self-rule. At this time he was actuated by the desire to destroy the rival to the panopticon. But one can claim wisdom for his final comment: 'Unhappily where dominion is concerned men cling to a dead burthen, with an attachment as obstinate, and much more blind, than if it were a revenue. Where dominion is to be given up, wisdom and economy will be deemed romantic and visionary in whatever shape they may present themselves.'[55] Here indeed he points the way towards the liberal ideals of peace and retrenchment.

Despite Bentham's forebodings, or hopes, New South Wales was to go on and flourish as a British colony. And the real Finance Committee Report failed to achieve the ends Bentham had hoped for. On 6 July 1798, nine days after the report was presented, Bentham wrote to Rose thanking him for suggesting the reference to the committee and trusting that the Treasury would now press forward with the scheme. Again, he confidently

[54] Ibid.     [55] Ibid. 361.

asked for the hulks contract and for approval of the temporary panopticon which would speedily put an end to them. At the end of the month he wrote again assuring Rose that his plans were fully prepared. But Bentham was deluding himself with false hopes. In August he suffered a humiliating interview with Rose who refused outright to consider giving him the hulk contract as compensation and derided the whole idea of a temporary panopticon as absurd. Rose would appear to have been dissociating himself from the business. Bentham was forbidden to approach him again, and told that in future he must deal with the Junior Secretary Charles Long. Thus the penitentiary project was relegated yet again. Even more hurtful for Bentham, Rose accused him of driving a hard bargain with the public.[56] But despite these humiliations and disappointments, hope was kept alive, for the Treasury was preparing notices for the enclosure bill and Bentham could look forward to acquiring Tothill Fields in the following year; a result that Bentham believed he owed to the Finance Committee Report.

But the Treasury could not, even if it would, make the way smooth. In a rare, if not unique, display of helpfulness and goodwill, Joseph White warned Bentham privately that the Dean and Chapter were nevertheless determined to oppose the bill at every stage. Colquhoun and his fellow magistrate Joseph Moser, whom he had recruited for the struggle, made determined efforts to induce the ecclesiastical authorities to withdraw their objections. But on 15 November the Westminster Chapter passed a resolution insisting that they had not consented to any bill for that purpose and that they would 'oppose such Bill if it should be brought into Parliament'. Later in the month, the parishes also officially resolved to fight the bill as injurious to the interests of their inhabitants.[57] In a final attempt to persuade Horsley, Bentham attempted to gain an interview to try the influence of his eloquence where his letters had failed, only to be rudely rebuffed, with the words: 'The Bishop of Rochester declines the honour of Mr Bentham's visits.'[58]

---

[56] *Correspondence (CW)*, vi. 61–4.

[57] UC cxvii. 132, 135. Westminster Abbey *Chapter Minutes 1791–1807*, 163. Joseph Moser (1748–1819), an author, artist, and magistrate; Deputy Lieutenant for Middlesex and Magistrate for Westminster, 1794–1819.

[58] *Correspondence (CW)*, vi. 127.

In the meantime, all hope for the new legislation was lost. In October Abbot, refusing to sponsor the bill himself, had warned that it would fall without the wholehearted support of the administration. Pitt and only Pitt would have the political authority to carry it through Parliament. The following month, the final legal obstacle emerged. The Speaker judged the bill private, so not only would it face far greater procedural hurdles than a government measure, it could not have the vital support of the administration. Long informed Bentham that no minister had the time to sponsor a private measure and, given the opposition of the Dean and Chapter, the bill would have to be abandoned. Thus was Bentham driven from his fourth site, where he had encountered a quagmire of legal complexities and the antagonism of powerful special interests; ironically the site of which he wrote: 'I betook myself at length to this ill famed spot as least likely to be contested.'[59] Another man might have despaired as failure followed upon failure, but Bentham persisted to the wonder of his friends. It is easy with hindsight to assume that the panopticon was doomed never to be built; that it was indeed visionary, romantic, and theoretical. Yet in 1798, Bentham felt himself to be near success despite setbacks; in June he was writing to Dumont: 'my Panopticon business wears at present a complection rather favourable.'[60]

As the years since 1786 had gone by, the idea of the panopticon had strengthened its hold on his mind. In 1797, far from despairing, he planned a vast extension of the principle to paupers. And he remained convinced that once the panopticon was built its manifest virtues would be immediately apparent and would ensure its wider adoption. It was the first step that mattered; the building and its management principles would persuade, proselytize, and convince; and inevitably the poor as well as the wicked would fall under his benevolent sway. There is no doubt that Bentham was ready to build his prison. In his papers are notes on multifarious practical details, including lists of essential equipment for each prisoner, recipes for soups, and estimates of the cost of coal.[61] Also, the frail structure of the 1786 building had acquired solidity. In a letter to Horsley in

---

[59] Ibid. 12.  [60] Ibid. 50.  [61] UC clvii. 24–64.

November 1796 Bentham listed the additional premises that would be needed, reception houses, infirmaries, a graveyard, yards for storing wood and stone, and turning and waiting spaces for visitor's carriages.[62] The panopticon had increased in size and was taking on some of the characteristics of a Howardian prison in deference to the accepted wisdom of contemporary reformers. Bentham would not have embarked on this project alone; he had expert advice and help readily available from his brother, Samuel, who would be his partner in this business venture. Bentham's evidence to the Finance Committee emphasized the central role that Samuel had played; he had invented not only the building, but also a great machine for wood- and stone-working; originally he had planned to acquire a steam engine to power this machine and the labour of the prisoners was to be a substitute for this. Much of Bentham's anguish over the shipwreck of the panopticon stemmed from the realization that he had deprived his younger brother of a fair prospect of fortune. At this juncture, Samuel was living at Queen's Square Place and, as Inspector-General of Naval Works, had responsibility for buildings; in 1797 he designed a Panopticon House of Industry making extensive use of iron and glass.[63] He was also concerned with preparing a structure on the inspection principle to accommodate French prisoners of war.[64] A colleague of his, Samuel Bunce, a naval engineer and architect, would have collaborated with the Benthams in the preparation of drawings for the prison.[65] Considerable expertise would therefore have been available; and Samuel had made extensive preparations, he had ordered iron struts for the building to his specifications which, as Jeremy struggled with the Dean and Chapter of Westminster, lay rotting only yards away in the wharves at Millbank.[66] As soon as he was given the opportunity, Samuel Bentham was to prove that his inspection house was a practical proposition. In 1805 he went to Russia for a second time and one of his first tasks was to plan a large wooden panopticon in St Petersburg capable of holding 3,000 workers. Within less than a year its foundations were rising

---

[62] *Correspondence (CW)*, v. 318–19.
[63] R. Evans, *The Fabrication of Virtue* (Cambridge, 1982), 222.
[64] *Correspondence (CW)*, vi. 21.
[65] Ibid. 139.
[66] Ibid. 128. Samuel's letters are at UC xxii. 1–30.

on the banks of the Neva and it was completed in 1808. Its object was to educate and employ young men in trades connected with the navy; and Samuel was to have a share in the profits. This structure lasted until 1818 when it burnt down—not a surprising fate since it housed a steam engine in its lowest storey by which all the machines were set in motion.[67]

Although Bentham had to contend with the inertia of the Treasury, the procrastination of Crown lawyers, and the antagonism of special interests, his panopticon had won the approval of a wide range of men from among the most able and intelligent of his contemporaries. Bentham came later to believe that almost all the members of Pitt's administration were in a conspiracy to destroy the panopticon, but at this time the project had its friends. Dundas had thought it worth devoting some time and energy to; at the Treasury Pitt and Rose, though inactive, were not hostile. Bentham was encouraged by the seemingly warm endorsement from the great men at the Home Office. Colquhoun had moved on his behalf and in January 1797, William Baldwin, the senior counsel dealing with criminal matters, wrote praising 'your great and good Plan'.[68] And later that month, the Home Secretary, the Duke of Portland himself, visited Bentham and through Colquhoun signified his approval of the scheme to set convicts to work. Evan Nepean, according to Bentham his only true friend in the administration, was unfortunately no longer at the Home Office but he continued to take an active interest and to give Bentham aid and comfort. Outside the immediate circle of government, the panopticon was considered as a practical proposition by hard-headed men of business. Colquhoun was unstinting in his praise and in his efforts to overcome obstacles: 'Never I believe did so many untoward Circumstances occur to obstruct one of the best measures that ever was devised for the public good.'[69] Another magistrate with long experience of dealing with crime in London, Joseph Moser, worked zealously to overcome the opposition of the parishes, the Dean and Chapter, and the Belgrave interest. He too was convinced of the merits of the scheme, writing: 'while I admir'd the ingenuity,

---

[67] *Correspondence* (*CW*), vii. 336, 389, and *The Gentleman's Magazine and Historical Chronicle*, 88 (Jan.–June 1818), 362–3.

[68] *Correspondence* (*CW*), v. 353.

[69] Ibid. vi. 123.

industry and benevolence which appeared in the patriotic plan . . .
I could not help lamenting that you should have had any difficulties to struggle against.'[70]

It was therefore not only Bentham's immediate friends, like
Wilberforce, Pole Carew, and Romilly who supported him, but
many other realistic, experienced men who were not impractical
dreamers, philanthropists, or philosophers. Charles Abbot himself, one of the most respected politicians of his time who later
became Speaker of the House of Commons, was 'very active in
his assistance, as well as intelligent in his advice'.[71] The family
connection might give the impression that the Finance Committee Report was concocted between them, perhaps the product
of the sinister interest of the Bentham/Abbot family. But the
laconic Abbot was not the man to make himself or his committee
ridiculous by publicly approving a bizarre project for the sake of
his stepbrother, and there is no evidence to suggest that he was
other than genuinely convinced of the merits of the scheme. He
indeed questioned the practicality of Bentham's commitment to
pay compensation for felonies perpetrated by released prisoners.
Bentham wrote of this plan:

It has hurt me, even with Abbot: it *had* hurt me with Nepean . . . I
satisfied him in three words . . . The loss could never befall me but in
company with a much greater gain. Either the man is *hanged*: and then
his superannuation Annuity is saved to me: or he comes back to me
again, and then I squeeze it out of him with interest.[72]

These words illustrate the fundamental dilemma facing Bentham
and the origins of many of the ambiguities of the panopticon. For
him it was an ideal, but to achieve this ideal he had to argue its
case in the arena of the real world. He had to appear a harsh
realist, capable of controlling daring and violent criminals. The
chilling, repellent insistence that work, and profit, must be
extracted from the men in his charge was the aspect of his prison
scheme absolutely necessary to convince men such as Abbot and
Nepean that the panopticon was practical and financially viable.
In this Bentham succeeded and the Finance Committee Report in
1798 was the apogee of his success.

It was a barren triumph. The site of Tothill Fields that the

---

[70] *Correspondence* (*CW*), v. 99.     [71] Ibid. v. 305.
[72] Ibid. vi. 331, Bentham's emphasis.

committee had recommended remained outside his grasp; the hulks contract and the temporary panopticon were also snatched from him. However, the report continued to provide him with ammunition and he referred frequently to its findings in subsequent attempts to further his plans. On the political front, the Finance Committee may have influenced the Treasury to find another site, for amidst the wreck of his hopes of acquiring Tothill Fields, the idle and devious Charles Long suggested a new site. In December 1798 Bentham saw himself as another storm-tossed Odysseus: 'four Ithacas each in its turn within a rope's length of my weather beaten back had already each in its turn vanished from my pursuit: after four such voyages little appetite was left to me for a fifth.' The destination of this fifth voyage, the Salisbury estate at Millbank, was casually indicated at a chance meeting in the park mockingly described by Bentham: 'The Honourable Secretary in the pomp of the fruit of royal favour, mounted on his prancer, overtook my solitary and feeble steps— I . . . pursuing my melancholy way by the only mode of conveyance which nature had given and Mr Long had left to me.'[73]

Millbank caused Bentham yet more bitter tribulation; for, although the land was acquired, he was never to build on it. It is ironic that the 1798 Finance Committee Report's endorsement of the panopticon prison may have been partly responsible for the only tangible result of all Bentham's endeavours, the great Millbank penitentiary, erected by his triumphant enemies on his site but on opposed principles of architecture and rival principles of management. And on the Millbank committee were George Rose and Charles Long.

[73] UC cxvii. 197, 201, headed 'Narrative History of the Purchase of Millbank Estate' dated, in pencil, 16 March 1802.

# 10

# A PICTURE OF
# A TREASURY

They have murdered my best days.
UC cxx. 466.

Long's offer of the Salisbury estate on Millbank altered the whole situation. It seemed to Bentham that the government were at last not only willing but able to honour their obligations and to press ahead with building the panopticon. But this renewed hope was to prove as illusory as all the others. Although Bentham actually gained possession of the land in November 1799, it lay idle. When Pitt resigned fifteen months later no final decision had yet been taken and Bentham had to wait another two years before Addington's administration had the compassion to inform him, in June 1803, that they were unwilling to find the necessary funds.[1] Altogether Bentham was kept in suspense for a further four and a half years.

These barren, wasted years are of significance in Bentham's life, for his sufferings fostered theories of government that were to find sober and considered expression in the *Constitutional Code*. It is a commonplace that Bentham's resentment over the government's abandonment of the panopticon nurtured a harsher radicalism and a more extreme democratic theory. These events and his reaction to them must therefore be of considerable

---

[1] It is difficult to be precise as to the date of the end of the panopticon. L. J. Hume, 'Bentham's Panopticon', in *Historical Studies*, argues that Mar. 1801 marks the effective end. But Addington's government did consider the matter, and June 1803, when they told Bentham that they would not provide the money to proceed, is a better candidate. But the publication of the latest volume of the *Correspondence* (*CW*), viii (ed. Stephen Conway), reveals that the panopticon was again considered by the Treasury in 1811–12 and that Bentham was willing to undertake the governorship himself even at that late stage. In Dr Conway's opinion it was not until Feb. 1813 that Bentham's hopes from the government were finally extinguished. (*Correspondence* (*CW*), viii, xxv–xxvii.) See Ch. 11, 263–81.

importance in understanding the evolution of his political philosophy. This chapter will give an account of the developments from the end of 1798, when the Salisbury estate at Milbank was first suggested as a suitable site for the penitentiary, to June 1803, when Addington finally abandoned the project. In conclusion, Bentham's reactions and the Constitutional points raised will be explored. The materials on which this account is based are threefold. First, the official Home Office letters and the Treasury Minutes, which chronicle the confused, contradictory, and dilatory decisions of the administration: second, the immediately contemporary account that can be reconstructed from the *Correspondence*: third, these can be elaborated and enriched by the unpublished manuscripts that Bentham wrote during 1802 and the early part of 1803. He called this indictment, 'A Picture of the Treasury under the Administration of the Rt. Hon. W. Pitt and the Rt. Hon. H. Addington with a Sketch of the Secretary of State's Office under the reign of the Duke of Portland'.[2] This gives an almost contemporary account of his dealings with officials and provides material for a case-study of British administration at the end of the eighteenth century. It is a fascinating insight for any student of government. We can come very close to these men, seeing the expression on their faces, hearing the tones of their voices, and penetrating the conduct of their meetings. A picture takes shape of the great men of the Treasury unprotected by guarded entrances and hierarchies of subordinates, working in rooms from which they would emerge into corridors full of anxious suppliants waiting to press their cases. Government was still casual and personal; physical presence was essential if one wanted business done. Bentham lurked in the passages and ante-rooms for days and weeks on end consorting with clerks and porters, awaiting a chance to pounce upon his prey. It was small wonder that Long felt desperate and hunted, and confessed to Nepean that he hated the very sight of Bentham.

The years between 1799 and 1803 were ones of crisis at home and abroad. In February 1801 Pitt resigned after almost twenty years as Prime Minister, after losing the confidence of George III over the issue of Catholic emancipation and the union with

---

[2] UC cxvi. 439.

Ireland. Abroad, Napoleon consolidated his hold on power, extended his grip over the Continent and, despite the short-lived peace of Amiens, posed a growing threat to the security of the realm. By the summer of 1803 invasion was again imminent. With Napoleon's grand army massing on the channel ports, it is not surprising that ministers had little time or inclination to consider the issues of penal reform. Bentham seems to have found it very hard to realize that the subject that obsessed his own mind must have been of small importance to the men he was dealing with. He was oddly aloof, seemingly untouched by patriotic fervour and undisturbed by fears of invasion. Like many of his contemporaries, he enjoyed a visit to Paris during the brief months of peace. He seems if anything to have approved of Napoleon, hoping at one time to interest him in his brother's invention of hollow fire-irons. In the 1802 plebiscite, using the honorary French citizenship bestowed upon him in 1792, he voted in favour of his appointment as Consul for life.[3]

In 1799 Bentham was still confident that he would succeed in building the panopticon. Charles Long himself had suggested the new site at Millbank and, despite the customary delays, the land was purchased. In June, on George Rose's motion, the Committee of Supply voted £36,000 to Bentham for purchasing the site and building the penitentiary. At this point the careful and experienced Abbot hoped that his stepbrother could now proceed 'with Confidence and Success'.[4] By November, after he had been created feoffee, he was actually in possession of the land. However, even this simple transaction had been bedevilled by delay seemingly caused by the wilful refusal of Joseph White to draw up a previous agreement with Lord Salisbury despite instructions to do so from the Treasury. White may have had respectable legal reasons for his reluctance. Bentham's desire that he should proceed by way of a previous contract, contingent on his becoming feoffee, stemmed from a continuing desire to obtain part of Tothill Fields. He hoped that by starting building on the Salisbury land he could make 'a sort of display of possession' that would persuade the Dean and Chapter to 'capitulate'—a suggestion, he wrote, that came from Long himself.[5] White,

---

[3] *Correspondence* (*CW*), vii. 5, 63.
[4] Ibid. vi. 168.     [5] Ibid. 147–8.

however, deeply disapproved of this method of proceeding and insisted on drawing up a contract in due form. This meant that Bentham was excluded from the land until the deed making him a feoffee was finally executed. In May bitterly resentful at this delay which was costing another precious year of his life, Bentham was haunting the Treasury corridors in the hope of persuading Long to force White to comply with his instructions. The humiliations he suffered can best be described in his own account of his encounters with Long:

sent in my name: and as it has more than once happened to me to pass morning after morning for weeks together not only without being able to get an audience of Mr Long but without being able so much as to learn whether then or at any future time whatever I should be able to obtain that favour, I ventured so far as to give general instructions to the Office . . . to ask Mr Long whether he could see me on that day or not:—the answer was in the negative—This negative was a favour: for in general, when I have sent in my name, no notice has been taken, in which case . . . I have been obliged to consume the whole morning there without seeing him after all. Apprehensive lest this sort of treatment should mark me out as an object of contempt to the Messengers and Porters, my way has been latterly not to send in my name, but to way lay Mr Long in his passage from one apartment to another . . . This day I called . . . I caught him just now in the Porter's washing room: I had just time to say that I came to thank him for his letter . . . His countenance expressed displeasure, he turned from me and entered into conversation with a somebody else . . . and for the evident purpose of avoiding me . . . turned off . . . with that somebody else. The intention was so evident, as to draw forth an universal smile upon the countenance of all the Messengers and Attendants in the room to the number of perhaps half a dozen. . . . If I give up sollicitation, the business perishes . . . if I persist in sollicitation, personal ignominy seems the only fruit I am likely to reap from it.

The pain Bentham suffered from this gross insult can be felt in his letter to his friend Pole Carew: 'I hate the sight of men, and dine with no such cattle . . . If I remain unshot, undrowned, unhung, it is to avoid burthening the public with Coroner's fees. Given at my dog-hole this 25 day of May, 1799—Bow, wow, wow.'[6]

The Millbank estate was sold for £12,000, still encumbered

---

[6] Ibid. 151–2, from an unsent letter to Wilberforce.

with leases. Salisbury's agent had been willing to buy them out prior to the sale for an extra £1,000 but the Treasury refused this option. Bentham himself suggested that he should be contracted to acquire the leases and he set to work negotiating prices and times with the lessees. This gave White another opportunity to delay the business by insisting on immediate possession and by refusing to pay out any money until all the negotiations had been completed. Another obstacle was the need to buy separately two strips of land owned by a Henry Wise, which were contiguous to the penitentiary site and essential to Bentham's building plans. Negotiations for this sale were in the hands of the government and no inclination to press ahead was apparent at the Surveyor-General's office. Excuses were made that the price demanded was exorbitant and that the powers for compulsory purchase under the 1794 act were doubtful. Long at the Treasury would not bestir himself to get involved despite Bentham's cogently argued pleas. Driven to distraction by the administration's inability to get business done, Bentham was reduced to writing Long's letters himself and sending them to him for signature.[7] As he commented later: 'in the art of doing nothing, nobody could be more expert than Mr Long.'[8]

Bentham also had the greatest difficulty in extracting a decision from the government on the vital question of the number of convicts that he would be given. He first raised the question in August 1799 pointing out that no plans for buildings could be started without certainty on this point. Long at the Treasury dismissed the subject, saying to his clerk, '*What can I say to this*? How can he expect me to know anything about the number to be built for?'[9] The question was referred to the Home Office. At this point, Bentham called on Evan Nepean for help. It was a clever move. Nepean, the Secretary at the Admiralty, was a friend of Pitt, Rose, and Long but also was, and remained to the end, a staunch believer in the panopticon. Bentham trusted him absolutely; he was the only member of the administration to emerge with any reputation for honesty, straight dealing, or good sense. He was always, 'my much loved and respected friend'.[10] During 1800 and 1801, he expended time and effort to help

---

[7] *Correspondence* (*CW*), vi. 150, 202.    [8] UC cxvii. 208.
[9] UC cxxi. 40.    [10] *Correspondence* (*CW*), vi. 193.

Bentham despite the pressures of his own arduous duties and the burden of ill-health. Bentham first approached Nepean through his discreet and delightful wife, Margaret, also a close friend. She assured him that her husband would speak to Mr Long, but later in September, she had to write again to confess that he had for the moment failed:

he went to Mr Long and talk'd the business over with him, which of course will prepare him for seeing you when you call at the Treasury— but as Mr Nepean does not in general say more upon any occasion than is absolutely necessary, I could learn no more from him about you otherwise than to join with me in assuring you we shall be very glad to see you here whenever it may be agreeable to you.

She goes on to advise the acquisition of 'a chearfull Pleasant Woman in the shape of a *Wife*' as a cure for Bentham's melancholy which she believed was inclined to afflict '*sedate single Men*'.[11]

Nepean did what he could, writing to tell Bentham that he had spoken to Long who had referred the matter to the Home Office, and he promised to mention the subject to King when he dined with him. Mr King at the Home Office gave Bentham audience, receiving him pleasantly, but letting slip the information that Long was 'cold' and that the Treasury 'did not express any great impatience to see the business forwarded'.[12] As for the question of numbers, this was a matter of very great difficulty since the information was so scanty. Bentham was referred to a clerk who was not at the moment in his office, and who did not return that day. On a subsequent visit, Bentham was passed on to another clerk who was reputedly the expert on the subject of transportation. Bentham's description of his conversation displays a sharp insight into the ways of the incompetent: 'it was more pleasant to him to display the extent of his knowledge by general demonstrations, than to furnish me with such particulars of it as were appropriate to my purpose. The topics were the scantiness of his salary contrasted with the firmness of his probity and the richness of his information.'[13] Bentham was referred to books, but was

---

[11] Ibid. 197–8, Margaret Nepean's emphasis.
[12] UC cxxi. 45. John King (1759–1830), Barrister; Law Clerk and Under-Secretary at the Home Office, 1791–1806.
[13] Ibid. 47.

scandalized to find that neither King nor his clerks were familiar with the essential information contained in the Finance Committee Report of 1798 nor in the recently published account of the new colony of New South Wales by David Collins.[14] So these officials in the department responsible for penal policy and the administration of the new colony were lent Bentham's copies of the Report and Collins's history.

Bentham was not told how many convicts he would have to provide for until March 1800, seven months after he had first raised the question. Ignorance and incompetence were not the only reasons for this delay. A serious difference between Bentham and the Home Office over the direction of penal policy was emerging. In estimating the number of convicts he should be given, Bentham assumed that most, if not all, transportable convicts would be sent to his penitentiary. This would have entailed the abandonment of the hulks and the running down of New South Wales as a penal colony. His calculations led him to press for 2,000 inmates rather than the 1,000 originally estimated. The policy of the Home Office was confused; they did not attempt to defend the hulks, but they were nevertheless planning to reform and extend the system. And they certainly did not envisage the end of transportation. Their position was laid down on 14 October 1799 in a letter from the Duke of Portland to the Treasury, which clearly shows that the Home Office did not regard Bentham's penitentiary as central to penal policy. The panopticon, like the hulks, was to be used as a temporary receptacle for convicts awaiting transportation. And they were to be sent there only if there was no room in the county gaols. This letter became a fundamental point in Bentham's indictment of the government and must be quoted at length. Portland wrote:

I understand the object of these Acts [of 1779 and 1794] to be, that such Penitentiary Houses should be used, principally as receptacles for such transportable Convicts as the several Jails of the respective Counties cannot contain, from the time of receiving sentence, till an opportunity may offer for their being transported . . . I am inclined to think it would

---

[14] D. Collins, *An Account of the English Colony in New South Wales*, 2 vols. (London, 1798–1802).

be very inexpedient to move such persons from the County Gaols unless the crowded state of those Gaols should render it absolutely necessary.

The Duke justified this policy by arguing, first, that if the county gaols were under-used it would 'check that spirit of improvement which now so universally prevails'; and, secondly, that the expense of prisoners in the national penitentiary would be 'borne by Government, instead of being defrayed by the respective Counties'.[15] The Home Office wanted to shift the financial burden from national taxes for which they were answerable to the poor rate for which they were not. And their interpretation of the legislation was certainly perverse; neither Howard's nor Bentham's Act can reasonably be read as setting up a temporary receptacle. Both their penitentiaries were to be idealistic experiments heralding a new era in penal policy. Bentham was later to dissect both the Home Office points at length, but at the time he kept his indignation largely to himself. The letter was not formally considered by the Treasury for five months, but King made no secret of it. On one of his visits to the Home Office in October, Bentham was received in a waiting-room. King was summoned away on other business, but before leaving, he pressed into Bentham's hands a book of manuscript letters, asking him to read it; he was told that he was allowed to take notes. In this book he found the offending letter. It was very difficult to reconcile this seeming open helpfulness with his theory of secret conspiracy. Bentham therefore ascribed it to King's incompetence, he had 'blabbed' and indiscretion was in any case no proof of innocence.[16]

However, the real obstacle to the panopticon was not confused thinking in the Home Office. The rock on which it foundered at this crucial stage was yet again aristocratic dislike of the chosen site. Bentham continued to hope that he would be able to build on Tothill Fields. He had been assured by Long that the Grosvenor opposition would be without effect. In December 1799 he sent a most ill-advised letter to Lord Belgrave asking him to use his influence with the Dean to persuade him to withdraw his opposition to enclosure. This request was accompanied by the threat to build his great penal structure next to Belgrave's garden wall, for only there could the foundations be solidly laid. It

[15] *Correspondence (CW)*, vi. 261.    [16] UC cxxi. 10.

seemed obvious to Bentham that it would be in Belgrave's interest to use his influence to ensure that another site was made available, particularly as he promised to put no obstacle in the way of Belgrave's plans to develop the neighbourhood. It was perhaps an indication of Bentham's relegation since 1792 that while Lord Spencer spoke and wrote to him, Lord Belgrave did not deign to communicate directly. His agent Mr Boodle answered for him in February 1800, writing that Bentham's plans would be destructive to the peace of his house and to his plans for the neighbourhood and that he was totally opposed to them. At the beginning of March, Bentham gave Boodle an ultimatum: 'I am . . . taking measures for setting down the building on the spot already pointed out.'[17] He delivered the letter by hand and was able to discuss the matter with Boodle. At that interview, Boodle told him that Lord Belgrave had been promised that the land would not be used for its only lawful purpose, that is for a penitentiary.[18]

The Treasury seemed to be speaking with two voices. There was total inaction on the matter of the site, but a decision was finally taken on the number of convicts to be accommodated. An official letter from Charles Long informed Bentham that 'the proposed Building of a Panopticon is to be calculated to accommodate Two Thousand Persons'.[19] Bentham had got his way and he was anxious to press on and negotiate the final terms of his contract. He wanted it phrased so as to leave open the question of the exact site in order to put pressure on Lord Belgrave and the Dean to release the waste of Tothill Fields. He also wanted more money, both for the building to accommodate twice the number and for the annual allowance payable by the government for each prisoner. He argued that the amounts must be calculated to take account of the rise in prices since 1792. His attempts to discuss these matters with Long met with evasion and he became increasingly suspicious that obstacles were being deliberately put in his way. In his later account, he related how he showed the official letter to Boodle to prove the government's determination to go ahead. But Boodle told him gently that it would make no difference; and a few days later he came up to

[17] *Correspondence* (*CW*), vi. 248.
[18] UC cxx. 24.
[19] *Correspondence* (*CW*), vi. 279.

him in the street and said: *'there was nobody but must sympathize with me.'*[20] Despite this, Bentham found it impossible to credit that the Treasury would betray him; he had right, reason, and Evan Nepean on his side. He was full of hopeful plans for his building, trying to persuade Long to allow him to seize an opportunity to buy a supply of almost incombustible wood for the floors of the prison; but he got no answer. He began again haunting the corridors of the Treasury, desperate to discuss the implications of the decision to build for 2,000 and to settle the details of the contract so that the building could be started that year. Long was as anxious to avoid Bentham as Bentham was to corner him. He was safe in his room but he had to emerge sometimes, and one day in April Bentham caught him flying past in the passage through the Treasury from Whitehall to the park. Bentham described later the use he made of this opportunity:

When first I spied him his pace was not a slow one: the sight of me did not slacken it. Accosting him immediately I entered upon the topic. . . . He ran and I ran: in this way we continued both running and me talking . . . I with my hand on the skirt of his coat . . . till we reached his chamber, into which I rushed with him as the besiegers will sometimes do with the besieged, after an engagement before the gates . . . His evil genius had betrayed him to his pursuer.

At any mention of Lord Belgrave, Long became impatient and agitated, and falling back on another device of the harried bureaucrat, he insisted that he was willing to consider views only if they were submitted in writing. Bentham must produce a Memorial. Bentham begged for another interview to discuss the contents and object of such a memorial. Long recoiled:

No—no—no: was the answer—not in words only but in the much more expressive and decisive language of voice and gesture. Another moment, and I should have been pushed out—I went out—and the door was clapt to in my face. What was to be done now? I was thunderstruck, dejected, confounded.[21]

So Bentham wrote a long, closely reasoned Memorial in which he argued for more land and more money.[22] He emphasized that

[20] UC cxx. 25, Bentham's emphasis.
[21] UC cxxi. 90–1.
[22] Reprinted in *Correspondence* (*CW*), vi. 471–85. Evan Nepean's copy of this Memorial is at BL Add. MS. 33122, along with copies of Bentham's

the $53\frac{1}{2}$ acres of the Salisbury estate was quite inadequate for his purposes, especially when the need for the subsidiary establishments for discharged prisoners was taken into account. At the very least he would need about 110 acres. This could be obtained partly by buying Mr Wise's land, which would add another $26\frac{1}{2}$ acres, leaving a shortfall of between 30 and 40 acres. This, Bentham was still trying to persuade the government, could be made up from the enclosure of the Tothill Fields waste. In his attempts to get Long to consider these issues, Bentham again appealed to Nepean for help. The contrast between the two secretaries was marked. Nepean regarded Bentham with affection and respect and went to very considerable lengths to resolve his problems. He was willing to act as intermediary and interpreter; Bentham saw him as a powerful protector who would not have doors slammed in his face. Long did, however, try to take evasive action. Bentham described how Nepean exclaimed: 'What is to be done? says he—Mr Long actually avoids me! Astonishment was printed on his countenance.'[23] But Nepean persevered and contrived to arrange a meeting with Long and White to resolve the issues. This meeting took place on 10 June 1800. Bentham believed that at long last hard decisions would be taken. He arrived with a heavy heart and had to wait outside while Long, White, and Nepean discussed his business. When he was called in: 'I found three long formal faces, to which I added a fourth, doubtless the longest of the four.' Long was 'in a state of visible uneasiness', his manner cold and discouraging. When the question of the Memorial was brought up, he denied having received any paper that could justly be described as a Memorial. At this point Nepean intervened and it was he who told Bentham that his demands would have to be presented in a shortened form on no more that one sheet of paper and that the terms must be made explicit and the amounts of money involved set out clearly. Nepean seems to have been acting as an interpreter of the Treasury's thinking and attempting to instruct his friend how he could best act to achieve his ends. But Bentham's hopes that the meeting would be decisive were shattered, the only upshot was that he had to submit another Memorial. He felt that

correspondence with the administration among some of Lord Pelham's papers concerned with prisons and police in London.

[23] UC cxx. 408.

the situation was out of his control and that he had suffered a major reverse; the terms were total capitulation, worse that those granted to the Carthaginians: 'in the fate of Carthage I read mine: and I read the fate of the Panopticon in the fate of Carthage.' He was reduced to 'the imbecility of childhood'.[24] In a letter he drafted, but did not send, to Nepean, he reveals his total dependence on his friend:

Did not you offer before them to draw up my *Memorial* for me? . . . Do so then:—it will not only afford me my best, not to say my only, chance—but even be the least troublesome course to yourself . . . you must be *known* to have drawn it . . . *You* think they mean to carry the business through: I am very glad you do: it was my only hope.[25]

However, Bentham recovered his nerve, set to work and abridged his Memorial, and sent it, shorn of verbiage and justification, to the Treasury on 19 June. It was barely a page long, it set out the changes he thought should be made in the financial terms, taking account of the doubling of the number of prisoners, the rise in prices of building materials, labour, and provisions, and the compensation that he considered due to him because of the change in the site from Battersea to Millbank. And he repeated his request for a new bill to acquire the requisite portion of Tothill Fields.

For once the administration acted with expedition. Within a month, the Treasury reported to the House of Commons that the penitentiary business had been delayed by Mr Bentham's increase in terms and that his Memorial was under consideration. Bentham was outraged; he had been outmanœuvred by Mr Long. He came to believe that the offer of 2,000 convicts was all part of a deep-laid plot designed 'to deceive and ruin me'.[26] He was convinced that he had been trapped into suggesting an increase in terms to give the Treasury an excuse to abandon the panopticon. The Treasury report to the Commons which, according to Bentham, neither Rose nor Long dared set their name to, was an example of sophistry and equivocation that 'might have commanded a premium from the Academy of Ignatius Loyola'.[27] Nepean, he believed, had been trifled with and deceived, he had

---

[24] UC cxxi. 137–41.    [25] Ibid. 144, Bentham's emphasis.
[26] Ibid. 252.    [27] Ibid. 165.

thought well of Long and had hoped to convert him, but he had not had Bentham's experience of the Treasury's perfidy and deviousness.[28]

After this 'anonymous' report to the House of Commons, the Treasury again moved with speed. In the following month, August, the Treasury Board again considered the matter and on the advice of the Home Office decided that: 'It may be advisable at the present time to relinquish the plan altogether.' But if the penitentiary were to be built, it should be on a reduced scale for only 500 prisoners by way of experiment; the money allowed to Bentham for the building was to be reduced accordingly. The reasons given for this decision were, first, the improved state of the colony in New South Wales, secondly, the improvements in the county gaols, and thirdly, 'the great increase of terms which Mr Bentham now proposes'.[29] In the event of the plan being abandoned, Bentham was to be offered compensation. Bentham heard of this, for him, momentous decision casually from Mr King whom he met accidentally in September. Bentham was doubtful as to the viability of a panopticon for only 500; as he pointed out, he could not pay for half a deputy, half a chaplain, or half a doctor, and the cost of the building would not be proportionately reduced. However, he was not given a chance to refuse; this last decision of Pitt's administration was not officially conveyed to him until it was out of office. In March 1801 a month after Pitt's resignation, Charles Long, in the task of clearing out his desk, saw fit to write to Bentham conveying the decision taken eight months before:

I am commanded by their Lordships to desire you will state, under what terms you are willing to Contract for building a Penitentiary House for *500 Persons* and for maintaining the Convicts, if the measure should be resolved upon: and if . . . the plan should be relinquished altogether, my Lords *desire you will inform them* what compensation you conceive yourself entitled to for your expenses and Loss of Time.[30]

Bentham was again outraged at what he stigmatized as this 'insidious' letter. In his 'last stroke of this picture of the Treasury', Bentham accused Long of deliberate procrastination; this vital

---

[28] UC cxvi. 409.   [29] *Correspondence (CW)*, vi. 352.
[30] Ibid. 383, Long's emphasis.

decision saw the light of day only because the change of government necessarily entailed the clearing of the Augean stables of
accumulated years of idleness:

> by the imperative of inexorable necessity heartened . . . in some degree
> by the intervening oblivion and amnesty of eight months, Mr Long took
> heart of grace . . . planted himself behind the screen [of the Treasury
> Board] and from that station of security and springing like a tygre from
> the jungle discharged upon me this *missive*.[31]

According to Bentham this letter showed an undisguised
resolution to relinquish the establishment; the proposal for 2,000
had served to extract a pretence to excuse this and the offer of
compensation was a cloak for injustice. Pride and caution, the
product of hard-won experience, prevented Bentham from
claiming compensation at this time. He imagined Mr Long and
Mr King, 'figuring to themselves the beggar Mr Bentham lying at
the bottom of the Treasury steps, a cap in hand ready and
anxious to receive into it such compensation'. He had no doubt
that his claim would be treated with the 'explicitness, candour,
civility, humanity, justice, and above all . . . dispatch' that he had
experienced over the past eight years.[32] And he made the legal
point that the Treasury would have to get Parliamentary sanction
for any payment and that would mean Bentham co-operating
with Pitt, Rose, and Long to petition for it: 'Torture has not been
in use since James the First's time: and nothing short of it would
have compelled me.'[33] He would not sink so low as to associate
himself with such men:

> I am not without my pride . . . I must have sunk in my own eyes before I
> could submit to rank myself in the same class or species of men as a Mr
> Rose, a Mr Long, a Mr Baldwin or a Duke of Portland . . . A burthen to
> my country I would not be made . . . But their only expedient for dis-
> burthening themselves from shame was by making me a burthen to the
> country—such a burthen as themselves.[34]

When Pitt resigned, not all the members of his administration
went with him, but there was a clean sweep at the Treasury.
Henry Addington, the Speaker of the House, replaced Pitt as
First Lord and Prime Minister; Addington's brother, John Hiley

---

[31] UC cxxi. 175, Bentham's emphasis.     [32] Ibid. 313, 319.
[33] Ibid. 321.     [34] Ibid. 331.

Addington, replaced Rose; and Nicholas Vansittart, Long. Abbot was elected Speaker in Addington's place. By July, the Duke of Portland had moved from the Home Office and was succeeded by Lord Pelham, a man not of high ability, but good-natured and prudent. To Pelham, Bentham was to address his denunciations of Pitt's government. But John King remained at the Home Office to become, much to Bentham's chagrin, Pelham's trusted adviser. Bentham's old adversary, Lord Spencer, left the Admiralty; but his staunch friend, Evan Nepean, remained. Bentham seems to have believed that this new government would be hostile to its predecessor and that it would signal new beginnings and new hope for the panopticon. But in this he misunderstood the political situation. Pitt had not been destroyed by defeat at an election or in the House of Commons, but had fallen only because he had failed to persuade George III to agree to the emancipation of the Catholics as part of the deal for the union with Ireland. The withdrawal of the King's confidence was to prove temporary and in the meantime, Addington's government was dependent on Pitt's neutrality, if not his support. And Bentham was soon to find that Addington's administration was as adept at procrastination as Pitt's and as disinclined to build the panopticon or to inform him definitely that the project must be abandoned. Bentham was 53 in March 1801, at an age when many men look forward to retirement rather than to undertaking the burden of arduous new duties. Yet he remained determined to spend his old age as a prison governor. In a manuscript note he asserted:

My faculties are certainly not what they might and would have been had they not been pounded and crushed by the innumerable and indescribable oppressions sustained in the course of so many anxious years... I do not yet perceive them to be in any such degree debilitated... but that with the help of an engine of such matchless and unexampled force... I may yet be found not altogether incapable to fill the situation of a Jailer.... Certainly neither can my faculties be so serviceable nor will my remaining years be so many, as they might have been, had it not been for Mr Pitt, Mr Rose and Mr Long.[35]

[35] UC cxxi. 297–8. John Hiley Addington (1759–1818), Secretary to the Treasury, 1801–2; Joint Paymaster-General, 1803–4; Commissioner Board of Control, 1806–7; Under-Secretary of State for Home Affairs, 1812–18. Thomas Pelham (1756–1826), Baron Pelham, 1801; 2nd Earl of Chichester, 1805;

Failing to get satisfaction from the new government, Bentham gave up trying to persuade and ingratiate himself and became aggressive. He was determined to defend his reputation from the slurs cast on it in the official record, and, by June 1801, he was threatening to publish his wrongs. This seems to have had some effect, for on 9 July he was granted another interview at the Treasury. Ominously for the panopticon, the old and new administrators were co-operating closely. Bentham had been summoned to the Treasury to speak with Nicholas Vansittart with whom he had been corresponding on the subject of his annuity note plan. After waiting an hour, 'I observed the late Secretary of the Treasury, Mr Long, going into the apartment of Mr Hiley Addington. I took notice of an appearance of alarm and anxiety upon his countenance.'[36] After waiting another two or three hours, he was summoned into Addington's, not Vansittart's, room where he found Long looking unusually sad, grave, and anxious. Despite the provocation of being unjustly accused of impatience, Bentham contrived to keep his temper. The two secretaries then brought the conversation round to the question of the penitentiary, and Bentham slowly realized that he was being offered a compromise; a panopticon for 500 would be built as an experiment and he would receive liberal compensation for the reduction in numbers. Bentham responded warily, pointing out that the government was bound by the law of the land and its own engagements to build the penitentiary. But he was treated with scorn and contempt, feeling himself regarded as a mere 'ignorant bookworm'.[37] He suspected that the two officials were trying to provoke him into an outburst of anger that would provide them with an excuse to break faith with him. Although he again contrived to keep his temper, he left the meeting deeply suspicious of the good faith of the new administration and convinced that the two secretaries were fellow conspirators, that their offer was a sham, and that Hiley Addington would find the promise to Lord Belgrave as insurmountable an obstacle as

---

Commissioner Board of Control, 1801–2; Home Secretary, 1801–3; Chancellor of Duchy of Lancaster, 1803–4. Nicholas Vansittart (1766–1851), cr. Baron Bexley, 1823; Secretary to the Treasury, 1801–4; Chancellor of the Exchequer, 1812–23; Chancellor of Duchy of Lancaster, 1823–8.

[36] Ibid. 334.
[37] Ibid. 342.

had Charles Long. As the weeks passed his suspicious were confirmed by meeting yet again with the familiar excuses and procrastination. By September Vansittart at the Treasury had still failed to find an opportunity of mentioning the matter to Lord Pelham at the Home Office. And later in the year, though Wilberforce was urging Lord Pelham to consider the question, the administration had still failed to come to any decision.

By the beginning of 1802 Bentham had determined to publish his grievances. It was to be an extraordinarily creative year in his life. Not only were two pamphlets printed, but voluminous manuscripts and copies of further works bear witness to his industry. Obsessively he went back, recording, analysing, and giving his version of the events of the past. These vituperative memoirs had a dual object: to destroy the reputation of Pitt's administration and to frighten Addington's into building the panopticon. His friends, Wilberforce, Romilly, Dumont, Abbot, and Nepean were recruited for the fray. His old ally and convert, Sir Charles Bunbury, was again pressed into service; his old acquaintance, Lord Auckland, disappointed a few years earlier in his ambition to become Pitt's father-in-law, again poured his oil on troubled waters. But Bentham failed in both these objects. Pitt's reputation never stood higher than in 1802 and in the next year Addington's administration finally plucked up courage to abandon the penitentiary.

Bentham's writings in 1802 took the form of letters to Lord Pelham.[38] Their theme was to refute the arguments put forward

---

[38] The published works are:

(1) *Letter to Lord Pelham giving a comparative view of the system of penal colonization in New South Wales and the home penitentiary system, Prescribed by two Acts of Parliament of the Years 1794 and 1799*, and *Second Letter to Lord Pelham, in continuation of the comparative view of the system of penal colonization in New South Wales, and the home penitentiary system, Prescribed by two Acts of Parliament of the Years 1794 and 1799*. Both of these letters were privately printed during 1802 and the last page of the second is dated 17 Dec. 1802. Bentham's original title was *Panopticon versus New South Wales*, and this title was revived when the pamphlet containing both letters was finally published in 1812. It was subsequently published in Bowring iv. 173–248. (2) *A Plea for the Constitution: Shewing the Enormities Committed to the oppression of British subjects, Innocent as well as Guilty, in breach of Magna Charta, the Petition of Right, the Habeas Corpus Act, and the Bill of Rights: as likewise of the several transportation acts; in and by the design, foundation, and government of the penal colony of New South Wales: including an inquiry into the right of the Crown to legislate without Parliament in Trinidad, and other British colonies.* Bentham's

by Pitt's administration for relinquishing the penitentiary and to attack the constitutional assumptions that underlay their actions. Only a small portion of these writings has been published under the titles of *Panopticon versus New South Wales* and *A Plea for the Constitution*. *Panopticon versus New South Wales* consisted of the first two letters to Lord Pelham and in them Bentham argued against the Home Office contention that the improvement in the colony made the building of the penitentiary unnecessary. It launched an attack on the whole concept of transportation both in theory and in practice. Bentham cunningly used the facts revealed in David Collins's panegyric account of New South Wales as ammunition for a horrific description of conditions prevalent in the colony. Transportation was branded as inferior to penitentiary discipline on the grounds of inspection, reformation, example, humanity, religion, and economy. He also argued that the government was illegally, unjustly, and unconstitutionally detaining prisoners after their terms had expired. This attack on the Australian penal colony made almost no impact at the time, partly because Bentham was seen to be an interested party, and it has been almost ignored in the context of penal history.[39] And his *Plea for the Constitution*, which revealed that the British government was acting illegally in setting up and administering its colonies, hardly fared better. In this pamphlet, Bentham undertook to prove that the government had no powers and so were acting in breach of all the most sacred cows of the Constitution, Magna Carta, the Petition of Right, the Habeas Corpus Act, and the Bill of Rights. The irony of a thinker with dangerous radical views defending the Constitution from the establishment of Honourable and Right Honourable gentlemen was not lost on Bentham. He confessed to 'a whoreson kind of

alternative title was 'The True Bastille, shewing the outrages offered to Law, Justice and Humanity by Mr Pitt and his Associates in the foundation and management of the penal colony of New South Wales'; this title was not used. The pamphlet was printed privately in 1803 and published in 1812 with *Panopticon versus New South Wales*. It was subsequently published in Bowring, iv. 249–84. Bentham had tried to publish both these polemical pamphlets in 1803 but they were rejected by his publishers (see *Correspondence* (*CW*), vii. 206). Most of the relevant MSS are at UC cxx. and cxxi.

[39] The Webbs date the beginning of outspoken condemnation of the transportation system to 1836. S. and B. Webb, *English Prisons* (London, 1922), 44–5.

tenderness' for the Constitution.[40] And he was amused as well as incensed that those who so smugly paid tribute to the glories of the British Constitution had driven a coach and horses through it. He argued that ministers were not only open to impeachment but also, under the Habeas Corpus Acts, to the penalties of Praemunire. In a letter to his brother, Bentham contemplated with glee the prospect of the Duke of Portland, Mr King, and Mr Baldwin being liable to imprisonment for life and forfeiture of all their property at the suit of any convict illegally detained after the expiration of his term.[41] Romilly, consulted on this point of law, was startled to find that Bentham was correct. And Bentham was convinced that he had manufactured a bomb that would blow up government and penal colony together; it would set 'the whole Colony in a flame' and might lead to 'the evacuation of that scene of wickedness and wretchedness'.[42]

But again he was to be disappointed. According to Hume, although Bentham's animadversions produced a certain uneasiness in Australia, they had 'no perceptible influence on the course of political life'.[43] Convicts from Botany Bay did not bring actions in the courts against the great men at the Home Office. Bentham may have been right in law but the ultimate sanction was in the hands of the House of Commons and if the House were disinclined to bestir itself ministers would remain unrebuked and go unpunished. Bentham understood this enough to press his friends to raise the matter in the House. In April 1802 he approached the famous guardian of the Constitution, Sir William Pulteney, asking him to bring to the notice of Parliament the whole question of the unconstitutional actions of the late government, in particular the exercise of the dispensing power. But Pulteney politely declined to take any initiative.[44] By the summer Bentham was asking Dumont to sound out members of the Opposition to see if they would take up the question. In September, writing to Charles Abbot, he depicts himself as a crusader against perfidy, treachery, and oppression, as a hunter

---

[40] *Correspondence* (*CW*), vii. 94.
[41] Ibid. 89.
[42] Ibid. 90.
[43] Hume, *Historical Studies*, 16 (1974–5), 40.
[44] *Correspondence* (*CW*), vii. 16–19. Sir William Pulteney (1729–1805), independent MP. He had gained his reputation as a defender of the Constitution by his opposition to Charles James Fox's East India Bill in 1783.

running down his quarry. By this time Addington was confounded with Pitt, both men hoped he would, 'die broken
hearted, like a rat in a hole'.[45] The Opposition showed a certain
interest; according to rumour Charles Fox himself became
'a zealous Panoptician'.[46] But a full-scale political attack on
ministers failed to materialize. Bunbury worked hard to interest
ministers in the penitentiary scheme but the best he could achieve
in Parliament was a debate on transportation in which the
panopticon was favourably mentioned.[47]

This lack of political interest can easily be explained and had
little to do with the merits of Bentham's case. Issues of peace and
war, the incompetence of Addington in comparison with Pitt,
and the possible return of Pitt as Prime Minister absorbed the
attention of the political nation. And wrongs to criminals are
never a favourite political issue. As Romilly cynically but realis-
tically told Bentham: 'neither Opposition, nor Ministry nor the
public at large care a straw about Convicts—or would manifest
any sort of resentment for any injustice that ever has been or
could be done to them.'[48] Also the very fact that time had gone
by made it impossible to abandon the colony of New South
Wales. Bentham sent his 'Letters to Lord Pelham' to the new
Attorney-General, Spencer Perceval, but although he found
Bentham's logic incontrovertible, he confided privately to Abbot
that the great obstacle to building a penitentiary was the consideration 'of leaving the Botany Bay Colony in the state to
which we have brought it' for it would continue to be a source of
great expense whether or not it were used for transportation.
Perceval also took exception to the tone of Bentham's communications, 'which I think his friends must allow, is not the best
formed to secure *dispassionate* attention'.[49]

This criticism was echoed by his friends, who united in trying
to restrain the more extreme manifestations of Bentham's wrath.
By the beginning of 1803 the first two 'Letters to Lord Pelham'

---

[45] Ibid. 114.
[46] Ibid. 200.
[47] Ibid. 189–90.
[48] Ibid. 100.
[49] Ibid. 180–1, Perceval's emphasis. Spencer Perceval (1762–1812), Solicitor-
General, 1801–2; Attorney-General, 1802–6; Chancellor of the Exchequer,
1807–9, and Prime Minister, 1809–12. He has the melancholy distinction of being
the only Prime Minister in British history to have been assassinated.

had been printed but in February they were refused for publication. A mass of even more vituperative polemic was lying waiting in Bentham's papers, some of it already marked up for the printer. During the final months, Bentham launched a last attempt to force the administration to honour its commitments. In January he suggested to Bunbury that the Attorney-General might be given full powers to settle the business, thus bypassing the normal procedures of government, in particular the Home Office where the devious Mr King still held sway. Lord Pelham, 'After kicking awhile . . . has sunk entirely into the pocket of Mr King.'[50] Nothing came of this. Bentham still hoped that ministers would be intimidated by his revelations and he also tried to shame them into action by exposing sodomy in the hulks: 'infinitely more shocking to John Bull than the most exquisite miseries.' As he wrote to the devout Wilberforce: 'from the very nature of the receptacle, *such things ever must be*. Such are the abominations of which Lord Grosvenor has *obtained*, and Lord Pelham and Mr Addington *decreed*, the perpetuation and diffusion.' And he begs Wilberforce and Thornton to join with Bunbury in an approach to the minister. Are they, he asks, to be 'good samaritans, or are they Priest and Levite?'[51]

With war imminent and Napoleon's army gathering at the channel ports, ministers were not very approachable. In May, Bunbury was writing to Bentham that he had no information as to the penitentiary: 'I . . . have been like many others waiting in daily Expectation of hearing whether we were to be at Peace or War—before that Great Question is decided, Ministers will not talk on any other Subject.'[52] Ten days later, on 18 May 1803, England was again at war with France. In early June the faithful Bunbury alone, unsupported by Wilberforce or Thornton, at last got audience with Pelham and finally obtained a definite answer. The panopticon was not to be built. 'He heard my Arguments in Favour of your Plan very patiently . . . but at last he said, that the Judges did not appear to wish it to be carried into Effect, and he did not suppose Mr Addington would furnish the money necessary to proceed with it at present.'[53]

[50] *Correspondence* (*CW*), vii. 187.
[51] Ibid. 208, 212–14, Bentham's emphasis. Viscount Belgrave had succeeded his father as Earl Grosvenor in 1802.
[52] Ibid. 225–6.        [53] Ibid. 240.

This answer came as no surprise to Bentham, though he bitterly accused Pelham of chicanery and being under the sway of the Grosvenor family. He also at long last abandoned hope, recognizing that for the time being at least there was no chance of the panopticon being built. He stopped his campaign; the first two 'Letters to Lord Pelham' and the *Plea for the Constitution* were not published until 1812 and the major part of his great polemic has remained undisturbed and virtually unread among his papers. Yet the years 1801 to 1803 were of vital importance in Bentham's life, marking the beginning of new ventures and the end of old friendships. His friends among the political establishment had, with varying degrees of success, urged caution. Even the loyal Bunbury found it impossible to believe that Lord Pelham was guilty of 'practising Evasions, and Artifices which would disgrace not only a Minister's Secretary, but even his Porter'.[54] And up to June 1803, he was warning Bentham not to publish his attacks. Charles Abbot was predictably caustic. He wrote: 'Of all the invectives and threats, I have not communicated one word. Of the Facts I have communicated so much as in my Judgment I thought desireable.'[55] Wilberforce reacted more emotionally to the vilification of his friends; he admitted that the government had procrastinated but warned Bentham that he would get little credence or sympathy; his indignation spills over into abbreviations and capitals:

But can you doubt, that it will be with the World a suffict. answer . . . that Mr Pit havg. the whole Machine of Govt. to superintend, during a period, such as never before was witnessed in the History of this Country, may be forgiven if he neglected one Subject, tho. of Importance, which was not within his immediate Department.

He leapt also to the defence of Lord Belgrave and his religion:

Ld Belg one of the best and most amiable Young Men in this Kingdom . . . you speak with Levity at least if not ridicule of his religious Character . . . I must condemn the Style and Spirit in which you have resented the Error of a most respectable and truly amiable Character on whom . . . this Country may look . . . for . . . the Elevatn of the Moral Standard and the preservation of our Manners and Habits from that taint of practical Infidelity . . . which is the true Jacobinical Contagion.

[54] Ibid. 102.    [55] Ibid. 131.

What must have been most irritating of all, Wilberforce preached Christian resignation to Bentham, praying that he might find patience to bear ill-usage and solace for his sufferings in the consolations of Religion.[56]

Romilly, too, frankly criticized Bentham's levity. In an unprinted preface to the *Plea* that he sent to Romilly, Bentham had accused Pitt of destroying the Constitution: 'To Pitt the second was reserved the glory of conquering, if not Britain herself, that constitution which is her choicest treasure.'[57] Romilly flatly contradicts him: 'The truth is that notwithstg what has been done at Botany bay the Brit Constitn is not conquered but still remains as it did.'[58] Romilly also warned Bentham that he was running the risk of action for libel: 'I have received your papers, and I see no objection to any part of them, but their violence. . . . That the pamphlet is, in point of law, a libel on the duke, and the more a libel for being true, cannot, I think, be doubted.' He too advised against publication: 'I should suppose that ministers were a kind of beings whom such a publication was likely to render implacable.'[59] This threat of libel alarmed Bentham and was probably instrumental in preventing the more vituperative papers being widely circulated.

Bentham's friends were certainly correct in warning him that it was unlikely that any attack on William Pitt would be given a fair hearing. Bentham could hardly have chosen a worse time for his assault. Pitt's departure from office had enhanced rather than diminished his reputation. His abilities shone the more bright in comparison with Addington's lack-lustre performance. And his temporary absence had forced the world to reappraise his achievements; they appeared formidable. He was widely seen as the saviour of the nation and as its one sure guardian against the perils of war and revolution. In May 1802, at the very time when Bentham was penning his invective, the great banquet was held in Pitt's honour where for the first time George Canning's verses were sung:

> And Oh! if again the rude whirlwind should rise,
> The dawnings of peace should fresh darkness deform,

---

[56] *Correspondence* (*CW*), vii. 117–23.     [57] UC cxvi. 478.
[58] *Correspondence* (*CW*), vii. 202.     [59] Ibid. 154–5.

The regrets of the good and the fears of the wise,
Shall turn to the Pilot that weathered the storm.[60]

And it was his old friend Earl Spencer, for whom Pitt had sacrificed the panopticon, who rose to propose the toast to 'The Pilot that weathered the storm'. It was unlikely, at this time of danger abroad and uncertainty at home, that Pitt's position as a national hero would be endangered by Bentham's fulminations.

The years between 1799 and 1803 marked a turning-point in Bentham's life; old friendships cooled. He could not forgive Wilberforce for his apostasy and never entirely trusted him again. He wrote to Dumont of 'a not unamusing or altogether unedifying contrast . . . between the ardour of his piety and the icy coldness of his love of public justice'.[61] And politically, if not personally, his and Romilly's paths began to diverge until in 1818, during the Westminster election, he publicly attacked Romilly's candidature.[62] But despite his growing disillusionment with the process of government, Bentham's overriding ambition to achieve practical reforms had remained unquenched. He tried to interest the government in an annuity stock note scheme that he believed would be the answer to the pressing problem of controlling the currency. And in January 1801, at the nadir of his relations with the Treasury, he had sent to Rose a pamphlet on circulating annuities. Rose replied courteously, paying graceful tribute to Bentham's 'Talents and Labor'.[63] Less happily, Bentham also turned his passion for improvement on the time-honoured practices of the House of Commons. He wrote to the then Speaker, Henry Addington, suggesting that large notice-boards should be erected in the Chamber; one displaying the subject currently under debate; the others a Table of the Rules of Debate, and a Table of Improprieties. The Speaker would be supplied with a rod and could then, with gentleness and dignity, restore order in the House by pointing to the rule infringed or the impropriety committed.[64] These somewhat ludicrous suggestions drew a measured rebuke from his stepbrother, Charles Abbot,

[60] Robin Reilly, *Pitt the Younger* (London, 1978), 313.
[61] *Correspondence* (*CW*), vii. 150.
[62] Romilly, *Memoirs of the Life of Sir Samuel Romilly Written by Himself* (London, 1840), ii. 512.
[63] *Correspondence* (*CW*), vi. 374.
[64] Ibid. 336.

who warned him that he was in danger of acquiring 'the character of a *Faiseur de projets* with people who are not too much disposed to carry into effect the one for which they are pledged'.[65]

Happily for Bentham, while the fortunes of the panopticon waned, new horizons were opening. At the beginning of 1802, Dumont was arranging the publication of the *Traités de législation civile et pénale* in Paris; this work immediately enhanced Bentham's reputation and enabled him to enjoy the unusual delight of basking in general admiration; an admiration that must have been balm to his soul after the humiliations he had suffered. His joy was apparent in his letters to Dumont: 'You have set me a strutting, my dear Dumont, like a fop in a Coat spick-and-span from the Taylors.'[66] And he was also coming to the gratifying realization that he was the leader of a band of disciples. 'Benthamiste?—what sort of an animal is that?' he asked, '. . . As to Religion—to be sure a new Religion would be an odd sort of thing without a name.' In the autumn of 1802 he took advantage of the precarious peace to visit Paris. The *Traités* helped Bentham to become a revered figure on the Continent. He was to be praised in the unlikely context of Napoleon's *Code pénal* for his 'traité récent et estimé', and his 'profondes méditations'.[67] He returned to philosophical speculation by starting his great study on judicial evidence. It is as though, after creating his picture of the Treasury, he was able to turn his back on his disappointments and free himself to embark on new ventures.

The significance of Bentham's account of the events surrounding the collapse of the panopticon has only recently been recognized and that only partially. Hume's clear exposition discusses some of the issues but is necessarily limited in scope. The whole of the work has not yet been studied and the text is still available only in the confused bundles of papers in the Bentham archive. Hume concentrates his attention on the Constitutional point of the relations between the legislature and the executive, but there are other strands which Bentham was later to use to construct his theories of constitutional government and democracy. In all, they spell out the lessons that Bentham learnt from his experiences. The main theme was, as Hume emphasizes,

---

[65] *Correspondence* (*CW*), vi. 342.
[66] Ibid. vii. 28.
[67] Ibid. 65. *Code pénal* (Paris, 1810), 62.

the absolute supremacy of the legislature over the executive and the wickedness and illegality of ministers using their power to nullify its will. But there were also several subsidiary themes that foreshadow the principles of the *Constitutional Code*. In these writings, Bentham maintained that government should be organized so as to counter the sinister influence of the aristocracy and of officials. It should be open, for secrecy was abhorrent and led to inefficiency and waste. Individual officials should be directly responsible for their actions and should not be allowed to shelter behind the decisions of boards or committees. He dealt with the problems of sinecure and salary and of officials wielding illegitimate power by manipulating the information on which decisions were made. Finally, he discussed public opinion; this is of especial interest given the central position that the public opinion tribunal holds in his constitutional theory.

The serious content of these writings can be overlooked in enjoyment of the magnificent invective with which Bentham lambasted the administration; if he had given free rein to this aspect of his genius, he could have become one of the greatest of political pamphleteers. In an echo of Mark Antony's funeral oration over the gory corpse of Julius Caesar, Bentham repeatedly pilloried 'the Honourable and Right Honourable Gentlemen' guilty of the murder of the panopticon; guilty of 'remorseless and persevering duplicity . . . cold unprovoked barbarity';[68] of perfidy, peculation, forgery, and murder. His vituperation is imbued with a sense of personal humiliation and betrayal; he was the sacrificial victim, a lamb to be devoured, he was a poor, unprotected worm.[69] His attempts to extract information from Long was 'begging mercy to *Blue Beard*: it was pleading for justice to Robespierre'.[70] Bentham seems to have been genuinely convinced that Pitt, Rose, and Long were trying to contrive his death, to murder him by legal means by a slow poisoning of the mind:

Had the scene laid in Italy, the prosecution of this design would have cost some Right Honourable or Honourable Gentleman a good dinner or at least a cup of chocolate, besides the characteristic ingredient in it . . . As it is the attempt has not cost so much as a cup of chocolate to any Right Honourable or Honourable Gentleman . . . but then . . . it has

---

[68] UC cxxi. 303.          [69] UC cxx. 35, 166.          [70] Ibid. 368.

failed . . . though unfortunately as to the destruction of eight years of the most valuable part of the life of the destined victim, its success has been but too manifest and complete—Yes, my Lord, they have murdered my best days.[71]

Bentham was convinced that the original source of his misfortunes was Pitt's betrayal of the Battersea site to his friend Lord Spencer. The Prime Minister had asked him to make his arrangements and then made it impossible for him to do so. 'In the year 1794 . . . Mr Pitt for the accommodation of his nobel colleague and table companion was prevailed upon to sell the interest which the public had in Battersea Rise for present ease.'[72] From that time Pitt was determined to give up the establishment 'and with it his honour and the authority of Parliament'. His guilt could be compared with that of Henry II in the murder of Becket—others performed the dread deed but his was the guilt.[73] Bentham interpreted the whole of his dealings with the government in the light of this belief in a deep-laid conspiracy. The 1794 Act was passed for no 'better or other intention or design than of serving as a bait for gulling me out of my money'.[74] The refusal to deprive Duncan Campbell of the contract for the hulks and the reference to the Finance Committee in 1798 were both proof of a plot to destroy the panopticon. And from the very first, the Treasury had no intention of using the Salisbury land for a penitentiary. This secret and dishonourable conduct, he insisted, was a conspiracy to obstruct the law and a deliberate waste of the public's money; and the key to all subsequent events was a clandestine assurance given to Lord Belgrave.[75]

Bentham had started his travails with a belief in the altruism of great men. Implicit in his letters to Spencer was the assumption of public virtue, that one of the greatest of pleasures was to work for the general good, and that this sentiment would be strong in statesmen. By the time Pitt's administration had finished with him, he was disillusioned and more than ever confirmed in his belief that the cause of good government could only triumph if sinister interest was strictly controlled. He had become cynically convinced of the wrong-headed selfishness of the vast majority of

---

[71] UC cxx. 466.   [72] Ibid. 458.   [73] UC cxvi. 444.
[74] UC cxx. 35.   [75] Ibid. 32, 20.

Lords, Honourable, and Right Honourable Gentlemen. Despite the purchase of the Salisbury estate it had not been settled where the panopticon was to be built, or indeed whether it was to be built at all. Bentham became assured that the Treasury officials were determined to prevent the erection of the prison. Looking back in 1802, he saw White's 'contemptuous and peremptory' refusal to obey his instructions over the contract with Lord Salisbury as the first breach of faith that brought 'the plan . . . of perfidy to light'.[76] His own involvement in the buying out of the leases was part of the plot; and the whole purchase of the estate was a job to accommodate the Marquis of Salisbury. He insisted that: 'It had been settled . . . that the land should not be bought clear of leases because it would thus have come into my hands in a state ready to be put immediately to its particularly destined use.'[77] The object of Long and White was 'to keep the business always doing and never done—to keep me in torture till they had destroyed me'. White's refusal to allow any money to be paid over for the leases until all negotiations were finalized and his insistence on immediate possession were all part of a conspiracy not only against Bentham, but 'against the peace and prosperity of eight and thirty industrious families'.[78] The very vote of the purchase money, he believed, had only been carried through Parliament without opposition because the Dean of Westminster had been given a private assurance that the penitentiary would never be built. Contemptuously, Bentham held Lord Salisbury himself blameless (despite his being Lord Chamberlain) not on the grounds of his probity but because the price for the land was not excessive and he could have done as well selling to another buyer.

The Millbank site was far from ideal for the beautiful and salubrious structure of Bentham's dreams. For one thing, it was far too small; Bentham wanted well over 100 acres and it comprised only 53. Much of the ground was a quagmire under water for most of the year and in urgent need of drainage. The acquisition of Mr Wise's land was essential, for on it were establishments for the disposal of the refuse of tallow chandlers and the boiling of putrid horse flesh and other rotting carcasses

[76] Ibid. 31–7.     [77] Ibid. 285.     [78] Ibid. 332–4.

both of which gave off 'an intolerable stench'.[79] In the ditches bubbles of gas formed, called in those days, 'bells'.[80] This would have been methane, indicative of a gross contamination of the water-table by human excrement and other waste. The site was notoriously unhealthy and it was difficult to find a place where firm foundations could be laid. These shortcomings noted at the time of purchase were amply confirmed when the building of the Millbank penitentiary was delayed by subsidence and the prison became infamous for the numbers of its inmates who died.

The site that Bentham threatened to use was on the northeastern edge of the Salisbury estate; Belgrave House was on the river just downstream. Originally Peterborough House, it was a seventeenth-century building remodelled on classical lines and had been bought by Earl Grosvenor in 1789 as a town residence for his heir, Viscount Belgrave, a young man famous for his piety and notorious for his thrift. The estate owned several of the streets around. In the early 1790s it was hoped that Lord Salisbury would develop the river frontage upstream but these plans came to nothing.[81] The Viscount and his wife had recently built a pleasure-garden in their grounds; Bentham's plans would have wrecked any pleasure or privacy. The great panopticon would have loomed over their grounds and the entrances to their house; it would have been so close, according to Bentham himself, that it might have been possible 'to have my Prisoners to shake hands with him and his lady from their windows'.[82]

Belgrave's influence was not negligible, he was very rich, very religious, and a commissioner of the Board of Control. Bentham became convinced that Belgrave's friends at the Treasury had given him a secret assurance that the penitentiary would not be built. There is contemporary evidence to support this story. Bentham wrote to Nepean at the time that he realized that Lord Belgrave believed that his opposition would prevent the penitentiary from being built.[83] There is confirmation also in the fact that the Surveyor-General's office was doing nothing whatsoever to acquire Mr Wise's land, and they were excusing their inactivity by saying that they did not believe that the Treasury Board had any desire to proceed in the business.

[79] *Correspondence (CW)*, vi. 211.     [80] UC cxxi. 156.
[81] Grosvenor Estate Minute Book, i. 59.     [82] UC cxx. 24.
[83] *Correspondence (CW)*, vi. 264.

Further confirmation of Bentham's suspicions can be found in the minutes of the Grosvenor estate, which show that by the end of 1800 they were taking for granted that the 'Ground which was purchased by Government for Mr Bentham's Penitentiary Houses will not be used for that purpose'; and that they were even contemplating purchasing the Salisbury estate themselves so as to prevent any further nuisance or injury to their interests.[84] But Lord Belgrave was considering leaving Millbank; in 1799 he was already looking for an alternative town residence and in 1801 decided in favour of Gloucester House in Mayfair.[85] Quite apart from the threat of the penitentiary, Millbank had many drawbacks. An open sewer ran into the Thames at the side of his grounds, the neighbourhood was becoming increasingly squalid, carts from the local brewers rattled past his doors, and the stench from the river was becoming ever more fetid. Belgrave House was left empty in 1805 and in 1808 there was a proposal that a tavern should be built in the gardens. No tenant could be found for the house and in 1809 it was demolished. Three years later the Millbank penitentiary was built on the site nearby, but by that time a road connecting to the new Vauxhall Bridge ran through the forecourt of the former mansion and there was no noble resident to object.

The most serious charge that Bentham brought against Pitt and his ministers was that they had illegally, indeed criminally, set aside two imperative acts of Parliament, the 1794 Penitentiary Act and the grant of £36,000 to buy the Salisbury estate and to build a penitentiary on it. Instead of implementing the will of Parliament, they had set it aside and had interpreted it to suit their own convenience. The panopticon had been treated as though it were a project 'which Gentlemen were at liberty to take up, or to leave upon the shelf, just as they happened to feel themselves disposed'.[86] And Bentham cited in support his old adversary Blackstone on the omnipotence of Parliament, which 'I acknowledge and bless and cherish as much as he or anybody.' When an Act of Parliament was turned into waste paper and the

---

[84] Grosvenor Estate Minute Book, iii. 90. In the archives and maps Belgrave House is called variously Millbank House or Grosvenor House.

[85] *Survey of London*, 39, *The Grosvenor Estate in Mayfair*, Part I (London, 1977).

[86] UC cxx. 139.

executive powers allowed to tread at pleasure on the legislature, 'the constitution is at an end'.[87] Pitt and his minions at the Treasury were guilty of complicity in this crime, but it was the Duke of Portland whom Bentham singled out for his most devastating attack. In a document entitled, 'On the Dispensing power exercised by the Duke of Portland and his Confederates'[88] he analysed the Duke's unhappy letter of 18 October 1799 in which he had conveyed his decision that the panopticon should be used only as a temporary receptacle for convicts prior to transportation, and then only when the county gaols were full.[89] Bentham argued that the Duke and Mr King were guilty of exercising a dispensing power to obstruct the implementation of an imperative Act of Parliament. Such an allegation, Bentham wrote, 'the reader will be apt to revolt from as incredible: it is as if one of those tales of Ghosts and Hobgoblins, which are told to Novel readers . . . were to be brought before Parliament . . . as if it were true'.[90] The Duke knew no 'repugnancy between his own will and that of the law . . . the proof of a blind and audacious despotism'.[91] Bentham argued that in overriding the law, the Duke had taken on himself the power to dispose of convicts. The law had laid down that convicts of all sorts should be sent to a penitentiary; the Duke's law was that no convict should be sent there except in extreme necessity. The avowed object of using the county gaols to capacity was denounced by Bentham; several times in his manuscripts he vehemently denied that the local gaols were improved and cited the notorious example of Cold-bath Fields to prove his point that even new structures were costly and uninspectable. Portland's idea of transferring the financial burden of the prisoners from national taxation to the rates was attacked as fiscally absurd as well as unconstitutional. 'Why not cost anything?—Because neither Mr King, nor the Duke of Portland . . . have to find the money for it. What the people pay, what the whole body of his Majesty's faithful subjects pays, they neither know nor care.'[92] And by his decision Portland had taken upon himself the power to transfer a burden of taxation from a fund marked out by Parliament on to the

---

[87] UC cxxi. 253.    [88] UC cxx. 570–91, in copyist's hand.
[89] See *supra*, p. 224–5 for text of this letter.    [90] UC cxx. 570.
[91] Ibid. 575.    [92] UC cxxi. 230.

overloaded contributors to the poor rate. This struck a blow at the very heart of the Constitution, the sole right of the Commons to propose new taxes.[93] Bentham emphasized the danger of creating a precedent. The authority of Parliament would be 'undermined gradually and silently for a time till an explosion comes, when it will be blown up and overthrown'. This was the road to despotism.[94]

According to Bentham's principles, legislation was an expression of the will and wisdom of Parliament; but many of his contemporaries interpreted the constitution very differently. It was widely held that legislation was an expression of the will of the executive. As Charles Abbot informed Bentham: 'nothing in which Govt. is directly or indirectly concerned will be carried through Parliament without their *cordial* support.'[95] On the different point of whether the executive had an obligation to implement their own Acts, Bentham's theories again got little support. In the eyes of his fellow politicians, the Duke of Portland's action in ignoring the 1794 Penitentiary Act was not improper, let alone illegal; any suggestion of criminality was bizarre. No member took up this point in Parliament and Bentham had to admit that even Wilberforce had 'a sort of implied notion' that Acts of Parliament were not binding on administration.[96] Long and Hiley Addington were expressing widely held assumptions when, as Bentham wrote, they treated Acts of Parliament as 'moonshine' and the idea of being obliged to implement legislation 'was rejected plainly and simply: rejected as inapplicable'.[97] These differences between Bentham's theories and those of most of his contemporaries in the political world were irreconcilable, for they stemmed from different interpretations of the Constitution. Pitt's administration worked on the unconscious assumption that it had the obligation, indeed the duty, to take decisions and to rule according to its own concept of the public good. This assumption was articulated in the twentieth century by L. S. Amery, who insisted that any British government was, and always had been, 'an independent body which on taking office assumes the responsibility of leading

---

[93] UC cxx. 575, 581.     [94] Ibid. 586.
[95] *Correspondence (CW)*, vi. 106, Abbot's emphasis.
[96] Ibid. vii. 129.     [97] UC cxxi. 343.

and directing Parliament and the nation in accordance with its own judgment and convictions'.[98] Conversely, Bentham assumed that government was an instrument responsive to the will of Parliament whose duty was to implement legislation.

Although this fundamental theoretical difference over the nature of the British Constitution was the most important issue in 'A Picture', other points of interest also emerged. His experiences taught Bentham a profound distrust of aristocratic influence and a determination to end the secrecy in which it flourished. He felt something near to personal hatred for the 'train of successive Lords', Spencer, Arden, and Belgrave, who had foiled his plans, and for Belgrave especially whose public piety exemplified the smug hypocrisy that condemned men to homosexual rape in the hulks while professing humanity and Christian beliefs. He seldom mentioned him without the adjective 'pious' attached; he was 'the Gospel-propagating Lord' who stole up the back stairs of government to whisper, *'the spot is too near me—it must not be made use of'*. And Bentham came sadly to the conclusion that 'nothing can be a matter of more profound indifference to any body than it is to great persons in what jail, or hulk, or improved Colony . . . human creatures starve or poison one another'.[99] It would have been better, he wrote, 'for morality, for religion, for human happiness', had Spencer and Belgrave never been born.[100] Pitt, Rose, and Long had sacrificed the panopticon to secret influence and they were able to conceal their nefarious plots by conducting the business in the 'thickest darkness possible'.[101]

Bentham believed that the fullest possible publicity for government and the clear responsibility of each individual official for his actions would prove an effective counter to sinister influence. These principles were to be worked out in detail in the *Constitutional Code* but many of the same ideas emerge in his attacks on the corruption, incapacity, and ignorance of the officials of his time. He argued that real despotism was the evasion of personal responsibility and that a committee, such as the Treasury Board, could be a screen for guilt and incompetence

[98] L. S. Amery, *Thoughts on the Constitution* (Oxford, 1947), 31.
[99] UC cxvi. 632–3.
[100] Ibid. 532.
[101] UC cxx. 574.

and could thus become 'an organ of despotism'.[102] 'It acts . . . as an extinguisher to all individual responsibility . . . the master spring of public virtue . . . and against that incapacity which in the service of the public is itself a crime. It serves as a cloak to all misconduct.'[103] By his own account Bentham had ample experience of the incompetence of officials. John King he held in particular contempt. He referred often to him as 'the ci-devant learned secretary' and was appalled by his ignorance of the most elementary facts about the colony he purported to administer. 'What did he know of the history of the Convicts down to that period?—Nothing. What did he know of the history of the part of his own empire down to that period?—Nothing.'[104] Government offices were 'hospitals for incapacity' and places where a man, 'who would starve if his bread depended upon his own faculties and exertions, makes a big figure'.[105]

Bentham also charged the administration with corruption. He strongly hinted that Rose had an improper connection with Campbell and so protected his interests. And Bentham regarded the Hulks Act of 1802 (42 Geo. III, c. 28) as a scandalous creation of a sinecure. This Act continued the powers to send convicts to the hulks as temporary places of confinement but also allowed the government to appoint, at a salary of £350 p.a., an inspector to report to Parliament. A Middlesex magistrate, Aaron Graham, was duly appointed by the Home Office. Bentham denounced this as a blatant sinecure; Graham was a friend of John King and King was 'the man behind the wainscot' in Pelham's office. Bentham made private enquiries and found that Graham was not in fact visiting the hulks as he should. But worse was that this salaried sinecure would be made a screen for the hideous evils of the hulks, 'the English Black Hole'.[106]

By one and the same operation abuse obtains concealment; favourites provision; Ministers patronage. By a metamorphosis as prompt as it was ingenious, out of the bitter thus cometh forth sweet . . . A new screen is bought for the abuse and the public pays for it. Lord Pelham taps the wainscot as usual for the gentleman by whom everything is done . . . in comes the gentleman with a friend in his pocket for the place.[107]

---

[102] UC cxxi. 255.  [103] Ibid. 182.  [104] Ibid. 82.
[105] UC cxx. 464.  [106] UC cxvi. 644.  [107] Ibid. 640.

And Bentham bitterly contrasted the alacrity with which the Ac
has been passed with the procrastination over the panopticon
'When is the time for waking?—when a place is to be created
When is the time for sleeping? when Parliament is to be obeyed
engagements fulfilled, reformation and economy planted
pestilence and famine stayed, and a system established which
puts an end to places.'[108]

Of even greater interest is Bentham's percipient criticism o
officials for exercising an undue influence by feeding minister
with partial and incomplete information—a charge which con
tinues to be levelled against the civil service. Bentham argued
that morally there is no difference between suppression of fact
and forgery. And for forgery men were hanged. He accused
Charles Long of such suppression; he who was 'the organ and
interpreter' of ministers. The meetings of the Treasury Board, he
asserted, had become fictions designed to come to decision
already agreed among the secretaries who would, 'suppress one
part of the documents, and put what colour they please in verba
and secret conversation on the rest, what is the whole ceremony
of the Board but a solemn mockery of truth and justice?'[10]
Bentham was later to lay down in his *Code* that individua
officials must be held personally responsible for their actions. Ir
this way he hoped to avoid the evils he had identified in hi
dealings with Messrs Long, Rose, and King.

In the *Constitutional Code*, public opinion plays a central role
as the main engine for reform and as the most effective check or
the pernicious exercise of power. According to Rosen, it was 'a
judicial body which applies the moral sanction to people and
institutions'.[110] And Bentham reasoned that with the progress
of civilization the dictates of public opinion would eventually
coincide with the greatest happiness principle. It is of consid
erable interest to find that in 1802 he was well aware of it
limitations and described its workings in a realistic, indeed
unfavourable, tone. The public opinion to which he then appealed
was a crude and harsh tribunal, more interested in gloating over

[108] UC cxvi. 637–8.
[109] UC cxxi. 184, 319, 161.
[110] F. Rosen, *Jeremy Bentham and Representative Democracy* (Oxford, 1983)
28.

the humiliation of the rich and the great than in seeing justice done and right triumph. He realized that at the time of the Finance Committee Report, the administration had manipulated opinion so that it would be indifferent to his wrongs and to the public good:

What did it all amount to? a squabble between the Treasury, and a man who had been kicking his heels there—a man who wanted to be a Jailer forsooth—and to *contract* for being one. Well—suppose the man waits for his jail a little while longer—what then? . . . And if he were to sink? What's that to us? Who cares for it? He'll get into a Jail, instead of keeping one.[111]

The 'John Bull' that Bentham pictured took delight in hunting down his quarry; and might be persuaded when he saw sport to run down Pitt and other members of his administration. 'John had rather race after a red herring that be idle.'[112] This is a different perception from the guardian of the greatest happiness principle that Bentham envisages in his *Code*. In 1802 he realized that public opinion could be irrational and vindictive and that it could be manipulated by appealing to humanity's worst instincts.

In his dealings with Pitt's administration, Bentham had been treated with indifference, contempt, and outright rudeness; his interests had been trampled underfoot, and his ideals shattered. Retribution, he felt, must be hanging over their heads and he himself would be the 'instrument of avenging justice'.[113] Using, in his extremity, the language of his philosophic adversaries, he appealed to Parliament to right his great wrongs:

But the more completely these Great men . . . have succeeded in forgetting the first principles of British Constitutional Law, together with the first principles of natural and universal justice, the more necessary it is that Parliament should take them in hand and . . . make their fate a lesson to Britain and to Europe.[114]

But Parliament turned a deaf ear, and the 'Picture of the Treasury' mouldered unread. There was neither justice nor vengeance for Bentham.

[111] UC cxxi. 276.   [112] Ibid. 278.   [113] Ibid. 287.   [114] Ibid. 258.

# II

# THE FINAL FAILURE

As he went through Cold-Bath Fields he saw
A solitary cell;
And the Devil was pleased, for it gave him a hint
For improving his prisons in Hell.

Samuel Coleridge, 'The Devils Thoughts'

In 1803 the Prime Minister, Henry Addington, had refused to fund the building of the panopticon; ten years later, as Home Secretary, and by then Viscount Sidmouth, he finally rejected the scheme. Until then, Bentham continued to hope. The repudiation of the panopticon during the years 1810 to 1813 was an important turning-point in the development of penal architecture and ideology. Up to then it remained possible that a contract penitentiary would be built and that Jeremy Bentham would manage it. The triumph of Howard's ideas was not preordained. This chapter will discuss why the panopticon failed; how the Press and the political nation responded to it; and what reasons were adduced for its rejection. It will also tell the story of Bentham's final battles with the politicians and civil servants.

The 1790s had been an unfavourable time to launch such an enterprise. The reasons for its failure went deeper than Bentham's political naïvety, government procrastination, the forces of 'sinister' interest, and the legal complexities of land acquisition. War and inflation had undermined political and economic stability. And the consensus among reformers on the direction of penal policy was shattered by the events following the revolution in France. The eighteenth century had been a time of enthusiasm for institutions, such as factories, workhouses, hospitals, penitentiaries, and asylums; they were widely perceived as engines for moral regeneration. The 1790s, in contrast, were a time of bitter disillusionment. The factories that had seemed a benevolent mechanism to educate and mould the future workers into sober, industrious citizens were all too often revealed as workshops where children were not only cruelly exploited but also, when not working, allowed to drink, gamble, and run wild, terrorizing their neighbourhoods, growing up ignorant, wicked, and godless. In 1802 Robert Peel's Factory Act, the first attempt to regulate conditions of work, was passed by Parliament. Workhouses too were under attack; the failure of the Suffolk Houses of Industry to relieve poverty by humane and rational methods was profoundly disillusioning. Ignatieff ascribes the rejection of the penitentiary and the wholesale use of outdoor relief to the doubts and divisions within 'the reform constituency'.[1] The very concept of penitential imprisonment was being questioned. The optimistic attitudes of the eighteenth century are well exemplified in the philanthropic eccentric John Jebb who advocated unrestricted suffrage in parliamentary elections and solitary confinement in the prisons. Revolution and war destroyed this consensus as the advocates of parliamentary reform were themselves subject to the new 'rational' and 'humane' methods of punishment. The suspension of the Habeas Corpus Acts and Pitt's persecution of the Jacobin corresponding societies sent many articulate reformers into the solitary cells of the new gaols; in particular to Sir George Paul's Gloucester penitentiary and into Coldbath Fields in London.[2] The experience of the horrors of solitary imprisonment resulted in a revulsion against the whole ideal of the penitentiary and it was now seen as a violation of the rights and liberties of Englishmen. The most eloquent of these sufferers was Horne Tooke, who in his influential analysis of language, *The Diversions of Purley*, expressed some of the outrage widely felt at the infliction of penitential discipline on political offenders; in his case he was imprisoned for seven months before trial and then triumphantly acquitted. In 1798 he inserted in his chapter on conjunctions a denunciation of his treatment:

The enemies of the *established* civil liberties of my country have hunted me through life . . . They have destroyed my fortunes: They have illegally barred and interdicted my usefulness to myself, my family, my friends, and my country. They have tortured by body . . . The antient legal and mild imprisonment of this country (mild both in manner and

---

[1] M. Ignatieff, *A Just Measure of Pain* (New York, 1978), 114–16.
[2] Ibid. 120–3.

duration, compared to what we now see) was always held to be *Torture* and even *civil death*. What would our old, honest, uncorrupted lawyers and judges . . . have said to *seven months* of CLOSE custody, such as I have lately suffered?[3]

In more measured terms, William Godwin in his *Enquiry Concerning Political Justice*, published in 1793, questioned the morality of inflicting either solitary confinement or hard labour on criminals. Godwin conformed to the doctrines of the Enlightenment that uncertainty of punishment multiplied crime and that punishment should be confined within the narrowest limits. But he totally rejected any justification for inflicting suffering other than the safety of the community. To confine men in order to reform them was 'contrary to reason and morality'.[4] And although he agreed with his contemporaries that the gaols were seminaries of vice, he argued that the solution of solitude was open to grave objections. Far from being a mild punishment it was barbarous cruelty, for 'Man is a social animal . . . Who can tell the sufferings of him who is condemned to uninterrupted solitude? Who can tell that this is not, to the majority of mankind, the bitterest torment that human ingenuity can inflict?' Solitude, by depriving a man of the opportunity to exercise benevolence or justice, would increase selfishness and nurture the gloomy and morose disposition that so often leads to crime. Godwin also condemned hard labour for reducing men to a state of slavery; man is an intellectual being, so 'There is no way to make him virtuous but in calling forth his intellectual powers.' Transportation, he argued, might be the best available method of providing criminals with the opportunity to exercise virtue, but Godwin's final conclusion was to shudder sentimentally away from the 'absolute injustice of punishment'.[5]

So the decade in which the most crucial battles for the panopticon were fought had seen radicals attack both its philosophy of punishment and the practices of the newly improved prisons. There was disarray among reformers. The circumspect *Morning Chronicle*, the leading newspaper of the radical party, denounced

---

[3] J. Horne Tooke, *The Diversions of Purley* (London, 1798), i. 246–7, Tooke's emphasis.

[4] W. Godwin, *Enquiry Concerning Political Justice* (London, 1793; Harmondsworth, 1985), 675.

[5] Ibid. 676–81.

solitary imprisonment and James Martin described it in Parliament as a 'cruel and mischievous' punishment.[6] The penitentiary was out of fashion with influential sections of the public opinion that Bentham might have hoped would further his views. He was especially unfortunate that the reputation of penitentiaries was further besmirched by the scandal of Coldbath Fields in Middlesex, one of the new 'improved' prisons opened as recently as 1794. In December 1798 members of the London Corresponding Society incarcerated there persuaded the radical MP Sir Francis Burdett to investigate conditions. They alleged that the inmates were subjected to absolute solitude, cold, brutality, and starvation. Burdett raised the question in the Commons and, although Wilberforce defended the management of the prison, the House appointed a committee of inquiry. The committee's report in April 1799 exonerated the management from the worst of the charges against them. Bentham or his friends do seem to have made some effort to counter the adverse effect that the inquiry might have on the fortunes of the panopticon. At this point, Bentham had just acquired the Salisbury estate on Millbank and was hoping that the Treasury would shortly accept his contract. In that spring there was a flurry of publicity for the panopticon. The *Morning Chronicle* carried a substantial story on 'the New Plan of Police'; Mr Bentham's project was 'so curious and so extensive that we give it in his own words'; and they reproduced the whole of the *Proposal*. Other newspapers copied the story.[7] These reports emphasized that the project was being seriously considered by the government, that it had been approved by the Finance Committee and that the iron struts for the building were already cast. It was seen as an alternative to the notorious Coldbath Fields; 'so it is possible', the *Morning Chronicle*, commented, 'that Cold Bath Fields may be superseded by the Iron Cage'. The following day the same newspaper carried a lengthy letter from 'A LOVER OF SPECTACLES'

---

[6] *The Parliamentary History of England*, 35 (22 July 1800), 470. British Library, Place Collection 36, p. 3. *Morning Chronicle*, 31 Dec. 1798.

[7] *Morning Chronicle*, 29 Mar. 1799. *Oracle and Daily Advertiser*, 30 Mar. 1799. *Courier and Evening Gazette*, 1 Apr. 1799. The *Morning Herald* did not reproduce the *Proposal* but had reports 30 Mar. and 1 Apr. A microfilm copy of these newspapers is available in the Burney Collection 942 at the British Library. At UC cxviii. 450 is a copy of the *Morning Chronicle*, 1 Apr. and at 168–70 are MS extracts of some of the comments from other newspapers.

which made a would-be humorous attempt to recommend the panopticon:

Give me leave to express my approbation of the plan published in your Paper on Friday for a prison on a new construction. Nothing I have seen of late years pregnant as this age is with reforms, so much deserving of attention . . . the plan of a prison constructed on the principles of *optics* was reserved to gild the declining rays of the eighteenth century. . . . I care not that one says it is a *visionary* scheme, and another that it may be easily *seen through*. The principle of it is certainly new and surprising and I may add *economical* for it reduces the number of senses formerly employed in reforming criminals to one only, namely the sense of seeing.

The writer went on to suggest that the name 'gaoler', 'must be changed into that of keeper and keeper . . . easily becomes *peeper*, an office peculiarly adapted to *lantern lucubrations*'. And the letter ends with a typically Benthamic suggestion that the principle of inspection should be extended to all human activity: 'I could not delay a moment in beginning to express my approbation of a plan which when perfected in *prisons* may be hereafter recommended in *private houses* as an effectual bar against all concealment, and tend more than anything yet invented to banish that scoundrel *secrecy* out of the world.'[8]

Other press reports were even less respectful. Contemporary journalists seemed unconvinced of the virtues of the panopticon and their comments were misinformed and malicious. True to their trade, they seized the opportunity for derision. They portrayed the panopticon as quite transparent with the prisoners subject to constant inspection from any chance passerby. The *Morning Herald* printed a letter dated All Fools' Day suggesting that, 'in the age of *new* lights and *wonderful reforms*', there might be transparent police officers as well as transparent prisons. The *Courier* mocked at 'the *fanciful* Glass Structure' which had already 'obtained the whimsical title of the *Penal Panorama*'; and, more harmfully for Bentham, pilloried him as a greedy projector. Bentham had certainly laid himself open to accusations of cupidity and the newspapers took full advantage of their opportunity. The *Courier* could not suppose 'that the *gain* arising from the novel exhibition had any influence on the mind of the

---

[8] *Morning Chronicle*, 1 Apr. 1799.

projector'.[9] The *Morning Herald* mocked, '*elucidations*, calculated so disinterestedly for the public good!'; and in a sly reference to Bentham's metaphor of a glass beehive, pointed out that: 'The contractor proposes for himself a *snug place* in the centre, where he may collect the honey...What a pity so ingenious a design should be so easily *seen through*.'[10] The *Morning Chronicle* did not impugn Bentham's motives but they were sceptical about the very principle of the scheme: 'We conceive Mr Bentham's proposals of an Iron Cage to be a pretty neat idea, but we extremely doubt whether the morals of the most notorious villains can be reclaimed by inspection.' And they laughed at his careful military preparations: 'There is one part of Mr Bentham's plan which deserves much praise and evinces great foresight—we mean that in which the building is to be properly fortified against all attempts from *without*. If our prisons are to be rendered so charming and comfortable, there can be no *safety* but in rendering them *impregnable*.' More seriously, when many radicals were languishing untried in the gaols, the paper made the topical point that the panopticon could be an efficient instrument of oppression. It was 'an additional proof of the vigilance of Ministers. They are determined that both out of prison and in it they are resolved to have their eye on the disaffected.'[11]

The panopticon seems to have made little impression on more serious journals. *The Annual Register* for 1800 printed the *Proposal* as a 'Useful Project'. In 1802 an outline of the plan was again brought before the public in Dumont's edition of *Traités de législation* but fared little better. Francis Jeffrey, in *The Edinburgh Review*, damned Bentham with faint praise: 'We take leave of this publication', he wrote, 'with some feelings of fatigue, but with sentiments of the greatest respect for the talents of the author.' He dismissed the panopticon as promising 'rather greater things from its adoption, than are very likely to follow'.[12] Otherwise the panopticon seems to have been greeted with silence. From 1803 to 1814 the *Gentleman's Magazine* featured prominently a series of 'Dr Lettsom's Letters on Prisons' which

[9] *Morning Herald*, 2 Apr. 1799. *Courier and Evening Gazette*, 2 Apr. 1799.
[10] *Morning Herald*, 2 Apr. and 30 Mar. 1799.
[11] *Morning Chronicle*, 2 and 3 Apr. 1799.
[12] *Annual Register* (1801), 396–8. *Edinburgh Review*, 4 (Apr.–July 1804), 'Bentham, Principes de Législation, par Dumont', 25–6.

publicized the results of James Neild's visits to the gaols. Full
of sentimental outrage, they eulogized Howard, but neither
Bentham nor the panopticon were mentioned. Another even
more startling indication of the invisibility of the panopticon is
that Sir George Paul, a considerable contributor to the debates
on penal reform, had never heard of the project; neither had
Matthew Wood the Sheriff of London concerned with the
building of new gaols.[13]

In 1803 the panopticon had been threatened by a very similar
but more practical scheme put forward by a Mr Robert Edington.
Bentham was warned that this was 'calculated intentionally as a
*Death blow* to your Plans'.[14] Edington praised Bentham, 'who
has added to the sum of political economy more intelligence
and more just reasoning than any person I know of'. But he
questioned the practicality of the panopticon. 'If it can be
executed', he wrote, 'it is a grand acquisition to social and
political reform. I fear that it is too great. I doubt not that the
individual gentleman is equal to the execution of it: but where
shall we find a successor or associate?'[15] Edington agreed that
labour would inculcate habits of honest industry and his solution
was to attach several penitentiary houses to the dockyards around
the country where the convicts could be set to work on naval
repairs such as rope-making, mending casks, and sail-making.
These prisons would have the dual purpose of employing convicts
and stopping peculation and pilfering from naval stores. Edington
insisted that his plan was superior to Bentham's for it would
avoid unmanageable concentrations of convicts; they would be

---

[13] *First Report from the Committee on the Laws Relating to Penitentiary
Houses. Ordered by the House of Commons to be printed, 31 May 1811*, 45, cited
as *First Report*, commonly referred to as the Holford Report. Part of this report
was reproduced in Bowring, xi. 148–51. The *Second Report from the Committee
on the Law Relating to Penitentiary Houses. Ordered by the House of Commons to
be printed on 10 June 1811* consisted of a letter from Bentham to Holford repr. in
Bowring, xi. 151–9, see *Correspondence (CW)*, viii. 135–46. A copy of both
reports is at UC cxv. 158. *Correspondence (CW)*, viii. 51–2. Matthew Wood
(1768–1843), Sheriff of London and Middlesex, 1809–10; Lord Mayor, 1815–16,
1816–17; MP for the City, 1817–43.

[14] *Correspondence (CW)*, vii. 229.

[15] Robert Edington, *A Descriptive Plan for Erecting a Penitentiary House, for
the Employment of Convicts; to which are added Plans for the Prevention of
Frauds and Thefts, so far as respecting His Majesty's Dock-Yards, Public Works
and Stores* (London, 1803), 3–4.

dispersed around the country and would be employed in the immediate service of the public they had injured. He attacked the design of the panopticon as a manufactory: 'Let me ask how, in a circular iron cage . . . could any of these great objects be effected? Good God! in what manner would Mr Bentham work up the twice laid rope; suppose a hawser of 140 fathoms, run metal, forge anchors, roll copper, in the circle of an iron cage.'[16] The government did not accept Edington's substitute for the panopticon.

During the vital twenty years between 1791 and 1811, the great bulk of the panopticon writings were not published and so were available to only a small number of people; by 1815 they were virtually unobtainable. The panopticon had made little impact on a wider public. It must, however, be remembered that in comparison with only a few years later, this public could be woefully ignorant and the channels of opinion sluggish and muddied. The newspapers were then thin and scrappy, some of them little more than advertisement and scandal sheets. Francis Place, writing in 1847, contrasted his own time with the 1790s. The middle classes were then, he wrote, mean and subservient, inferior in knowledge and manners; and there was no public opinion in the sense of a 'considerable number of men who acted together for the sole purpose of promoting the intelligence of the public'.[17] It is perhaps not surprising that Bentham made so little attempt to appeal to a wider tribunal of the world. The first systematic attempt to publicize the panopticon in the Press was the work of James Mill not Bentham. In a series of articles between 1811 and 1816, he launched a zealous exposition and defence of his mentor's brain-child. 'In truth', he wrote, 'we believe that under such a system of management . . . it would be hardly possible for any human being to remain unreformed.'[18] But by then it was too late.

In the years after 1803 Bentham appeared to accept that the panopticon had been laid aside. By 1808 he was writing, 'J.B. has next to no expectation of seeing Panopticon set on foot . . . and at his time of life scarce a wish about it: but that with him it has never been more than a secondary object, his primary object

---

[16] Ibid. 47.
[17] British Library, Place Collection 36, p. 1.
[18] *The Philanthropist* (1816), vi. 105.

being a reform in the state of the law.'[19] His life was not uneventful. In 1805, quite by chance, he met his old love, Caroline Fox, at Holland House and made his rather pathetic attempt to persuade her to become his wife. He misunderstood her pleasure in his friendship, and perhaps her condescension, for he was aiming high socially. She kindly but emphatically rejected him. Another link with the past was broken with the death of the original instigator of the panopticon project, Lord Lansdowne, though he had ceased for several years to be an intimate friend. And Bentham again lost the company of his brother and family when they set off for a second stint of service in Russia. He was able to derive some vicarious satisfaction from their accounts of the building of a panopticon on the banks of the Neva and in the construction of a conservatory and hothouse garden at the Bentham residence in St Petersburg. He even contemplated a visit to Russia to see the realization of his dream. In 1808 he was planning to escape from the bitter English weather by settling in Mexico, but was dissuaded by the difficulties that would have attended such an enterprise. He was becoming increasingly valetudinarian in his habits. His eyesight was failing; he suffered terribly from the cold London winters; and he was preoccupied with the necessity of having access to a water closet.[20]

At the end of 1807 the memory of the panopticon was revived in a way particularly irritating to Bentham. The commissioners for auditing public accounts asked him to account for the £2,000 of public money voted to him in 1794. A long and acrimonious correspondence followed. Bentham found it very difficult to comply with this request. Fourteen years had elapsed and despite his theoretical insistence on the importance of careful and accurate records, he and his brother had failed to get or to retain receipts for the work commissioned or the wages paid. Bentham collected what documentation he could but this did not suffice for the audit board and he was driven to plead with them to accept verbal testimony in lieu of written evidence. Bentham felt himself persecuted and outraged by the secrecy of their methods. And, as so often in his dealings with the government, he wrote a private self-justificatory account of his troubles in which he accused the board of 'anonymousness and invisibility', insisting

---

[19] *Correspondence* (CW), vii. 507.　　　[20] Ibid. 378.

that individual members of the board should be individually and publicly responsible for their actions, and so act on 'the principles of an English Court of Justice' and not on 'the principles of a Venetian Senate . . . or a Spanish Inquisition'.[21] However, in December 1808 the audit board agreed that verbal testimony could be accepted and Bentham's difficulties in accounting for the £2,000 were at an end.

During Bentham's skirmishes with the audit board, the idea of penal reform and the possibility of building a penitentiary revived. In 1808 Samuel Romilly began his courageous but vain campaign against the death penalty for trivial offences. James Abercromby, a Foxite MP, was inspired by reading *Letters to Lord Pelham* and *A Plea for the Constitution* to suggest that a parliamentary committee should be set up to investigate transportation. Nothing came of this. But general unease at the workings of the criminal law was growing both among reformers who wished to see a more rational and humane penal system and among those who feared that crime was increasing and the law was losing its terror. The proportion of those convicted of capital offences in the metropolis who went to the gallows was declining steeply; by 1808 it was scarcely more than 10 per cent. The only alternatives available were transportation or imprisonment in the hulks. Transportation was beginning to be perceived as a soft option and Australia a land of opportunity for English criminals. The evils of the hulks were too notorious to be disputed. With the restoration of Habeas Corpus and the freeing of political prisoners, much of the emotional reaction against penitential imprisonment had evaporated. The time was ripe for a revival of Howard's dream of a national penitentiary or for new initiatives in punishment. Bentham's panopticon was waiting in the wings.

At first Bentham's friends seemed to have little doubt that the panopticon project again stood a very good chance of success. Bentham did not take the initiative, believing that sinister interests were still at work to ensure his failure. But he was enticed by William Wilberforce to overcome his reluctance and once more to enter the fray. In June 1809 Wilberforce wrote an effusive apology for past coldness, telling Bentham that he was again active in promoting the panopticon. He had mentioned it

[21] UC cxxii. 254, 285.

in the House and had spoken 'with one of ye Treasury people'.
This conversation led him to the belief that, 'ye present was a
favourable moment for carrying into Execution your great
Project'. And he wrote to ask if Bentham 'had still ye *Heart* to go
forward after all your former disappointments'.[22] Bentham's
answer has not survived but his reaction must have been wary for
almost a year later, in May 1810, he was expressing his reluctance
to get involved, 'having no such ambition as that of passing
the short remainder of my life among the Treasury Porters'.[23]
Wilberforce, blandly optimistic, replied exhorting Bentham to
action not so much in hope as in assurance of success:

After all you have experienced Unless ye way is smooth'd and the doors
thrown wide for yr triumphant passage, I would not have you stir from
ye Chimney Corner—But if ye Hos. of Coms does awake from its long
Slumber and wish to establish a System in ye highest degree beneficial
and humane, Surely you will not refuse to tend yrself to those who
are eager to bring it forward . . . I am delighted by seeing with my
mind's Eye, your Honour like a great Spider seated in ye Center of yr.
Panopticon.[24]

This letter did incalculable harm; first by luring Bentham with
false hopes that were to embroil him in further fruitless labour
and public humiliation; and secondly in the use of vivid metaphor
to stamp for ever the image of him as a spider in the midst of his
penal web. At this point the Treasury also wrote to Bentham
asking him for a reply to the points raised in Charles Long's letter
of 1801; that is on what terms he would now be prepared to
undertake the contract for the prison and what compensation he
would claim if it did not go ahead. Bentham replied promptly
that he still held himself bound to carry out his side of the
bargain and that he had never asked for compensation. He was
also encouraged by expressions of support from his old ally Sir
Charles Bunbury, who wrote that he would be 'happy for the
Public Benefit, and for yours, to see The Panopticon firmly
established, and filled with *improving* Inhabitants'.[25] In 1810 the

---

[22] *Correspondence* (*CW*), viii. 32–3, Wilberforce's spelling and emphasis.
James Abercromby (1776–1858), cr. Baron Dunfermline, 1839; Speaker of the
House of Commons, 1835–9.
[23] Ibid. 63.
[24] Ibid. 64, Wilberforce's spelling.
[25] Ibid. 69, Bunbury's emphasis.

rejection of the panopticon was far from a foregone conclusion.

On 5 June a motion put down by Romilly, urging the government to implement the Penitentiary Acts of 1779 and 1794, was debated in the House of Commons. Romilly and the other radicals, James Abercromby and Samuel Whitbread, were joined by Wilberforce in urging the immediate adoption of the statutes. The Home Secretary, Richard Ryder, and government supporters resisted this demand arguing for delay and the setting up of a new inquiry in the next session. This debate had several remarkable features. No member on either side of the House seems to have realized that the 1779 Act had in fact lapsed in 1802 and so could not be implemented without further legislation. None of the advocates of the motion made any attempt to differentiate between the two Acts or to deal with the problems of reconciling them. And, although Howard, Blackstone, Eden, and even Paul were singled out for praise, Jeremy Bentham was not mentioned. Romilly confined himself to a general advocacy of the penitentiary system and the shortcomings of the hulks and transportation. Abercromby spoke in similar terms. Samuel Whitbread spent much of his time condemning solitary confinement and insisting that Howard had abhorred the practice. Wilberforce came nearest to mentioning the panopticon itself lamenting that a plan to reform by discipline, religion, and education had been on the statute book for sixteen years unused and should now, he urged, be instantly implemented. Richard Ryder for the administration was on strong ground in arguing that the legislation was defective and more consideration was imperative: 'the state of things', he said, 'at present renders it impossible to carry it into execution'. The ministry won the vote as well as the argument. Romilly's motion was defeated by 69 votes to 52, a majority of 17. But the House did resolve to consider the matter again in the next session. [26]

The administration honoured its assurances and, on 4 March 1811, a committee was appointed, 'to consider of the expediency of erecting a Penitentiary House or Penitentiary Houses, under the Acts of the 34th and 19th of His present Majesty'.[27] Several

---

[26] *Parliamentary Debates*, xvii. 322–52, 5 June 1810. Richard Ryder (1766–1832), Home Secretary, 1809–12. Samuel Whitbread (1764–1815), MP 1790–1815.

[27] *The Journals of the House of Commons* (1810–11), lxvi. 144.

of Bentham's friends and allies were on the committee, Bunbury, Romilly, Nepean, Morton Pitt, Wilberforce, and Abercromby; but of the twenty-one members at least fifteen could be reckoned as supporters of the ministry; and five could form a quorum. Most ominously of all, the chairman, George Holford, was a man antipathetic to Bentham. He enjoyed great wealth from a fortune inherited from his father, a director of the East India Company. He was a fervent, almost fanatical, Christian and had a few years previously published a pamphlet arguing that the destruction of Jerusalem was a sure proof of the divine origin of Christianity. He had been brought into Parliament by Addington and remained a supporter of the administration. He was opposed both to parliamentary reform and to the abolition of sinecures.[28] And, most unfortunately of all for the panopticon, he himself nursed ambitions in the field of penal reform. Of Bentham's friends, none could be expected to die on the barricades for the panopticon. Romilly was primarily concerned with fighting his tenacious battle for humanizing the sanguinary penal law; Bunbury was losing interest in politics; Wilberforce had always been a Tory and in the last analysis a friend of administration; and Nepean, primarily a civil servant, was dependent on the goodwill of ministers. (The following year he was appointed Governor of Bombay.) Unlike the Finance Committee of 1798, this committee would seem weighted against the panopticon, especially as among its members was Bentham's old enemy, Charles Long. Bentham, appalled by his presence, wrote to Romilly suggesting that their new ally, James Abercromby, should be given part of the 'Picture of the Treasury' so that he could realize the depth of Long's turpitude. This might help in 'keeping of Panopt. on its legs'. For 'Sitting over me as Judge to pronounce himself guiltless and me guilty here is a man (L) who for these 16 years and more has been the instrument of all the evil that has been done to me.'[29]

The committee got down to work quickly. Holford had completed his report by the middle of May and it was presented to

[28] R. G. Thorne, *The History of Parliament* (London, 1986), iv. 214–16. George Peter Holford (1767–1839), MP, 1803–26; Secretary, Board of Control, 1804–9. Author of *The Destruction of Jerusalem, an Absolute and Irresistible Proof of the Divine Origin of Christianity* (1805).
[29] *Correspondence (CW)*, viii. 117.

the House of Commons at the end of the month. Bentham was examined on 27 March and again on 1 April as to what were the terms and conditions on which he would be willing to manage a penitentiary house. Bentham, despite the presence of Charles Long, seems to have been confident of success. Perhaps he could not conceive that anyone could fail to be convinced by his arguments; perhaps he retained a faith in the legislature as an impartial arbiter of sectional interests; perhaps also he now believed that with the unfortunate King quite sunk in madness and Lord Grosvenor happily ensconced in his new home, the sinister opposition centred on the Court would no longer prevail. A measure of his confidence was that he again made detailed plans, jotting down points on the construction of the building and the requirements of the inmates; he wondered whether it might be illuminated by the new device of gas light. He also drafted a bill to exempt the panopticon from the provisions of the Statute of Apprentices.[30] In old age, he recalled his certainty that the committee would report favourably: 'In my intercourse with Mr. Holford, I assumed all along as a matter of course, that the determination of the Committee and thereafter of the government would be favourable to me.' His friends knew better; he told of how Wilberforce and Nepean came to conduct him, 'in their custody . . . to the destined place of my examination', he talking confidently of his future plans, while they uncomfortably tried to avoid the subject but failed to disabuse him of his false hopes.[31] He behaved at the time as one assured of acceptance. The substance of his evidence to the committee was that he could not now undertake the design and construction of the building especially as he had lost the expertise of his brother and of Samuel Bunce, who had died in the interim. But he insisted that he both would and could undertake the management of the penitentiary and that he had a right to the beneficial contract promised by the government. He even argued that the government was obliged to provide him with his additional 26 acres of land despite this needing new legislation; he had originally contracted to build a prison on 79 acres at Battersea Rise, and an equivalent site was therefore due to him. The panopticon was still a grandiose project. In his answers to questions, it emerged that

---

[30] UC cxvii. 317–18.    [31] BL Add. MS 33550, 409–13.

the convicts themselves would build their prison; the rotunda itself would be enclosed within a square wall; the rest of the site would be developed as gardens and farms and for the subsidiary panopticons. Eventually a great wall would enclose the whole 79-acre site of the vast penal colony stretching from Pimlico to Westminister.[32] At the age of 63, Bentham was certainly not lacking in courage or resilience.

He might have been alerted to danger by the hostile nature of his examination. He was pressed on a variety of issues; some of his answers were vague, others evasive. On the vexed question of sleeping arrangements, he was asked several times if he saw any objection to seven or eight men sleeping in the same cell, an insinuation that this would encourage homosexuality; he answered that there could be no objection because throughout the night the cells would be lit and constantly inspected. The committee was also concerned that the extensive powers of the governor would be open to abuse. It was pointed out to Bentham that it was illegal for the governors of houses of correction to sell supplies to inmates and he was asked if this were not an important safeguard to ensure the wholesomeness of provisions and to prevent the sale of improper luxuries. The committee was concerned too with the unregulated hours of labour and the lack of protection for prisoners from exploitation. Many times Bentham gave assurances that his mechanisms of book-keeping, insurance, reports to the King's Bench, and public inspection would safeguard the health and lives of his prisoners for it would be easy to complain within the panopticon and he would himself be the loser if any inmate died. He would not accept that there was any objection to the governor's charging the inmates what-ever price he wished for articles and he reserved the right to put convicts to work at unhealthy trades providing they had been bred up to them.

According to his logic, Bentham had to protect his prison's profit potential. This worried the committee; he was asked what would happen if the chaplain objected on moral or religious grounds to profitable combinations of prisoners working together, or to any other aspect of the regime of the prison. The position of the chaplain and the emphasis given to religion and repentance

---

[32] *First Report*, 62–7.

were central to the committee's concerns. He was asked if the long hours of labour would allow time for religious instruction and education, and whether the imperative to make profit would not favour the good workman as against the inmate who showed true penitence. Bentham reiterated that his system of checks would be sufficient, he argued that contrition could be more apparent than real and that he would have to be governed by appearance: 'I am', he said, 'no searcher of hearts.'[33] On the vital question of conflict of authority, he was driven to admit that the governor might have to be subject to outside control, possibly to an inspector appointed by the government; and he also conceded that the court of the King's Bench could have no sanction short of dismissing the governor and voiding the contract and so was a defective instrument for the day-to-day supervision of a prison. In his answers, Bentham failed to make a convincing case for his ultimate safeguard, the gallery where members of the public could overlook the cells. This emerged as an eccentric and flawed device, for the public could not be freely admitted at all hours, they could talk with the prisoners only through conversation tubes, and there were no official channels of complaint. The inmates would be at the mercy of chance and caprice. Bentham relied on the 'superintending authority of the newspapers, and I imagine the eyes of the newspapers will not be closed upon such an establishment as this'.[34] With a levity discordant with the solemnity of the committee's deliberations he opined that the public would be brought to the panopticon by 'curiosity and love of amusement (the most universally operative springs of action that apply to such a case)'.[35] Bentham mounted a very much more impressive defence of public inspection in manuscript notes that he drafted eight days after his examination; but these were not conveyed to the committee. He linked the panopticon gallery to the fundamental place of publicity within the Constitution applicable to all governments:

Against abuse . . . there is but one effectual security, and that is the scrutiny of the public eye . . . the division of power, though in practice a very salutary principle is so no otherwise than in so far as it is a promoter of publicity . . . Publicity of the acts . . . in the exercise of power with

---

[33] Ibid. 78.     [34] Ibid. 80.
[35] *Correspondence (CW)*, viii. 124.

liberty to contest the propriety of them is the only immediate and
intrinsically efficient security . . . If you have division of power without
publicity you have nothing, if you have publicity, though it be without
division of power you have everything.[36]

Bentham supplemented his verbal evidence with long letters to
Holford elaborating on points concerning the terms on which he
would undertake the management, the temporary provision for
female convicts and the modifications of the building that might
be necessary. And finally, on 6 May, he wrote again: 'For such of
the Convicts, whose conviction shall have taken place in London
or Middlesex . . . the provision made by the existing Contract
may, it seems to be supposed, suffice.'[37] And he went on to argue
at length that several panopticons built at Tothill Fields would be
the best provision for convicts from other parts of the country.
The expense, he argued, should be chargeable to national
taxation rather than the rates. The letter is also concerned with
the erection of subsidiary establishments for discharged convicts
who wished for employment. Bentham was clearly assuming that
Holford's recommendation of the panopticon was a foregone
conclusion and that his prison and all its ramifications would go
ahead. He wrote a little later, 'I really did understand that . . . it
was the sense of the Committee, and even nem. diss. that the
Contract was a Contract, and that so compleatly such as to
preclude all further enquiry into the subject.'[38] Samuel Bentham
was infected with his brother's optimism. 'I rejoice to hear', he
wrote, 'that poor Panop. appears once more to be raising its
head.' He still saw the project as a fair way to fortune and was
confident enough to suggest that the name of his 12-year-old son
might be substituted for his own in the contract, 'which on
account of his age would be much more valuable'.[39] Samuel, an
entrepreneur before he was a philanthropist, was perennially
short of money and anxious to amass a fortune for himself and
his family from the panoption or any other enterprise. Bentham
was, as always, willing to advance his interests. An odd light is

---

[36] UC cxvii. 379, 380, 394.
[37] *Correspondence (CW)*, viii. 135. The first letter to Holford, 29 Mar. 1811,
pp. 111–16; the second, 1 Apr., pp. 119–27; and the third, 6 May, pp. 135–46.
This third letter constituted Holford's *Second Report*.
[38] Ibid. 151.
[39] Ibid. 128, 130.

cast on the dubious mores of the time by a proposition he put to his brother that he might act as an adviser to a certain Captain Johnson who was proposing to set out on a privateering expedition to attack Napoleon's fleet by submarine. This Johnson whom Bentham recommended as an associate to his brother might well have ended as an inmate of the panopticon for he had twice been convicted of smuggling offences. Yet he was an acquaintance of Abercromby and Bentham saw no objection in his meeting Samuel at Queen's Square Place.[40]

Samuel Bentham was not destined to make a great fortune either from privateering or from the panopticon. Three years later he was forced to take his family to France where they could live more economically. The brothers' optimism had been misplaced. The Holford Committee took evidence from two other experts in the field of prison management, the Revd John Becher, a Nottingham magistrate responsible for the house of correction at Southwell and an exponent of work in association, and from Sir George Onesiphoros Paul from Gloucester, who favoured solitary confinement. They were both disciples of Howard and scathing in their criticism of the panopticon. Becher was particularly vehement in his attack; he seems to have intensely disliked both Bentham and his project. When asked if the proposed contract would be advantageous, he answered straightly— no. He argued that the authority of such a governor would be too great and the reports to the King's Bench would be an inadequate check, for 'his prejudices may obscure his judgment'. He insisted that the conduct of the governor must be supervised by visitors of high rank 'actuated solely by pure emotions of commiseration', so that, 'That principle of inspection, so frequently sounded in our ears by Mr Bentham should pervade not merely the fabric . . . but the whole institution.'[41] The chaplain and the doctor had, he emphasized, a crucial role to play in preventing the abuse of power and they must therefore be independent of the governor. He questioned whether the architecture of the panopticon was the best way of ensuring inspection: 'The name, and the explanatory treatise detailing its imaginary

---

[40] Ibid. 133–4.
[41] *First Report*, 40. John Thomas Becher (1770–1848), clergyman and writer on social economy; Visiting Justice of Nottingham.

advantages, might induce many to believe, that inspection had not engaged the attention of prison architects; such an intimation will, however, be found erroneous.' Blackburn's prisons had been designed to ensure inspection deemed sufficient by Howard and Blackstone who based their conclusions not on 'theoretical speculations' but on practical experience of prisons on the Continent. These great and good men, Becher declared, had concluded that prisoners should not work and sleep in the same room and that they should be separated at night; nocturnal solitude would be conducive to reform, for the criminal might be 'impelled to the duty of penitent meditation'. Becher also cast doubts on the economy of the panopticon, stating that at Southwell the cost per head was considerably less than that demanded by Bentham. He also challenged the whole concept of the building; Mr Bentham had cut expense, but only at the price of 'violating every principle which his indefatigable predecessors had established'. He had achieved his economy in the fabric of the building by omitting all day and work rooms, baths, airing rooms, and gardens. And Becher's onslaught culminated in a description of the panopticon as it might have been at its worst, a place of horror and nightmare:

To convey an adequate representation of a Panopticon Penitentiary, we may suppose a watch tower encircled by an external gallery, and surrounded at a small distance with six rows of cages, nearly similar to those used for the restraining wild beasts. Let the whole be connected under the same roof, with a sky-light over the area, and we shall have a Panopticon. Occupy these cages with 1,000 convicts, and the whole will exhibit an assemblage of human beings with the same ferocious dispositions, the same offensive exhalations, and the same degrading propensities, that characterize the brute creation.[42]

Paul was more measured and more just in his estimate, but as damning. He had not previously been aware of the panopticon scheme and admitted that: 'I cannot fairly judge between a favourite child of my own nurture, and an untried theory of an ingenious and inventive imagination, placed before me but yesterday.' But he took exception to the levity with which Bentham had ridiculed the Penitentiary Act of 1779, 'the result of the united labours of the most profound lawyer and the most

---

[42] *First Report*, 41–2.

distinguished philanthropists of the time'. His evidence was somberly unfavourable. He disliked the idea of the contract which must either be adopted whole or 'rejected from general doubt'. He found the sleeping arrangements 'extremely objectionable' and had grave doubts as to the powers given to the governor. He distrusted the insurance schemes; there was, he declared, 'no *conviction* to my mind that men will not die or escape, or that they *will not* return to their former vicious habits'. He was dubious about the role of the King's Bench and insisted that there was need for independent personal inspection by official visitors.[43]

The Holford Committee had thus become a forum for a discussion, indeed a confrontation, between the principles of Blackstone, Howard, and the 1779 Penitentiary Act and of Jeremy Bentham, the panopticon, and the 1794 Act. The rift was complete, there could now be no compromise; and George Holford came down firmly on the side of Blackstone and Howard. Just as Bentham and Pole Carew had dictated the terms of the 1798 Finance Committee Report so did Holford dictate the terms of his report. Bentham's supporters could do nothing to stop the committee approving it. In any case they seem to have abandoned the unavailing struggle. Bunbury was seldom in town, Nepean often absent, and Morton Pitt never attended the hearings at all. James Abercromby, whom Romilly had asked to take charge of the panopticon in committee, was the only one constant in his attendance. When Holford produced his report it was the only proposition before the committee.[44] Bentham had written to Nepean: 'You bid *me* prepare t'other day to have my liver and soul plucked out';[45] and he frantically pleaded with his friend to return to London to rescue the panopticon. But Nepean remained in Dorset. By this time the panopticon was a lost cause. Abercromby, Romilly, and Wilberforce either would not or could not stop Holford's report being presented to Parliament on 31 May; it was, as Romilly wrote to Bentham, 'very unfavourable to your Contract I attended the last day but one of their meeting but found it quite impossible to do anything'.[46]

---

[43] Ibid. 45–7. Paul's emphasis.
[44] *Correspondence (CW)*, viii. 155.
[45] Ibid. 149.
[46] Ibid. 158.

Holford's report was devised to enable him to achieve his own ambition to manage a great new penal experiment based on the faith that penitential confinement, seclusion, employment, and religious instruction would reform criminals. It recommended a penitentiary for London and Middlesex which would be managed in accordance with the principles of the 1779 Act. The Crown would appoint three commissioners who would erect the building and supervise the management of the institution. The whole would be superintended by a committee of great and good men who would lay down regulations and appoint governor, chaplain, and doctor. The penal regime was a compromise between the ideas of Paul and Becher. The convicts were to be divided into two classes; those at the beginning of their sentence would be subject to a severer separation similar to that at Gloucester; they would later be allowed greater association as at Southwell. Both Paul and Becher were highly praised, Paul for his 'meritorious exertions in improving and correcting the state of imprisonment in the County of Gloucester'; and Becher as 'a very active and intelligent magistrate'. Bentham was described less effusively as 'a gentleman of great respectability'.[47] If Holford were to achieve his ambitions, the panopticon had to be destroyed. His report is a classic statement of the ideology that has dominated penal policy for the past hundred and fifty years and a cogently argued exposition of the objections to punishment by contract and to the panopticon. It emphasized the dangers of entrusting the governor with such absolute power over his inmates; it argued that the virtues of these principles of management were too dependent on the character of one man and that the total control insisted on by Bentham for himself could all too easily pass into less worthy hands—a point of some relevance when one considers that had Jeremy and Samuel Bentham died the contract would have passed to Samuel's young son. The report also argued that to abandon statutory control over the wholesomeness of provisions was also dangerous not so much because prisoners might be starved or poisoned, but because the governor would be tempted to gain profit by introducing luxuries into the prison. Even if this objection were removed by new clauses in the contract, it would still leave the problem of ensuring due atten-

---

[47] *First Report*, 4, 10.

tion to religious instruction in a prison where profit was the main objective. The recommendations of the chaplain as to which prisoners should consort together could too easily be ignored: 'Your Committee see much reason to apprehend that under a system, in which pecuniary advantage is thus made the most prominent object of attention, the experiment of reformation could not be fairly tried.' The committee also rejected the safeguards of Bentham's insurance system; the report dismissed as 'of very little importance' his argument that compensation payments for a relapse into crime would ensure that the contractor would pay due regard to reformation. They were, in any case, nugatory for the scheme was not financially viable because no funds were set aside for payments falling due after the contractor's death. As for the life insurance that Bentham believed would safeguard the health of his prisoners, the report merely observed that in their opinion, this protection was insufficient: 'the health of the prisoners will be more effectually guarded by the exercise of the judgement of a professional man, not dependent upon the governor, and acting under the direction of other disinterested persons, than by the payment of any sum of money to fall on the governor in the case of the prisoner's actually dying within the walls of the prison during his confinement.'[48] A similar argument that opportunity for complaint and redress of grievances must be instantly available was used to insist that doctor and chaplain must be independent of the governor and that resort to the King's Bench was an insufficient check, indeed, 'totally inapplicable'. There must be day-to-day supervision by a committee appointed by Act of Parliament to correct bad practices instantly.

Bentham's idea of a public gallery and inspection by the tribunal of public opinion was again dismissed as self-evidently defective. Mr Bentham, the report almost contemptuously declared, 'seems to lay some stress on the vigilance which the newspapers are to exert in watching his conduct'; but such casual visitors could not be a substitute for superintendence by persons with power not only to inspect all aspects of the regime but also to require that the abuses be immediately corrected. The Holford Report therefore denied both the premises and the conclusions

[48] Bowring, xi. 150.

of Bentham's plan; it brought harshly to light the irreconcilable differences between his and Howard's ideas; and it shattered his carefully constructed engine to join interest and duty. The only part of the report that could have given him any satisfaction was the final recommendation that he should be given liberal compensation without further delay.

Bentham's reaction was predictable. He was convinced, once again, that a secret conspiracy of sinister interest had robbed him of his contract and his rights. He wrote to Dumont of 'an originally preconcerted plan for setting aside Panopticon, concerted I mean before the appointment of the Committee'.[49] And he feared that even Wilberforce was party to the deceit. As usual, he sought solace by writing during the next few months, 'Observations on Holford's Report' in which he confided his outrage that the committee was able 'to perform the office of Pope and dispense with engagements'. He listed 'backsliding friends' as a cause of failure and complained that Holford had given Paul and Becher an unfair advantage over him by allowing them copies of the panopticon writings whereas he had had no chance to refute 'the absurdity, the nonsense and the confusion' of their evidence. And he bitterly resented that he, 'at the end of a twenty years course of unmerited injury and oppression . . . a person without reproach and free[?] from all suspicion of blame in any shape . . . was not to be permitted to have any part whatsoever in the management of the concern upon any terms'.[50] Bentham also accused Holford of producing a self-serving report for he would himself benefit, at Bentham's expense, from its findings. *The Philanthropist* held Holford up to public opprobrium: 'A gentleman of the name of Holford was chairman of the committee who reported unfavourably of Mr Bentham's Panopticon plan. And that gentleman is the person chosen, with very considerable emoluments, to be the superintendent of the new penitentiary.'[51] At the end of his life, Bentham still nursed his resentment and suspicions; he wrote that, 'Mr Holford who in quality of chairman of the Committee was the prime instrument in the business and upon my extinction was decked . . . with the prime part of my spoils.' Wilberforce, however, was half

[49] *Correspondence* (*CW*), viii. 159.
[50] UC cxviii. 318, 327.
[51] *Philanthropist*, 5 (1815), 133.

forgiven: 'he approved J.B.'s plan while any chance of success—when none he supported the next best.'[52]

Despite the damning and unequivocal nature of the Holford report, Bentham and his friends did not entirely abandon hope. Early in the following session of 1812 Holford introduced a bill to implement his proposals. He paid tribute to Bentham as an ingenious and learned gentleman but argued that it was 'impossible to ingraft on a system of contract a provision for apportioning the duration of punishments to the conduct and demeanor of the prisoners'. In the debates on the bill, Bentham's friends made a last-ditch stand to save the panopticon. But in what was a major victory for Holford's ideas, they had jettisoned management by contract. Abercromby, while praising the talents and benevolence of Mr Bentham, suggested that even if contract were rejected, there was merit in the architectural design.[53] And Romilly conceded Holford's argument that management by committee was preferable to that by an individual answerable only to the King's Bench. But he pleaded that the principle of public inspection should not be abandoned for there were 'no inspectors or guardians as good as the public themselves'. But Bragge Bathurst, a member of the committee and a supporter of the bill, took the opposite view: 'the plan of making the prisoners a public spectacle . . . had a tendency to defeat the main object, namely, that of affording them every opportunity of solitary reflection upon the nature of their offences, and the justice of their punishment'. Wilberforce allowed that Bentham's plan was not perfect, but he praised the provision of employment for discharged prisoners to prevent their return to a life of crime. In a dramatic final plea, Romilly reminded the House that Pitt and Dundas had approved the panopticon; and in a last desperate move, he turned to Charles Long, appealing to him to corroborate the truth of this. Long rose and did Bentham his last disservice. He had to admit that the two illustrious statesmen had approved the panopticon, but 'he was not prepared to say that they were particularly attached to Mr Bentham's plan which . . . t was impossible any person could wholly approve who had attentively examined it'. Romilly's motion to delay the passage of the penitentiary bill to allow further consideration for the panopticon was defeated in a thin House by 35 votes to 18.[54] The bill became law in April.

Even this was not quite the end for the panopticon. In May 1812 the Prime Minister, Spencer Perceval, was assassinated and his place taken by Lord Liverpool. Richard Ryder, a strong supporter of Holford's proposals, was replaced at the Home Office by the former Prime Minister Lord Sidmouth. And the indefatigable Bentham soon extracted from him an undertaking that the panopticon would be reconsidered. Even at this late stage, Bentham still hoped that the Penitentiary Act would be set aside and the panopticon after all be built on Millbank. But if that proved impossible, he believed that his plan could still be used to replace the hulks. In June, to Bentham's renewed fury, the Holford Committee produced its anodyne third report on the hulks. It does seem to have applied a double standard in comparison with the way it had dealt with the panopticon. It appeared determined to approve the hulks, for it admitted that the prisoners were battened under hatches at night uninspected and unsupervised with the guards remaining on deck afraid to go down among them; but, the report suavely pronounced, 'they do not often ill-use each other'. And the atrocious vice which rumour imputed to them, 'appears to be held in as much abhorrence on board the Hulks as in other places'.[55] The committee did concede, however, that the hulks were not ideal instruments of reformation and it recommended a series of palliatives, in particular that the chaplains should be more active and a hierarchy of salaried supervisors should be appointed. Bentham was allowed a meeting with Lord Sidmouth to put his case and he followed this up with a lengthy letter enclosing all the panopticon writings from *A View of the Hard Labour Bill* to *A Plea for the Constitution*. This somewhat frenetic letter rehearsed the arguments for a contract panopticon prison and indignantly refuted, point by point, the arguments of the Holford Reports. Bentham was particularly incensed by the insinuation that his

[54] *Parliamentary Debates*, xxii. 101–3, 20 Mar. 1812. Charles Bragge Bathurst (1754–1831), MP, 1790–1823; Chancellor of the Duchy of Lancaster, 1812–23; President of the Board of Control, 1821–2.

[55] *Third Report from the Committee on the Laws Relating to Penitentiary Houses. Ordered by the House of Commons to be printed 27 June 1812*, 139.

sleeping arrangements would foment homosexuality. 'Thus,' he alleged, 'and with so delicate a touch as scarce to leave a soil on Honourable fingers—thus was *Panopticon blackened.*' He boasted yet again of the endorsement of Blackstone and Eden, and again claimed the friendship of Howard. And again he extolled the panopticon as the most economical, rational, and humane way to manage a penitentiary. And he accused Holford and his associates of creating a mountain of patronage as a remedy for the evils of the hulks. 'Now, my Lord,' he asked, 'what is this panacea? Oh, my Lord, considering who the Physicians are, an answer is almost a superfluity—*Offices*! *offices*! Yes my Lord: the nests of offices promised, with the expences attached to them, innumerable.'[56] And he was still convinced that his right to the contract had been stolen from him by a group of conspirators who were now themselves enjoying the spoils. But Bentham's angry eloquence failed to move the Home Secretary. Sidmouth's refusal to overrule Holford and his reports was gently conveyed to Bentham by Dumont on 22 February 1813: 'He spoke with admiration of Mr Bentham etc. etc. but could not hesitate when a committee of the H. of C. was at variance with him.'[57] The panopticon project was dead at last.

Bentham's claims for compensation were, however, very much alive; and once all hope was finally extinguished, he turned his mind to extracting the best possible terms from the Treasury. The Penitentiary Act had provided for the appointment of two arbitrators, one by the Treasury and one by Jeremy Bentham to determine the amount; the payment was to be made one month after the award. Bentham complained vehemently that the Act had 'my name posted up . . . in the joint character of a public burthen and a recorded outcast'. And to Romilly, he ostentatiously paraded his repugnance to compensation:

Oh, how grating—how odious to me is this wretched business of *compensation*! Forced, after twenty years of oppression—forced to join myself to the Baal-peor of blood-suckers, and contribute to the impoverishment of that public, to which, in the way of economy . . . I had such well-grounded assurance of being permitted to render some signal service.[58]

[56] *Correspondence (CW)*, viii. 278–9, Bentham's emphasis.
[57] Ibid. 308.
[58] Ibid. 264, 290.

These scruples did not prevent Bentham pressing his claim with guile and tenacity; he was determined to squeeze the last penny from the public purse. During the passage of the bill, he persuaded Romilly to propose amendments that strengthened his case. Instead of being entitled to claim compensation only for 'loss of time and for his trouble', he had substituted the words, 'for all Loss and Damage by him and the said Samuel Bentham or either of them sustained by reason of the non-fulfilment' of the contract.[59] His brother's rights were subsumed in his and this vague open-ended clause enabled him to argue for very substantial damages indeed. He had unbounded faith in Samuel's inventions and a firm conviction that only ill-fortune had prevented his becoming one of the most successful of entrepreneurs. In a manuscript draft the wide scope of his ambitions is apparent:

As to the loss of commercial profit supposing any one of the most fortunate adventurers in the line of scientific invention, a Sir Richard Arkwright, a Mr Bolton, or a Mr Wedgwood suppose his venture nipped in the bud and he called upon to ask for compensation. Suppose him to have named but the half or the quarter of what he afterwards realized, what scorn ... would have been poured upon his castles in the air.[60]

So in his claim for compensation he listed the grounds for damage as: first, expenditure of capital for the development of Samuel Bentham's mechanical contrivances; secondly, the loss of profits that might have accrued from their development; and, thirdly, the loss of profit that might have accrued from the fulfilment of the panopticon contract itself. Bentham computed the lost profits from September 1795 to March 1813 at the rate of £37,500 p.a.; from that he deducted 25 per cent to cover the wages and superannuation payments to the inmates; and he ended with the grand total of a claim for £689,062. 11s.[61] Bentham was living in Cloud-cuckoo-land if he believed that the Treasury would pay him compensation even remotely in that area. Such an amount would have made him one of the richest men in England—or have built three penitentiaries. But the monstrous size of his claim is the last indication of the size of his aspirations.

The arbitrators were finally appointed in March 1813; they and

[59] *Correspondence (CW)*, viii. 242, 52 Geo. III, c. 44, p. 737. UC cxviii. 345.
[60] UC cxvii. 299.
[61] UC cxxii. 351–486.

their legal advisers met several times in June and July. John Koe, Bentham's close friend and disciple, attended on his behalf. Fortunately, notes of some of these meeting have been preserved in Bentham's papers so the reception of his claim has been recorded. On 28 June William Cooke for the Treasury suggested that Mr Bentham had better approach the Treasury direct, as 'the sum he had demanded was so enormous that there was no dealing with it'. John Koe defended his mentor saying that 'the claim was not inserted as a demand but merely put there as the unavoidable conclusion from the Evidence taken before the Committee of the House of Commons in 1812'. A few days later, William Vizard, representing Bentham, informed the meeting that the Treasury was suggesting an annuity. On 6 July at the third meeting, Bentham's arbitrator, John Whishaw, made it clear that he would be unable to support Bentham's claim and that the amount of compensation would have to be based on the amount of expenditure incurred and that there was a lamentable deficiency in the accounts.[62] The arbitrator's award given in July was for £23,000. But because of Treasury regulations the payment could not be made until October; they did, however, grant him interest for these three months. Whether Bentham was disappointed is not recorded, but he was certainly determined to extract the last possible penny from the Treasury. In August, he wrote to the Lords Commissioners maintaining that he was entitled to his expenses for going to arbitration. The Treasury rebutted this additional claim arguing that the £23,000 covered all dealings with the government. This money was finally paid to Bentham on 19 October 1813. But this was not quite the end of the matter. Later that month he wrote again, alleging that the amounts due to him in interest and as reimbursement of fees had been miscalculated and he requested an additional £779. 3s. to make up the difference. The Treasury conceded this demand.[63] So Bentham at least won the final skirmish in his twenty-year battle with his country's political and administrative system.

---

[62] Ibid. 347–50. William Cooke (1757–1832), barrister at Lincoln's Inn. John Herbert Koe (1783–1860), barrister at Lincoln's Inn; Bentham's secretary and protegé, c.1800–c.1820; County Court judge, 1847–60. William Vizard (1774–1859), Solicitor to Princess Caroline, 1811–20. John Whishaw (c.1764–1840), Commissioner for auditing public accounts 1806–35.

[63] *Correspondence* (*CW*), viii. 356.

# PLANS, VISIONS, AND UTOPIA

A Dovecot full of doves and pigeons
Shudders Hell through all its regions.

William Blake, *Auguries of Innocence*

Scattered among Bentham's papers are many pages of casual, inchoate notes jotted down in columns, that are like pieces of a jigsaw which, when fitted together, give detail and substance to his plans for a prison and afford a new insight into the nature of his ideal society. There are two separate bundles of papers seemingly the product of two climaxes of the panopticon saga.[1] The collection dating from 1794 at the time of the Penitentiary Act are more grandiose and bizarre than the later notes inspired by the Finance Committee Report and the possibility of a temporary panopticon in 1798. They were both times of hope but, by 1798, Bentham's private vision had become more sober. He seems to have been less intoxicated with the visionary and more concerned with mundane detail. These private musings reveal many facets of his character, his taste in architecture, interior decoration, and art. For any study of Bentham's personality they are essential reading.

Bentham was much concerned with the minutiae of domestic details, combining a crass disregard for the sensibilities of his inmates with endless care for their comfort. Women's caps were dispensed with as a needless expense and a receptacle of filth; better that the women, like the men, should have their heads

---

[1] UC cvii and clvii. It is difficult to date this fragmentary material with any certainty. Many of the sheets in UC clvii are endorsed in pencil, 'Temporary Panopticon' and dated 1798. UC cvii is earlier, some sheets are dated 1794 and the metasylum is mentioned which again suggests the date of 1794. Some of the schemes might seem to fit more readily with the Poor Plan but they are interspersed with notes that clearly apply to felons. This would strengthen the theory that the pauper panopticon derived directly from the prison.

shorn. Perhaps shoes were unnecessary: 'Bare legs and feet will prevent offensive smells' and be an obstacle to escape.[2] But a list of apparel and equipment needed for each inmate is comprehensive, including coat, waistcoat, knee-breeches, pocket handkerchiefs, water jugs, salt cellars, and head brushes. The building should have a striking clock, a bell, and a wind dial, as over the chimney piece at Sam's Coffee House in Change Alley, to determine the direction of the wind so windows could be opened accordingly to increase comfort.[3] Bentham scribbled down ideas and suggestions at random; a recipe for 'Birmingham soup' at one halfpenny a pint, consisting of meat, onions, rice, and oatmeal; a note that coals brought from Oxford by canal are cheap; that beds should be 6 feet by $2\frac{1}{2}$ feet, though some might be smaller or larger; that there should be a movable board over each man's cell specifying his name and offence; that each man should have a three-legged stool with back support provided by ropes; that the inmates' own clothes should be carefully preserved, to this end each prisoner would have a wooden label provided with their names ready to be attached.

As well as being a great workshop of wheel-driven machinery, the panopticon would also have been a farm. Potatoes, vegetables, fruits, and flowers were to be grown and pigs were to be reared. Nothing was to be wasted. The excreta of the convicts was to be mixed with lime, earth, and straw from the beds and used as compost. 'Will hogs', Bentham pondered, 'eat chaff?' If so, used straw could be mixed with uneaten potatoes and fed to them. He also devised a panopticon for hens, the ptenotrophium, which has many of the features of the modern battery and gives to Bentham the dubious distinction of being a precursor of factory farming. The birds were to be kept in cells in a multi-storey coop with sufficiency of room, but, as Bentham carefully inserted between the lines, 'no superfluity of room'. And when the time came for them to be slaughtered, each operation, the killing, the plucking, and the gutting were to be performed separately by different female convicts on a conveyor-belt system. The hens were subject to experiment, the coop being turned at different angles to the sun to find the optimum position and their happiness was analysed on familiar Benthamite lines.

[2] UC clvii. 39.    [3] Ibid. 28, cxix. 23.

The advantages of their regime were listed as warmth, dryness, cleaning, equality of feeding, prevention of fighting, and security against vermin and disease.[4]

Many of the inmates of an eighteenth-century prison would have been little more than children and although Bentham dealt sketchily with their education in the published proposals, his private marginal notes show that this was nevertheless a matter of considerable interest to him. Education need not be confined to Sundays; even on weekdays, 'allowing twelve hours for work, there would be four to employ in learning, writing, music etc.'. A 'book to learn to read in' is listed with other essential equipment. Thought was given to how the young could be persuaded to work and learn: 'Boys and young men that appear promising, treat them at first with cold severity, that they may enjoy the difference.'[5] Their wishes and inclinations were to be collected and registered, in order the better to choose indulgences for them. Some, on their consenting to be tattooed, might be trained as bookkeepers and so provide a pool for parish clerks to keep parish schools; some were to be gardeners, others attached to the surgeon. Bentham's love of music pervades his educational plans, and an inmate would have had ample opportunity for the exercise of his talents. Any with a voice would be taught singing and the more proficient would learn an instrument. Choirs and orchestras would be formed, to sing at meals and services and to perform concerts: 'Bands in the two wards to perform alternately and responsively—sometimes to join in full chorus.' They were to learn psalms, anthems, and finally oratorios; they might even be permitted to spend some of their working time practising music. And, if tattooed, might be allowed out of prison to perform at public concerts. Even those unable to perform could contribute to the creation of melody by copying music as one of their sedentary tasks.[6]

In his notes Bentham sometimes referred to 'Panopticon Town' or 'Panopticon Hill', and was clearly envisaging a wider neigh-

---

[4] UC cvii. 93. The management of poultry in this way was not unknown at the time. The Duke of Bedford had a large coop warmed by a stove for better fattening in cold weather, *Annals of Agriculture and Other Useful Arts*, 39 (1803), 426. See also R. Evans, *The Fabrication of Virtue* (Cambridge, 1982), 439.

[5] UC clvii. 39, 28, 39.

[6] Ibid. 39.

bourhood than the prison factory of his public schemes. He
hoped to be allowed to undertake the upkeep of the roads all
around and to build along and over them.[7] In this neighbourhood
he would have found scope for his talents as an architect, a
town-planner, and a landscape gardener. He intended to build a
covered way between the river and Panopticon Town for the
convenience of visitors in rainy weather.[8] This structure was to
be 15 feet high and on the outside terraced houses were to be
built into the wall. A frigidarium could be accommodated in the
passage and a lift with counterweight would give access from the
ground to the promenade above the arches. A garden would be
created here, each of the houses having a bulkhead on the top
floor with a door into the garden. Access for the inhabitants of
the houses was limited, for the governor of the panopticon would
hold the keys to these doors and they could be locked at any time
he wished in the interest of security and seclusion. The houses
were to be built in brick, flint, or old stone—if it could be got
cheap. Each house would have a projecting beam for the easy
raising of flowerpots to the promenade gardens and these beams
would be adorned with the cast-iron heads of an animal, King
George III, or the likeness of one of the convicts. The façades
would vary, some having large fronts, others projecting bows,
the whole in the Gothic style surmounted by battlements; the
most imposing of the buildings being the Castle Tavern for the
reception of visitors, its terrace suitable for firework displays.
In the crenellation of the battlements would be inserted vast
stone letters, large enough to be read from below, constituting
an appropriate legend, for instance: 'Instituit J.B. Primus
Gubernator A″ X″ 18 . . .'[9] Other areas outside the grandiose
structure of the battlemented prison complex would have provided
further fields for the exercise of his genius. In 1794 he proposed
to pull down Tothill Street and build in its place a wide street
with shops at ground level, dwellings above, and a covered walk
with pillars, supporting balconies above which would form a
continuous garden. The wood- and stonework for this development would have come from the panopticon. Bentham himself

[7] UC cvii. 103.
[8] The details of this scheme are in disjointed notes in UC clvii. 58, probable
date 1798.
[9] UC clvii. 58.

would have undertaken the watching, paving, and lighting, he would also manage the upkeep of the garden with plants renewed annually from the panopticon nurseries. Female convicts could be employed in the gentler occupations of horticulture, grafting, budding, gathering, sowing, and planting.[10]

Some of these fragmentary jottings open a window on to Bentham's dream world; he seems to have communed with himself, confiding in the lined columns of his paper thoughts that other men would have kept hidden in the recesses of their minds or expressed as poetic imaginings. It is as though he was compelled to write down every fugitive thought lest it escape. These notes often consist of no more than a list of disjointed phrases, but pieced together they present a picture of a bizarre fantasy world, a world in which 'J.B.' is the central figure, the Walter Mitty of the panopticon, performing heroic roles which were in reality denied him. He would be an officer educating and drilling a corps of men to serve with the East India Company.[11] The panopticon was to be the centre of new trading and exploration ventures. Ships would be sent across the oceans of the world to West America, 'Cook's shores', and California to collect specimens of plants and seeds, especially valuable hardy timber trees, the raw material for the woodworking machinery of the panopticon. These new specimens would be propagated in the panopticon nurseries; and the voyages could be made profitable by the sale of these plants and the proceeds from the publication of illustrated accounts of the expeditions. In an ambiguous note, Bentham suggests that a ship in home port might have women assigned to it, 'Say one woman to 4 men'. They were to do 'what women's work there is to do such as cooking, sewing, washing ect.'.[12] Whether they would also have provided sexual services is not specified. Gardens, botany, and the study of plants from all over the world were real and lasting passions. In organizing such expeditions from the panopticon, Bentham would have been realizing, by proxy, an ambition from his youth. Before he read Helvetius, he had imagined himself sailing the oceans and exploring the interior of South America where he believed a study of the plants and animals would increase scientific knowledge and confer great benefit on mankind—a remarkably prophetic

---

[10] UC cvii. 72, 74.     [11] Ibid. 71.     [12] Ibid. 67.

anticipation of the voyage of the *Beagle*. A weak constitution and the alternative ambition of reforming the laws prevented this voyage from becoming more than a pipedream. But into old age, he instructed friends to send him back seeds of useful and beautiful plants from their travels and himself took great pleasure in distributing them in the service of humanity. And at the age of 60 he was again making plans to travel to Mexico.[13]

In Bentham's vision, the panopticon would not only be a vehicle for botanical study and discovery but a centre for wider scientific and technical experiment. The scope of his ambitions is made clear in his draft advertisement for a surgeon for the establishment. He asked for: 'A young Gentleman who has received a compleat Medical Education, such as would qualify him to officiate in the capacity of Surgeon to a ship of the first rank.' But in the salubrious prison, 'the immediate duty of his situation will probably occupy but a very small proportion of his time', and a man with wide-ranging knowledge and an interest in research would find ample scope for his talents. For it was proposed to set up an experimental laboratory, and the surgeon would share in the work and in the profits from any experiments or discoveries that might be made. 'A taste for Botany, Experimental Horticulture or Music will also be likely to meet with gratification.' The salary for this post would be determined by the lowest offer received; Bentham believed that the pleasures of the pursuit of knowledge would incline a talented young man to work for small remuneration, and indeed that a lust for money was not compatible with a thirst for knowledge: 'it being presumed that the stronger a man's passion may be for the pursuits in question, the more indifferent he will be to inducements of a mere pecuniary nature.'[14]

Scattered among his fragmentary notes are suggestions for mechanical and other contrivances, some of which show a remarkable prescience; his panopticon would indeed have been in the vanguard of technical progress. He sketched a 'hanging bridge' made 'of cable strained in the manner of the warp of a loom', clearly a precursor of the suspension bridge. He anticipated some of the comforts of modern travel in his improved Phaeton

[13] *Correspondence (CW)*, ii. 98–9, vii. 561–73.
[14] UC cxviii. 137.

Stage, a low-slung coach on springs; 'the gentry' separately accommodated above the ordinary passengers on reclining seats, seats which could be shut off from their neighbours at pleasure; the back might even let down on a hinge for sleeping.[15] Other notes suggest water closets, portable houses, and the preservation of food by the exclusion of air. If only food could be preserved in an unaltered state, it could be available at all seasons; poultry could be killed at any age and all types of foodstuffs could be imported from distant lands. He speculated on the practical application of processes *in vacuo*—distillation would take less heat and butter might be more easily preserved. He also planned to attempt a whole range of different processes, silkworm culture, trout-farming, vegetable-drying within the heating system, distillation, dyeing, mushroom-growing, an aviary for guinea fowls, and the breeding of angora rabbits. Panopticon was to have its own coinage, newspaper, almanac, and maps. And it was to be the centre of a national effort of applied technology under the direction of the Board of Agriculture: 'J.B. to make any such labour saving agricultural instruments as the Board shall recommend.'[16] Religion and poetry were to be pressed into service to uphold his austere society. Songs holding out the 'prospect of a happy immortality after a life of innocence' would be composed; J.B. laying down the theme, others providing the versification—a subordinate task which he proposed to delegate to William Cowper among others.

In his old age, Bentham recalled the panopticon as 'a magnificent instrument with which I then dreamed of revolutionizing the world'.[17] One of his dreams was of subsidiaries to the parent panopticon, one of them for infants, the paedotrophium. The infants would be acquired in various ways; some would be the children of prisoners; some the offspring of soldiers or seamen killed in the war; others might be paupers taken by contract or apprentices on the footing of adoptive children. He calculated their value in monetary terms estimating how long they must live to pay back the cost of their maintenance in work. Bentham gave his love of coining neologisms free rein. This establishment he called the 'Paedotrophium, Abyssinia or the sequestered Empire containing the Brephoconi or infant nursery . . . the Neaniskion

---

[15] UC cvii. 84, 87, 91.     [16] Ibid. 88.     [17] Bowring, x. 572.

or apprentice nursery'.[18] His plans for the management and subsequent education of these infants are in themselves interesting
and at times extraordinarily prescient. He anticipated the division
between grammar and technical education. Boys (girls are not
mentioned in this context) should be divided into two groups,
those suitable for a literary education and those better fitted for
one in handicrafts. Each boy should be directed to the subject for
which he had the most talent; and physical exercise should be
combined with intellectual. The literary education would have
been formidable, a far cry from the limited practical education he
planned for the panopticon inmates. A study of Linnaeus would
teach both Latin and Botany; no classics, at least for the ordinary
boy, and no poets except possibly Horace. French should be
taught from Voltaire's *History*; German from Crill's *Annals
of Chemistry*; mineralogy from the best book available in any
language. Bentham revealed his own preferences and artistic
priorities when he avers that drawing need be taught only as far
as it is needed in mechanics, but music must be available at all
times. In the teaching of infants, Bentham anticipates Maria
Montessori in emphasizing the importance of instruction by play
and suggesting ivory letters and wooden geometrical figures,
maps, and cards.[19]

The problems of feeding a large number of babies also occupied
Bentham's mind. One of his less-convincing contrivances is a
trough for the mass suckling of infants, laying them 'round a
vessel full of milk with an artificial nipple for each'. He was,
however, aware of the dangers of infection: 'possibly in the case
of a contaminating disease this mode might be infectious, if so,
each child should have an artificial breast to itself.'[20] The milk
might be woman's, sow's, ass's, bitch's, or cow's. He devised five
different diets: (1) potatoes alone; (2) potatoes with milk; (3)
potatoes with fish; (4) potatoes with soup; (5) potatoes with
meat; and suggests that experiments could be made by feeding
different groups of children on the various diets and observing
the results. Even under the age of 4 these infants were not to
be idle and useless; their time could be spent reading, writing,
gathering things, or looking for worms, snails, and caterpillars to
feed to the birds in the ptenotrophium. After the age of 4, these

---

[18] UC cvii. 55, 58, 61.     [19] Ibid. 54.     [20] Ibid. 56.

children, like those in the pauper panopticons, would be set to work to pay for their maintenance.

The most unforgettable of all Bentham' subsidiary schemes and one that reveals a great deal about his attitude to women is the 'timoioterim,' or, as he preferred to call it, the 'sotimion'.[21] This was a refuge for fallen women, which in Bentham's mind emerges as a grotesque cross between a Magdalen and an amusement park. The sotimion would have been blazoned to the world by vast symbolic pictures over the entrance to the great road to the panopticon; Charity with her children, Reputation with eyes uplifted to Heaven, and Secrecy with her finger to her lips. It was to be another commercial venture; as soon as the land for the prison was secured he planned to circulate a prospectus inviting subscriptions from investors in an establishment: 'for the preservation of female delicacy and reputation. The advantages of optional solitude and necessary concealment combined with the comforts of innocent society. With which is connected the Nothotrophium or Asylum for the innocent offspring of clandestine love. Bene vivat qua bene latuit.'[22]

There was certainly a market for such a service. The newspapers at the time regularly carried advertisements directed to pregnant women who needed a safe and secret refuge for the delivery of their babies. A gentleman at 44 Goodge Street offered help in pregnancy to:

Ladies who, from the consequences of indiscretion, may be desirous of medical aid, or perhaps find temporary seclusion from the world necessary, may be accommodated with a furnished house or appartments, in town or its vicinity, and every requisite appendage for the month, or any time previous to it, according to circumstances, by a Medical Gentleman whose honour and secrecy may be safely confided in.

Although the word abortion was not mentioned, this accommodating gentleman hinted that he might be able to help in less legal ways, his 'advice and friendship if early sought for, may be productive of unexpected benefit, and the means of preserving reputation unsullied'. To repress curiosity and improper applications, any consultation cost a guinea. Another gentleman, Mr Watson, a surgeon and man mid-wife, offered to dispose of unwanted children, arranging for them to be 'put out to nurse

---

[21] UC cxvii. 100–7.     [22] Ibid. 103.

and humanely taken care of'. He also offered help in another form, his Pill Benedicta at £1. 1*s*. a box was 'an effective remedy to remove all obstructions and irregularities'.[23] It seems a reasonable inference that the rate for abortion in London was a guinea and that it was widely available. The reputation of such gentlemen as Mr Watson was deplorable and to seek their aid was an enterprise full of misery and peril; these unfortunate women were quite at their mercy, as Bentham realized: 'as no woman can complain of them without betraying herself they are out of reach of the popular sanction.'[24] Under the bland surface of Bentham's happy contrivance of the sotimion, we can catch glimpses of a grim world. Death in childbirth was all too common and for these women the risks were greatly enhanced. As for their babies, most unwanted infants died from neglect, malnutrition, or disease; and the survivors faced the chances of the workhouse and foundling hospitals and eventual apprenticeships into trades such as chimney-sweeping or in the textile manufactories in the north. Their mothers would often have little alternative but to resort to prostitution. Bentham's sotimion attached to his carefully organized children's home might have seemed a refuge indeed for these unhappy women. As Bentham argued, the advantages were manifold, they would not be degraded or humiliated: 'thus modesty will not have been blunted by the habit of ignominy', subsequent marriage would therefore be easier to achieve. Also, 'The pleasantness of the place and the character of the Manager would give this establishment the advantage over the advertising private ones.'[25]

Bentham would have spared no effort to minister to the needs of his ladies in distress. Each was to be accommodated in a cabin with a sitting-room large enough to house a piano and chair, two other chairs, a table, a fireplace and a coal-scuttle; the ceiling was to be no more than 7 feet high to make the room easier to heat; two small carpets were provided. Notes on how the chairs could

---

[23] UC cviii. 101; *Morning Herald*, 7 Apr. 1796.

[24] UC cvii. 100. Under the common law, abortion was not a crime before 'quickening' at 4–6 months of pregnancy. In 1803 Lord Ellenborough's Act for the first time made procuring abortion before quickening a criminal offence punishable by fine or transportation. Death was the penalty for the offence if performed after quickening.

[25] Ibid.

be designed for the comfort of women in an advanced state of pregnancy cover a whole page of Bentham's notes. They would have shoulder and leg screens, adjustable side-rails, a footboard, and elbow supports. Samuel Bentham's ingenuity would again be brought into service, his sick-chair and new armchair were to set the standard, and Jeremy Bentham's frame was to be the standard of measurement: 'Height of the back to be equal to the height of J.B.'s back.' 'The *depth* of the seat to be equal to the length of J.B.'s thighs.'[26] At night convenience was not forgotten, a commode at the end of the bed would be provided with a hinged cover which would close automatically; it would be emptied every morning: 'The soil to drop upon a drawer lined with a bed of lime and to be conveyed away every morning at twilight by a female convict'—probably to add to the heap of fertilizer for the garden. The food was admirably devised to provide a healthy diet: poultry, new-laid eggs, milk, fresh fruit and vegetables, and hot rolls. Wine and even liquors from some neighbouring public house could be supplied. But although living in the sotimion would be luxurious, the ladies were not immune from regulation, each would be supplied with a Book of Rules and Bentham discussed with himself whether sumptuary laws prohibiting or taxing expensive dress and display might not be desirable—he even suggested a uniform, which, although an extra expense, would be picturesque.

The amusement of the ladies was not neglected; a place would be allocated to them in the panopticon chapel and they would process there on Sundays, perhaps dressed in their uniform—Bentham does not explain how this public spectacle of a crowd of pregnant women could be reconciled with their need for secrecy. They would be entertained by the music from the panopticon and could themselves take instruction to improve their music and drawing; they could play at cards (but not for money); there would be lambs to cosset and hens to feed. Outside, Bentham seems to have envisaged the environs of the sotimion, and the panopticon, being turned into a fun-fair. Sailing, punting, paddling, and rowing would be available on ponds and canals; on land, roundabouts, swings, an 'up and down', and a chamber-horse would provide entertainment. Bentham's *tour de force* is a

---

[26] UC cvii. 101, Bentham's emphasis.

Russian flying chariot whose velocity and degrees of smoothness could be regulated and which might develop into 'The Panopticon Flying car', which might be prescribed by doctors as a healthy exercise. It is not clear whether Bentham envisaged his pregnant ladies taking their turns on these fairground rides. More appropriate to their condition was the provision of a coffee-room for members only, which in Bentham's mind began to take on the characteristics of an exclusive gentlemen's club. Members could be expelled for indelicacy; at the discretion of the other members, three black balls, or black balls from a quarter of the whole number, being sufficient to exclude an immodest female from the coffee-room. Thereafter she could be excluded from the garden and finally expelled altogether on the vote by ballot of a majority of the members. So, although Bentham's schemes for the amusement of the inhabitants of the sotimion show scant respect for the female intellect, the women were to be allowed this practical exercise in democracy. Bentham certainly believed he could make the women content with their lot. He speculated as to the terms on which they might be permitted to stay on after the birth; the amusements, and the difficulties of finding asylum elsewhere, might make this desirable, perhaps they could buy their cabins or possibly pay double or triple rates. Bentham discussed the question of visitors with sensitive sympathy; at one point he considered allowing the women's lovers to visit and stay with them, but at another point suggested it might be better to allow only females to visit; in any case, visitors must send in their name and be approved by the member before being admitted and the member should be able to inspect the visitor before showing herself. The ladies were to have a garden to walk in, carefully secluded and locked; but Bentham himself might be able to slip in to enjoy the gentle female companionship that he craved: 'Quere,' he wrote, 'J.B. to have a key?'[27]

Domestic needs were not forgotten. The washing would be done at the panopticon. The panopticon surgeon would provide medical and obstetrical services and the panopticon chaplain would christen the babies and church the women. Other domestic services might be provided cheaply by taking in, for no charge or on low terms, necessitous pregnant women who in return would

[27] Ibid. 100.

wait on the rich ones, help with the infants, and wash and sew. But the sotimion was a commercial enterprise and its profits would come from the fees paid by the women or their families. They would pay in advance and the fees would not be remitted in any circumstance: 'The fee must be the same, child or no child and whether it lives or dies, payable on admission that there may be no temptation to destroy or neglect it on the part of the parents.'[28] This care for the infant was not disinterested, neither is there any hint whatsoever that Bentham would have contemplated abortion. This was not from sentimentality or a scrupulous regard for the law: he had a use for these children; they, like their mothers, would be a source of profit. They would be taken at birth and placed in the paedotrophium. And a strict anonymity was enforced, an anonymity unbreakable until the child's service had expired, until he had worked long enough to earn enough profit to repay the manager for the expense of his upbringing. But careful records would be kept, a register of identity and identification marks would enable the maternity and, in some cases, the paternity of the child to be ascertained; parents could pay to obtain knowledge of their child, and if 'the child turned out anything extraordinary its parentage might be communicated to the Parents'.[29] Bentham, a childless bachelor in his mid-40s might be forgiven for taking no account of the anguish his schemes would have inflicted on the unhappy mothers; it is more difficult to sympathize with his measurement of the value of the life of a child in monetary terms. He later estimated that:

According to the calculations which had then been . . . made, the pecuniary value of a child at its birth,—that value which at present is not merely equal 0, but equal to an oppressively large negative quantity, would, under that system of maintenance and education which I had prepared for it . . . have been a positive quantity to no inconsiderable amount.[30]

For Bentham money was an objective standard of measurement; and his attitude to children must be seen in the context of a horrendously high infant mortality rate. Bentham in his own family had suffered grievously, five of his younger brothers and

---

[28] UC cvii. 100.     [29] Ibid.     [30] Bowring, xi. 103–4.

sisters had died in early childhood, the youngest, Samuel, being the only survivor. This fact of eighteenth-century life is illustrated by the words of Edward Gibbon writing at this time: 'The death of a new-born child before that of its parents may seem an unnatural, but it is strictly a probable event; since of any given number the greater part are extinguished before their ninth year, before they possess the faculties of the mind or body.'[31] The fate of children in the workhouses of London was horrendously cruel. Many were entrusted to 'killing nurses', so called because no child survived their care. Jonas Hanway found that in the parish of St Andrew Holborn and St George the Martyr, of 284 infants received only sixty-two survived.[32] As Bentham saw it, a child might live if it were a source of profit, if it were not, it would most assuredly die. Death of the young was commonplace and would also assuredly have been the lot of many of the ladies of the sotimion; despite their comforts and amusements many were doomed. But even in death, Bentham, unsentimental as he was uncensorious, would have had a use for them. Buried in the panopticon graveyard, their memorial stones could be laid so as gradually to form a pavement that would be useful as a path to walk on in wet weather.

The sotimion was a sequestered, secret place in direct contrast to the panopticon. According to Bentham's inspection principle, public access to the prison was essential to its successful management. He constantly reiterated that it must be near London, 'the great seat of inspection'. He planned not just to allow visitors, but to encourage them to come in large numbers by the provision of exotic entertainment. The Panopticon Hill that Bentham dreamed of creating at Battersea Rise would have been a little distance from London, and in the summer the journey could be a pleasant excursion in one of his brother's veriminicular boats. These boats could be rowed up the river by some of the more orderly of the convicts, many of whom would have been seafaring men. Bentham shatters this tranquil summer picture by suggesting that these boats should be shadowed by others carrying armed guards in pulpits ready to shoot any offender who should

---

[31] Edward Gibbon, *Autobiography* (London, 1796), Everyman edn. (London, 1939), 22.
[32] J. S. Taylor, *Jonas Hanway Founder of the Marine Society, Charity and Policy in Eighteenth-Century Britain* (London and Berkeley, Calif., 1985), 105–6.

attempt an escape. On arrival, the visitors would refresh themselves in the Panopticon Tavern, a place full of fantastical devices, coloured lights, mirrors, and exotic scents. In these bizarre plans, the cardinal principle of economy seems to have been jettisoned and the austere philosopher becomes the advocate of a sumptuous lifestyle. The tavern was to be built of brick glazed in a pearl colour. In the refreshment bar, silver-plated copper fountains would spray jets of rose-water, orange-flavour water, lavender-water, and Hungary-water; other, invisible, electric fountains would perfume the rooms. Ironically given his later opinion of George III, he proposed that the words 'God Save the King' should be written by lamps enclosed in coloured water-bottles, and a transparent colossus of the monarch should be erected, illuminated from within. Lenses full of coloured water would refract light; lamps would illuminate columns, arches, and pilasters. The apogee of this Aladdin's cave of colour, perfume, and lights was the garden balcony, wide enough to walk along, full of plants, ornaments, columns of hollow glass, and gilt balustrades; at each end a door inlaid with mirrors would, when opened, reflect and re-reflect the gilt, the flowers, the ornaments, and the coloured columns into eternity.[33]

The most elaborate, fantastical, and expensive devices were reserved for Bentham's own dwelling. He planned a home for himself and his brother with a hall, common parlour, dining parlour, drawing room, a two-storey study for J.B., a study for S.B., and a laboratory. It was to be built of white Highland marble. But the real glory of this residence was yet another garden. J.B.'s study would open on to it. It was to be glazed and was to have a lawn, an artificial swamp, rock-plants, and hothouse plants. It could be decorated with shells from the panopticon voyages and stocked with plants from the panopticon explorations: 'The best part of it for prospect to be enlarged into a circular area inclosed in a circular basin for gold fish, crowned by a Dome...The balcony at each end, to terminate in a looking glass door made of lattice work under a copper gilt fretwork.' One side of the garden was to be 'of a different elevation from the other, of such an elevation that neither shall impede the prospect of the other'.[34]

---

[33] UC cvii. 56, 85.     [34] Ibid. 75, 103, 104.

Bizarre and fantastical though these designs and architectural plans may seem, they were capable of achievement. Bentham finally took leave of reality in a project to build, literally, a castle in the air, a skyscraper, 'to take advantage of coolness—useful E & W Indies living'. It was to be immensely tall: 'for the extent of proposal compare it with the height of the highest hill near London, Highgate, Hampstead, Shooters, Box Hill.' It was to be extraordinary, comparable with the pyramids of Egypt or the Colossus. And in a parody of his own logic, Bentham argued that it would be safe, for 'The danger to visitors will be completely disproved by the workers who will live in the castle as they build it.'[35]

Bentham's private vision of the development of the panopticon prison suggests that the utopian elements have their roots firmly in the original scheme and are thus an essential part of his thought. This theory is difficult to reconcile with the traditional picture of Bentham as a humdrum rationalist who rejected emotion and sentimentality. Bentham is not generally seen as a utopian thinker. H. L. A. Hart maintained that Bentham, 'envisaged no millennium and no utopia'.[36] Manning argued that his low opinion of human nature made utopia impossible.[37] Thomas also insisted that he 'was not a utopian, dreaming like so many of his contemporaries of some state of perfection'.[38] Bentham himself rejected the possibility of a golden age, arguing that: 'The unequal gifts of nature and of fortune will always create jealousies: there will always be opposition of interests . . . Pleasure will be purchased by pains; enjoyments by privations'; and that the fate of great numbers of mankind must always be 'Painful labour, daily subjection, a condition nearly allied to indigence'.[39] He stigmatized Thomas More's 'Romance' itself as an anti-rational fallacy, for its whole concept ignored causes and effects and produced 'a felicitous result, flowing from causes not having it in their nature to be productive of any such effects, but having it in their nature to be productive of contrary effects'.[40]

[35] Ibid. 84, 85.
[36] H. L. A. Hart, *Essays on Bentham* (Oxford, 1982), 24–5.
[37] D. J. Manning, *The Mind of Jeremy Bentham* (London, 1968), 84.
[38] W. Thomas, *The Philosophical Radicals* (Oxford, 1979), 20.
[39] Bowring, i. 194.
[40] Ibid. ii. 459.

Yet from its inception he described *Pauper Management Improved* as a romance and a utopia.[41] And this scheme was a natural extension of his metasylum, which, in its turn, was an essential of the prison; and it has clear affinities with the private imaginings confided to his manuscripts. He planned a National Charity Company that would build 250 workhouses at equal distances throughout the country. They would be run as profit-making organizations and would, of course, be built on panopticon principles. The labour of the inmates would be maximized. Bentham delighted in devising tasks for children, the infirm, the disabled, and the blind. But they would be protected from exploitation and brutality in the same way as were his prisoners, by life insurance and public inspection. These workhouses would be a refuge from the economic hazards of the world, an asylum for the indigent and unfortunate and an alternative society and economy. Bentham was planning on a grandiose scale. These pauper panopticons were to be self-sufficient communities; the company was to be empowered to purchase compulsorily enough waste or common land to support its population and the basic task of the workforce would have been to produce their own food. These proposals were a solution to the fundamental problem of how to increase wealth and food supply by putting the commons to productive use. The *Annals of Agriculture* had been founded in 1784 to achieve just this end. Arthur Young had written:

While the American dream lasted, we were told that the growing population of that Continent would create such a system of employment for our manufacturers and sailors, that the prosperity of the mother country would be as boundless as the wastes of her transatlantic dominions.[42]

Now, however, it was necessary to cultivate 'the wastes which disgrace this country' by easier enclosure and by improved methods of agriculture. Bentham devised the pauper panopticons to achieve this purpose and to be engines for the creation of wealth. But he saw the dangers of relying exclusively on the market to achieve a good society. According to his principle of self-supply, production for use within the community rather than

---

[41] *Correspondence* (*CW*), v. 377.
[42] *Annals of Agriculture and Other Useful Arts*, 1 (1784), 45.

for sale outside would avoid many disadvantages and go some way to achieve social justice. He listed the advantages as:

Value in the way of *use*, not susceptible, like value in the way of *exchange* of being destroyed or reduced by glut, competition, stagnation, change of fashion, war . . . nor by imperfections in workmanship affecting *appearance* rather than use . . . Under the principle of self-supply, neither *market*, i.e. *demand*, nor capacity of production, are exposed to failure.—Each hand working, for the most part, not only for the establishment of which he is a member, but in some degree, individually for himself, natural justice holds out its sanction to this arrangement, sympathy helps to promote it, and self-advantage to sweeten it.—Acknowledged community of interest will enable the willing to spur the lazy, without exposing themselves to the reproach of officiousness or ill-nature.[43]

Poynter has perceptively described the profound ambivalence of Bentham's solution to the problems of poverty:

The Pauper Plan grew into a Utopia, and is not the least interesting of the species. If, in much of his work, Bentham preserved a delicate equilibrium between economic liberalism and public planning, in this scheme the planner ran riot. Enough systematic regimentation was involved to make the plan horrible to modern minds: Bentham the Big Brother was no doubt benevolent in intent, but was as dogmatically authoritarian as most of the kind. Not always, perhaps. Flashes of a third Bentham appear behind the planner and the defender of free capitalist competition, Bentham the patron of co-operation between free individuals. The Pauper Plan became, in the end, a pattern for a new society, to exist within a free capitalist economy; a society which would be planned, but with a productive system based on mutual co-operation; the whole serving to remedy the flaws in the free economy, and to lead it in the search for knowledge and social improvement.[44]

In the National Charity Company panopticons, children would be brought up sequestered from the evils and temptations of the world, separated from their natural parents, educated up to the age of 4, but at that stage set to work and taught thereafter only on Sundays. They would be the subject of educational, medical, dietary, and social experimentation; the industry house was a 'crucible for men'.[45] And when they grew up they would become

---

[43] Bowring, viii. 382–3, Bentham's emphasis.
[44] J. R. Poynter, *Society and Pauperism* (London and Toronto, 1969), 109.
[45] Bowring, viii. 437.

the subject of breeding experiments to find out, for instance, the optimum age for marriage. This society Bentham called 'my Utopia'. It has been subject to the fiercest ridicule and condemnation. Himmelfarb argues that the touchstone of the benevolence of any scheme for the poor is its treatment of children and the unfortunate. On that basis Bentham failed lamentably—extending indigence, subjecting little children and the aged infirm to grindingly hard labour, and destroying the liberty of an increasing number of the poor. She concluded that *Pauper Management Improved* was retrograde and an antithesis of humanity, generosity, and civilization. Bahmueller's fuller study follows in Himmelfarb's footsteps: 'if a poorhouse is Utopia', he asks rhetorically, 'what is Inferno?'[46] Modern revisionist or Foucaultian history depicts the panopticon as a cruel contraption ingeniously designed to subjugate the human spirit, a strait-jacket for both body and soul, an instrument to degrade man, to strip from him the last vestiges of dignity. It is a dystopia of horrifying proportions, a terrifying premonition of the worse excesses of totalitarianism.

There is no necessary contradiction in perceiving the panopticon both as a utopia and as an instrument of oppression. Bahmueller implies that utopia should be equated with Heaven, but it can mean many other things, 'nowhere', an unreal or impractical world, or absurd speculation as to the future. And most of the classic utopias are authoritarian; even the anarcho-communist societies of Kropotkin and William Morris exert control through the pervasive and inescapable influence of groups of neighbours. Indeed, it can be argued that regimentation, conformity, and compulsion are the very essence of ideal communities. Lewis Mumford expresses this eloquently: 'every utopia is, almost by definition, a sterile desert, unfit for human occupation.' And he explains this paradox in words wholly apposite to Bentham:

the abstract intelligence . . . is actually a coercive instrument: an arrogant fragment of the full human personality, determined to make the world over in its own over-simplified terms, willfully rejecting interests and values incompatible with its own assumptions, and thereby depriving

---

[46] Himmelfarb, 'Bentham's Utopia: The National Charity Company', *Journal of British Studies*, 10 (1970), 80–125. C. F. Bahmueller, *The National Charity Company* (Berkeley, Calif., Los Angeles, London, 1981), 104.

itself of any of the cooperative and generative functions of life—feeling, emotion, playfulness, exuberance, free fantasy—in short, the liberating sources of unpredictable and uncontrollable creativity.[47]

Thus Mumford suggests that utopia would doom to destruction the very forces that create it.

Bentham does display a certain frightening arrogance. He wrote of himself: 'J.B. the most ambitious of the ambitious. His empire—the empire he aspires to—extending to, and comprehending, the whole human race, in all places . . . at all future time.' The panopticon was: 'A new mode of obtaining power of mind over mind, in a quantity hitherto without example.'[48] It would be easy to interpret these words as symptoms of an incipient paranoia and to depict Bentham as a megalomaniac held in check by the iron bars of a superlative intelligence and a certain humour. But Bentham was not insane; yet neither was he a rationalist humdrum exponent of a drab utilitarianism. He was a man with a vision; a vision that had its origins in the English utopian tradition and in the Arcadian romance of the pastoral idyll. The panopticon was an enclave of reason isolated from the temptations and disorders of the ordinary world. It originated in pre-Freudian Hartlian concepts of human nature as a product of experience. According to these theories, men could be manipulated and changed by manipulating and changing their education and environment. Sequestered from the sources of evil and idleness, men would learn to love labour, they would be inured to habitual industry, and live peaceful, innocent, productive lives. The panopticon shared in the characteristics of other Enlightenment utopias, of which Kumar writes: 'Their overriding aim is the elimination of social discord and individual unhappiness caused by unrestrained desires and strivings.'[49] This is a central element in Thomas More's Utopia and the similarities between it and the panopticon are so striking that it is difficult to believe that Bentham was not deeply influenced by More's work.

More's utopian capital city, Amaurotum, was built on a gentle slope above a great tidal river, like the River Thames in London. Water was supplied in pipes; houses were solid and spacious and

[47] L. Mumford, 'Utopia the City and the Machine', in F. E. Manuel (ed.), *Utopias and Utopian Thought* (Boston, Mass., 1966), 10.
[48] Bowring, xi. 72; iv. 39.
[49] K. Kumar, *Utopia and Anti-Utopia in Modern Times* (Oxford, 1987), 37.

their back doors opened on to gardens luxuriant with herbs and fruits. In Utopia, chickens were hatched in special incubators and music was played at mealtimes. Those convicted of serious crimes were enslaved. In words that Bentham himself might have written, More justified this enslavement as an alternative to execution: 'Their labour is more profitable than their death, and their example lasts longer to deter others from like crimes.'[50] These slaves worked continuously as their punishment; the Utopians themselves were never overworked but would apply themselves happily and industriously to the trade best fitted to their talents. More assured his readers that each Utopian would 'be not wearied like a beast of burden with constant toil from early morning till late at night. Such wretchedness is worse than the lot of slaves, and yet is almost everywhere the life of working men—except for the Utopians.'[51] More was envisaging work of only six hours a day. In Utopia, as in the panopticon, idleness was the most heinous sin; More compared other societies where the noblemen and their retainers 'live idle . . . like drones'. There was no scarcity in Utopia for there was no crowd of idle women, priests, gentlemen, or beggars. Only essential goods were made for there was no ministering to luxury or licentiousness. The inhabitants were sequestered from the corruptions of the world and work was unavoidable; for there was no privacy in Utopia: 'no wine shop, no alehouse, no brothel anywhere, no opportunity for corruption, no lurking hole, no secret meeting place.'[52] The only way of avoiding work would be, as with those inmates of the panopticon who showed exceptional talent for music, to show some especial promise in one of the branches of higher learning.

More's Utopia was a place of authoritarian regulation and its inhabitants valued security above liberty. 'For what can be greater riches for a man', More writes, 'than to live with a joyful and peaceful mind, free of all worries . . . but feeling secure about the livelihood and happiness of himself and his family.' And an essential ingredient of this security was, in Utopia as in the panopticon, a provision for old age. More pictured the workmen

[50] T. More, *Utopia* (Louvain, 1516), ed. Edward Surtz (New Haven, Conn., and London, 1964), 112.
[51] Ibid. 69–70.
[52] Ibid. 83.

in other lands who not only toil for the present but 'agonize over the thought of an indigent old age'. But in Utopia, 'there is no less provision for those who are now helpless but once worked than for those who are still working'.[53] This financial security was a product of labour and so, in the last resort, Utopians were forced to work. Anyone travelling within his own district would be expected to do his daily stint; if he wished to travel further afield a certificate from the Governor would be necessary and, if he had the temerity to stray outside his own territory without such a certificate, 'he is treated with contempt, brought back as a runaway, and severely punished. If he dares to repeat the offence, he is punished with slavery.'[54] The parallels with the panopticon and the Vagrants Acts are obvious.

There are, of course, profound differences as well as resemblances between Utopia and the panopticon. In his plans for separating children from their parents, Bentham drew on Plato rather than More. And, more crucially, Bentham did not envisage property held in common as in Utopia. The panopticon was to be a capitalist enterprise within a capitalist economy. Bentham's primary purpose was to sketch a blueprint for a practical scheme that would find acceptance in his own time; the elements of an ideal society were incidental and largely secret. More himself seems to have shared Bentham's doubts as to whether his Utopia was realizable in the world as it was. 'I readily admit', he wrote in his final sentence, 'that there are very many features in the Utopian commonwealth which it is easier for me to wish for in our countries than to have any hope of seeing realized.'[55]

The panopticon is even more closely akin to Francis Bacon's *New Atlantis*. This was the first scientific utopia where the application of knowledge would have ameliorated the lot of man. Bentham greatly admired Bacon as a thinker in advance of his age; his work was, he wrote, 'a precocious and precious fruit of the union of learning and genius'. The *New Atlantis* was a utopia realizable through scientific advance; its dynamic was Solomon's house, the centre of scientific study. 'The End of our Foundation', Bacon wrote, 'is the knowledge of Causes and secret motions of things; and the enlarging of the bounds of Human Empire, to the

---

[53] Ibid. 147–8.     [54] Ibid. 82.     [55] Ibid. 152.

effecting of all things possible.'[56] In its details the *New Atlantis* presaged many of Bentham's enthusiasms. Bacon's ideal society experimented in the breeding of animals, fish, silkworms, and bees; it discovered the cure for diseases; it invented new plants and engines. It multiplied, reflected, and refracted light and it produced artificial rainbows and sweet perfumes to nullify unpleasant smells. It conducted experiments in caves 600 fathoms deep in the mysteries of refrigeration and the conservation of bodies; it created artificial metals; and invented conversation tubes to convey sounds through pipes. Bacon dreamed of building high towers up to half a mile in height for meteorological observations and of flying machines and submarines. 'We have', he wrote, 'some degrees of flying in the air: we have ships and boats for going underwater.'[57] In the *New Atlantis* Bacon had created a world very close to Bentham's heart.

The panopticon therefore closely resembles the two classic utopias in English literature. It is also deeply imbued with the Arcadian tradition. Bentham is not usually portrayed as a sentimental romantic; but he does seem to have shared some of the assumptions and preconceptions of that literary genre. He was an avid novel reader. He himself asserted that Fénelon's *Telemachus*, though at times disappointingly vague, was the inspiration of his utilitarianism. 'That romance,' he wrote, 'may be regarded as the foundation-stone of my whole character; the starting-post from whence my career of life commenced. The first dawning in my mind of the principles of utility may, I think, be traced to it.' And Fénelon's heroine in her glass palace was the archetype of the panopticon.[58] Fénelon's ideal society was a pastoral Arcadia where shepherds and shepherdesses live in small family groups under the benevolent rule of a Father-King. They were sequestered from the evils of luxury, envy, and violence. The idea of innocence protected from corruption by rural isolation is the very stuff of the pastoral idyll. It is a world where men, uncorrupted by cities, were moderate in their desires because their knowledge of evil was limited and where their tastes were temperate for they knew nothing of luxury and strong drink. For Rousseau, cities

[56] F. Bacon, *The Philosophical Works of Francis Bacon*, ed. J. M. Robertson (London, 1905), 727.
[57] Ibid. 731.
[58] Bowring, x. 10; xi. 105.

were 'the abyss of the human species'.[59] Gray's 'Elegy Written in a Country Churchyard', the classic poetic expression of eighteenth-century romantic melancholy, evokes a happy rural innocence where:

> Far from the madding crowd's ignoble strife
> Their sober wishes never learn'd to stray;
> Along the cool sequester'd vale of life
> They kept the noiseless tenor of their way.

Goldsmith's Vicar of Wakefield described his refuge in similar terms:

The place of our retreat was a little neighbourhood, consisting of farmers, who tilled their own grounds, and were equal strangers to opulence and poverty . . . they seldom visited towns or cities in search of superfluity. Remote from the polite, they still retained the primaeval simplicity of manners, and frugal by habit, they scarce knew that temperance was a virtue.[60]

The cloistered virtue of the panopticon inmates is of the same kind. Bentham's vision can be seen as sharing the assumptions of the pastoral idyll, that true happiness comes from curbing desire, from restraint of the passions, and from the absence of temptation. And these same assumptions underlay the common eighteenth-century perception that poverty and crime had their roots in luxury, extravagance, and idleness.

Bentham was defensive about the utopian elements of the panopticon and himself rejected the comparison with More on the fundamental point of viability. In a private note concerning the panopticon he wrote:

This no Utopia. In Utopias, effects are represented as produced when no adequate causes have been assigned . . . happiness is represented as existing without adequate means of happiness . . . virtue without adequate [. . . ?] and motives to virtue. Persons are represented as regulated and subsisting in a state of regulation, without anything to regulate them. The selfish affections are represented as in a state of uniform subordination to the social . . . In this place happiness is provided for not by an unfounded assumption or confident prediction, but by the care

---

[59] J. J. Rousseau, *Émile*, cited F. E. Manuel and F. P. Manuel, *Utopian Thought in the Western World* (Cambridge, Mass., 1979), 439.
[60] Oliver Goldsmith, *The Vicar of Wakefield* (London, 1766, Harmondsworth, 1974), 23.

that is taken to bring together the means of happiness and to exclude the efficient causes of unhappiness. The interest of him on whom everything depends is identified with his duty.[61]

In this emphasis on the junction of interest and duty as the basis of his ideal society, Bentham looked forward to the *Constitutional Code*, and back to *A View of the Hard Labour Bill*. He had written in 1778: 'The Utopian speculator unwarrantably presumes, that a man's conduct (on which side soever his interest lie) *will* quadrate with his duty, or vainly regrets that it will *not* so.'[62] And his insistence on viability presages the dynamic scientific utopias of the nineteenth century. Robert Owen, for instance, derived from Bentham the concept that the object of government and society should be to maximize human happiness. And he shared with him the perception of man as an animate mechanism which could be moulded by training and environment. They both discounted heredity. The end result was similar disciplinarian utopias. The panopticon has obvious affinities with contemporary model paternalistic factories, such as Quarry Bank Mill at Styall in Cheshire as well as Owen's New Lanark mills in Scotland. Any visitor to New Lanark must be struck by the panoptic quality of the counting-house where from a bow-window Owen could survey his mills and the terraces of his township. His workers were provided with sanitary housing, shops, schools, good wages, and excellent working conditions. But they were under strict surveillance both at work and in their private lives, even to the extent of sending a 'bug officer' into their homes to check on cleanliness. Owen believed that his New Lanark system of paternalist co-operation, if applied nationally and internationally, would herald the end of war, crime, depravity, and idleness. Bentham had similar hopes for the panopticon. In an unpublished note among the manuscripts connected with *Panopticon versus New South Wales*, he analysed the causes of crime and war: 'Rapacity is a disposition resulting from the preternatural strength of the self-regarding affections.' Drunkenness, sexual attraction, and prodigality were among the strongest incitements to rapacity. And sloth was the root of all these evils for it encouraged men to avoid labour, 'the natural and . . . the only beneficial . . . medium

---

[61] UC cvii. 58.
[62] Bowring, iv. 12, Bentham's emphasis.

through which the instruments of enjoyment can be acquired'. Murderousness, he argued, was a form of insanity nurtured by cruelty, for the spectacle of animal suffering led all too easily to a disregard for human life and to the final madness of war: 'It is in the love of cruel sports in the Bear garden and the bear-baiting ground that men train themselves up for the love of needless war. In the same spirit . . . the agonies of a lacerated animal would . . . in the Cabinet sate its gratification by the maintenance of useless and endless war.'[63] Bentham was much attracted by the New Lanark experiment and invested some of his panopticon compensation money in it. And, according to Owen, found it, 'the only successful enterprise in which he ever engaged'.[64]

Too much weight should not be put on the similarities between Owen and Bentham; the differences between them are substantial. Owen was more paternalistic in the sense that he did not believe in democracy and was more sentimentally humane, carefully considering the dignity of his workforce. Above all, he differed radically from Bentham in his refusal to contemplate the exploitation of small children. He would not employ any under the age of 10 and advocated full-time education up to the age of 12. In the later development of his thought he threw caution to the winds and preached a social harmony that could and would be created easily and quickly on the basis of co-operation. Bentham remained more dubious of the basic goodness of men. He had a low opinion of Owen's intellect: 'Robert Owen', he said, 'begins in vapour, and ends in smoke. He is a great braggadoccio. His mind is a maze of confusion.'[65] Owen's cloudy vision took him thousands of miles to found New Harmony on the banks of the Wabash in Indiana; Bentham's cooler enthusiasms allowed him to remain in comfortable seclusion in London.

The bizarre paradox of a prison as an ideal society was not peculiar to Bentham. There is a utopian element in the Quaker penitentiaries in Philadelphia, in Millbank, and in Pentonville. It

---

[63] UC cxvi. 484–6.
[64] R. Owen, *The Life of Robert Owen Written by Himself* (London, 1857), ed. J. Butt (London, 1971), 96. See *Correspondence* (*CW*), vii. as index for the beginning of Bentham's relationship with Owen, and Bowring, x. 476–7 for its continuation.
[65] Bowring, x. 570.

had its fullest expression in the twentieth century at Stateville penitentiary near Chicago under the rule of its most authoritarian governor Joseph Ragen, who saw his rigidly disciplined prison as morally superior to the petty politics and sordid corruption of the society outside.[66]

Although the panopticon can be seen to be in the utopian tradition, it was not a true utopia. It may have been an enclave of reason, but the delicate mechanism of checks and balances essential to achieve the junction of interest and duty was dependent on a world outside enabling profit to be enjoyed and the sanction of public opinion to be brought to bear. A utopia must be self-perpetuating; but Bentham's devices suppose external regulation. He himself emphasized that the essential utopian element was that the interest of the governor should coincide with his duty. But according to his plans, the governor's reward would come from profits earned and spent in the outside world; a world where he might become a peer of the realm and enjoy the plaudits of society. His inmates would be protected from cruelty and exploitation by the surveillance of the court of the King's Bench and the inspection of the public. There is thus a fundamental flaw in the panopticon as an ideal society for its smooth, humane organization would have depended on the law courts and the public opinion of another world. Hardly surprisingly in a practical prison scheme there is no indication that the panopticon inmates would be able to control or influence the management, or become managers themselves. They could not be treated as citizens of a free society. As a utopia, the panopticon can best be seen as a step towards Bentham's true ideal society in the *Constitutional Code* in which the mechanisms to create harmony are internal. In the panopticon the reconciliation of interests was forced by external pressures, but in the *Code* a framework is constructed which would enable and encourage, but not force, self-regarding men to consider the interest and happiness of others.

[66] J. B. Jacobs, *Stateville: The Penitentiary in Mass Society* (London and Chicago, 1977), 31.

# 13

# CONCLUSION

Bentham never ceased to abominate the uninspectable 'hermetically-sealed Bastile' at Millbank.[1] And it gave him considerable pleasure to contemplate the troubles that beset it. The three commissioners were his old antagonists, George Holford, the Revd John Becher, and Charles Long. They started to build at once, but the doubts raised when the Salisbury estate was first acquired proved only too well founded. The ground was too swampy and unstable to sustain the building; whole sections subsided and had to be underpinned at vast expense. In the end, the building cost £500,000, more than twice the original estimate. Beatrice and Sidney Webb observed that it was doubtful if the Taj at Agra, the Cloth Hall at Ypres, or the cathedral at Chartres cost anything like as much.[2] Unlike these creations of human genius, the Millbank penitentiary was grossly ugly, a vast pile dominating the skyline just upstream from Westminster. This labyrinth of a building was full of dark corners and passages, winding staircases, and innumerable doors and gates. So confusing was it that warders would blaze their trails with chalk marks on the walls.[3] The regime was no more successful than the architecture. At first, the prison was the plaything of benevolent philanthropists. The supervising committee included, as well as Holford, Becher, and Long, several other protagonists in the history of the panopticon, Charles Abbot, George Rose, Richard Ryder, and William Morton Pitt. They made serious mistakes. Discipline was so lax that in 1817 the inmates rose in open mutiny. And the regime was so soft and the diet so lavish that there was a public outcry. In reaction, the food allowance was cut. This, combined with the unhealthiness of the swampy site and the fetid miasma from the river, caused an epidemic which

---

[1] Bowring, i. 256.
[2] S. and B. Webb, *English Prisons* (London, 1922), 49.
[3] A. Griffiths, *Memorials of Millbank and Chapters in Prison History* (London, 1875), 33.

killed many of the inmates. In 1823 the whole prison had to
be evacuated and the prisoners transferred to the hulks where
their health improved. The ideals that Holford had shared with
Bentham of imposing discipline by moral persuasion had to be
jettisoned and in 1830, for the first time, inmates were whipped.
The Millbank penitentiary also failed to reform its patients. As a
desperate remedy in 1837, the Revd Daniel Nihil was appointed
to combine the office of chaplain and governor. This was the
apogee of the doctrine that had been held so fervently by
Howard and Hanway that criminals could be saved by the
Christian ministry. It was also the apogee of hypocritical morbid
religiosity in the gaols. The warders were expected to lead sober,
godly lives, to forswear strong drink, and to interlard their
conversation with biblical phrases. They were dismissed for
swearing. Prisoners could curry favour with lurid displays of
piety, ostentatious penitence, and hymn singing. In the 1840s
Millbank was superseded by the new generation of penitentiaries
exemplified in Pentonville, and its failure was admitted. It ceased
to be a penitentiary and became merely a depot to hold convicts
prior to transportation. With the end of the sailings in 1853, it
became an ordinary prison. Finally, it was demolished and made
way for the Tate Picture Gallery in 1892. Bentham had been
amply justified in his conviction that Holford's penitentiary would
be a costly failure.

The rejection of the panopticon presaged the end of contract
punishment. It was never again seriously considered, and the
remnants of private enterprise were gradually eliminated from
the gaols. The influence of Bentham's scheme on the direction of
penal policy seems to have been minimal, although Benthamite
ideas on the need for uniformity of administration and government regulation were among the pressures that resulted in the
Prison Act of 1835. This Act destroyed the autonomy of the local
magistrates; thereafter they merely administered the gaols under
Home Office regulation, scrutinized by government inspectors. In
1877 the great Prison Act placed the prisons directly under the
control of the Home Office where they have remained. Although
reformation remained the ostensible object of imprisonment, the
emphasis changed. Productive labour came under attack from the
manufacturing interests as unfair competition, and it aroused
general resentment as being too soft on criminals. Economic

recession after the war and the development of steam power made prison labour increasingly unprofitable. The ideology of penitence demanded that prisons should be places of pious misery. The Revd John Clay, an eminent prison chaplain, was scandalized by Preston gaol: 'a scene of active and much too cheerful industry; and the discipline, lax generally, was very lax indeed in the case of lucrative felons.'[4] These complex pressures led to the adoption of treadmills and cranks, and to the imposition of sad, sober, penitential regimes, of which solitary confinement became an integral part. Disillusionment with the failures to reform criminals encouraged the reimposition of solitude, now concealed under the euphemism, 'the separate system'. This was fervently embraced by William Crawford and Whitworth Russell, the first government inspectors of prisons appointed in 1835. It seemed to them the only way to prevent corrupting association. Crawford's seminal *Report on the Penitentiaries of the United States* was responsible for the establishment of solitary confinement in the English gaols and for the building of Pentonville. In this, Bentham's panopticon is scarcely mentioned.[5]

In the years after 1811 the panopticon was the subject of desultory controversy. Bentham's freakish ambition to become a prison contractor continued to cast a shadow over his reputation. William Cobbett derided him as an 'everlasting babbler' who 'was made a Reformer by PITT's *refusal to give him a contract to build a penitentiary and to make him prime administrator of penance*, that is to say, Beggar-Whipper General'.[6] *The Quarterly Review* anticipated Himmelfarb and many others, in its comparison of the panopticon with Napoleon's France where:

the jailer (the most unhappy wretch of all) sits in the centre of his transparent dominion, and sees to the utmost recesses of its crimes and its filthiness, all the proceedings of his aggregation of slaves. The poets give us a terrible idea of eternal *solitude*; but eternal solitude is paradise

---

[4] J. Clay, *The Prison Chaplain* (London, 1861), 105.
[5] W. Crawford, *Report on the Penitentiaries of the United States*, addressed to Viscount Duncannon, Principal Secretary of State for the Home Department, 1835.
[6] W. Cobbett, *Cobbett's America*, ed. J. E. Morpurgo (London, 1985), 202, Cobbett's emphasis. I am indebted to Mrs Judy Gilbert for drawing my attention to this passage.

to *society* under such everlasting inspection. The panopticon would soon become Bedlam, the keeper going mad first.[7]

The *Quarterly* continued to snipe at Bentham, deriding his prose style as, 'that peculiar quaint *patois* in which he delights to enshrine his lucubrations', and the panopticon as, 'wholly visionary' and without any proper checks or lasting securities.[8] And finally, after mocking 'Jeremy Bentham's illustrious project of manufacturing rogues and harlots into honest men and women', it launched the unkindest of accusations that Millbank was 'a monument at once of Jeremy's philosophico-philofelon-philanthrophy, of national folly, and of the futility of all such schemes of reformation'. This earned it a measured rebuke from the *Westminster Review*: 'a political party is badly led, whose leaders compromise it by mis-statements.'[9] The desire to refute this libel was one of the reasons why, in his last years, Bentham wrote his final contribution to the panopticon saga, the 'History of the War between Jeremy Bentham and George the Third. By one of the Belligerents.'[10] Little credence can be given to this account. Bentham's powers and memory were failing; it is slipshod and inaccurate and reads like the unconsidered maunderings of an old man. But it shows that he never ceased to mourn his panopticon.

Several of his immediate followers remained loyal. James Mill and John Bowring were convinced of the virtues of the panopticon. At the height of Bentham's influence in European radical circles, the Spanish Cortes, convened in the aftermath of the 1820 uprising, approved of the use of the panopticon in prison establishments throughout that kingdom.[11] But the Spanish revolution was soon crushed. Étienne Dumont actually built a panopticon prison in Geneva; but although it faithfully produced many of the architectural features, down to conver-

---

[7] *Quarterly Review*, 10 (Oct. 1813 and Jan. 1814), 489, *Review*'s emphasis.
[8] Ibid. 47 (Mar. and July 1832), 183; 30 (Oct. 1823 and Jan. 1824), 427.
[9] *Quarterly Review*, 44 (Jan. and Feb. 1831), 277. *Westminster Review*, 14 (Jan.–Apr. 1831), 454.
[10] Bowring, xi. 96–107. See Appendix for a full discussion of this document and the related MSS in the British Library.
[11] *Diario de las Actas y Discusiones de las Córtes Legislatura de los anos de 1820 y 1821* (Madrid, 1820–1), viii, Sesion de dia 6 de octubre de 1820, pp. 19–36. Report of the Prison Commission.

sation tubes, for reasons of economy only a semicircle of cells was built. Contract management was not adopted and open public inspection was rejected for fear of disorder. Dumont's penitentiary was a publicly managed institution inspected by officially appointed visitors; it was a Howardian rather than a Benthamic institution. It was demolished in 1862.[12] The panopticon did not become an important aspect of the utilitarian approach to penal policy. Edwin Chadwick, the Benthamite who achieved most in the field of practical reform, stressed the need for uniformity of administration and central regulation of prisons, but he preferred to address himself to the causes of crime, poverty, housing, and social indiscipline, rather than to institutional punishment. Bentham's intellectual heirs, the Fabian socialists, rejected the concept of reformatory penitentiaries. The ideological wheel turned full circle with Bernard Shaw's denunciation of prisons as part of the coercive structure of society in terms similar to Foucault or Himmelfarb. 'Prisons', he wrote, 'are horribly cruel and destructive places . . . no creature fit to live should be sent there.'[13]

As an architectural concept the panopticon has influenced prison building particularly in the United States. The Western penitentiary at Pittsburgh built between 1820 and 1826 followed the panopticon design closely, but 'in so doing, gave the final proof of the impracticability of carrying out Bentham's idea in its original form'.[14] Ten years later it had to be demolished. In the twentieth century the most famous example of a panopticon prison is Stateville penitentiary at Joliet near Chicago. It was started in 1916 to astonish the world as a perfect penological structure, but it was a travesty of Bentham's plan, fatally flawed by the failure to understand that unseen inspection was of the essence. The central inspection towers were devised so that the inmates could observe every move of the guards; supervision became a mockery. And the building became notorious as one of the 'most awful receptacles of gloom which were ever devised and put together with good stone and brick and mortar'.[15]

---

[12] R. Roth, *Pratiques pénitentiaires et théorie sociale* (Geneva, 1981).
[13] S. and B. Webb, *English Prisons*, Introduction, p. viii.
[14] T. A. Markus, 'Pattern of the Law', in *Architectural Review*, 116 (1954), 254.
[15] *Handbook of American Prisons and Reformatories* (New York, 1933), i. 144.

If Bentham's own panopticon had ever been built, it would almost certainly have failed in the sense that other penal institutions have failed. It would have been subject to the same economic, social, and religious pressures that shaped the direction of penal policy towards Pentonville. But one may question the perception of failure. Historians and penal reformers of every generation have proclaimed the failure of prisons. But, as Margaret DeLacy points out, two-thirds of the inmates released from Lancaster gaols in the 1820s did not return, the same proportion as now.[16] And historians in Foucault's mould have not suggested how society should have dealt with the problem of crime, given that a regime of treating criminals with gentle persuasion would have been intolerable to the public. If the gaols had been left as they were, cholera, a virulent new disease of the nineteenth century, would have wiped out untold thousands. If the policy of general maximum deterrence had been maintained, there would have been a holocaust of executions. During the first half of the century, the population trebled; the streets of London would have become slaughter-yards. Sanitary, disciplined prisons were surely a better alternative.

The concept of a philanthropic prison, so alien to modern minds, was a commonplace idea in the eighteenth century. The panopticon should not be seen as a paradigm of government, but as an instrument; an agency of government, not government itself. But in the wider context, it was designed to create an environment for co-operation, foreshadowing a utopia where the interests of the rulers and the ruled could be reconciled. In the context of the callous brutality of its time it was essentially humanitarian. It must be seen against the cesspits of the gaols and the hulks and the horrific and irresponsible experiment of the penal colony at Botany Bay. Bentham addressed himself to these problems and he also pointed to another way forward than the road taken by penal reform that led to the secret evil world of the nineteenth-century prisons where, cloaked in a stifling officialdom, cruel tortures were inflicted on minds and bodies and were sanctified in the name of discipline and religion. Bentham was not a sentimental dreamer but a realistic, kindly man looking

---

[16] M. DeLacy, *Prison Reform in Lancashire, 1700–1850* (Manchester, 1986), 13.

for ways to ameliorate the lot of the poor and the outcast in his own time. He applied his considerable intellect to the practical problems of poverty and crime. He produced a system that is far more than a bizarre contraption. His ideas presage measures for public health, education, pensions, and secure employment. Inevitably, he made mistakes; he could not have the benefit of hindsight or of the doubts and reservations that are the product of two centuries of hard-won experience.

Yet prisons remain repellent institutions; and the panopticon is no exception. It is almost beyond belief that a man of Bentham's intelligence and humanity should have died still grieving for this mechanism of punishment. And there seems a fundamental difficulty in reconciling Bentham's concept of justice as respect for expectation utilities with his denial of a man's freedom to walk out of a prison at the end of his sentence. How could the rigidly controlled and manipulated inmates of the panopticons have exercised their rational powers in the exercise of individual judgement? It is possible to make some attempt to resolve these contradictions. If we apply Bentham's rigorous logic and look again at the arguments he used to justify his metasylum, it becomes apparent that, within his definition, he was committing no injustice. It cannot be too often reiterated that the panopticon must be seen in the context of eighteenth-century law and practice. And the expectations of prisoners were grim indeed. Death, maltreatment, filth, starvation, the horrors of the transports and the hulks were their common lot. And, after the expiration of their terms, their expectations were little better; the likelihood of perpetual servitude in Botany Bay, or at the very best, a precarious freedom, living in the shadow of vagrancy, pauperism, and crime. If a component of justice is security of expectation, it is easier to understand the relevance of Bentham's constant comparisons between discharged prisoners and others innocent of any crime caught up in the brutal and capricious web of the eighteenth-century system which created the framework of expectation for those on the margins of society. The metasylum and the National Charity Company would have changed this framework and so have changed the expectations of the poor. And this new framework might have been more secure, more certain, and so more just. Paul Kelly in his study on Bentham and distributive justice maintains that expectations are dependent upon the minimization of contingency: only security can ensure the sphere of personal inviolability within which men can make rational choices.[17] The panopticon certainly minimized contingency, and Kelly's argument becomes even more relevant when he suggests that for Bentham the enjoyment of the fruits of productive labour is the precondition of social stability. So again, the panopticon, by providing employment for all the outcasts, the criminals, the disabled, and the poor would have enabled them to achieve personal autonomy, the precondition of all freedom.

There is, however, something profoundly disturbing about the panopticon. The concept of ceaseless invisible inspection all too graphically conjures up the nightmares of Orwell's Big Brother, Tolkien's Dark Lord, or the hideous reality of the clattering surveillance towers along the old Berlin Wall. The panopticon can too easily become the prototype of a fiendishly efficient instrument of totalitarian control, of ruthless social engineering, and of psychological manipulation. It has been deployed by his philosophic adversaries to suggest that the whole of Benthamite political theory is authoritarian and repressive. Gertrude Himmelfarb calls emotively for the exorcizing of these devils from our heritage, Manning raises the spectre of the Holocaust by suggesting that in the Benthamite state the unfit might be eliminated. And for Michel Foucault, the panopticon is a cruel and ingenious mechanism of the new physics of power designed to subjugate the individual. Michael Ignatieff with a cooler vision nevertheless pictures the philosophical, radical state as a calm, dispassionate eye holding the deviant in thrall.

In many ways Bentham himself is to blame for these profound misunderstandings. By a strange irony, he who was so acutely aware of the delusive power of language, used words in such a way as to create an impression of ossified, frigid, rule-bound bureaucracy. Words such as 'functionary', 'tribunal', 'dislocability', and 'melioration' do indeed evoke visions of totalitarianism. But this is a false impression. He did not stop thinking after the failure of his panopticon scheme. He went on to perfect his theory of institutions and in it there is no concept of the state as an entity separate or greater than the individuals who serve

---

[17] P. J. Kelly, *Utilitarianism and Distributive Justice: Jeremy Bentham and the Civil Law* (Oxford, 1990), 93–4.

it. For almost another twenty years he reflected and wrote on government, working out the ideas that reach their apogee in the *Constitutional Code*. During these years he applied the lessons he had learnt at the cost of such anguish. He took and transmuted the two fundamental principles of the panopticon, the junction of duty and interest and inspection and applied them to government. What emerged was a tough, realistic theory of democracy. Underlying it was his harsh belief that the interests of rulers are always and always will be in diametrical opposition to the interests of their subjects. Whatever the rhetoric or ideology of these rulers, whether a paternal monarch, freedom fighters, or intellectuals, they will inevitably sacrifice the interests of their subjects. Whether they rule in the name of Marx, Allah, Christ, or the Market, they are men and will accumulate money and privileges for themselves. They will, as night follows day, plunder and oppress their people. Bentham did not deny the possibility of the odd altruistic action, but he argued that it would be imprudent to found a system of administration on such an unlikely contingency. He wrote, in 1821, when considering the government of Spain:

vain would it be, to bring to view any of those sacrifices, which, in particular conjunctures, under this or that violent and short-lived excitement, have sometimes been seen made. It is to the general tenor of human conduct, and not to any extraordinary deviations from it, on pain of being ineffectual all such arrangements must be adopted.[18]

Ruling élites would automatically close ranks to protect their own, to cover up mistakes, to spend money on schemes to their own benefit, to protect and extend their powers and privileges. Such corruption pervades all government and becomes so instinctive that it no longer seems corrupt. Bentham compared the reactions of public functionaries drooling after power and patronage with the behaviour of cats at feeding time. In a moment of rare self-parody, he describes cats as 'four-legged domestic functionaries' and disclaims any intention to insult them by comparing them with politicians: 'Far be it from this pen to seek to degrade the ever vigilant and faithful functionary to a level with

---

[18] UC clxxii. 228.

any such unfaithful ones.'[19] This is not a comfortable insight. It undermines the basis of many of the assumptions on which government rests. It threatens civil servants who want a quiet life and politicans who try to conceal their incompetence and affect a disdain for press and public. Government can no longer be a sacred mystery and any tradition, however hallowed, can be challenged.

Bentham came to believe that the only form of government that could safeguard the people against this exploitation and oppression was representative democracy, because only therein were subjects able to control their rulers. It was the only form of government that would consistently aim at the greatest happiness of all, for the people were themselves sovereign. To achieve this end Bentham devised a complex system of assemblies and elections that would ensure that the executive was subordinate to the legislature and that each functionary was removable and punishable by the people. But democracy cannot in itself ensure good government, for the people's representatives would soon succumb to the temptations of power unless they were closely watched. In the *Constitutional Code* he constructed an architectural extravaganza which quite overshadows the panopticon. Panoptic offices were devised in which government functionaries, from the Prime Minister down, were overlooked by their superiors, their inferiors, and by the public at large. Open accountable administration under the constant scrutiny of the public could solve the age-old dilemma, 'Quis custodiet ipsos custodes'.

To achieve this miracle Bentham conjured up the genie of the 'public opinion tribunal', by which he meant public opinion informed and educated by free discussion. In the *Code*, Bentham obscures rather than clarifies his ideas. He tortures the English language in his vain quest for an impossible precision and has thereby created a barrier which has vitiated his influence—it needs a very special dedication to embark on this work. The very phrase 'public opinion tribunal' itself creates difficulty. In ordinary modern usage, the word 'tribunal' implies a formal assembly with power to judge and impose sanctions; and Bentham's use of the word might suggest that he was envisaging

---

[19] *First Principles Preparatory to Constitutional Code*, ed. Philip Schofield (Oxford, 1989) (*CW*), 21–2.

some sort of people's court before which the peccant functionary would be arraigned and condemned by acclamation. This is far from the truth. Bentham's public opinion tribunal can best be translated as public opinion informed by publicity. It was informal and pervasive and comprised every person within a community, indeed, 'every individual of the human species'.[20] It was the one direct expression of sovereignty, for 'the sovereignty is in *the people*'. It is 'the will and undefinable power of the people'.[21] Bentham admitted that it was a fiction and could be seen to work only as a committee. He analysed his concept of what he called this 'half and half imaginary tribunal' and his breakdown of the different classes which comprise the tribunal is enlightening. First of all those with the power of speech, secondly those who can also read, thirdly those who can speak, read, write, and publish. Those who publish writings on matters of government are presidents or leading members, and editors of political newspapers are 'presidents of all these presidents, king of these kings, Lord of these lords of the dominion of liberty and independence'.[22] This tribunal could impose the ultimate sanctions of the withdrawal of obedience and even the execution of the tyrant. So, although the tribunal was fictitious and invisible, it was real for its existence could be deduced from the force it exerted; for example, even the government of England, which Bentham described as a 'monarchico-aristocratical despotism with a spice of anarchy' was tempered by the force of public opinion.[23]

This fictitious imaginary tribunal was essential to the proper working of Bentham's constitution. It was one of the 'counter-forces to official power'. It had broadly two functions; it was first a check against oppression, corruption, and inefficiency, in Bentham's language, 'the censorial and executive functions'. Secondly, it was an engine of reform, providing information and suggesting improvements, in Bentham's language, 'the statistic or Evidence furnishing function and the Melioration suggestive function'. In this Bentham presages important themes in sub-

---

[20] *Constitutional Code*, i, ed. F. Rosen and J. H. Burns (Oxford, 1983) (*CW*), 39.

[21] Ibid. 25, 128.

[22] Bowring, viii. 561–6.

[23] *Constitutional Code*, i, 25.

sequent constitutional theory of responsible government, in the sense of responsive to the needs and wishes of the country, and of ideas of the ultimate sanction of popular disapproval. It was through the medium of the public opinion tribunal that the interest of the functionary was joined with his duty. Open government, maximum publicity, and Press freedom would overpower the sinister interest of authority and ensure that it acted in accord with the greatest happiness principle. To the pernicious exercise of the powers of government it was the only check. This check would work by physical oversight of the workings of government, by attendance at plays or public meetings and through the Press. Bentham envisaged every meeting of the legislature or law courts open to the public. Even the executive business of government was to be conducted under the eye of casual observers. All government offices were to be clearly labelled, their entrances easily scrutinized, and their doors open to the public. Ministerial offices were to be arranged in a cresent or a circle with the Prime Minister's at the centre and the whole observed by visitors from numbered waiting-boxes arranged so that any who had business would not be delayed unreasonably or unfairly. This, Bentham wrote, in words surely inspired by the humiliations he had suffered in Whitehall, would avoid 'needless delay, vexation and expense: vexation, by haughty or negligent demeanour on the part of the functionary, and by unjust favour in respect of priority of audience'.[24]

Freedom of the Press was essential for the proper working of the public opinion tribunal. Halévy's much quoted dictum that Benthamite utilitarianism 'is not, in origin and in essence, a philosophy of liberty',[25] should be set against Bentham's own insistence that freedom of the Press and of information was the bedrock of his constitution. In emotive terms he denounced;

Every act, whereby . . . a man seeks to weaken the effective power of the Public Opinion Tribunal, or by falsehood, or . . . by suppression of truth, to misdirect it, is evidence, of hostility on his part to the greatest happiness of the greatest number: evidence of the worst intentions, generated by the worst motives . . . he may, without fear of injustice, be numbered among the enemies of the human species.[26]

[24] *Constitutional Code*, 445.
[25] Halévy, *The Growth of Philosophic Radicalism* (London, 1928, 1972), 84.
[26] *Constitutional Code*, i, 41.

The principles that sustain the *Constitutional Code* are similar to those of the panopticon but they have been reversed. Bentham's democracy is a structure full of light, as was the panopticon, but the light falls on those in authority. Around the perimeter in the position of the criminals—a fit place given Bentham's opinion of officials—were the functionaries under the unremitting surveillance of the public, liable to be dismissed and punished if they failed in their duty. There would be no secrecy in this structure; the functionaries would see freely into the workings of the public opinion tribunal in their midst, they would study and be guided by it. But this transparency would extend only to official matters; Bentham specifically asserted that a functionary's private life, his sexual appetites for instance, should not be disclosed because of the suffering this might cause, 'evil to a deplorable amount may be produced . . . a whole life may be filled with misery'.[27] One may doubt if government under these conditions of unremitting publicity is possible—whether this would not be a recipe for paralysis. But it is certainly not a paradigm of absolutism for every government action would be open to question and debate. It is also perhaps unlikely to be tyrannical for the exercise of tyranny would threaten the security of all and a properly functioning democracy would reject it. Constant debate would educate people in the need to protect the well-being of minorities, for they would soon realize that everyone's security was threatened by oppression.

Foucault appears to have paid little attention to Bentham's mature theory of government: and in making him an exemplar of modern subjection he has done him a grave injustice. By an odd irony, Bentham shared many of Foucault's fears; fear of secret, furtive power, fear of oppression, and fear of delusive language. He also shared his insight that people might collaborate in their own subjection. Foucault attempted to turn transparency itself against Bentham. The eighteenth century, he suggested, was haunted by the fear of darkened spaces and the panopticon is 'an apparatus of total and circulating mistrust'. Light becomes a trap: 'An inspecting gaze, a gaze which each individual under its weight will end by interiorising to the point that he is his own overseer, each individual thus exercising this surveillance over,

[27] *First Principles*, 290.

and against, himself.'[28] Again it is impossible to argue with such oracular declarations. They say more about Foucault's claustrophobic distrust of his world than they do about Bentham's theory of representative democracy. Why should not light and free debate inspire trust rather than mistrust and co-operation and goodwill rather than fear?

Bentham himself was no idealistic optimist—he realized that democracy is a fragile structure for rulers will always be tempted to use delusion and secrecy to blind the people to their oppressions and subjects will always wish to believe in the integrity and good intentions of their rulers. Good government can only be achieved by constant vigilance and without liberty of discussion, democracy will falter and die. Or in panopticon terms, the junction of interest and duty can only be achieved by inspection. The distrust of government that pervades his later thought was nurtured by his experiences with the panopticon when, as he believed, a scheme of great advantage to the public was destroyed by the sectional interest of great men. But it was not just hatred that inspired him. Before this experience, he regarded himself, by and large, as an insider, a gentleman, clever, well educated, with influential connections, who could manipulate his society to his financial advantage. Afterwards, he saw the world in a harsher light. He had been excluded from the cosy world of power and privilege, he had been ignored and cold-shouldered. It left him with a sympathy for the outsider, the deprived, the poor, and the dispossessed that gave an edge and a passion to his theory of democratic radicalism.

New insights into Bentham's philosophy go some way to explain the hold the panopticon had on his mind and his heart. It would have been a framework within which men could make rational choices freed from temptations; a framework in which work was rewarded and idleness punished. But Bentham was no transcendent prophet and his panopticon remains profoundly ambivalent. He lacked an imaginative tolerance for the shortcomings of others; he was over-optimistic, he was ruthless, and he was pre-eminently egocentric. The panopticon mirrors these

---

[28] M. Foucault, 'The Eye of Power', in *Power/Knowledge* (New York, 1980), 155–8. Foucault's theories on Bentham and the panopticon are fully considered in my article 'Foucault and Bentham: A Defence of Panopticism', in *Utilitas*, 4 (May 1992), 105–20.

faults. But his concept of man as a creature responsible for his actions is no less derogatory to human dignity than Foucault's man who is a plaything of forces beyond his comprehension, a victim of circumstance, fated to suffer and to sin without remedy. Utilitarian man is at least master of his fate; his passions are not ungovernable and he can make rational choices. One of these choices is to join duty with interest and the panopticon would have demonstrated the efficacy of this junction. Bentham dreamed of a myriad of such institutions working in perfect harmony with the effortless efficiency of precision engineering. The panopticon is not a paradigm of government or society but a harbinger of humane competence, a light leading through the darkness of error and superstition to a new heaven and a new earth. It would also have made Jeremy Bentham a very rich man.

# APPENDIX

## 'History of the War between Jeremy Bentham and George the Third, By one of the Belligerents'

This work is at Bowring, xi. 96–107. Several of the documents from which it was drawn survive at BL. Add. MS 33550, 365–415, dated 1827–31. Bentham was not well served by his editors. His powers were clearly failing; at one point his usually precise, if illegible, writing straggles down the page. He was aware that substantial correction would be necessary; he wrote that looking up facts had become a 'disproportionate burden . . . The task of completion must, I fear, be left to those who come after me' (Add. MS 33550. 402). 'The History of the War' is full of major errors of fact and seriously misleading as to the chronology of events. This appendix will go through the account page by page correcting the mistakes.

Page 97: 'In the year 1786 or 1787.' The date must have been 1786 for the panopticon *Letters* had been written before the end of that year. Bentham absolves Pitt from blame: 'to which no just condemnation can be attached.' This was certainly not his view in 1802–3.

Page 98: 'I published, anno 1789, a tract, entitled, "View of the Hard-Labour Bill".' The correct date is 1778. The account of the *View* is misleading: (1) It implies that it was written after, rather than considerably before, the panopticon *Letters*. (2) It states that the bill proposed a plan of management in which interest would in no way be coincident with duty. In fact the bill provided for the governor to profit from the work done in the prison. (3) It states that *A View* was 'a complete demonstration of its inaptitude', whereas it was laudatory. Bentham also maintains that under the terms of the subsequent Act, the government was empowered to buy the land at Battersea Rise and transfer it to anyone. As this history of the panopticon has shown, this was not so; under the 1779 Act only powers to pass the land to the three commissioners designated in the statute were given.

'In the year 1790, the return of my brother to England, furnished me with requisite architectural skill.' Samuel Bentham returned in May 1791. Bentham had already consulted the architect Willey Reveley in 1790.

Page 99: 'in March 1792, I sent in to Mr Pitt . . . a proposal for the taking charge of convicts.' In fact he first sent his project to Pitt on 23 January

1791; in November he sent a reminder, and on 3 February 1792 a further letter offering to execute the scheme on terms more favourable to the government.

Page 100: 'In the year 1797 was instituted the . . . Finance Committee.' This is strictly speaking correct, but it can be misleading. The panopticon was not referred to the committee until the following year, 1798.

Pages 100–1: Here the chronology becomes very difficult to follow. Bentham writes that after the passing of the 1794 Act, 'The lingering continued; nobody knew why.' In fact everyone knew exactly why. An amendment to the Act had made it possible for Lord Spencer to refuse to give up his land in Battersea. This is mentioned out of order on p. 101 implying that Bentham's negotiations with Spencer took place after the reference to the Finance Committee. Hanging Wood is also mentioned as being lost after the Committee Report.

On Colquhoun's involvement Bentham writes: 'How this happened I never knew', but he had conducted a lengthy correspondence with him in which they had discussed their plans in detail.

Page 102: Bentham ascribes the failure to build on the Salisbury estate entirely to George III's refusal to allow the authorization of the expenditure to be signed. This is not borne out in the contemporary evidence. Bentham fails to mention the problem of persuading the administration to consider the terms of the contract, the opposition of the Grosvenor interest, of the Dean and Chapter of Westminster, or of the parishes.

He has, 'In 1797 Pitt the First', obviously a slip for Pitt the Second.

Page 103: The description of George Rose as 'Senior Secretary of State' could be misleading. Pitt was First Lord of the Treasury and Prime Minister. Rose was the Senior Secretary to the Treasury not Secretary of State.

Bentham certainly exaggerates the likelihood that the government would have adopted his poor panopticons; and he jumps suddenly from 1797, when his claim to be 'Sub-Regulus for the Poor' was being considered, to 1811 when the Holford Committee rejected contract management for penitentiaries.

It is clear, therefore, that the 'History of the War' must be treated with very great caution and not used as evidence for events or opinions unless there is contemporary confirmation.

Bentham's central contention that George III's personal intervention was responsible for the ruin of the panopticon has been given short shrift by historians. There is no evidence to support it in the record. Yet silence in these circumstances is not entirely conclusive. A more credible version of the situation is given in a letter Bentham wrote to his brother in 1804 conveying information given to him by Lord St Helens and Evan Nepean (*Correspondence (CW)*, vii. 284–6). He ascribed his unpopularity at Court to his reputation as a Jacobin as well as to the Anti-Machiavel Letters. Lord Grenville, Pitt's Foreign Secretary, as well as the King, had been infuriated by his activities. The Queen also disliked him and Lord Belgrave, a favourite at Court, had used his influence. It is certainly easier to give credence to the possibility that there was a pervasive hostility to the project in royal circles than to believe that George III, amid his preoccupations with war, intermittent madness, and family scandals, marked out Jeremy Bentham for ruin and over several years hounded him to destruction.

# SOURCES

## Manuscript Sources

Bentham manuscripts in the University College London Library.
Bentham manuscripts in the British Library, Additional MSS 33122 and 33550.
Place Collection and Burney Collection in the British Library.
Grosvenor Estate Minute Books in the City of Westminster Victoria Library.
Chapter Minute Books, Westminster Abbey.

## Bentham's Works

*The Collected Works of Jeremy Bentham*, gen. eds. J. H. Burns, J. R. Dinwiddy, and F. Rosen (London and Oxford, 1968– ).
*Chrestomathia*, ed. M. J. Smith and W. H. Bustin (Oxford, 1983).
*The Correspondence of Jeremy Bentham*, i–ii, ed. T. L. S. Sprigge (London, 1968); iii, ed. I. R. Christie (1971); iv–v, ed. A. Taylor Milne (1981); vi–vii, ed. J. R. Dinwiddy (Oxford, 1984, 1988); viii–ix, ed. S. Conway (1988, 1989).
*First Principles Preparatory to Constitutional Code*, ed. Philip Schofield (Oxford, 1989).
*Securities against Misrule and other Constitutional Writings for Tripoli and Greece*, ed. Philip Schofield (Oxford, 1990).
*The Works of Jeremy Bentham*, published under the superintendence of his executor, John Bowring, 11 vols. (Edinburgh, 1838–43).
*Étienne Dumont recensions.*
*Traités de législation civile et pénale*, 3 vols. (Paris, 1802).
*Théorie des peines et des récompenses*, 2 vols. (London, 1811).

## Secondary Sources

Cobbett's Parliamentary Debates.
Code pénal (Paris, 1810).
The Journals of the House of Commons.
*The Parliamentary History of England.*
Reports from Committees of the House of Commons.
Statutes of the Realm.

*Journals*

*Annals of Agriculture and Other Useful Arts.*
*The Annual Register or a View of the History, Politics and Literature.*
*The Edinburgh Review or Critical Journal.*
*The Gentlemen's Magazine and Historical Chronicle.*
*The Philanthropist: or Repository for Hints and Suggestions calculated to promote the Comfort and Happiness of Man.*
*The Quarterly Review.*
*The Westminster Review.*

# SELECT BIBLIOGRAPHY

ABBOT, C., *The Diary and Correspondence of Charles Abbot, Lord Colchester*, ed. Charles, Lord Colchester, 3 vols. (London, 1861).

ALLEN, L. B., *Brief considerations on the Present State of the Police of the Metropolis with a Few Suggestions towards its Improvement* (London, 1821).

AMERY, L. S., *Thoughts on the Constitution* (Oxford, 1947).

ASPINALL, A., *The Later Correspondence of George III*, 5 vols. (Cambridge, 1962–70).

ATKINSON, C. M., *Jeremy Bentham His Life and Work* (London, 1905).

BABINGTON, A., *The Power to Silence: A History of Punishment in Britain* (London, 1968).

BACON, F., *The Philosophical Works of Francis Bacon*, ed. J. M. Robertson (London, 1905).

BAHMUELLER, C. F., *The National Charity Company: Jeremy Bentham's Silent Revolution* (Berkeley, Calif., Los Angeles, London, 1981).

BARNES, H. E., *The Evolution of Penology in Pennsylvania* (Indianapolis, 1927).

BARTLE, G. F., 'Jeremy Bentham and John Bowring: A Study of the Relationship between Bentham and the Editor of his *Collected Works*', *Bulletin of the Institute of Historical Research*, 36 (1963), 27–35.

BAUMGARDT, D., *Bentham and the Ethics of Today* (Princeton, NJ, 1952).

BEALES, H. L., 'Jeremy Bentham Social Engineer', *The Listener*, 3 August 1932, 148–50.

BEATTIE J. M., 'The Pattern of Crime in England, 1600–1800', *Past and Present*, 62 (1974), 47–95.

BECCARIA, C., *Dei delitti e delle pene* (1764), trans. J. A. Farrer (London, 1880).

BENDER, J., 'Prison Reform and the Sentence of Narration in *The Vicar of Wakefield*', in F. Nussbaum and L. Brown (eds.), *The New Eighteenth Century* (New York and London, 1987), 168–88.

BENTHAM, M. S., *Life of Brigadier-General Sir Samuel Bentham, KSG* (London, 1862).

BORALEVI, L. CAMPOS, *Bentham and the Oppressed* (Berlin and New York, 1984).

BOSWELL, J. *Life of Johnson* (London, 1791), ed. R. W. Chapman (Oxford, 1980).

BRANCH-JOHNSON, W., *The English Prison Hulks* (London, 1957).

BROWN, J. B., *Memoirs of the Public and Private Life of John Howard the Philanthropist* (London, 1823).

BUTLER, J., *Sermons by Joseph Butler DCL*, ed. W. E. Gladstone (Oxford, 1897).

CARPENTER, M., *Reformatory Schools for the Children of the Perishing and Dangerous Classes and for Juvenile Offenders* (London, 1851).

CHRISTIE, I. R., 'Jeremy Bentham and Prince Potemkin', *The Bentham Newsletter*, 10 (1986), 17–21.

CLAY, J., *The Prison Chaplain* (London, 1861).

COBBETT, W., *Cobbett's America*, ed. J. E. Morpurgo (London, 1985).

COLLINS, D., *An Account of the English Colony in New South Wales*, 2 vols. (London, 1798–1802).

COLQUHOUN, P., *A Treatise on the Police of the Metropolis, explaining the various crimes and misdemeanours which at present are felt as a Pressure upon the Community; and suggesting remedies for their prevention, By a Magistrate* (London, 1796).

CRAWFORD, W., *Report on the Penitentiaries of the United States*, addressed to Viscount Duncannon, Principal Secretary of State for the Home Department, 1835.

DeLACY, M., *Prison Reform in Lancashire, 1700–1850: A Study in Local Administration* (Manchester, 1986).

DENNE, S., *A Letter to Sir Robert Ladbroke, Knt. Senior Alderman and One of the Representatives of the City of London* (London, 1771).

DICEY, A. V., *Lectures on the Relation between Law and Public Opinion in England during the Nineteenth Century* (London, 1905; 2nd edn. 1914).

DINWIDDY, J., *Bentham* (Oxford and New York, 1989).

EDEN, F. M., *The State of the Poor* (London, 1797).

EDEN, W., *Principles of Penal Law*, 2nd edn. (London, 1771).

EDINGTON, R., *A Descriptive Plan for Erecting a Penitentiary House, for the Employment of Convicts; to which are added Plans for the Prevention of Frauds and Thefts, so far as respecting His Majesty's Dock-Yards, Public Works and Stores* (London, 1803).

EHRMAN, J., *The Younger Pitt: The Years of Acclaim* (London, 1969).

EVANS, R., *The Fabrication of Virtue: English Prison Architecture, 1750–1840* (Cambridge, 1982).

EVERETT, C. W., *The Education of Jeremy Bentham* (New York, 1931).

—— *Jeremy Bentham* (London, 1966).

FAY, C. R., *Life and Labour in the Nineteenth Century* (Cambridge, 1920).

FIELDING, H., *A Proposal for Making an Effectual Provision for the Poor* (London, 1753).

FINER, S. E., 'The Transmission of Benthamite Ideas, 1820–1850', in

Gillian Sutherland (ed.), *Studies in the Growth of Nineteenth Century Government* (London, 1972), 11–32.

—— *The Life and Times of Sir Edwin Chadwick* (London, 1952).

FITZGERALD, M., and SIM, J., *British Prisons*, 2nd edn. (Oxford, 1982).

FORSYTHE, W. J., *A System of Discipline: Exeter Borough Prison 1819–1863* (Exeter, 1983).

FOUCAULT, M., *Discipline and Punish: The Birth of the Prison*, trans. A. Sheridan, 1977 (Paris, 1975; Harmondsworth, 1985).

—— *Le Panoptique* (Paris, 1977), Précédé de L'Œil du Pouvoir entretien avec Michel Foucault. Postface de Michelle Perrot.

—— 'The Eye of Power', in *Power/Knowledge* (New York, 1980).

FRY, M., 'Bentham and English Penal Reform', in G. W. Keeton and G. Schwarzenberger (eds.), *Jeremy Bentham and the Law* (London, 1948), 20–57.

FURBER, H., *Henry Dundas, First Viscount Melville, 1742–1811* (Oxford, 1931).

FURNEAUX, R., *William Wilberforce* (London, 1974).

GARDNER, A., *The Place of John Howard in Penal Reform*, Howard League for Penal Reform (n.p., 1926).

GEIS, G., 'Jeremy Bentham', in Hermann Mannheim (ed.), *Pioneers in Criminology* (London, 1960).

GIBBON, E., *Autobiography* (London, 1796), Everyman edn. (London, 1939).

GODWIN, W., *Enquiry Concerning Political Justice* (London, 1793; Harmondsworth, 1985).

GOLDSMITH, O., *The Vicar of Wakefield* (London, 1766; Harmondsworth, 1974).

GRIFFITHS, A., *Memorials of Millbank and Chapters in Prison History*, 2 vols. (London, 1875).

GUY, W. A., *John Howard's Winter Journey* (London, 1882).

HALÉVY, E., *The Growth of Philosophic Radicalism*, trans. M. Morris (London, 1928; repr. 1972).

*Handbook of American Prisons and Reformatories*, i (New York, 1933).

HANWAY, J., *The Defects of Police* (London, 1775).

—— *Solitude in Imprisonment* (London, 1776).

—— *Distributive Justice and Mercy* (London, 1781).

HARRISON, R., *Bentham* (London, 1983).

HART, H. L. A., *Essays on Bentham: Studies in Jurisprudence and Political Theory* (Oxford, 1982).

HARTLEY, D., *Observations on Man* (London, 1749).

HASKELL, T. S., 'Capitalism and the Origins of the Humanitarian Sensibility', *The American Historical Review*, 90 (1985), 339–61, 547–66.

HASKELL, T. S., 'Foucault, Humanitarianism and the Blameworthy Self', unpublished paper given at the conference on the Welfare State, Murphy Institute, Tulane University, in February 1986.

HAYNES, F. E. F., *The American Prison System* (New York and London, 1939).

HAYTER, T., *The Army and the Crowd in Mid-Georgian England* (London and Basingstoke, 1978).

HEATH, J., *Eighteenth-Century Penal Theory* (Oxford, 1963).

HENRIQUES, U. R. Q., 'The Rise and Decline of the Separate System of Prison Discipline', *Past and Present*, 54 (1972), 61–93.

HERTZLER, J. O., *The History of Utopian Thought* (New York, 1922).

HIMMELFARB, G., *Victorian Minds* (London, 1968).

—— 'Bentham's Utopia: The National Charity Company', *The Journal of British Studies*, 10 (1970), 80–125.

—— *The Idea of Poverty* (London, 1984).

—— *Marriage and Morals among the Victorians* (London, 1986).

HOME, H. (Lord Kames), *Historical Law Tracts* (Edinburgh, 1761).

THE HOWARD ASSOCIATION, *Defects in the Criminal Administration and Penal Legislation of Great Britain and Ireland* (London, 1872).

HOWARD, J., *The State of the Prisons in England and Wales* (London, 1777).

—— *An Account of the Principal Lazarettos in Europe* (London, 1789).

HOY, D. C. (ed.), *Foucault: A Critical Reader* (Oxford, 1986).

HUME, L. J., 'Bentham's Panopticon: An Administrative History', in *Historical Studies*, 15 (1971–2), 703–21, and 16 (1974–5), 36–54.

—— 'Revisionism in Bentham Studies', *The Bentham Newsletter*, 2 (1978), 3–20.

—— *Bentham and Bureaucracy* (Cambridge, 1981).

IGNATIEFF, M., *A Just Measure of Pain: The Penitentiary in the Industrial Revolution, 1750–1850* (New York, 1978).

IVES, G., *A History of Penal Methods* (London, 1914; repr. Montclair, NJ, 1970).

JACOBS, J. B., *Stateville: The Penitentiary in Mass Society* (London and Chicago, 1977).

JEBB, J., *Thoughts on the Construction and Polity of Prisons with Hints for their Improvement*, Preface by Capel Lofft (London, 1786).

JOYCE, H., *The History of the Post Office* (London, 1893).

KELLY, P. J., *Utilitarianism and Distributive Justice: Jeremy Bentham and the Civil Law* (Oxford, 1990).

KENYON, E., *The Dilemma of Abortion* (London, 1986).

KUMAR, K., *Utopia and Anti-Utopia in Modern Times* (Oxford, 1987).

LETWIN, S. R., *The Pursuit of Certainty* (Cambridge, 1965).

LONG, D. G., *Bentham on Liberty: Jeremy Bentham's Idea of Liberty in Relation to his Utilitarianism* (Toronto, 1977).

LUKER, K., *Abortion and the Politics of Motherhood* (California, 1985).

LYONS, D., *In the Interests of the Governed* (Oxford, 1973).

McCONVILLE, S., *A History of English Prison Administration*, i (London, 1981).

MacDONAGH, O., *Early Victorian Government* (London, 1977).

MACK, M., *Jeremy Bentham: An Odyssey of Ideas* (London, 1962).

—— *A Bentham Reader* (New York, 1969).

MADAN, M., *Thoughts on Executive Justice* (n.p., 1785).

MAESTRO, M., *Cesare Beccaria and the Origins of Penal Reform* (Philadelphia, 1973).

MANDEVILLE, B., *An Enquiry into the Causes of the Frequent Executions at Tyburn* (London, 1725).

MANNING, D. J., *The Mind of Jeremy Bentham* (London, 1968).

MANUEL, F. E., and MANUEL, F. P., *Utopian Thought in the Western World* (Cambridge, Mass., 1979).

MARKUS, T. A., 'Pattern of the Law', *The Architectural Review*, 116 (1954), 251–6.

MELOSSI, D., and PAVARINI, M., *The Prison and the Factory: Origins of the Penitentiary System* (Bologna, 1977), trans. G. Cousin (London, 1981).

MILL, J., *Essays*, repr. from the Supplement to the *Encyclopaedia Britannica* (London, 1827).

MILL, J. S., *Utilitarianism On Liberty: Essay on Bentham*, ed. M. Warnock (Glasgow, 1990).

MORE, T., *Utopia* (Louvain, 1516), ed. E. Surtz (New Haven, Conn., and London, 1964).

MORGAN, Miss, *The Gaol of the City of Bristol compared with what a Gaol ought to be By a Citizen. With an appendix containing a brief account of the Panopticon, a prison upon a new plan proposed by Jeremy Bentham* (Bristol and London, 1815).

MORGAN, R., 'Divine Philanthropy: John Howard Reconsidered', in *History*, 62 (1977), 388–410.

MORTON, A. L., *The English Utopia* (London, 1952).

MUMFORD, L., 'Utopia, The City and the Machine', in F. E. Manuel (ed.), *Utopias and Utopian Thought* (Boston, Mass., 1966).

NELSON, R. R., *The Home Office, 1782–1801* (Durham, NC, 1969).

OWEN, R., *The Life of Robert Owen Written by Himself* (London, 1857), ed. John Butt (London, 1971).

PAREKH, B., *Bentham's Political Thought* (London, 1973).

PATTERSON, M. W., *Sir Francis Burdett and his Times* (London, 1931).

PAUL, G. O., *Considerations on the Defects of Prisons and their Present System of Regulation* (London, 1784).

PHILLIPSON, C., *Three Criminal Law Reformers* (London, 1923).

PORTER, R., *Mind-Forg'd Manacles: A History of Madness in England from the Restoration to the Regency* (London, 1987).

POSTEMA, G. J., *Bentham and the Common Law Tradition* (Oxford, 1986).

POSTER, M., *Foucault, Marxism and History* (Cambridge, 1984).

POYNTER, J. R., *Society and Pauperism* (London and Toronto, 1969).

RADZINOWICZ, L., *A History of English Criminal Law and its Administration from 1750*, 4 vols. (London, 1948–68).

REILLY, R., *Pitt the Younger* (London, 1978).

ROBERTS, W., 'Bentham's Poor Law Proposals', *The Bentham Newsletter*, 3 (1979), 28–45.

RODGERS, B., *Cloak of Charity: Studies in Eighteenth-Century Philanthropy* (London, 1949).

ROMILLY, S., *Memoirs of the Life of Sir Samuel Romilly Written by Himself*, 3 vols. (London, 1840).

ROSE, G., *The Diaries and Correspondence of the Right Hon. George Rose*, ed. L. V. Harcourt, 2 vols. (London, 1860).

ROSEN, F., *Jeremy Bentham and Representative Democracy: A Study of the Constitutional Code* (Oxford, 1983).

ROTH, R., *Pratiques Pénitentiaires et Théorie Sociale* (Geneva, 1981).

ROTHMAN, D. J., *The Discovery of the Asylum* (Boston, Mass., 1971).

SALAMAN, R. N., *The History and Social Influence of the Potato* (Cambridge, 1949).

SEMPLE, J., 'Bentham's Haunted House', *The Bentham Newsletter*, 11 (1987), 35–44.

—— 'Foucault and Bentham: A Defence of Panopticism', *Utilitas*, 4 (May 1992), 105–20.

SHAW, A. G. L., *Convicts and the Colonies* (London, 1966).

SMART, B., *Michel Foucault* (London, 1985).

SMITH, A., *The Wealth of Nations* (London, 1776–8).

SPECTOR, B., 'Jeremy Bentham—His Influence on Medical Thought and Legislation', in *Bulletin of the History of Medicine*, 37 (1963), 25–42.

SPENCER, H., *The Man versus the State* (London, 1884).

STEINTRAGER, J., *Bentham* (London, 1977).

STEPHEN, L., *The English Utilitarians*, 3 vols. (London, 1900).

A STUDENT OF POLITICS, *Proposals to the Legislature for Preventing the Frequent Executions and Exportations of Convicts* (London, 1754).

*Survey of London*, 39, *The Grosvenor Estate in Mayfair*, Part I (London 1977).

SWEENEY, C., *Transported in Place of Death; Convicts in Australia* (Melbourne, 1981).

TAYLOR, C., 'Foucault on Freedom and Truth', *Political Theory*, 12 (1984), 152–83.

TAYLOR, J. S., *Jonas Hanway Founder of the Marine Society: Charity and Policy in Eighteenth-Century Britain* (London and Berkeley, Calif., 1985).

TEETERS, N. K., and SHEARER, J. D., *The Prison at Philadelphia* (New York, 1957).

THOMAS, W., *The Philosophical Radicals* (Oxford, 1979).

THORNE, R. G., *The History of Parliament: The House of Commons, 1790–1820*, 5 vols. (London, 1986).

TOOKE, J. H., *The Diversions of Purley*, 2nd edn., 2 vols. (London, 1798, 1805).

TOWNSEND, J., *A Dissertation on the Poor Laws* (London, 1786).

TWINING, W. L., and P. E., 'Bentham on Torture', in M. H. James (ed.), *Bentham and Legal Theory* (Belfast, 1973).

WAGNER, RICHARD, *Das Rheingold*, ed. N. John, trans. A. Porter (London, 1985), 70–1.

WALKER, N., *Crime and Punishment in Britain* (London, 1965).

WARD, W. R., 'Some Eighteenth-Century Civil Servants: The English Revenue Commissioners, 1754–98', in *English Historical Review*, 70 (1955), 25–54.

WEBB, S. and B., *English Prisons under Local Government* (London, 1922).

—— *The Development of English Local Government, 1684–1835* (Oxford, 1963).

WEDDERBURN, A. (Lord Loughborough), *Observations on the State of the English Prisons and the Means of Improving Them* (London, 1793).

WILBERFORCE, R. I., and WILBERFORCE, S., *The Life of William Wilberforce*, 5 vols. (London, 1838).

WILBERFORCE, W., *Private Papers of William Wilberforce*, coll. and ed. A. M. Wilberforce (London, 1897).

WILSON, W. E., *The Angel and the Serpent: The Story of New Harmony* (Bloomington, Ind., 1964).

WOLIN, S., *Politics and Vision* (Boston, Mass., 1960).

# INDEX